Thinking Its Presence

ASIAN AMERICA
A series edited by Gordon H. Chang

The increasing size and diversity of the Asian American population, its growing significance in American society and culture, and
the expanded appreciation, both popular and scholarly, of the importance of Asian Americans in the country's present and past—all these
developments have converged to stimulate wide interest in scholarly
work on topics related to the Asian American experience. The general
recognition of the pivotal role that race and ethnicity have played in
American life, and in relations between the United States and other
countries, has also fostered the heightened attention.

Although Asian Americans were a subject of serious inquiry in the
late nineteenth and early twentieth centuries, they were subsequently
ignored by the mainstream scholarly community for several decades.
In recent years, however, this neglect has ended, with an increasing
number of writers examining a good many aspects of Asian American
life and culture. Moreover, many students of American society are
recognizing that the study of issues related to Asian America speak to,
and may be essential for, many current discussions on the part of the
informed public and various scholarly communities.

The Stanford series on Asian America seeks to address these interests. The series will include works from the humanities and social
sciences, including history, anthropology, political science, American
studies, law, literary criticism, sociology, and interdisciplinary and
policy studies.

A full list of titles in the Asian America series can be found online at
www.sup.org/asianamerica.

Thinking Its Presence

FORM, RACE, AND SUBJECTIVITY
IN CONTEMPORARY ASIAN AMERICAN
POETRY

Dorothy J. Wang

STANFORD UNIVERSITY PRESS
STANFORD, CALIFORNIA

Stanford University Press
Stanford, California

© 2014 by the Board of Trustees of the
Leland Stanford Junior University. All rights reserved.

Printed in the United States of America
on acid-free, archival-quality paper

Library of Congress Cataloging-in-Publication Data

Wang, Dorothy J., author.
   Thinking its presence : form, race, and subjectivity in
contemporary Asian American poetry / Dorothy J. Wang.
      pages cm — (Asian America)
   Includes bibliographical references and index.
   ISBN 978-0-8047-8365-1 (cloth : alk. paper)
   ISBN 978-0-8047-9527-2 (pbk. : alk. paper)
      1. American poetry—Asian American authors—History
and criticism. 2. American poetry—History and criticism—
Theory, etc. 3. Literary form. 4. Poetics. I. Title. II. Series:
Asian America.
PS153.A84W36 2013
810.9'895—dc23

                                          2013018373

ISBN 978-0-8047-8909-7 (electronic)

For my parents,
Alfred Shih-p'u Wang (王 世 璞)
and
Veronica Ch'eng-fang Chow (周 成 芳)

and whatever is said
in the world, or forgotten,
or not said, makes a form.

    —ROBERT CREELEY, "THE FINGER"

alles is weniger, als
es ist,
alles ist mehr.

all things are less than
they are,
all are more.

    —PAUL CELAN, "CELLO ENTRY," FROM *ATEMWENDE*

Contents

Acknowledgments

An intellectual journey is long and winding in its making. I have had the fortune to be guided and inspired by superb teachers and mentors along the way.

The late Robert F. Gleckner taught me English Romantic poetry in the most exciting class I took in college, lighting a spark for poetry that has never left me.

Perry Meisel first introduced me to "theory," opened unknown gates of perception, and changed my life.

Michael Davidson represents an exception to my critique of the politics of poetry: his understanding that the social and the poetic are intertwined and his professional integrity continue to model for me the highest standards—and possibilities—of the work of being a scholar-teacher. For his support and careful reading of my work, I am grateful.

Henry Abelove shows me every day what it means to be a committed scholar and human being. His intellectual acumen, sensitivity to poetry, understanding of bigotry in its various forms, and courage to challenge orthodoxies find expression in writing that manifests near-perfect stylistic and critical pitch. His belief in me and my ideas have sustained me for more than a decade and a half. I am honored to call him a friend.

Finally, David Lloyd has been the greatest intellectual and political influence on this book. He possesses the rarest of combinations: an acute analytical mind; a nuanced feeling for poetry; an understanding of race and racism; and fearlessness in the face of institutional power to speak uncomfortable truths. It is not an exaggeration to say that it was David who taught me how to really think about poetry and to understand the workings of culture. This book, on whose pages the impress of his ideas is felt throughout, serves as just a small offering of my deep respect and gratitude.

My heartfelt thanks go out to other friends who have read various parts of the manuscript over the years. David Eng and Mae Ngai, in particular, read the book in its entirety and provided key support and tough love, especially during the later stages of this project. Their personal and professional generosity and their commitment to Asian American studies prove that it is possible to become a successful senior academic without losing one's soul. I have also gained much from the perspicacious readings and support of Lily Cho, Julie Joosten, Fred Moten, Jeff Santa Ana, Shuang Shen, and Helen Thompson. Greg Mullins has been an example of uncommon decency and loyal friendship, a combination not often found in the academy.

Toward the end of my time at Berkeley, Craig Dworkin introduced me to contemporary avant-garde poetry and transformed my idea of poetry. Marjorie Perloff and Charles Altieri were important—though mostly internalized—interlocutors throughout this book. While I have often disagreed with their conclusions on race and minority poetry, the oppositional arguments they raised were never far from my mind, and my respect for their scholarship and their willingness to forthrightly engage with a junior colleague was not dimmed by these disagreements. This book is better for the objections they raised, explicitly or not, to various arguments within it.

Others who have helped this project, directly or indirectly, come to fruition include, at the University of California at Berkeley, Tony Brown, Eric Chandler, Mark Chiang, Jeannie Chiu, Candice Fujikane, Jane Iwamura, Daniel Kim, Marie Lo, Khashayar Pakdaman, Ken Saragosa, Victor Squitieri, Karen Su, Theresa Tensuan, and Shelley Wong; in San Francisco, Alvin Lu; at Wesleyan University, Christina Crosby, Harris Friedberg, Joel Pfister, Claire Potter, Joe Reed, Richard Slotkin, and Khachig Tololyan; at Northwestern University,

Kevin Bell, Brian Edwards, Jillana Enteen, Betsy Erkkila, E. Patrick Johnson, Dwight McBride, and Alex Weheliye; in Chicago, Thomas Kim, Jason Ku, Mary Margaret Sloan, and Timothy Yu.

At Williams College, I have been fortunate to have found attentive and sympathetic readers of my work: Gail Newman, Mark Reinhardt, and Karen Swann, who understood the intellectual and disciplinary stakes of my project and encouraged me to do the kind of work I do. I have also enjoyed literary discussions with my colleagues Lynda Bundtzen, Gage McWeeny, David L. Smith, and Christian Thorne. Thanks to Gene Bell-Villada for clarification on some fine points of grammar. Stéphane Robolin and Maria Elena Cepeda were and are comrades-in-arms with a rare sense of humanity. Kiara Vigil and Ji Um have been supportive American Studies colleagues; Robin Keller and Donna St. Pierre provided key administrative help. Laylah Ali, Carsten Botts, Monique Deveaux, Joyce Foster, Peter Mehlin, Marcin Lipinski, Michael Nixon, Omar Sangare, and Tanseli Savaser have made my life in Williamstown not only habitable but possible.

Significant portions of this book were written during my year and a half as a visiting scholar at the Center for the Study of Ethnicity and Race (CSER) at Columbia University. I thank the director, Frances Negrón-Mutaner, for giving me access to Butler Library—and its gorgeous Reference Room—and the opportunity to teach a wonderful group of students in "Experimental Minority American Writing." The writing of this book was also supported by a University of California President's Postdoctoral Fellowship and a Hellman Fellows Grant from Williams College.

Versions of chapters have been given as talks at other institutions: audiences at Australian National University, Simon Fraser University, Smith College, UC Irvine, UCLA, UC Santa Barbara, UC Santa Cruz, University of Cambridge, University of Chicago, University of London, University of New Hampshire, University of Texas at Austin, University of Washington, University of Wollongong, Westmont College, Vanderbilt University, and Vassar College gave valuable feedback. I am especially grateful for the hospitality of Vereen Bell, Kingkok Cheung, Chris Connery, Helen Gilbert, Robert Hampson, Neville Hoad, Cheri Larsen Hoeckley, Simon Jarvis, Tseen-Ling Khoo,

James Lee, Jacqueline Lo, Robyn Morris, Wenche Ommundsen, Michael Szalay, Bob von Hallberg, Priscilla Wald, Rob Wilson, and Karen Tei Yamashita, among others. Alan Golding, Lynn Keller, Dee Morris, and Aldon Nielsen also gave useful comments.

My research and teaching are not separate enterprises. My students at Wesleyan, Northwestern, Williams, and Columbia have invariably given me fresh insights into texts I thought I knew. Their openness, willingness to be persuaded, and enthusiasm provided, and continue to provide, sustaining moments of brightness amid the institutional dystopia of academe.

All the poets in the book—Mei-mei Berssenbrugge, Marilyn Chin, Li-Young Lee, Pamela Lu, and John Yau—sat down with me to talk about their work at one point or another over the years. I am appreciative to them for having given me their time. I constantly learn from talking to poets, especially Will Alexander, who never lets me forget the big picture; Tan Lin, who expands possibilities; and Prageeta Sharma, whose poems and bravery inspire me. Thanks to Lyn Hejinian, for providing supportive advice when I needed it. Ken Chen and Sunyoung Lee run the Asian American Writers' Workshop and Kaya Press, respectively—two rare and necessary entities that further the long, rich, and hard-fought history of Asian American literature.

Many thanks to Gordon Chang for seeing promise in the project and to Stacy Wagner for taking a chance on a literary critical monograph at a time when this genre is fast becoming extinct. Stacy has been the most steadfast editor a first-time author could ask for; Jessica Walsh provided valuable help as editorial assistant. This book is all that much better for the efforts of Tim Roberts, a responsive production editor, and Cynthia Lindlof, who, in her careful copyediting, has taught me new things.

Marie Lee Marchesseault was, in a real sense, the first person to introduce me to the notion "Asian American" during our freshman year of college; her friendship continues to be bedrock. I am also thankful for the loyal friendships of Anne Schiffman, Gary Idleberg, and Terri Briley Williams, who has been there for me since junior high school. Some of the most intense conversations about literature I have had in my life were with Gwen Leen (1929–94) at 2 Washington

Square Village more than twenty-five years ago. Gwen had a passionate attachment to literature I have seldom seen equaled. I can still hear her voice and will never forget her. And though I never met him, I would like to acknowledge the memory and spirit of my uncle, Wang Shih-kuei (王 世 珪), 1934–52.

There are five people to whom I must give special thanks for pulling me through the last hard stretch, for never doubting I could finish: Leslie Wingard, writing partner and friend, whose e-mails, always encouraging, kept me going; Boris Thomas, who guided me with kindness and wisdom; John Keene, poet-brother and fellow fighter, who understands, without words, the stakes of this project; Joanna Klink, beloved fellow traveler, whose feeling and feel for poetry—and whose own words—never cease to astonish me; and David Russell Paul, whose love, companionship, and gentle nature sustained me through "a lonesome wild." To all five, I am forever grateful. I would not have been able to complete this book without them.

Finally, this book is for my parents, Alfred S. Wang and Veronica Chow Wang. Their abiding love for English literature and their forced diaspora—from coastal towns in Northern China, upended by war and imperialist violence, to small Presbyterian colleges in Jim-Crow North Carolina, to New York City, to the English PhD program at Tulane University in New Orleans, and then back to North Carolina, where they taught, with courage and dignity, as professors of English literature at East Carolina University for more than thirty years—showed me firsthand the inseparability of aesthetics and politics in art and in life, and the necessity of poetry. This book is dedicated to them with love.

Preface

This book is as much a rethinking of how poetry is critically discussed today by critics—in the academy mainly but also, to a lesser extent, in the wider poetry-reading public—as it is a focused study of five contemporary Asian American poets. *Thinking Its Presence: Form, Race, and Subjectivity in Contemporary Asian American Poetry* adds a voice to the long and ongoing conversation about poetry and poetics, even as it will be read more topically as a study of Asian American literature, minority American poetry, and diasporic literature. I see no contradiction in claiming that a "minor" literature, not only minor but also secondary among American minority literatures,[1] provides a crucial lens through which to view fundamental questions concerning what is, arguably, still *the* major genre in the English literary tradition, even as critics bemoan the fact that no one reads it: poetry. Indeed, Asian American poetry—which occupies a unique place in both the American national body and the American literary imaginary as the nexus of constitutively and immutably "alien" racialized subjects and the vaunted English-language poetic tradition[2]—puts to the test many of our widest held beliefs, not only about minority literature but also about English literature, poetry and poetics, American literature and society, and the value of the literary.

This claim that minority poetry can contribute importantly to American (and English-language) poetry and poetics flies in the face of the reception of ethnic poetry in English literary and poetry studies, among critics of both "mainstream" lyric and avant-garde poetry. Poetry by racialized persons, no matter the aesthetic style, is almost always read as secondary to the larger (and more "primary") fields and forms of English-language poetry and poetics—whether the lyric, prosody, rhetorical tropes, the notion of the "avant-garde"—categories all too often presumed to be universal, overarching, and implicitly "racially unmarked." Within colleges and universities, poetry is almost always studied in classes and departments that are nationally based, monolingual,[3] and internally organized by periods or eras, each studded with a few "stars": for example, a Modernist poetry survey would feature Eliot, Stevens, and Pound certainly, and then, give or take a few other white poets, perhaps Williams or Crane or Marianne Moore.[4] Langston Hughes might be included as the token black— or what amounts to the same thing, the exceptional exception—but surely no other Harlem Renaissance poet (not to mention an Asian American poet such as Jose Garcia Villa). Hughes is much less likely to be linked to Modernism—never "High" Modernism—than to the category of African American poetry or African American literature.

Because of our investment in such schemata, it might be difficult to imagine that studying the poetry of, say, Asian American poet John Yau, the author of more than a dozen volumes of poetry, can teach us as much, though differently, about "poetic voice" and the poetic "I" as does reading the works of John Ashbery. The question here is not "Who is the greater poet?"—one could substitute e. e. cummings for Ashbery in the example—but why there exists a double standard in discussing the work of poets of color and those who are supposedly racially "unmarked." Critics look at the work of Ashbery as contributing to "universal"[5] questions of subjectivity and poetics while Yau, with rare exception,[6] is seen as occupying a narrower historical or partisan niche—as one of the post–New York School poets or, more recently, as "merely" an Asian American poet.

The double standard extends to how we read works of poetry. Critics are more likely to think about formal questions—say, poetic tone and syntax—when speaking about Ashbery's poems but almost certainly to focus on political or black "content" when examining the work of Amiri Baraka, a poet who has pushed the limits of formal invention for more than half a century—certainly as long as Ashbery has. How likely would a critic be to approach Li-Young Lee's poems by studying his use of anaphora? How likely would a critic be to examine Louise Glück's poems by turning to her autobiographical background—for example, her having grown up Jewish on Long Island—in the same way that critics often invoke the "Chinese" background of Marilyn Chin when speaking of her poems? Glück's having been born to a Jewish-Hungarian immigrant father (who helped invent the X-Acto knife), having been exposed (or not) to non-English languages as a child, having suffered from anorexia, and having attended Sarah Lawrence College and Columbia University should not be irrelevant to a reading of her poetry. Where she grew up, her racial ethnicity, her class, her knowing other languages—these factors, among many, have influenced her writing; likewise, her knowledge of the English literary tradition, her grappling with poetic precursors, and her knowledge of languages should not be irrelevant to a reading of her poetry.

There is, as Edward Said reminds us in *The World, the Text, and the Critic*, a "connection between texts and the existential actualities of human life, politics, societies, and events"[7] (these actualities also include, of course, literary and aesthetic engagements). I am not arguing for reading biographically in a simplistic manner but, rather, for taking into account all the factors and contexts—literary and extraliterary—that undergird and help to determine poetic subjectivity and that, consciously or unconsciously, manifest themselves in the language of poems. All sorts of linguistic and sociopolitical considerations (race and class, among others) influence the formation of a person and her relationship to the English language and the poetic tradition; these factors are at one and the same time embodied in the person of the poet but are also inseparable from institutional, ideological, social, and other structures that function in realms beyond the personal world of the individual poet. There are, as Raymond Williams puts it, "profound connections between formations and forms."[8] We should, I argue, be reading both minority poets and canonical poets with attention to formal concerns *and* the social, cultural, historical, and literary contexts that have shaped the work.

Whereas critics of more "mainstream" minority lyric poetry—such as that by Elizabeth Alexander and Li-Young Lee—tend to read for "content," critics working on the other end of the aesthetic spectrum, the "avant-garde," do a similar disservice to experimental minority writing when they completely ignore references to race or ethnic identity, even when the poets themselves (for example, Mei-mei Berssenbrugge or Will Alexander) speak about the importance of issues of race and of ethnic and racial identity formation to their work. It is not that critics of avant-garde poetry are unable to speak about other social concerns—for example, scholars writing on Language poetry are attuned to formal structures that implicitly critique the structures of capitalist market economies; others write trenchantly about how gender differences manifest themselves in the forms of writing by poets such as Lyn Hejinian. It is that race alone seems unspeakable.

Although the situation among literary critics I have just delineated may be changing slightly with the rise of Internet culture and the increasing numbers of younger critics of color who have been trained in the wake of "multiculturalism," I still contend that, in the main, poetry critics both inside and outside the academy—including some younger minority critics—continue to misread minority poetry along these lines.[9] Even if some critics may be willing to acknowledge formal experimentation in an Asian American poet's work, what is lacking are sustained critical analyses that pay serious attention to both the literary and social properties of Asian American writing.

Thinking Its Presence: Form, Race, and Subjectivity in Contemporary Asian American Poetry is, I hope, the first of many such studies. In this book, I argue for a capacious and complex mode of reading Asian American, minority American poetry, and poetry in general by making the case that a poem's use of form is inseparable from the larger social, historical, and political contexts that produced the poet's subjectivity. Just as all human lives are complex, layered, multidimensional, and sometimes contradictory, so are poems—and the subjectivities that produce them—and to have insight into their workings, one must pay careful attention to the *particularities* of the persons and the writing, by means of close reading, in historical time and place. All writing is situated in both aesthetic and social realms.

Critics should accord the same degree of complexity and respect to the whole stylistic range of minority poetry as they do to "racially unmarked" poetry—to pay the same serious attention to language (its literary, linguistic, and rhetorical aspects) so as to understand the nuanced and complex interplay between "form" and "content" and to avoid the sorts of reductive binary categories that oppose form and content, the cultural/social/political and the literary, and so on. A poem manifests formally—whether in its linguistic structures or in its literary and rhetorical presentation—the impress of external forces and contexts.[10] This relationship pertains as much in an abstract avant-garde poem as in an overtly "political" poem. And it holds as much for a poem by Li-Young Lee as it does for a poem by Mark Strand; likewise, the poetic language of a Strand poem bears the impress, explicit or unconscious, of the ethos and effects of social and political contexts no less than does the language of an "ethnic" poem.

In other words, what is true for white poets is true for minority poets. And vice versa.

If my arguments in *Thinking Its Presence: Form, Race, and Subjectivity in Contemporary Asian American Poetry* seem to highlight the role of racial interpellation and racialized subjectivity on these poets' work, the reason is not that I think that race is the only—or necessarily the primary—factor at work in the poetries of these Asian American poets or other minority poets but that the overwhelming body of critical discourse has occluded this significant issue. One must never overlook the political (institutional, intellectual) and aesthetic stakes at work in the academy and in the work literary critics do. One must never forget what one is fighting *against.*

In other words, an exhortation to not forget that politics and aesthetic concerns are intimately intertwined, even in the most abstract and racially "unmarked" poetry, flies in the face of powerful institutional and humanistic discourses that dictate literary value and the terms of literary discussion. Culture has, says Said,

> the power . . . by virtue of its elevated or superior position to
> authorize, to dominate, to legitimate, demote, interdict, and
> validate: in short, the power of culture to be an agent of, and perhaps

the main agency for, powerful differentiation within its domain and beyond it too. (*WTC*, 9)

What is more important in culture is that it is a system of values *saturating* downward almost everything within its purview. (original emphasis; 9)

Criticism in short is always situated. (26)

We as literary critics might ask ourselves these questions: "Why is it so difficult for poetry critics to talk about race?" "Why is race so often occluded in discussions of American poetry, or, if the issue is raised at all, why is it so often discussed in reductive terms?" "Who has the power to decide who gets to sit at the table of 'real' poetry, and what kind of table it will be?"

"For as long as social relations are skewed," reminds poet-critic Charles Bernstein, "who speaks in poetry can never be a neutral matter."[11]

Introduction

Aesthetics Contra "Identity" in Contemporary Poetry Studies

A Few Snapshots of the Current State of Poetry Reception

In the January 2008 issue of *PMLA*—the official publication of the Modern Language Association (MLA) sent to more than thirty thousand members in one hundred countries[1]—a cluster of essays by eight distinguished literary critics appeared under the title "The New Lyric Studies."[2] The pieces took as their jumping-off point the eminent poetry critic Marjorie Perloff's MLA presidential address, "It Must Change," given in December 2006 at the annual convention in Philadelphia and later reprinted in the May 2007 issue of *PMLA*. In that talk, Perloff asks, "Why *is* the 'merely' literary so suspect today?" (original emphasis), contending that "the governing paradigm for so-called literary study is now taken from anthropology and history."[3]

Because lyric has in our time become conflated with the more generic category of poetry,[4] the *PMLA* forum serves to address not only the state of lyric studies but, more broadly, the state of poetry studies today. Nine critics may seem a small number—hardly representative of the larger numbers of academic poetry critics in the country—but because of the influential reputations of the critics involved (Perloff and Jonathan Culler in particular);[5] because the MLA, despite the ridicule to which it is sometimes subjected, is the largest, most powerful and influential professional organization for professors and academic critics of literature; and because the *PMLA* reaches a wider and broader audience than any other literary-critical journal,[6] the views of these particular critics are highly visible and influential and cannot be easily discounted or dismissed. The MLA is one of what Edward Said calls the "authoritative and authorizing agencies" of culture in the Arnoldian sense (*WTC*, 8). Individual articles in *PMLA* may be overlooked, but statements by high-profile members about the state of the field of literary criticism—especially when marked by an adjective such as "New"—are often noticed and by a not insignificant number of readers.

In quite a few respects, the arguments made in "The New Lyric Studies" were varied: from Culler's making the case for the specialness of lyric—with its "memorable language" and its being "characteristically extravagant"[7]—to Rei Terada's calling that we "[be] release[d] from lyric ideology" and "let 'lyric' dissolve into literature and 'literature' into culture"[8] (Robert Kaufman, the requisite Marxist contributor, splits the difference by claiming, via Adorno and Benjamin, that lyric is special precisely because it operates ideologically by the same "version of aura or semblance" that the commodity form does[9]); from Stathis Gourgouris's and Brent Edwards's urging that lyric scholars engage with truer and more incisive forms of interdisciplinarity;[10] to Oren Izenberg's assertion that "it makes good sense to bring literary study into closer proximity with the disciplines that give accounts of how the mind works," such as "the philosophy of mind, philosophical psychology, and metaphysics that deal with the nature of mental phenomena and their relation not so much to the determinations of culture as to the causal structure of reality."[11] Virginia Jackson and Yopie Prins both argue for more and better historicization: Jackson—pushing against the tendency to make poetry and lyric abstract, idealized, and transhistorical—urges that we "trace . . . the history of lyricization"; Prins, that we examine "the cultural specificity of poetic genres" and the history of poetics and prosody.[12]

Yet despite the various methodological, disciplinary, and aesthetic inclinations of the respondents, there are moments of agreement, some expected and others less so, sometimes cutting across the familiar "literary versus cultural" divide within literary studies. Not surprisingly among scholars committed to the "literary," Culler, like

Perloff, makes the familiar validating move of tracing the history of lyric back to the Greeks. Gourgouris, too, bolsters his arguments by appealing to the authority of ancient Greece (not so unexpected given that he works on Greek literature), taking Perloff slightly to task for too narrowly conceiving of *poietike*, which she translates as "the discipline of poetics." But Gourgouris—who makes the point that Perloff "does not inquire if 'poetics' can be conducted nowadays in a fresh language"—does agree with her claim that literary studies has taken a wrong turn, though for him the reasons are internal to the field and not, as Perloff suggests, because interdisciplinarity, in the form of anthropological and historical paradigms, has been a bad influence. Gourgouris writes in *"Poiein*—Political Infinitive,"

> For a decade or more since 1990, the microidentitarian shift in theory precipitated a failure of self-interrogation, especially regarding the paradoxes of the new disciplinary parameters that emerged out of the practice of interdisciplinarity. As a result, literary studies (and other disciplines) suffered, not so much a defanging, as Perloff implies, but rather carelessness, perhaps even arrogance—one is a symptom of the other—which led the discipline to abandon self-interrogation and instead hop on the high horse of identity politics. In other words, if Perloff's scenario for the relegation of literary studies to a secondary practice is legitimate, the devaluation is not external but self-induced. (224)

This moment is surprising in that Gourgouris, who strongly advocates for, in effect, a "truer" form of interdisciplinarity—one that "requires, by definition, the double work of mastering the canonical and the modes of interrogating it" (225)—and who emphatically states that "[p]oetry cannot be understood except in relation to life" (227), places the blame for the fall of literary studies so firmly and unquestioningly on "the high horse of identity politics"—presumably not "relat[ed] to life"—the end result of "carelessness" and the abandoning of "self-interrogation." Indeed, "identity" has already been referenced as a dirty word earlier in the quote when Gourgouris speaks of the "microidentitarian shift in theory" and its having "precipitated a failure of self-interrogation." Let me delay my discussion of this critique of "identity politics" for now and turn to another moment of agreement in *PMLA*.

On page two of his essay "Poems Out of Our Heads," Oren Izenberg—before asserting that literary studies be brought in closer proximity with more scientific "disciplines that give accounts of how the mind works"—makes common cause with Perloff, quoting her:

> I share much of Perloff's resistance to viewing poetry as "symptoms of cultural desires, drives, anxieties, or prejudices" and to the sometimes haphazard forms of interdisciplinarity that this view fosters. (217)

This move is also somewhat surprising, for aesthetic and methodological rather than disciplinary reasons: not only has Izenberg been harshly critical in print of the Language poets, of whom Perloff has been a pioneering and fierce champion, but his privileging of analytic philosophy's methods do not align with Perloff's more Continental proclivities and her more literary historical approaches to poetry.[13]

Thus, whatever other aesthetic, methodological, and disciplinary differences may separate them, Gourgouris, Izenberg, and Perloff do converge when thinking about one of the reasons—if not the major reason—for the fallen state of literary studies: forms of sloppy (careless, haphazard) thinking, slightly differentiated but fundamentally linked, that privilege, variously, the sociological over the literary (Perloff); identity politics over rigorous self-interrogation (Gourgouris); the cultural over the literary or philosophical or something called "reality" and its "causal structure" (Izenberg). In other words, scholarly overconcern with the cultural, including the political—dismissed as unspecified "anxieties" and "prejudices"—has seduced serious literary scholars away from the proper study of the literary, specifically poetry. Perloff posits this binary quite starkly in her presidential address:

> Still, I wonder how many of us, no matter how culturally and politically oriented our own particular research may be, would be satisfied with the elimination of literary study from the curriculum. (656)

Despite her use of the first-person plural pronoun, Perloff suggests that such "culturally and politically oriented" research is precisely the research that "use[s] literary texts" instrumentally, as "windows through which we see the world beyond the text, symptoms of cultural drives, anxieties, or prejudices" (654). She ends her address by forcefully exhorting,

> It is time to trust the literary instinct that brought us to this field in the first place and to recognize that, instead of lusting after those other disciplines that seem so exotic primarily because we don't really practice them, what we need is more theoretical, historical, and critical training in our own discipline. (662)

More rigorous training in the discipline of literary studies—though oddly, a discipline rooted in an "instinct" that brought "us" into the field in the first place (who is included in this "us" and "we"?)—is posited as the antidote to the deleterious cultural and political turn, seen as a "lusting after" the "exotic."

For Perloff, this either-or choice obtains not only with literary methods and disciplines but also with individual authors and texts themselves. In her spring 2006 "President's Column" written for the *MLA Newsletter*, she writes more explicitly and directly of what choices are at stake:

> Under the rubrics of African American, other minorities, and post-colonial, a lot of important and exciting novels and poems are surely studied. But what about what is not studied? Suppose a student (undergraduate or graduate) wants to study James Joyce or Gertrude Stein? Virginia Woolf or T.E. Lawrence or George Orwell? William Faulkner or Frank O'Hara? the literature of World Wars I and II? the Great Depression? the impact of technology on poetry and fiction? modernism vis-à-vis fascism? existentialism? the history of modern satire or pastoral? Or, to put it in the most everyday terms, what of the student who has a passionate interest in her or his literary world—a world that encompasses the digital as well as print culture but does not necessarily differentiate between the writings of one subculture or one theoretical orientation and another? Where do such prospective students turn?[14]

What is one to make of this suggestion that Joyce and Woolf and Faulkner or any of the other canonical authors listed are not being studied because curricula are crammed full with the works of, say,

Chinua Achebe and Gwendolyn Brooks?[15] (Since Perloff does not mention the names of minority or postcolonial writers—only that "a lot" of their work is "surely" being studied—one can only guess which writers she is referring to.)[16] What is most noteworthy in this passage is not that Perloff opposes the "important and exciting novels and poems" of "African American, other minorities, and postcolonial" writers against the great works of Joyce et al. (Joyce himself a postcolonial writer) but that, rather, she explicitly sets up an opposition, "in the most everyday terms," between the "literary" and the writings of these racialized[17] and postcolonial subjects who are members of "subculture[s]."[18]

For Perloff, the problem is not the death of literary print culture at the hands of the digital, as some critics lament—she is forward-thinking in championing new technologies and rightly sees no contradiction between the literary/poetic and the digital, or even between the literary and the cultural (there is no problem in studying a topic as sociological as "the Great Depression")—but that the works of "African American, other minorities, and postcolonial" writers leave no room in the curricula for those works that satisfy "the student who has a passionate interest in her or his literary world."[19] Perloff explicitly frames the choice as one between "passionate" and "literary" writing by famous named authors, all white, and an undifferentiated mass of unliterary writing by nameless minority authors.[20] Perhaps because she is writing in the more informal context of an organizational newsletter, Perloff feels freer to be more explicit about what exactly threatens the "literary" than in her MLA presidential address "It Must Change," where she uses more generic terms such as "culturally and politically oriented" research—though we can fairly accurately guess what the indefinite pronoun "It" in the title refers to.

My critique here is directed not at Perloff's views as an individual scholar but at an ideological position that she articulates in her MLA presidential address and the newsletter—one widely held in the academy but not usually so straightforwardly stated. Indeed, I admire the forthrightness with which Perloff expresses what many literary scholars think and feel but do not say except, perhaps, between the enclosed walls of hiring meetings: the frightening specter that, because of "politically correct" cultural-studies-ish pressures in the academy, presumably the detrimental legacy of both 1960s activism and the culture wars of the 1980s, worthy, major, and beloved works of literature—whose merits are "purely literary"—are being squeezed out of the curriculum by inferior works penned by minority writers, whose representation in the curriculum is solely the result of affirmative action or racial quotas or because their writings have passed an ideological litmus test, not literary merit. This sentiment is usually expressed in a manner much more coded though, nonetheless, clearly understood.

What makes it particularly disappointing that Perloff is the one using the powerful forum of the MLA presidency to express these conventional (and literary-establishment) views on minority writing and race is that for decades, she has fought hard to open the academy to unconventional modes and forms of poetry, which were often not considered poetry or even literature, at a time when there was no institutional reward for doing so. She was one of the first, and certainly the most prominent and vocal academic literary critic, to champion the Language poets and is almost single-handedly responsible for their now having become officially canonized and holding appointments at various prestigious English departments across the nation, such as the University of California, Berkeley, and the University of Pennsylvania. Anyone who works on avant-garde poetic writing in this country owes a debt to her—including myself.[21]

In the particular 2008 issue of the *PMLA* in question, it is left to Brent Edwards—the only critic in the group of eight respondents who writes on ethnic literature (and is himself African American)—the task of explicitly making the argument for the social in his response, "The Specter of Interdisciplinarity," to Perloff's "It Must Change" address and her posited binary of the "cultural" and the "political" versus the "literary":[22]

> Perloff uses "merely" [in her rhetorical question "Why *is* the 'merely' literary so suspect today?"] to suggest that the literary, even if threatened or "suspect," can nevertheless be considered in isolation, as the core of a disciplinary practice. (189)

In whatever form, literary criticism must not relinquish its unique point of articulation with the social. (191)

To reinforce this latter point, Edwards turns to the work of the black Martinican poet Monchoachi—"a pseudonym . . . the name of an infamous Maroon who led a violent insurrection against French slavery in Martinique" (191)—active in the *creolité* movement in the Francophone Caribbean:

> It is suggestive to read Monchoachi's speech [made in 2003 on accepting the Prix Max Jacob] in juxtaposition to Perloff's, at once for his "social interpretation" of the role of poetry, his different call for a "return," and his implicit departure from some of her framing gestures, perhaps above all her turn to Greek sources as foundations for the discipline of poetics. (191)

On the previous page, Edwards spoke of "the unique experimental character of postcolonial poetics," adding that "[s]till, only a handful of scholars have begun to theorize the relation between postcoloniality and poetics in a broader sense." That Edwards turns to a Francophone postcolonial poet, rather than an African American one, and speaks of the "comparative literature of the African diaspora," rather than US ethnic literature, is understandable, given the minefield that awaits anyone, especially a minority scholar, who dares to invoke the term "identity" (much less "race or "identity politics") in a US context. This treacherous terrain is a synecdoche of the fraught nature of any discussion about race in the larger national context—even, or especially, in this "post-race" era.

As it turns out, of the nine or so poets discussed with more than passing reference by Perloff and the eight respondents, Monchoachi is the only nonwhite writer and the one with the least name recognition among American academics.[23] In other words, even as the nine literary critics here evince a variety of aesthetic proclivities and allegiances (traditional versus avant-garde, major versus minor, and so on), methodological approaches (literary criticism, analytic philosophy, Frankfurt School), disciplinary stances (intra- versus inter-), and ideological commitments (classical, Marxist, postmodern, among others), the poets they choose to speak about constitute a much more

homogeneous and narrow group. This is not an insignificant observation: the selection of which authors critics consider worth devot-
ing time and energy to study speaks volumes about whom they consider truly literarily important. And, despite what we would like to
believe, the occlusion of minority poets here is not unrepresentative
of aporias in the field of poetry studies at large, even with the work of
those (nonminority) critics of modern and contemporary poetry who
have sought to link aesthetics and politics—Rachel Blau DuPlessis,
Michael Davidson, Alan Golding, David Lloyd, Cary Nelson, Aldon
Nielsen, Jerome McGann, Susan Schultz, Donald Wesling, and Shira
Wolosky, to name a few.[24]

Here, I must confess that, even as I tallied the list of poets in the
previous paragraph, I felt guilty—or was it pre-accused?—of having
taken precisely the sort of instrumental approach opponents of "identity politics" decry: of having come down on the side of the political and the social and the cultural against the "literary." I felt and
feel this indictment even though I am someone who has spent my
life, academic and otherwise, devoted to poetry; someone who is the
daughter of two English professors—a Romanticist and a Victorian-
ist—and someone who feels that there is indeed something distinctive
and valuable about literature and literary criticism and that literary
critics make a mistake when they become would-be analytic philosophers or scientists or legal scholars or economists.[25] I, too, feel wonder
at "how and why the art called poetry exert[s] such a magic spell"[26]
and believe that what literary and poetry critics have to contribute
to the field of knowledge is an attunement to and understanding of
language and the various literary forms it takes. I, too, agree that we
must have "theoretical, historical, and critical training in our own
discipline" (including prosody and poetics—knowing what an ode or
a terza rima is—and, in Gourgouris's words, "mastering the canonical
and the modes of interrogating it" [225]).

But—and this is a big but—I do not at all see why we must make
an either-or choice between reading Beckett *or* reading Aimé Césaire,
between calling out and into question "cultural desires, drives, anxieties, or prejudices"—the supposed realm of the cultural, the social,
and the political, cordoned off from the pure realm of the literary—*or*

analyzing metonymy, chiasmus, sprung rhythm, lineation, anaphora, parataxis, trochees, and so forth. The posited choices are false ones.

As Shira Wolosky, a scholar of nineteenth-century American poetry (and of Paul Celan), writes, "The notion of poetry as a self-enclosed aesthetic realm; as a formal object to be approached through more or less exclusively specified categories of formal analysis; as metahistorically transcendent; and as a text deploying a distinct and poetically 'pure' language: these notions seem only to begin to emerge at the end of the nineteenth century, in a process that is itself peculiarly shaped in response to social and historical no less than aesthetic trends."[27]

That critics of avant-garde writing fall into these traps is perhaps even more perplexing given that they have long had to fight off the same sorts of dismissive arguments about "literary value" and "literariness" that are now made about minority writing. But being marginalized in one arena, as avant-garde poets and critics have been, does not guarantee that one understands forms of marginalizations in other arenas—here, specifically racial.

What seems to me so drearily familiar in this exchange in *PMLA* is how much the readers both intuit and are expected to intuit, in a myriad of ways, spoken and unspoken, precisely what the terms invoked "really" mean and what is at stake here, at stake not just in the debates about the state of the profession but in the very conditions—the framework and terminologies—of the forum itself. In other words, what is even more operative here than what is explicitly stated is what is *not* stated, what does not *need* to be stated, or what needs to be stated only by shorthand: "identitarian," "identity politics," "cultural," "social," "political," "anxieties," "prejudices," "exotic," "carelessness," "haphazard" versus "literary," "classic," "classical," "discipline," among other terms. These terms (as does the term "avant-garde") act as placeholders for larger assumptions and beliefs, many of which have largely become normative in shoring up the supposed opposition between the cultural against the literary.

For, even as we have entered the twenty-first century—with a black man in the White House for two terms, avant-garde Language poets now holding major posts at our most prestigious universities, a globalized world with non-Western countries "on the rise," new forms of technology and media cropping up faster than we can assimilate them (including new forms of digital poetries and archives and forums of literary criticism)—many members of our profession continue to rely upon assumptions, beliefs, categories, and norms that operate unquestioningly in English departments across the country.[28] So it is that critics who might diverge quite strongly in their poetic allegiances, or who might disagree about how disciplinarity has or has not played itself out, can easily come to agreement across the aesthetic and institutional divides about what threatens the literary and the poetic. (Yes, the MLA and *PMLA* represent a certain "official" or perhaps institutionalized segment of poetry critics, but their influence has no close rival in the field.)

And I do not think that the views expressed in "The New Lyric Studies" are idiosyncratic or marginal to literary studies, despite, as noted earlier, the important work of a dozen or so poetry critics who do attend to the inseparability of the aesthetic and the sociopolitical. The conceptions and reception of minority poetry are concerns that are not quirky and individual matters of, say, "taste" but deeply ideological, institutional, and structural ones—framed and reflected by the curricula of departments of English, disciplines and units within colleges and universities, (in)visibility within the pages of *PMLA*, and decisions made by the NEH, and so on.

The framing of the state of decline of poetry studies as an opposition between social context and the literary is, of course, not new. Debates about poetry's role and relevance in society, "form" versus "content," and so on, extend back through the history of poetry—to the Greeks, surely, but more significantly and urgently for those of us in the modern era, to the Romantics (German and especially British, who witnessed firsthand capitalism's brutal triumph and the concomitant splitting off from the sullied market-driven world a realm of "pure" artistic sensibility). To understand how little we have traveled, imagine how William Blake and Percy Shelley might feel about their poetry's being discussed in purely "literary" terms. As Raymond Williams reminds us:

> What were seen at the end of the nineteenth century as disparate
> interests, between which a man must choose and in the act of choice

declare himself poet or sociologist, were, normally, at the beginning of
the century, seen as interlocking interests. . . . [A]s some sort of security against the vestiges of the dissociation, we may usefully remind
ourselves that Wordsworth wrote political pamphlets, that Blake was
a friend of Tom Paine and was tried for sedition, that Coleridge wrote
political journalism and social philosophy, that Shelley, in addition to
this, distributed pamphlets in the streets, that Southey was a constant
political commentator, that Byron spoke on the frame-riots and died
as a volunteer in a political war; and further, as must surely be obvious
from the poetry of all the men named, that these activities were neither marginal nor incidental, but were essentially related to a large part
of the experience from which the poetry itself was made.[29]

Since the revolutionary and world-changing period we now call
Romantic, urgent grapplings with the question of the aesthetic's
relation to the social and the political have made themselves felt
in distinct and vibrant poetic movements and groupings: various Modernist movements (Italian and Russian Futurism, Dada,
Surrealism, Harlem Renaissance, among others), the Frankfurt
School, Négritude, Black Arts, Language poetry, to name the most
noteworthy. In the English literary tradition alone, poet-artists and
poet-critics such as William Blake, Percy Shelley, Ezra Pound, Allen
Ginsberg, Amiri Baraka, Adrienne Rich, and Harryette Mullen, to
name but a few, have thoughtfully and incisively interrogated the
intersection of the aesthetic and the social.[30]

But what *is* new in the discussions of the last two decades or so—
in the aftermath of the various political movements of the 1960s and
1970s, which inevitably led to furious "culture wars" about the literary canon in the 1980s—has been the firm clicking into place of the
terms "identity," "identitarian," and, most overtly, "identity politics"
as the antithesis of (opposite to and opposing) literary value and critical rigor. So it is that one can group the terms "identitarian," "identity politics," "cultural," "social," "political," "anxieties," "prejudices,"
"exotic," "carelessness," and "haphazard" together and know exactly
what is being invoked (that is, demonized).

In the US academy and society at large, the words "identity," "identitarian," and "identity politics" are often automatically conflated. Used

synonymously, all three function as a reductive shorthand to refer to an essentializing and unthinking "identity politics"—almost always regarded, explicitly or not, as the provenance of minorities with grievances. "Identity politics" is a straw-man term. This is what I meant earlier when I called many of the words used by half of the *PMLA* critics "placeholders": they index something understood by readers as troubling but whose precise contours are amorphous and indistinct—and, I would argue, ultimately incoherent and indefensible. Indeed, if one were to put pressure on Gourgouris's singling out of the "high horse of identity politics," one might ask him, "Who exactly are the practitioners of this 'identity politics' in the academy? What specifically do they believe? Is 'identity politics' really the demon that has overtaken the study of literature and wrecked the disciplines of poetry studies and theory?"

This negative reaction to the term "identity" finds consensus across ideological and aesthetic differences, though for reasons varying in degree of nuance. And here we come to my second snapshot: While Gourgouris teaches in the Classics Department at Columbia and has translated the fairly mainstream poetry of Carolyn Forché into Greek, another scholar, Steve Evans, a major critic of more formally "radical" poetry (and of capitalism), has noted a not-dissimilar reaction among young avant-garde poets toward "identity," but for more complex and radical reasons than are evident in Gourgouris's *PMLA* piece. In "Introduction to *Writing from the New Coast*," an essay originally written in 1993 to introduce a collection of new experimental writing (and later reprinted in a 2002 anthology of essays on avant-garde poetics of the 1990s), Evans takes up Yeats's declaration that "the only movements on which literature can found itself . . . hate great and lasting things":

> It is my contention that such a hatred as Yeats speaks of does ani-
> mate the present generation [of post-Language avant-garde writers]
> although it is a hatred so thoroughgoing, so pervasive, and so unre-
> mitting as to make the articulation of it seem gratuitous, even fal-
> sifying. It is the hatred of Identity. . . . It is the hatred of those who
> have learned that, given current conditions, there exists not a single
> socially recognized "difference" worth the having.[31]

Evans is specifically talking about the conditions under capitalism in which everyone and everything are done violence to and flattened—what he describes as "capital's need to manufacture and mark 'difference' (commodification) while preserving and intensifying domination (its own systemic identity)" (14):

> As social space is forced to yield more and more of its autonomy to "the market"—where the mundane logic of the commodity dictates that nothing appear except under the aspect of identity—even progressive demands for the recognition of ethnic, linguistic, and sexual difference are converted into identity claims and sold back to the communities in which they originated at a markup. (14–15)

This sentence is a forceful rejoinder to critics, like Gourgouris, who indict those—one assumes members of various minorities—who supposedly make "identity" claims. Evans perceptively points out that, under late capitalism with its commodity logic, genuine claims of difference are "sold back" to the communities in which they originated "at a markup": for example, repackaged either as the illegitimate accusations of "identity politics" or in the form of an "inclusive" "multiculturalism" that exacts its own hidden high price.[32]

Yet, while I agree with Evans that no one and nothing escape Capital's maws, I cannot help feeling a lingering disquiet about the broad sweep of his claim that, under capitalism, "only one meaningful distinction remains—the distinction between identities-in-abeyance (markets awaiting 'penetration') and Identity as such (penetrant capital)" (15)—and for these reasons:

First, despite the fact that under capitalism "there exists not a single socially recognized 'difference' worth the having," the reality is (and I do not think Evans would disagree) that there are those who must unequally bear the burden of the material and psychic marks of these differences' continuing to be enforced and perpetrated, even if these differences are illusory.

Second, even within the airless and closed system of capitalism, there do exist varying ethical and political responses, specific ways to acknowledge and respond to the ongoing reality and effects of "socially recognized differences," even if they are produced under capitalism's corrupt aegis and are ultimately illusory—both the differences and the responses.

Third, such broad economically based analyses such as Evans's have the unfortunate outcome of producing their own flattening of differences and identities, even as Evans explains that "this generation's hatred of Identity"

> does not mean that all traces of the abstract idiom of "otherness" and "difference" developed in the poststructuralist and multiculturalist discourses have been, at a single stroke, erased from this emergent discourse [avant-garde poetries of the 1990s]. (15)

While Evans surely understands that those who find themselves on the wrong side of otherness and difference know that there is more at work and at stake than abstract idioms, he somehow fails to acknowledge the privilege that allows him—someone who is not an ethnic, linguistic, and/or sexual minority—to make such sweeping pronouncements with ease.

In this regard, Evans is not atypical of many smart and hip white male theorists and practitioners of avant-garde poetry who make cogent critiques about institutionalized forms of knowledge, power, and class (and poetry's relation to them) but do not seem to take into account their own (racial) privilege. Kenneth Goldsmith, the most famous of the Conceptual poets and a Perloff favorite, writing two decades later in *Uncreative Writing*,[33] evinces an even more myopic cluelessness about the privileges of his own subject position, as he lobbies for "uncreative writing":

> Uncreative writing is a postidentity literature. (85)

> If my identity is really up for grabs and changeable by the minute—as I believe it is—it's important that my writing reflect this state of ever-shifting identity and subjectivity. (84)

Goldsmith's token acknowledgment that "[t]he rise of identity politics of the past have [*sic*] given voice to many that have been denied. And there is still so much work to be done: many voices are still marginalized and ignored"[34] does not negate the raced, gendered, and classed tone-deafness and thoughtlessness of his somewhat glib claim that identity is "up for grabs and changeable by the minute."

As with Goldsmith's espousal of "postidentity literature," so with Evans's "hatred of Identity," there is the danger that, despite Evans's clarification about "multiculturalist discourses," such a broad use of the term "Identity" inevitably conjures for readers the specter of race and, especially for less discerning ones, an essentializing and unthinking racial "identity politics"—not the least because, as I have said, in the US context, "identity" and "identity politics" are often automatically conflated and associated with the aggrieved and "unearned" demands of racial minorities.

The reality is that we currently live in a system in which socially recognized differences operate. If they exist at all, conversations on race in this country suffer from, variously, inhibition, defensiveness, a paucity of signifiers, a narrow range of possible preordained positions, caricatures of thought on all sides—in short, a spectacular failure of memory and imagination. Thus, in invoking "Identity," even with his multiculturalist caveat, Evans puts into play in the mind of readers the bugaboos of "identity politics" and racial essentialism and all the knee-jerk, unexamined responses, assumptions, expectations, categories, and beliefs about race that swirl around the terms "identity" and "identity politics." Even used neutrally or "benignly"—as in discourses of "multiculturalism" and "diversity"—these terms are viewed as code words, and woe to the minority critic who foolishly invokes the term "identity"—or worse, "race." In polite company, some things are better left unsaid.

At the same time, we academics, whatever our political affiliations, understand that one black critic should be included at the party—in this case, a soiree of *PMLA* respondents. Brent Edwards, whether he wants to or not, serves a preordained role in the system: as the exceptional exception, hailing from an Ivy League institution, of course, but also the representative, in both senses of the term, of the social in the realm of the literary, the one who is given the unspoken (and unenviable) distinction of speaking for and about minority critics and poets.

Charles Bernstein is correct in seeing links between multiculturalism's so-called inclusiveness and a barely concealed (neo)liberal
politics:

> I see too great a continuum from "diversity" back to New Criti-
> cal and liberal-democratic concepts of a common readership that
> often—certainly not always—have the effect of transforming unre-
> solved ideological divisions and antagonisms into packaged tours of
> the local color of gender, race, sexuality, ethnicity, region, nation,
> class, even historical period: where each group or community or
> period is expected to come up with—or have appointed for them—
> representative figures we can all know about.[35]

That Edwards chooses to discuss a Francophone black Caribbean
rather than an African American poet makes, as I mentioned earlier,
perfect sense—and one does not need to ascribe a personal motive to
Edwards to see that. As the token black critic in the *PMLA* forum,
why should he also have to take on the burden of having to convince
other critics that a particular American black poet is really as "literary" and "rigorous" and worthy of study as, say, Robert Frost (or
Susan Howe)? This is the Catch-22 situation in which minority literary scholars all too often find themselves trapped.

While "hard-core" or "real" literary and poetry critics talk about
questions of etymology, prosody, and form, minority poets and poetry
are too often left out of the conversation about the literary (or simply
left out). How is it possible that among nine poetry critics, speaking
about poets across centuries and "The New Lyric Studies," not a single poet of color writing in English is cited? How is this possible when
and especially when—if we are to take such claims as Perloff's seriously—hordes of minority and postcolonial writers are taking over
our literature courses? This occlusion is, as we have seen, as true of
critics emphasizing literary issues, whether traditional or avant-garde,
as those interested in history (and historicizing) and ideology.

My third snapshot of the current reception of minority poetry
is a more experimental counterpart, if you will, to "The New Lyric
Studies": The "Rethinking Poetics" conference, held in June 2010 at
Columbia University, was a three-day gathering, convened by the

Penn-Columbia Poetics Initiative and organized by Bob Perelman, one of Language poetry's major figures and a University of Pennsylvania professor, and Michael Golston, who teaches avant-garde poetry and poetics at Columbia University and wrote his dissertation under Perloff. Like the *PMLA* forum and as its title indicates, "Rethinking Poetics" was conceived of as a "rethinking" of poetry and poetics, though more specifically by way of contemporary avant-garde writing (a.k.a. non-official-verse-culture poetry) rather than through a specific category of poetry such as lyric.[36] Prominent figures from Language and post-Language poetries participated or were in attendance: Susan Howe, Charles Bernstein, Bruce Andrews, Joan Retallack, Craig Dworkin, Juliana Spahr, Lisa Robertson, among others. "Rethinking Poetics" did include minority American poets and critics, though predominantly African American ones: of forty-one speakers—poets and/or academics—four were African American (including Brent Edwards), one Native American, and two Latino/a.[37] There was not a single Asian American included, despite the fact that New York City is the home to several prominent and established avant-garde Asian American poets, most notably John Yau and Mei-mei Berssenbrugge.

The minority invitees were tastefully dispersed across such panels as "Ecologies of Poetry" (the Native American poet was slotted here), "Globalism and Hybridity," and "Social Location/Ethics," though not in the crucial "Poetics as a Category" panel, which, not surprisingly, was all-white. Again, as in *PMLA*, the minority poets and critics served a certain preordained function: as representative tokens of the gathering's inclusiveness and open-mindedness, but their presence did not give rise to either a serious grappling of issues of race in American poetics and poetry—eco-poetics, by contrast, got its own panel—or an acknowledgment that minority poets and critics have something to say about avant-garde poetics "as a category."

In other words, neither "The New Lyric Studies" nor the "Rethinking Poetics" conference actually did a rethinking of the fundamental category of American poetry, including the intrinsic role of race in that category's formation[38] (that is, the inseparability of minority poetry and American poetry). This oversight is especially indefensible in the US context, given how crucial—indeed, fundamental—the question of race has been to the formation of the US nation-state and to the very notion of what is "American": our history, ideologies, myths, psyches, and, of course, our art forms, including our literatures.[39] The primacy of race in the US imaginary and reality is not simply a question of sociological "content" but has been, and continues to be, determinant of the forms of our textual productions—including our sacred foundational documents, the Declaration of Independence and the US Constitution.[40]

Poems are never divorced from contexts and from history, even as they are, among other things, modes of thinking philosophically through an engagement with formal constraints.[41] Likewise, what constitutes the social, the cultural, and the political must be analyzed for their linguistic and structural forms. Poetry works by conscious and unconscious means and arises from the complex interplay between the poetic imagination and the larger world. To be an American poet or poetry critic and *not* think about this larger world and its history seems like an incredible act of repression. "[W]hatever is said / in the world, or forgotten, / or not said, makes a form," reminds Robert Creeley.[42]

Race and American Poetry

That well into the second decade of the twenty-first century, we as literary critics are still perpetuating the either-or binary of the social versus the literary in the pages of our most prominent professional organization's journal says as much about the state of American poetry studies as it does about the larger US inability to face its history and the consequences of that history, especially in relation to issues of race. Race seems to me the most salient, contested, and painfully charged social difference in the American context,[43] and one that imbues—and must be disguised by— the more generic terms "cultural" and "political" when they are raised in opposition to the "literary." That said, I understand clearly that issues of race are inseparably intertwined with issues of class, and that class, too, produces painful differences. But in the minds of those who decry "identity" and "identity politics," it is race, not class, that drives the engine of "identity" and "identity politics," though this belief will not likely be explicitly articulated for fear of seeming to appear "racist."

To discuss American poetry and not discuss a single American minority poet—or include only the token one or two—speaks volumes about both a delusive blindness and a double standard in poetry studies. Because minority subjects and cultures are viewed in the American imaginary as occupying the realm of the bodily, the material, the social, they are often overlooked when considering questions of the literary and the cultural (in the sense of cultural value and high culture).[44] Form, whether that of traditional lyric or avant-garde poems, is assumed to be the provenance of a literary acumen and culture that is unmarked but assumed to be white.[45]

And if minority writers are acknowledged as producing literature at all, it is a literature that functions mimetically and sociologically as an ethnographic window into another "subculture"—or, in Founder Thomas Jefferson's words, a poetry of the "senses only, not the imagination."[46] Elaine Showalter, a major critic of women's writing who taught for two decades at Princeton University, expresses a not atypical view of minority literature's character:

> During the 1960s and 1970s, teaching literature became an explicitly political act for radical and minority groups in the university. English departments were the places where feminist and African-American critics first began to initiate courses and put pressure on the curriculum to include black and women writers. Their efforts heralded a paradigm shift in canon formation and literary studies generally, and a repudiation of formalism in favor of a more engaged and partisan reading that saw the goal of literary study as the formation of personal identity and political struggle. . . .
>
> But the theory revolution of the 1970s quickly shifted attention away from the mimetic use of literature.[47]

Note Showalter's smooth elision of "radical" and "minority." And while her facts are not quite accurate about English departments' being the first sites of struggle—they were arguably the sites of the most bitter struggles, given how resistant English departments in general were (and in too many instances, still are) to the inclusion of minority writers in the curricula[48]—she expresses the not uncommon view among English professors that minority literature "repudiates formalism," is "partisan" (in contrast to racially "unmarked" canonical literature, which presumably is unpartisan) and mimetic, and emphasizes the "formation of personal identity" as a "goal" of literary studies.[49]

In assuming the interchangeability of "minority" and "mimetic" forms, Showalter may not know her American literary history very well. Modernist writers such as Jean Toomer and Langston Hughes and the Filipino American poet Jose Garcia Villa were experimenting with form well before the 1960s and 1970s. The mixed-race poet Sadakichi Hartmann, whose mother was Japanese, was writing Symbolist poetry at the end of the nineteenth century (he also served as a secretary to Walt Whitman).[50] Even during the "radical" 1960s and 1970s, Black Arts writers, such as Amiri Baraka, and Asian American writers, such as Mei-mei Berssenbrugge,[51] were acutely interested in pushing the limits of the English language—a project that did not contradict (indeed, helped to further) the struggle to attain the full equality that had been promised all Americans, not just white men of property, since the eighteenth century. (Baraka, as LeRoi Jones, was, of course, centrally involved with downtown avant-garde culture in New York City in the 1950s, and close to poets in various avant-garde and countercultural movements, such as Ed Dorn and Frank O'Hara.)

Baraka is a perfect example of a formally innovative and politically engaged poet who almost always gets typecast as a "radical" minority writer and is marginalized by both mainstream and avant-garde poetry groupings. As a key figure in the New York City literary scene in the 1950s and 1960s, Baraka has incorporated all sorts of formal and political concerns in his poetry and in his work in various communities. His writing has had crucial links to American Surrealism, Black Mountain, the New York School, the Beats, Black Arts (which he largely founded), jazz poetry,[52] jazz criticism, leftist poetry, avant-garde poetry, minority poetry, and minority and avant-garde fiction. He is perhaps the most polyvalent American poet and critic of the twentieth century. Baraka's work has been endlessly inventive over the decades, never standing still, yet he is for the most part largely categorized as an "angry," "radical" black poet stuck in the 1960s and Black Nationalist and Marxist thinking.

The problematic nature of the rhetoric and forms of how minority poetry gets discussed is a function of several factors—of which the endemic American inability to deal head-on with the legacy and reality of racial oppression and disparities is one. First, there remains a lingering tendency within literary studies and in the wider reading public to view prose as the bearer of social analysis, and poetry, especially the lyric, as the genre addressing more personal, private, and "purely" literary concerns. Even as illustrious a critic as Bakhtin, despite some later revising of his ideas, held this bias (as I discuss more fully in Chapter 6).[53]

Second, since the racialized poet, subject, and person is often apprehended in terms of the bodily,[54] the material, and the political, her poetry is inevitably, though often not consciously, posited in opposition to the abstract, the intellectual, the literary. Minority writing, including poetry, is inevitably read as mimetic, autobiographical, "representative," and ethnographic, with the poet as native informant (for example, Chinatown tour guide), providing a glimpse into her supposed ethnic culture. Since poetry remains, even in the twenty-first century, the epitome of high literary culture, minority poetic production is often treated as a dispensable add-on to this long tradition—the recent inclusion of minority poets in poetry anthologies such as the *Norton Anthology of Poetry* functions largely as a concessionary bone (market-driven) in this so-called multicultural age.

Third, since the terms "minority" and "poetry" are conceived of in the academy as intrinsically opposed—content versus form, sociological versus literary, and so on—minority poetry is often seen as belonging more properly to the provenance of cultural studies or ethnic studies. As we can see in the *PMLA* presentation of "The New Lyric Studies," the place at the table for minority poetry in discussions about, say, meter or poetic form, is barely there, if it exists at all— and this holds true, again, for critics of both mainstream lyric poetry and avant-garde work. When critics read "real poets" such as Jorie Graham or John Ashbery, they almost always examine the "poems themselves," paying attention, for example, to their use of tone or parataxis. When they read a literary work, fiction or poetry, by an Asian American writer, they almost inevitably assume that the work functions as a transparent window into the ethnographic "truth" of a hyphenated identity and an exotic "home" culture—in other words, as if there were no such thing as the mediatedness of language.

On the other side of the aesthetic spectrum, critics of avant-garde Asian American poetry (such as that by Tan Lin or Mei-mei Berssenbrugge) tend, in their analysis of the poems, to completely ignore the ethnicity of the poet,[55] even when the poet makes clear that racialized/ethnic identity is not a trivial concern in the work. Ironically (and self-contradictorily), critics of avant-garde poetry, who privilege a focus on form and who usually excoriate thematic readings of poems, will dismiss the relevance of race in the work of, say, Berssenbrugge, by recourse to the very sorts of thematic rationales they abhor: in this case, by citing the lack of racial themes or markers. But a perceptive reader, especially an experienced reader of formally innovative writing, would know to look closely at what the poem's form, and not simply its content, tells us.[56]

Asian American Poetry and the American Body Politic

I turn now from the broader category of "minority poetry" to the particular case of Asian American poetry, which, like Latina/o and Native American writing, is seen as marginal to the category "minority literature"—and is thus doubly marginalized within the academy (triply, if one takes genre into account). Most critics use the term "minority" to mean "African American," as typified by the previous Showalter quote and demonstrated by the demographic representation of the *PMLA* and the "Rethinking Poetics" groupings. If discussed at all, Asian American writing is treated as ancillary in the current academy and viewed as being of interest mainly to Asian American students; unlike African American literature, Asian American literature is almost wholly studied by specialists of Asian American literature, who are almost all of Asian descent. If Asian American literature is included in American literature courses at all, it is represented by the token inclusion of Maxine Hong Kingston's *The Woman Warrior* or, perhaps, Jhumpa Lahiri's and Chang-rae Lee's fiction (both having been anointed in the pages of the *New Yorker*). The poetry is almost never taught—except perhaps in specialized Asian American literature courses, but even then not so much.

Indeed, most critics of American literature or poetry can hardly name one Asian American poet, or at most one or two, and view the work as being tertiary to the American literary canon. This is the case even though Asian American poetry has been written for more than a century by an array of authors whose ethnic origins, genres, and styles are widely varied. In terms of its breadth of aesthetic styles and time span, Asian American literature as a category is certainly more variegated and wide ranging than, say, Modernist writing. All too often in English departments Asian American literature seems to be taught not so much as a body of work with literary merit but as texts that Asian American undergraduates can "relate to."[57]

So why focus on such a "narrow" stratum of American poetic writing? My answer: because of Asian Americans' unique form of racial interpellation—inextricably linked to the view of them as culturally and linguistically unassimilable—Asian American writing offers a particularly illuminating "limit case," for thinking not only about the relationship between a poet's interpellation (including racialization) in American society and her relationship to the English language but also, more broadly, about the assumptions and preconceptions undergirding our notions of poetry, English-language poetry, American literature, "Americanness," the English language, and questions of literary value, among others.[58]

To explain what I mean requires a knowledge of history.

Like all groups of minority Americans, Asian Americans have experienced unique forms of racial interpellation within the United States, but unlike other minority groups, "Orientals," "Asiatics," and "Asians" in particular came to exemplify a racialized form of *constitutive and immutable* alienness from what it means to be "American."

A little over thirty years after the arrival of Chinese immigrants to this country in the mid-nineteenth century, this perception of utter foreignness, nonassimilability, and un-Americanness—which, to a greater or lesser degree, has persisted to this day, albeit in slightly variant guises—had already hardened into pernicious, and legalized, form. The Chinese Exclusion Act, passed in 1882 and not repealed until 1943, was the first and only immigration exclusion law in American history to exclude a specific named group on the basis of race.[59]

In fact, the Chinese were seen as more unassimilable than even ex–chattel slaves. As Supreme Court Justice Harlan wrote in 1896 in his oft-lauded dissent in *Plessy v. Ferguson*, arguing against the logic of the majority opinion upholding "separate but equal," "There is a race so different from our own that we do not permit those belonging to it to become citizens of the United States. Persons belonging to it are, with few exceptions, absolutely excluded from our country. I allude to the Chinese race."[60]

Yet, as US history has unfolded, this interpellation of Asians and Asian Americans as perpetually and constitutively foreign, alien, and threatening to the very idea of "Americanness" itself has also become intermixed with or, some may think, supplanted by what is mistakenly viewed as more benign or even "positive" images of them as "model minorities"[61] and "honorary whites." In reality, these hollow honorifics (stereotypes) "reward" Asian Americans precisely for their compliance, docility, submissiveness—and function to generate more (nameless, faceless, and interchangeable) workers in our capitalist economy and ensure their invisibility and voicelessness within the American national and political body.[62] "Honorary whites" are, of course, not "real" whites and are granted none of the benefits of white privilege; at the same time, Asian Americans also experience the drawbacks of not being perceived as "real" or "true" minorities either.[63]

For all minority groups in this country, two facts obtain: First, the processes of racialization have entailed the pressure to assimilate, the struggle to prove one's true "Americanness," and have been enforced by forms of violence and domination. Second, proving one's "Americanness" has always been inextricably tied to the imperative to master English[64] and to erase any foreign tongues and accents.[65] But, Asian Americans in particular have been singled out in US history as *constitutively* and immutably foreign and "nonnative" to American culture and the body politic[66]—threatening to the very idea of "Americanness"[67]—a pernicious and unwavering ideological characterization that has been inseparable from the belief that "Orientals" are also constitutively nonnative speakers of English and thus can never overcome, no matter how hard they try, this deficit to the English language because it is foundational.[68] Even Asian Americans who are fourth-generation American, with a perfect command of English, are often asked if English is their native tongue.[69]

One might ask, "What is the link between the perception that Asian Americans are not 'real' Americans and are nonnative speakers of English, and the belief, largely unconscious, that Asian American poets are not 'real' poets?" It is clear that this perception of Asian Americans as utterly alien to Americanness and to the English language—a view that persists even in this "post-racial" era—cannot *not* be a factor in the reception of Asian American poets.

Given these assumptions and stereotypes, an Asian American poet, whether knowingly or not, often faces a particularly vexed and compensatory relation to the English that is always already not hers, and to an English literary tradition in which poetry continues to be seen as the genre most tied to high culture, literary tradition, formal mastery, and "native tongue"—a literary tradition from which minority writers were largely excluded for centuries and into which they were granted entry only recently, after the furious canon wars of the 1980s, and only begrudgingly—in limited and policed fashion—allowed to occupy circumscribed academic and aesthetic Bantustans because of the generosity of enlightened liberals. While many writers feel an "anxiety of influence" in relation to a dominant literary tradition, for Asian American writers, the usual questions of literary culture, tradition, and reception confronting an individual writer take on an added, if not more intense (and intensely painful), urgency and burden for all the reasons detailed.

How then does an Asian American poet situate herself in an Anglo-American poetic tradition when she is marked as constitutively alien and unassimilable and excluded from the category of "native speaker" of English? How does an Asian American poet labor under and contend with the foregone conclusion that her English will never be "good enough"?

It is my contention that the answers surface as much in the formal structures as in the thematic content of Asian American poetry.

Many of the poets in this study focus obsessively on the question of language and writing, even as their poems deal with a wide range of concerns. Of course, to some extent all poets are hyperaware of the act of writing itself, but for Asian American poets, this relation to the writing—and wished-for mastery—of English takes on a heightened sense of self-consciousness because of their constitutive exclusion from the category of native speaker. When Li-Young Lee says, "Everything is language,"[70] he may be speaking primarily as a poet, but one has the strong sense that his poems' obsessive concern with getting names and naming right is more than just a function of his simply being interested in words.

Since Asian American poetry occupies a unique place in the American national body and literary imaginary—as a body of American writing that inextricably ties the racial group seen as having the most alien/alienated relationship to the English language and the most exalted and elite English literary genre[71]—it can be argued that Asian American poetry is not only not marginal to thinking about American poetry and poetics but is *especially* resonant for thinking about such literary and literary historical concerns.

There is also a strong case to be made for studying a sizable but largely neglected body of American writing: Asian American poetry. While Asian American fiction has had some visibility with the reading public, primarily through the popularity of two works—Amy Tan's *The Joy Luck Club* and Maxine Hong Kingston's *The Woman Warrior*—few Americans, including literary scholars of American literature, are familiar with Asian American poetry.

While I am highly aware of the many contradictions of and tensions within the category "Asian American," I also understand the practical realities and strategic necessity of such a term. Just as in the 1960s and 1970s, various Americans who (or whose ancestors) emigrated from China, Japan, the Philippines, Korea, Vietnam, and other Asian countries shared an experience of racism and discrimination in American society—of being seen as "gooks"[72] and "all looking alike"—and, thus, found political power in coming together as "Asian American," so in the twenty-first century, the presence of the categories "Asian American studies" and "Asian American literature" in the academy enables Asian American literature to be taught at all. Indeed, one could make a strong case that without these institutional slots, even *The Woman Warrior* would rarely be taught, whether in classes on American literature or contemporary fiction. The same was the case with the categories "women's studies" and "African American studies": the institutional existence of these disciplines was necessary so as to get writing by women and blacks into the door and onto curricula. These writings did not just magically appear in universities—their presence was the result of hard-fought battles and struggles taking place over many years, and still being fought today, with professional and personal costs to minority professors and students.[73] In other words, in order to interrogate the category "Asian American," one needs the category to begin with.

Asian American literature occupies the paradoxical position of being both emergent—many English departments across the country are just now filling their first positions in Asian American literature long after they have hired specialists in African American literature and women's literature—and disappearing at the same time: not a few English departments at prestigious institutions across the country are now turning toward "transnational" or "global" or "diasporic" conceptualizations and contextualizations of Asian American writing, moving away from having to deal with issues of US racial politics—and racism.

When confronted with how little college and graduate students and faculty colleagues know about either Asian American history or literature, I often have to remind them that in the last century the United States fought four wars with Asian countries (the Philippines, Japan, Korea, and Vietnam,[74] with many millions killed), that an Asian country was the only one in history to have had a nuclear bomb (two, in fact) dropped on it, that the only group of potential immigrants to the United States to have been specifically identified and systematically excluded on the basis of race was Chinese (government

enforcement of the Chinese Exclusion Act in 1882 necessitated the creation of the precursor—and foundation—of our current US Citizenship and Immigration Services, an agency within the Department of
Homeland Security),[75] and that the only group of American citizens
ever interned in concentration camps on the basis of their ethnicity
was Japanese Americans. One is almost surprised at how consistent
and continuous the yellow-peril rhetoric has been over the past century and a half, from Chinese exclusion to, now in the twenty-first
century, the "rise of China."

I am not saying that there is an easy one-to-one correlation
between how Asians and Asian Americans have been apprehended in
American history, society, and in the public imaginary and how their
writers have been received in the literary realms, but I am confident
that the common (mis)perception that Asian Americans are perpetual
foreigners bearing a constitutively nonnative relationship to the English language cannot have not influenced the ways in which Asian
American writing has been read—or rather, misread.

For example, in 1982, when Cathy Song became the first Asian
American poet to win the Yale Younger Poets Prize for her first
book, *Picture Bride*, the selecting judge, poet Richard Hugo,
described the Honolulu-born, Wellesley-educated poet as one who
"accommodates experiential extremes with a sensibility strength-
ened by patience that is centuries old, ancestral, tribal, a gift passed
down."[76] One wonders if Hugo would have invoked the "ancestral,
tribal" and "centuries-old" patience and sensibility of a white American Yale Younger winner or focused on the poet's "accommodat-
ing" nature and the "experiential."

One would think that things are different now, in the wake of multiculturalism and the changes wrought by the canon wars. Yet almost
thirty years later, when Ken Chen won the same prize in 2009, reviewers' responses to his work split into two distinct and opposed categories.
As Chen puts it in an e-mail, "My book confuses them [reviewers] bc
[because] they either think it's all Asian all the time and ignore the rest or
they only focus on the avant-garde formal stuff and ignore the content."[77]
As an example of the former, the reviewer on the Poetry Foundation's
Harriet blog reads Chen's volume *Juvenilia* almost wholly thematically:

> The speaker's upbringing is marked by his parent's [*sic*] disaffected marriage ("faces that would not kiss in life") and eventual separation. The inability to communicate, an affliction that spans across generations for this Chinese American family, manifests itself as a mysterious illness on [*sic*] the young speaker who sees his relatives succumb to the ills of unhappiness bottled up within.[78]

This sort of reception is not atypical. Reviewers and scholars, when writing about Asian American poetry, almost never pay attention to linguistic, literary, and rhetorical form (perhaps because of their ingrained perception of Asian Americans' generations-old "inability to communicate"?)—an oversight that is all the more puzzling when the object of attention is a poem, whose very being depends on figures of speech, meter, rhythm, and other formal properties. This seems to be the tendency, though less pronounced, even when the critic works within the field of minority literature or is a minority person himself (as is the case here).

Anyone who has written even a few lines of poetry knows how crucial a decision it is that someone chooses to write a poem—and not, say, a journalistic essay or political manifesto—and how essential are the myriad formal decisions made at every turn in a poem: where to break the line, what rhythmic or metrical pattern (or none) will govern, what will constitute the unit of the stanza, how the poem will look on the page, and so on. It is not only a matter of conscious authorial choice but also of the submerged or unconscious structures of language that make themselves felt in the particular language of individual poems.

Certainly in the United States, where race has been absolutely fundamental to the formation of national identity and national history and to the texture of everyday life, one's racial identity—or presumed universality in being racially "unmarked"—must play a role, consciously or unconsciously, in the formation of the American poet, black or yellow or white. Racial interpellation is absolutely inescapable in the formation of American subjectivity, not just the subjectivity of "visible minorities."

Thus, the occlusion or ignoring of race by critics and poets at the avant-garde end of the critical spectrum is equally as disturbing as the fetishization of racial and ethnic content and identity by more mainstream poetry critics. Critics of avant-garde writing, despite their openness to radical new poetic forms, often fall into the same traps as more formally conservative critics when thinking (or, more accurately, not thinking) the link between poetry and the subjectivity—which includes the racialized subjectivity—of the poet. They overwhelmingly tend to ignore race by focusing exclusively on formal properties or other themes in the writing (for example, emotion or science in Berssenbrugge's poetry); to explicitly oppose political and social "content" (including racial identity) against formal literary concerns; or to distinguish between "bad" ethnic poetry (autobiographical, identity-based) and "good" poetry (formally experimental) that just happens to be written by a person of color.[79]

An example of the third route appears in the review of Chen's *Juvenilia* in *Publishers Weekly*. While not writing for an avant-garde publication, the anonymous reviewer nonetheless privileges certain kinds of formal experiment and expresses a firm view of what constitutes bad ethnic writing:

> The latest Yale Younger Poet writes about his Chinese-American heritage; he draws on classic Chinese poets, such as Wang Wei and Li Yu. Yet his verse and prose stand at the farthest possible remove from the memoirlike poems, and the poems of first-person "identity," that have characterized so much recent verse about U.S. immigrant life. Instead, Chen is "experimental" in the best and broadest sense of the term: each new page brings an experiment in self-presentation, in sentence, syntax, or (long) line.[80]

Here, good minority poetry is set against bad minority poetry, which focuses on "identity" (that hated concept, again), and to be experimental in the "best and broadest sense of the term" is, implicitly, not to discuss race or ethnic identity.

One could make the case that the categories "experimental," "innovative," and "avant-garde" are often implicitly coded as "white"— as Harryette Mullen and a few other experimental minority poets and scholars have argued—and that not only do the few minority writers included in experimental anthologies and conferences tend to function as tokens (Mullen describes the situation as "aesthetic apartheid"[81]) but also, as we see in the case of Baraka's poetry, certain modes of experimentality, such as jazz poetics, are excluded from definitions of the avant-garde and "experimental." The criteria of what counts as avant-garde, even in the twenty-first century, is judged according to High Modernism's purely formalist repertoire: disruption of syntax, fragmentation of the line, and so on.[82]

We should interrogate this monolithic view of what constitutes the avant-garde and what criteria of linguistic experimentation pass the test. In "Language and the Avant-Garde," a chapter of his book *The Politics of Modernism*, Raymond Williams writes,

> Thus what we have really to investigate is not some single position of language in the avant-garde or language in Modernism. On the contrary, we need to identify a range of distinct and in many cases actually opposed formations, as these have materialized in language. This requires us, obviously, to move beyond such conventional definitions as "avant-garde practice" or "the Modernist text."[83]

We can see that, just as much as the term "identity politics," the term "avant-garde" comes with its own set of (racialized) assumptions and implications.

Experimental minority poets are often included in the avant-garde fold either because their work and stylistic choices are universalized as part of an avant-garde movement ("she's just like us, but, oh, isn't it great that she also happens to be black?") or because they are seen as "exceptions" to the general tendency of minority poets to write badly and to focus mistakenly on identity politics (or is it that they write badly *because* they focus on issues of race and identity?). As I have demonstrated, racial identity often becomes conflated with the strawman term "identity politics."

In the last section of *Thinking Its Presence: Form, Race, and Subjectivity in Contemporary Asian American Poetry*, I examine the work of Mei-mei Berssenbrugge and Pamela Lu, whose poetry manifests virtually no ethnic themes or markers at all. By looking at this avant-garde writing, I put to a more strenuous test my argument that it is in the formal and rhetorical manifestations, particularly the linguistic structures, of the poems that one sees evidence of the impress of social and historical influences. For instance, Berssenbrugge's having been born in Beijing to a Dutch American father and a Chinese mother, with Chinese as her first language, but then raised in New England, have made her acutely aware of the contingency and relationality of not only human identity but also language and natural phenomena. This awareness deeply informs her poetic lines, which are rife with a syntax of contingency and conditionality (frequently marked by use of the subjunctive mood and/or the conditional mode). One example: "She wonders what the body would reveal, if the cloud were transparent" (from "Honeymoon," published in *Empathy*).[84]

In making a claim for the link between a minority avant-garde poet's work and her racialized ethnic subjectivity, I make a critical intervention in current discussions about avant-garde writing. Whether critics focus solely on ethnic content in more mainstream Asian American poetry or whether critics ignore issues of race in avant-garde Asian American poetry and privilege the "purely" literary or formal (against the ethnic), the full complexity of Asian American poetry—and minority American poetry—has not been acknowledged. These critical approaches profoundly impoverish our understanding of the complex multidimensionality and contradictions of American and English-language poetry.

Thinking Its Presence

In *Thinking Its Presence: Form, Race, and Subjectivity in Contemporary Asian American Poetry*, I argue against such reductive modes of reading Asian American poetry. The book builds its case by focusing with great particularity on the writings of five contemporary Asian American poets who range in age from their early forties to late sixties[85]— Li-Young Lee, Marilyn Chin, John Yau, Mei-mei Berssenbrugge, and Pamela Lu—and whose poems represent a spectrum of literary styles, from expressive lyric to less transparently representational and more formally experimental. For each poet's body of work, I consider, through detailed readings, a formal crux or mode (metaphor, irony, parody, a syntax of contingency, the subjunctive mood) whose deployment is central to his or her poetic project and whose structure articulates and enacts in language the poet's working out of a larger political (in the broadest sense of that term) and/or poetic concern or question.

These specific formal aspects of the poems simultaneously reflect and manifest aesthetic influences[86]—compositional decisions, structures of language (conscious and unconscious), the shadow of literary precursors, and so on—but also, importantly, the influence of sociopolitical forces and historical context, such as geographical location, current events, and his or her socialization in the world as a person of a particular, race, gender, sex, class, and educational level.[87] This is as true for "mainstream" lyric poets as it is for "avant-garde" poets. And it is as true for white poets as for minority ones.

Even supposedly as "hermetic" and "enigmatic" a poet as Paul Celan—who certainly knew firsthand what it meant to be a minority (and racialized) poet in a hegemonic European language—understood that "the poem does not stand outside time. True, it claims the infinite and tries to reach across time—but across, not above." This from a speech he gave in 1958, thirteen years after the end of the Nazi death camps.[88]

By doing intensive and serious readings of these particular Asian American poets' use of language and linguistic forms—what Susan Wolfson calls "theory in action"[89]—I aim to show how erroneous we have been to view Asian American poetry through a simplistic, reductive, and essentializing lens: as a homogeneous lump of "nonliterary" writing by "Asians." As with white poets' work, each Asian American poet's practice is different from another's, and how language is deployed in his or her work is particular to that writer.

Thinking Its Presence: Form, Race, and Subjectivity in Contemporary Asian American Poetry joins in its analytical framework methods and areas of study usually considered disparate, if not mutually exclusive: formal analysis, literary history, reader reception, race studies, avant-garde writing. By juxtaposing form, sociohistorical context, and poetic subjectivity, it questions customary methodological, literary-historical, and disciplinary practices and assumptions—such as the supposed dichotomy between cultural-studies approaches and formal literary analysis. Must a poetry or cultural critic be forced to choose between an interest in form (with its implied anti-cultural-studies stance) and the desire to understand the historical conditions, social and aesthetic, of the production of a poem? In the twenty-first century, is it not time to rethink these ingrained poetic and literary-critical categories and assumptions?

The phrase "thinking its presence" in my book's title comes from Mei-mei Berssenbrugge's poem "Chinese Space" (from her 1989 volume, *Empathy*) and evokes both the ineffability of certain phenomena and their very real materiality and presence. Being able to cognitively grasp ("think") these phenomena—in this case, politics, history, race, and their effects on subjectivity and language—does not in any way reify or essentialize or make reductive the not always definite (note the indefinite pronoun "its"[90]), often mysterious, but very real relation between and among the social (racial), subjective, and poetic. As Boris Ejxenbaum writes in "Literary Environment," "The relations between the facts of the literary order and facts extrinsic to it cannot simply be causal relations but can only be the relations of correspondence, interaction, dependency, or conditionality" (61).

Paying close attention to what poems tell us—not so much in their stated content but in their formal manifestations—is itself a praxis-based methodology of theorizing. As poems in their linguistic specificity are powerful means of philosophically thinking about the world through language, so my close readings are, in their detailed unfolding, a theoretical engagement with the poem and the social world. [91] For example, in the poetry of Li-Young Lee, the structure of metaphor, with its almost-but-not-quite equivalences, isomorphically captures both the poet's Romantic struggles to have an unmediated connection to his authoritarian, Chinese, Presbyterian-minister father; to God; to his Chinese ancestry and language; and to the felt pressure to assimilate to American culture in rural Pennsylvania and to the English language.

Let me make clear that I am not positing a simplistic causal or reductive link between the world—in this case, being "Asian American"—and the poem (Ejxenbaum again: "The relations between the facts of the literary order and facts extrinsic to it cannot simply be causal relations" [61]). Nor am I arguing that Li-Young Lee is deploying an "Asian American" (or even Chinese American) way of using metaphor, that there is an "Asian American" way of writing poetry, that there is a reifiable Asian American "essence" that can be found in various formal elements and structures, or that there is one "Asian American" or "Chinese American" essence or link joining the work of Asian American poets (or even the half dozen Chinese American poets in my study). In other words, as a category, "Asian American literature" encompasses texts that are as heterogeneous and varied as those in other conventional literary categories, such as "women's literature" or "African American literature" or "American literature" or "Victorian literature."[92]

Thus, the use of participial phrases in the poetry of Mei-mei Berssenbrugge works differently and springs from different sources than the use of such phrases in the work of Myung Mi Kim (or Robert Lowell). The lived experiences of all three poets as poets of particular social and historical formations are as much a part of their poetic subjectivities as are their readings in the poetic tradition, and these influences emerge in the form of language in the poem. Each poet's life history is particular to her—as is her poetic practice—but that is not to say that certain shared general experiences do not obtain (for example, the Great Depression) and make an impact on one's subjectivity and work, even though that impact will be expressed in ways specific to each poet. For the racialized poet, a significant part of her lived and psychic experience is the fact of having moved in the world and been apprehended as a racialized subject. Given the importance of race and racialization in the formation and history of these United States, one could argue that for *American* poets, white or minority, to ignore such fundamental sociopolitical issues consistently and broadly over time constitutes serious acts of omission.

While the precise nature of the link between the world and a poetic text can never be fully explicated, what is clear is that the path to understanding that relation can come only through close readings of particular poems themselves—and an understanding of the poet's and text's place, both temporal and spatial, in historical context. Whether reading the poems of Li-Young Lee or Gerald Stern, Mei-mei Berssenbrugge or Leslie Scalapino, one must pay careful attention to the nuances and specificities of the poet's particular use of language and the sociopolitical environment, whose particular residues (some different, some shared) have suffused each poet's subjectivity and influenced the production and reception of poems.

I cannot emphasize this point enough. For in bringing race into the critical conversation about avant-garde writing—in particular, by positing a link between racial subjectivity and the forms of poetry—one runs the risk of being accused of conjuring up a link that is not there or artificially "imposing" the issue of race onto "racially unmarked" writing, usually by smuggling in some reductive essentialist version of racial identity.

A typical objection might run: "If John Yau and T. S. Eliot in their poetry both question a stable and transparent subjectivity, then why is what Yau is doing specifically 'Asian American' or 'Chinese American'"? The fallacious assumption here is that because Yau and Eliot both seem to be making similar poetic (and metaphysical) moves, these moves are formally and substantively identical. But Eliot and Yau are *not* actually doing the same thing in their poetries. Given how radically different their persons, subjectivities, histories, contexts, and so on are, there is no way that their projects of destabilizing subjectivity are the same. Nor can the resulting poems be the same.

Poetic subjectivities and poetic practices are not interchangeable. It would be just as wrong to claim that Eliot's and Yau's are interchangeable as it would be to claim that Yau's and Tan Lin's are interchangeable. Sadly, though, our idea of ethnic Americans is often to (unconsciously) render them as abstract, one-dimensional, homogeneous, and interchangeable.

While it may initially appear that Yau and Eliot are doing the same thing with the subject, their reasons for doing so stem from different contexts and are specific to, and part of, their own histories, subjectivities, and poetic projects. Thus, it would be misguided to claim that Yau's emphasis on destabilized identities itself is specifically "ethnic" or "Chinese American" or is necessarily limited to Chinese American subjects.[93]

The variegated and complex particularities of Yau's experiences as a racialized person cannot be reified into some practice or thing called "Chinese American." There is no one stable Asian American or Chinese American identity or subjectivity or point of view or poetic practice. The subjectivity of an ethnic American is not a thing or a content. Of course other poets who are not Chinese American—such as T. S. Eliot—destabilize the subject, too. Eliot's reasons, conscious or unconscious, for his poetic choices will be different from Yau's.

To underscore how the element of race skews these discussions about poetry; how it elicits reductive, contradictory, conflationary thinking; how it throws the burden of proof over and over again back onto the critic who raises the issue of race, one need only do two thought experiments.

The first would be to continue with the comparison of Yau's and Eliot's poetry, but to switch the burden of proof from Yau's minority poetry to Eliot's canonical poetry and to change the extratextual feature from race to some nonracialized experience or feature—for example, Eliot's experiences in Europe in World War I. How likely would a critic of Modernist poetry be given a hard time for claiming that these experiences influenced the fractured subjectivities and the broken lines in *The Wasteland*? How likely would this appeal to the extratextual be shot down for being extratextual? How likely would this critic be rebutted with the argument that, because no unproblematic correlation between Eliot's extratextual experiences and his poetry can be proven, then the fractured lines and subjectivities in *The Wasteland* were not influenced at all by Eliot's wartime experiences in Europe?

And, to push the point further, how likely would it be that someone would then say to that critic, "Well, John Yau also fractures subjectivity and breaks lines in his 'Genghis Chan' poems, and because Yau does the same thing as Eliot, but Yau never lived in Europe during the war, then Eliot's having lived in Europe was not a necessary influence on *The Wasteland*. And not only was it not necessary but it was not an influence at all"?

The second thought experiment: remove race from the equation completely and compare not a white and a minority poet but two white poets—say, Eliot and Stein—using the same scenario of a critic's claiming that Eliot's experiences in wartime Europe had influenced the form of *The Wasteland*. How likely would this critic of Modernist poetry be rebutted by the counterargument that since Stein also fractured poetic subjectivities and lines, but did not have the same experiences as Eliot in Europe, then Eliot's particular wartime experiences were not a "necessary" influence on the lines in *The Wasteland*—again, not only were not necessary but were not a factor at all?

The arguments in *Thinking Its Presence: Form, Race, and Subjectivity in Contemporary Asian American Poetry* about the interplay between racial subjectivity and poetic writing depend crucially upon paying close attention to the language and structures of the individual poems of particular poets, including—or especially—minority poets. This praxis-based critical argumentation, in which the poems themselves suggest theoretical orientations, resists abstract generalizations that can easily oversimplify (and render reductive and one-dimensional) arguments about racial subjectivity and minority poetry. Let us pay nuanced attention to what the language and forms of poems—*all* poems in the American body—tell us.

Chapter Summaries

Thinking Its Presence: Form, Race, and Subjectivity in Contemporary Asian American Poetry builds its arguments by moving between focused attention on the linguistic, literary, and rhetorical workings of specific Asian American poems and a larger meditation on how we think about form in American poetry and poetics.

In Chapter 2, I examine the work of arguably the most well-known Asian American poet writing today, Li-Young Lee. This chapter considers what makes Lee's poetry so desirable to mainstream non–Asian American audiences by examining the rhetorical trope of metaphor, whose form instantiates the Romantic sensibility that permeates his four books of poetry. The structure of metaphor, which is often called the trope of desire, isomorphically expresses the structure of the poet-narrators' yearnings to merge with, variously, an "authentic" cultural past (represented by his formidable

Chinese Presbyterian-minister father), the Absolute Text, a pure language, the beloved, an Old Testament God—and the simultaneous recognition that this fulfillment is impossible.

In Lee's poem "The Cleaving," the central metaphor of cleaving captures the structural logic of metaphor and assimilation's imperatives, marked by a gap—spatial, temporal, linguistic—that signifies both a permanent separation and an asymptotic coming together. At the same time, unlike the use of metaphor in his first book, Lee's more nuanced and overarching metaphoric practice in "The Cleaving," one that does not inhere in discrete countable metaphors, deconstructs a simplistic binary model of metaphor by demonstrating how metaphor can hold both likeness and difference in tension without making its two terms identical, as the logic of assimilation demands. This more open and less regulative model of metaphor offers the possibility of rethinking binary ways of thinking about both metaphor and the interpellation of minority Americans in the political and literary (critical) spheres.

That said, the chapter leaves open two questions: first, whether both the tendency of metaphors to concretize abstract ideas and feelings into concrete images and the Romantic transcendental tendencies of Lee's poetry encourage readers to reify Lee's metaphors and his poetry itself, as "poetic" nuggets of ethnic immigrant experience,[94] without having to grapple with more specific, material, and difficult immigrant and racial histories and realities; and second, whether critics' and readers' own tendencies and desires to read in such depoliticized ways limit the more interventionary potential of Lee's poetic form, specifically his use of metaphor.

The next chapter deals directly with the question of reception of an Asian American poet very different from Li-Young Lee: Marilyn Chin, one of the few Asian American poets who openly declares her poetry as "political" and herself a feminist, and the author of three books of poetry. Though also written in the same first-person lyric mode as Lee's, Chin's poetry is markedly different from his in its voice, a mix of female sass and melancholy (the latter emotion Lee also shares), and in its overt, though often ironic, political critique.

In Chapter 3, I examine the vitriolic battle between Chin and three white men affiliated with Copper Canyon Press that broke out in the pages of *Poetry* magazine in 2008. At issue was Chin's translation of a poem by an eighteenth-century Vietnamese woman poet and Chin's response to a letter by Copper Canyon's sales and marketing director, who unfavorably compared Chin's translation to one done by a Copper Canyon translator. Chin called out what she saw as the veiled sexist, racist, and imperialist assumptions in his letter. In subsequent issues of *Poetry*, Chin was skewered by various white male letter writers for "playing the race card" and for being a Chinese imperialist, among other accusations.

I use this incident as a springboard to discuss several larger issues that arise from the incident and that frame the question of the place and reception of Asian American poets in the academy and in the poetry world at large. For example, who has the right to translate and who has the right to write English-language poetry? Why do skeletons from earlier cultural and military wars continue to reemerge in the newly multicultural and prosperous pages of *Poetry* magazine and, more broadly, in the "post-race" era? Why does the "American" keep dropping out of the term "Asian American poet" in the popular and critical imaginary? What is the place of an Asian American woman poet in the poetry world, especially one who is outspokenly political and who refuses to conform to the model minority stereotype?

I conclude the chapter by asking why Chin's straightforward calling out of racism in *Poetry* elicited such rage, whereas her poems—which are often as bitingly critical of racism, sexism, and imperialism—are met with much more critical approval. I argue that because the use of irony always entails the possibility of misreading by readers, irony's multiple voices in Chin's poems allow some readers to miss her sharper critiques. How well does irony "translate" between poets and readers who come from different contexts (political, racial, aesthetic, among others), and does this potential for mistranslation limit irony's political efficaciousness? The relationship between irony, audience, and translation is crucial in poems and in everyday life, where minority subjects are themselves read literally (phenotypically) and whose societally acceptable range of interpretation of racism's multiple guises is often limited to literal readings of overt manifestations.

In Chapter 4, I examine Chin's use of irony in her poems in greater detail. As a woman writing at the nexus of two patriarchal traditions and as an avowedly political poet, Chin uses the trope of irony to engage and parry the demands of Chinese and American cultural purists, both of whom view her as "barbarian," and to make sharp critiques of racism and sexism in both American and Chinese cultures. This ironic voice is gendered and, variously, sassy, melancholic, sexy, and sober, but always fierce. Using a multivoiced irony allows her to mimic, express, and confront conflicting states of self-hatred, self-colonization, and erotic desire for white male domination, even as she hits hard at forms of colonialism.

The female speakers of Chin's poems often occupy more than one ideological position and tonal register; their ironic voices thus cannot be analyzed according to the general view of irony as "saying something other than what is understood"[95] (or a simple binary between a stated "false" meaning and an unstated "true" message). Following the work on irony by such scholars as Paul de Man, Kenneth Burke, Linda Hutcheon, and Claire Colebrook, I argue that irony operates in Chin's poems across multiple registers that interpenetrate each other and that irony always has a social function as well as a figurative one. Likewise, the psyche of Chin's female poetic narrators cannot be characterized by any either-or "Chinese or American" formulation. They have often internalized both resistance to and desire for assimilation, epitomized by their desire for the white male body and what it represents—colonial, national, linguistic, and sexual power and domination. Again, one might question how interventionary and efficacious Chin's use of irony is, given the marginalization of Asian Americans and Asian American writers in the American political and literary arenas.

In Chapters 5 and 6, I focus on the work of John Yau, who occupies a unique position in the contemporary poetry world as an Asian American poet who has published more than fifty books— poetry (well over a dozen since 1976), art criticism, fiction, collaborations with artists (such as Thomas Nozkowski and Archie Rand), monographs on artists, gallery

catalogues (not to mention essay contributions to various other books)—
and who has also achieved prominence as a critic in the art world. In
its eschewing of the classical lyric form and in its aggressive linguistic
wordplay, Yau's poetry differs significantly from that of Lee's and Chin's
first-person lyrics. His work can be situated in the more avant-garde tradition of poetry—both American (à la Pound and New York School) and
European Surrealist—though his poetry generally has not been considered formally experimental "enough" by the Language poets.

Chapter 5 begins with the analysis of another critical controversy:
this time a heated debate in 1994 in the pages of *American Poetry
Review* between the critic Eliot Weinberger and Yau, a confrontation
that was as vitriolic as, or even more so than, the one between Marilyn Chin and the Copper Canyon men in *Poetry*. In reviewing Weinberger's anthology, *American Poetry Since 1950: Innovators and Outsiders*, Yau strongly criticized him for the paucity of poets of color represented in the volume, which included only Langston Hughes and
Amiri Baraka. Not unlike the response by the *Poetry* letter writers
against Chin fourteen years later, Weinberger responds by charging
Yau with "race-mongering" and "race-baiting" and implies that after
years of writing and publishing poetry, Yau has become interested in
playing the "race card" only when it is expedient and profitable.

Yet a quick review of Yau's career reveals that, even from the very
beginning, his subject position as a Chinese American poet and its
attendant concerns and anxieties clearly permeated his work. The
second half of this chapter examines the arc of Yau's early to midcareer, before his canonical inclusion as an "Asian American poet"
in various anthologies in the 1990s. I argue, contra Weinberger, that
Yau, far from shying away from the topic of race and racial identity
throughout his career, has dealt with these concerns by more oblique,
often nonthematic, means. Because critics such as Weinberger tend
to look only for thematic manifestations of "Asianness," they have
missed Yau's more subtle, non-content-based grappling with issues of
racial identity, including racial self-hatred, and his critiques of racist
representations and discourses.

In Chapter 6, I look specifically at Yau's use of parody—both
defensively and offensively, as rhetorical strategy and as weapon—

to critique and undermine dominant racial discourses (for example, Hollywood's stereotypes, narratives of assimilation) and, in particular, representations of Asian American men. Parody allows Yau to occupy multiple subject positions to express conflicting feelings of racial self-hatred, feelings of racial emasculation, anger at American society's treatment of Asian Americans, and a vexed yet productive and playful relationship to the English language. I begin by examining the history and nuances of parody as a genre, with a particular focus on the work of Mikhail Bakhtin, before turning my attention to Yau's series of "Genghis Chan: Private Eye" poems, which manifest most forcefully Yau's biting use of parody. Parodic language mimics and exposes the discourse of yellowface movies—with its chop-suey Chinglish and depictions of inhuman "Orientals" (servile or barbaric), among other demonizations (and dehumanizations) of Asian Americans—while also submitting, in the very act of ventriloquizing, to the truth of racial self-hatred and of minority internalization of these dominant representations.

While my discussion of parody is indebted to Bakhtin's work, I disagree strongly with his view that parody belongs most properly to what he considers the more social and heterogeneous realm of fiction rather than poetry, which he considers more "private" and purely literary. Bakhtin's narrow conception of poetry can no longer account for the diverse poetries of twentieth- and twenty-first-century American society—with its multiple cultures, languages, and discourses—of which Asian American poetry is a vibrant part. Yau's poetry, like that of the other poets studied in this book, contributes to a more complex, nuanced, and multifaceted view of English-language poetry and, hence, of poetry in general.

In the final two chapters, I turn to two even more formally experimental Asian American poets, one a veteran of the multicultural struggles of the 1960s and 1970s and the other a Bay Area writer in her early forties. Like Yau's work, the writing of Mei-mei Berssenbrugge and Pamela Lu brings into relief the relationship between race, writing, and the avant-garde: the ways in which Asian American avant-garde writing is almost always read as de-raced and the ways in which avant-garde writing is almost always implicitly coded as "white."

Thus, I put to a hard test my hypothesis that writing by Asian Americans formally manifests the effects of social and historical forces on the poets' subjectivity and language, not only in what is consciously and explicitly stated but also in what is unstated or said obliquely and—crucially—in *how* something is said (for example, syntax, tone, word choice). If the tendency is to consider the connection of formation and form in poetry by racial minorities only at the level of recognizable "ethnic" content, then how does one apprehend a poem, written by a minority American poet, in which racialized subjectivity is not overtly realized, whether by means of an autobiographical "I" and/or markers of ethnic culture and whose poetry is viewed as abstract and "difficult"?

Mei-mei Berssenbrugge's poetry has recently been embraced by those in avant-garde circles. A few critics have written on her poetry's links to, say, nature and affect and mothering, but few mention Berssenbrugge's Chinese American identity, the fact that Chinese was her first language, or that she was an early participant in the fight for the recognition of minority literature. Berssenbrugge tends to get read as one of the successful experimental minority poets who has avoided the trap of identity politics and "bad" identity writing.

In Chapter 7, I argue that, while Berssenbrugge is indeed interested in amorphous, seemingly immaterial states, such as emotions and natural phenomena, which are difficult to quantify and touch yet are very real—such as a horizon, color, fragrance, fog—she is equally interested in the issue of ethnic identity and "mother tongue," as she herself has explicitly stated. It is in her use of a syntax of conditionality that this Beijing-born, Massachusetts-raised, mixed-race poet reveals her own contingent relationship to language, both English and Chinese, and her sense of the contingency and relationality of natural phenomena *and* identity. There is no contradiction here. Berssenbrugge's poems, while appearing abstract and largely devoid of racial markers, nonetheless strongly bear the impress of social and historical contexts, including processes of racialization and the influence of her first language—Chinese—which shaped and continue to shape her subjectivity as both an Asian American and a poet. To ignore these contexts and their formative influence on her poetry is, to a large extent, to misread her body of work.

In Chapter 8, I examine Pamela Lu's *Pamela: A Novel*, a text that refuses easy categorization by almost any criteria. Though its title makes knowing reference to one of the founding texts of the English novelistic canon and its syntax often takes the form of "well-written," somewhat formal, sentences, this *Pamela* is nonnarrative, filtered solely through the consciousness of a twenty-something Chinese American Californian ("I" or "P"), eschewing plot and dialogue, lacking in fully fleshed-out characters and character development, and almost completely devoid of any ethnic or racial markers. Even more so than Yau and Berssenbrugge, Lu, who works in the tech industry in Silicon Valley, completely refuses genre-based, literary classificatory, and formal categories to such an extent that one does not know whether to call *Pamela: A Novel* a novel, prose poetry, or memoir, "Asian American," "American," traditional, or avant-garde.

Markers of race are almost completely erased or nonexistent in the text, yet, I argue, this is not a "post-race" novel, as some have averred. While *Pamela: A Novel* displays almost no thematic references to race, the consciousness of the narrator—who, it is obliquely suggested, is, like Lu, a Chinese American from Southern California—cannot be separated from the tale the book tells, if it could be said to tell any tale at all, nor from the very form of its poetic sentences. Indeed, the text is so fully infused with the consciousness of this triply minoritized (in terms of race, gender, and sexuality) narrator that it need not mark its speaker's identity overtly or thematically.

Subjunctivity is crucial to *Pamela: A Novel*. Not only is it a topic of philosophical speculation but it is inseparable from the subjectivity evinced in the text and from the language of the text itself. The "as thoughs" and "as ifs" bring out the constructedness, indeterminacy, and imagined dimensions of identity, memory, history—to a great extent raising many of the same questions that come to light with the terms "diasporic" and "Asian American": questions of identification with a larger ethnic group, shared cultural memory, racial interpellation, and so on. I argue that the subjunctive mood captures the postmodern diasporic subject's relationship to a "home" country and the English language. Lu forces us to ask, "What is 'relative' (in both senses of the term)?" What makes "I," "P," and "Pamela" and diasporic subjects relative(s) is not blood but their being yoked—brought into being—through and in the shared English language.

Thinking Its Presence: Form, Race, and Subjectivity in Contemporary Asian American Poetry ends with a brief epilogue in which I argue that exciting new forms of experimental minority poetry; the emergence of scholars who have been trained to see no contradiction between ethnic studies and poetics, prosody and postcolonialism; and new digital technologies and possibilities may be catalyzing forces for the reframing and reconceptualizing—the genuine *rethinking*—of American poetry, down to its very historical and conceptual foundations.

TWO

Metaphor, Desire, and Assimilation in the Poetry of Li-Young Lee

When asked to name Asian American fiction writers they recognize, or are familiar with, most serious readers, including English professors,[1] are likely to cite Amy Tan, Maxine Hong Kingston, or, perhaps, more recently, Jhumpa Lahiri and, just maybe, Chang-rae Lee.[2] But if asked to name a single Asian American poet, this same group might draw a blank, hard-pressed to think of a single name. Even in ethnic literature and Asian American literature courses, it is works of fiction, drama, and nonfiction—not poetry—that largely represent Asian American literature.

And within the field of Asian American fictional and nonfictional prose, autobiographical narratives—often bildungsroman, usually written by women[3]—have largely been the preferred form of Asian American literature in the mainstream publishing marketplace of the past few decades (especially so in the 1990s and the first decade of this century). These books often contain familiar themes: the clash between immigrant and American-born generations, poverty and gender oppression in the Asian home country, a patriarchal Asian immigrant father, the saving grace of the love of a good white man, and the liberating process of self-discovery in the land of the free. This trend continues to some extent among the major New York publishers though, thankfully, more and more experimental and formally inventive Asian American works of fiction and nonfiction are being published—mainly by small, mostly unknown, presses across the country.[4]

Yet there is no obvious reason why Asian American poetry should necessarily be precluded from readers' appetite for ethnic or multicultural literature; after all, poems, particularly in their common lyric manifestation, could just as easily as a memoir or novel hold the descriptive and narrative promise of autobiographical revelation or of familial practices—perhaps even more so, since poetry is viewed as the genre of expressive interiority. One might argue that this overlooking of minority poetry is merely a symptom of American culture's larger denigration of poetry—poetry's status in society has been the object of much debate in recent decades, what literary critic Christopher Beach has characterized as "discussing the death of poetry to death"[5]— but, as I lay out in the Introduction, the reasons for Asian American poetry's treble marginalization[6] within the literary marketplace and the field of literary studies (and even its second-class status within Asian American studies and Asian American literary studies) are both various and specific to the question of the place of Asian American literature in the academy and in the literary marketplace and to the question of the place of Asian Americans within the US nation-state.

Of the not insignificant number of Asian American poets writing today, who are largely unknown to the wider public and even to academics, Li-Young Lee (b. 1957) is arguably the most recognizable and recognized among academics, having been officially canonized in *The Norton Anthology of Poetry*—the only Asian American poet included.[7] Though not widely known among general readers, Lee and his poetry have been acknowledged in a greater array of venues than most Asian American poets: not only the *Norton* but also Bill Moyers's 1995 PBS series *The Language of Life: A Festival of Poets*, and even the fashion magazine *Elle*, where the long-haired Lee peers out from the pages intensely, looking every bit the hip, brooding poet ("Musing on the Poet's Plight: Li-Young Lee Puts Verse Things First").[8] Lee is firmly rooted in and assimilated into an English lyric tradition, as evidenced by his inclusion in the *Norton* and many other poetry anthologies. His poems most often picked for mainstream volumes are those dwelling on his family and scenes from a "Chinese" domestic life, such as eating steamed fish around a kitchen table. While critics and Lee himself have mythologized his history as the son of a Chinese Indonesian political prisoner under President Sukarno's regime in Indonesia,[9] this type of political residue—distant, foreign, a question of other Asian countries' "human rights" violations—is neutralized in Lee's poetry by the Romantic sensibility and lyricality of his language and by readers' own reading proclivities, into a "universal" "human" experience of dislocation.

That Lee is the sole Asian American poet allowed entry into the hallowed halls of the *Norton* and that he has been awarded prestigious national grants (from the Guggenheim, the National Endowment for the Arts, and others) signals that his popularity extends beyond a solely Chinese American, or even Asian American, readership. The attraction of Li-Young's Lee poetry lies largely in its style—eloquently "lyrical" in both its rhetorical resonances and its expression of intense emotions, such as nostalgia, love, and grief—and his equally compelling themes—a poet's grappling with issues of family, memory, and exile from an "imaginary homeland"—which allow anyone who struggles with the thorny issues of parentage and history to "relate to" his poems. Thus, his alluring "nonconfrontational" style and his skill at transmuting personal life details, even some that are quite traumatic, into a "timeless" (dehistoricized) and abstracted (thus, not overtly political) human experience ensure that, like other more popular Asian American writing, Lee's poetry is read as both "exotic" and "universal" at the same time.[10] And in true American fashion, his poetry can also be read as the story of a personal and a private, not a political, self—not unlike the ways in which lyric poetry, the dominant mode of poetry today, is often misapprehended by general readers as the unmediated record of a poet's feelings.

In other words, unlike the writings of Frank Chin, which are often read as the rantings of an "angry minority" man, or even the poems of Marilyn Chin, who identifies overtly as an activist feminist poet, Lee's poems—though they do not shy away from addressing the sadness and trauma of emigration, dislocation, and living as a Chinese American in the United States—are not viewed as overtly "political." This reading of Lee's poetry reflects both the usual tendency by readers and critics to prefer the consumption of ethnic poetry that offers morsels of an exotic culture (one dish among many in a global literary food court) rather than poetry that makes one uncomfortable by overt racial critiques of American realities,[11] and Lee's tendency himself to write of his experiences in terms of a dehistoricized seeking of eternal truths: "Poets should traffic in the ideal," he has said.[12]

In response to a question in 1999 about "having reacted very strongly against being pigeonholed as an 'Asian-American' writer," Lee answered:

> The fine print of that question—"Where do you stand as an Asian-American writer?"—is a question about one's dialogue with cultural significance. I would say the answer is nil: I have no dialogue with cultural existence. Culture made that up—Asian-American, African-American, whatever. I have no interest in that. I had an interest in spiritual lineage connected to poetry—through Eliot, Donne, Lorca, Tu Fu, Neruda, David the Psalmist. But I've realized that there is still the culture. Somehow an artist has to discover a dialogue that is so essential to his being, to his self, that it is no longer cultural or canonical, but a dialogue with your truest self.[13]

These are clearly not the words of an "angry minority" American who harps on "identity politics," by making explicit references, for example, to the wounds of US racism or the effects of US wars and imperialist intervention in Asia (for example, CIA attempts to overthrow President Sukarno in Indonesia).[14] Not surprisingly, Lee's brooding poetic ruminations can often come across as abstracted, dreamlike, and decontextualized. The poems' lack of overt politics make them attractive to readers; even details of personal and family travails under Asian despotic regimes or those occasioned by the more abstract notion of "exile" only further enhance their appeal to audiences (vicarious suffering without guilt).

A review of Lee's first book, *Rose* (1986), by Roger Mitchell underscores this point:

> Lee is one of a rising number of Asian-American writers, though in *Rose* that background is not an issue. One line refers to someone "exiled from one republic and daily defeated in another." Two other lines recall someone "who was driven from the foreign schoolyards by / fists and

yelling, who trembled in anger in each retelling." There is a poem, too, about relatives singing and remembering China. But Lee does not dwell on grievances.[15]

Between Mitchell's two unvexedly declarative assessments— "background is not an issue" and "Lee does not dwell on griev- ances"—the quoted lines, which are rife with examples of the violence and difficulties of assimilation in the United States (not Asia), illustrate how in error his judgments are. More revealing than what is stated in this passage is what is left unsaid: the reviewer's assumptions, which (pre)determine how he will interpret this Asian American poetry, no matter the evidence. Mitchell makes unam- biguously clear that Lee is to be praised precisely for *not* emphasizing ethnicity or history or politics; these racial residues are equated with (anti-American) "grievances"—and bad poetry.[16] Mitchell is certainly not alone in holding this view.

Yet to see Lee's poetry solely in "universal" dehistoricized terms— as the verse equivalent of *The Joy Luck Club*[17]—elides the effects of a specific context and racially marked history, which have molded the poet's sensibility and his poems. Claiming that Lee's poetry speaks for the mythic Immigrant, or for all Americans or humans, erases the specific marks attesting to the violence of each racialized group's assimilation into American culture. To minimize the impact of such histories and conditions glosses over the particularities that manifest themselves in the poet's practice and leads, ultimately, to a misreading of his work. The danger of such a misreading goes beyond mere questions of literary niceties, having repercussions in the wider cultural sphere, such as bolstering, for example, the poetic establishment's regulative ideal that minority poets assimilate both as poets and as citizens.

Because Lee is not viewed as a poet concerned with sociopolitical issues and because he himself has disavowed the influence of "culture" on his poetry—instead, preferring to speak of what is "essential" about his "truest self"—Lee's poetry provides an excel- lent test case for my argument that the experience—the always politicized experience—of living as an Asian American subject and poet makes itself felt on the level of language, even in poetry whose content is more often read as personal and familial than political and/or ideological.

As I asked earlier, "What would it mean to take Asian American poetry seriously as literary writing and to read these poems for their formal properties, *without* divorcing these properties from the social, political, and cultural contexts of the poets who wrote them?" To read Asian American poetry as writing that is both literary and intrinsically linked to the conditions of its making would be to run against the flow of critical currents, whether that of cultural studies or of formalism—both in its conservative (New Critical, neoformalist) and antifoundationalist (deconstructive, postmodernist) guises. What I am arguing for is an examination of how social, political, and cultural conditions and context—the lived experience of the poet in his or her historical moment—manifest themselves *in* language, by means of (and having shaped) the subjectivity of the poet. One could examine any number of formal properties: syntax, line breaks, meter, tone, figures of speech, rhythm, rhyme, and so on. I choose to focus on Li-Young Lee's deployment of metaphor because it is the trope that best captures the Romantic sensibility permeating his poems—a sensibility that, not surprisingly, accounts for the relatively wider appeal of his poetry to readers and audiences[18]—and several of his key poetic concerns.

By advocating that critics pay close attention to such formal specificities as tropes, I am by no means calling for a return to New Criticism or to the various "new" formalisms that have emerged as reactionary forms of countercriticism to the opening of the canon and the emergence of literatures and topics that were formerly marginalized or rendered invisible. What I *am* saying is that the language and content of poems are never divorced from the conditions of their making—those conditions being the historical, cultural, political, and social influences that, in Raymond Williams's words, are "essentially related to a large part of the experience from which the poetry itself [is] made."[19] These are equally as important as the influence of literature and literary tradition.

Like all poets, the Asian American poet is a product of history, ideology, and prior discourses, and the constructions of his subjectivity become explored and (re)articulated in the poetic text through language and form. Even when he claims to be free of the effects, pernicious or not, of being a racially marked person in the United States, his subjectivity and poetry have not escaped this context. As Theodor Adorno writes in his 1962 essay "Commitment,"

> There is no material content, no formal category of artistic creation, however mysteriously transmitted and itself unaware of the process, which did not originate in the empirical reality from which it breaks free.[20]

As I argue throughout this book, to be a member of a racial minority in the United States means that, whether consciously politicized or not, one is always already imbricated in a fabric of laws, stereotypes, historical accretion, and popular culture—represented before the fact, as it were. In this sense, no writer of color can remain unwritten by the political. Race itself is a deeply political concept, a political concept that takes particular forms. No matter how much one may willfully blind oneself to the fact, the material and psychic realities of race and racism in this country are embedded in the American collective psyche as well as the psyches of individuals, and they constitute the scrim through which the minority poet is perceived. Thus, it is impossible that the effects of the processes by which the "hyphenated" American poet is produced could be absent from the language, even if they are not the subject, of his or her poems.

An examination of certain formal concerns can reveal much about the construction of the "hyphenated" American subject.[21] What is the hyphen, after all, but a metaphor? This particular metaphor has dictated the ways in which Asian Americans have been read and misread and other material consequences beyond the realm of the purely linguistic. The clichéd model of Asian Americans as having dual personalities and dual allegiances has not only grossly oversimplified the complexities of their experience but also perniciously marked them as unstable and untrustworthy ("inscrutable"). In the preface to their 1974 anthology of Asian American writing, *Aiiieeeee! An Anthology of Asian American Writers,* Frank Chin and his fellow editors described the consequences of this stereotype of the bifurcated Asian American:

This myth of being either/or and the equally goofy concept of the dual personality haunted our lobes while our rejection by both Asia and white America proved we were neither one nor the other. Nor were we half and half or more one than the other. Neither Asian culture nor American culture was equipped to define us except in the most superficial terms.[22]

One need only look back at the past 150 years to see the concrete effects of rhetorical categorizations that have stamped Asian Americans as treacherous, traitorous, devious, inscrutable, and un-American:[23] the Chinese Exclusion Act, Japanese American internment, the Wen Ho Lee "spy" case, and more recently the resurgence of yellow-peril rhetoric around China's possible dominance ("taking over") in the twenty-first century. Rhetorical (re)presentation has had a great deal to do with shaping political representation.

Most critics acknowledge that poetry functions as a way of thinking through form—that poetry works both ontologically and epistemologically. Of literary tropes, such as metaphors, Paul de Man writes, "[C]oncepts are tropes and tropes concepts."[24] Poetry does not merely paint images but creates knowledge, and what it mines lies close to the unconscious, individual or collective. What may not always be conscious to the individual poet can be belied by the language of her poems (Donald Davidson calls metaphor "the dreamwork of language"[25]).

Poetic language, like dreams, makes manifest—though not necessarily in direct or straightforward fashion—the processes that have produced the individual poetic subjectivity, but it also actively contributes to the constitution of the subject. For example, figures of speech can constitute formal means of mediating the extraliterary forces that have shaped the particular history and subjectivity of the poet—in Lee's case, the experience of having grown up the son of Chinese Protestant immigrants in rural Pennsylvania; intimate exposure at home to a non-American language, culture, worldview, and literary tradition; spatial and temporal displacement from an imagined cultural-linguistic "center," whether Chinese or American; the pressure to assimilate in American society; demands of "authenticity" from Chinese and American cultures; the struggles to contend with a hyphenated identity; the task of situating the self in an Anglo-American poetic tradition; and so on.[26]

To say that Li-Young Lee's use of metaphor has distinct characteristics because of the influence of his experiences as an Asian American is not to say that the *substance* of these effects is necessarily generalizable to other writers but to make both a claim that is specific to Lee's poetry project and a broader argument: that the experience of living as a racially marked subject and poet produces an observable impact at the level of language, not just subject matter. In other words, I am not claiming that Lee has come up with a new "Asian American" or "Chinese American" way of using metaphor. And in no uncertain terms am I implying that what is manifested in Lee's poetry is a racialized "blood knowledge" or a transhistorical Confucian culture[27]—there are no "Chinese" or "Asian" essences in the poetry.[28] Various influences—such as the Bible, Lee's wide reading in other Western canonical texts, city life in Chicago—are as important for his poetry as the fact of his ethnicity. Lived experiences and histories influence both minority and nonminority poets alike, and their effects become manifested in a poem's form, not just its content.[29] We can see this process at work by examining Lee's use of a specific rhetorical trope, metaphor, whose presence and character permeate the spirit of his work and whose very structure parallels and makes manifest the logics of displacement, yearning, and assimilation that mark his history and experiences as an Asian American immigrant.

The titles of three of Lee's four poetry collections, *Rose* (1986), *The City in Which I Love You* (1990; hereafter, *City*), and *Book of My Nights* (2001)—as well as his 1999 memoir, *The Winged Seed*[30]—suggest a poetic practice heavily invested in metaphor. Metaphor, what many call the trope of desire, captures the Romantic sensibility that permeates his poems: the simultaneous yearning to merge with, variously, an "authentic" cultural past (represented by his formidable father), the Absolute Text, the English language, the Beloved, God—and the recognition that this fulfillment is impossible.

David Simpson writes that "[t]he making of metaphor serves to bind the subject into a wished-for relation to its context, in that the conjunctions which it establishes are the wished-for features of an imaginary world which the subject can then reflect back in order to constitute itself."[31] Insofar as metaphor can be thought of, in Paul de Man's words, as "a language of desire and as a means to recover what is absent,"[32] its force—and that of the poetry in which it is embedded—lies precisely in never attaining what it desires. Poetry reenacts this desire, and it is, says Donald MacKinnon, in the "groping, a *tatonnement* . . . [that] one is seeking to find one's way, to establish a sense of direction."[33] The flip side of desire, of course, is loss.

In this chapter, I focus on Lee's first two books of poetry, *Rose* and *City*, primarily because I believe that these are his strongest collections; the poems in his latter two books continue the themes and melancholic rhetoricity set up in the first two books:[34] that of the exilic son, who seeks some sort of "authentic" truth about his father and a connection to a home(land). (The titles of some of these later poems—"My Father's House," "The Eternal Son"—suggest an almost self-imitating performance of the brooding poet, who laments his condition of existential displacement.)

Analyzing how metaphor works in Lee's poetry opens up five main ideas raised by (and about) his poetic practice.

First, the structural logic of metaphor, the trope of desire (and loss), is not only similar to but isomorphically captures the structural logic governing social and psychic processes this particular Chinese American poet has been subject to and has grappled with: for example, the poet's displacement from and yearning for an imagined past/center of cultural authenticity and authority—symbolized by his father, who represents the weight of Chinese (and Western) cultural tradition and authority;[35] the aporias of memory heightened by immigration and geographical displacement; his interpellation as a hyphenated American; and the imperatives of assimilation. In the first two cases, the poet imposes his Romantic sensibility on a situation that resists it and attempts to bridge what seems separate; in the third, he is forced to live the gap of being seen as neither fully Chinese nor fully American; in the fourth, he must experience the violent strictures of assimilation that force the unlike to become like (here, an "American").[36] Thus, we can see that the "split" nature of metaphor works simultaneously in multiple dimensions: those of language, politics, and culture—realms in which the minority subject is necessarily embedded. This tension between like and unlike, near and far, together and apart, identity and difference is intrinsic to the structure of metaphor.

Second, one could argue that Lee's use of metaphor inheres not so much in discrete instances of metaphor—though there are examples of these—but in an overarching metaphorical practice, if not quite a system, that is strongly influenced by his having lived as an immigrant, an exile, and an Asian American.[37] Thus, discrete, countable metaphors do not fully capture the metaphoric nature of Lee's work; for example, in the poems, the poet's father becomes the metaphor for China, Chinese culture, and an essentialized "Chineseness"[38] but also for a certain cultural authority that is not only Chinese.[39] But even more important, Lee's poetry as a whole—his entire poetic practice and *effort*, as well as the final products of this process—can itself be said to be metaphoric in its striving, in its reaching toward what the poet knows is impossible to attain: certainty and fulfillment in the father, the Absolute, the Ideal.

Third, Lee the poet is well aware of the dangers of an unexamined deployment of metaphor, particularly a too-easy conflation of the thing itself with the figurative other. Lee's decision to withhold observable metaphors in most of the poems of his second book, *City*, bespeaks a conscious attempt to resist the temptations and possible pitfalls of metaphoric language, especially a too-easy conflation of the two terms of the metaphor, of the thing itself with its figurative other. As David Simpson writes, when summarizing Wordsworth's distrust of figurative language, which the poet saw as a product of reduction, "items in th[e] comparison lose something of their individuality in order for this 'just' comparison to be achieved."[40] Lee is aware of how metaphor increases the risk of a poet's speaking for an unknown other—his ventriloquizing effectively silencing the other.

Fourth, his poems offer a means of apprehending metaphor that not only resists the separation of "tenor" and "vehicle" but brings metaphor's two "halves" into a relationship, not of separation or conflation but of productive tension. Lee's understanding of the complexity of metaphoric signification is captured by the central metaphor of his most accomplished poem, "The Cleaving," discussed in more detail later. More broadly, Lee's metaphoric practice has implications for our understanding of the link between the forms of aesthetic representation and the structures of ideological and political representation as well as the very forms (metaphoric) of these political and ideological concepts.

Finally, with metaphor's possibilities come its limits (as is also the case with irony and parody): while Lee's use of metaphor, the result of conscious and unconscious choices, reveals an awareness of the trope's complexities and dangers, such as tendencies toward reification, and his use of metaphor raises the possibility of rethinking larger political issues, the reality of his poetry's *reception* by readers and critics—not to mention Lee's own tendency to speak of his work in dehistoricized and depoliticized terms—might limit the trenchant possibilities and political potential of his metaphoric practice.

Before turning to Lee's specific uses of metaphor, let us briefly examine the trope of metaphor itself. An overview of the vast amount of writing devoted to theories of metaphor—from Aristotle to German Romanticists to I. A. Richards and Paul de Man—cannot be adequately dealt with here.[41] But a few words about the structure of metaphor are necessary.

What is metaphor? The definition in the current fourth edition of *The Princeton Encyclopedia of Poetry and Poetics* strikes me as overly broad and vague: "A trope, or figurative expression, in which a word or phrase is shifted from its normal uses to a context where it evokes new meanings." The entry goes on to say, "Despite . . . arguments and attempts to create a more satisfactory classification of figures, the definitions of the major tropes have remained unchanged since the cl. [classical] period."[42]

Aristotle considered metaphor the most significant feature of poetic style and viewed the trope as a condensed simile. Quintilian agreed: He described a simile as the "compar[ison of] some object to the thing which we wish to describe," whereas in a metaphor "the object is actually substituted for the thing"—in other words, not "A is like (or as) B" but "A is B."[43] Philosopher Donald Davidson disagrees with this formulation: "For if we make the literal meaning of the meta-phor to be the literal meaning of a matching simile, we deny access to what we originally took to be the literal meaning of the metaphor."[44] Northrop Frye tried to define metaphor as a statement of identity: "In its literal grammatical form metaphor is a statement of identity: this is that, A is B."[45] But while logical identity—that is, identification *as* (for example, to say, "The queen of England is Elizabeth II" is to say she is herself)—stays fixed, poetic metaphor goes beyond, for, as Frye notes, "in poetic metaphor things are identified with each other, yet each is identified as itself, and retains that identity. When a man, a woman, and a blackbird are said to be one, each remains what it is, and the identification heightens the distinctive form of each. Such a metaphor is necessarily illogical (or anti-logical, as in 'A violent disorder is an order') and hence poetic metaphors are opposed to likeness or similarity" (170).

Although Frye firmly asserts that metaphor is opposed to similarity, the subject of the piece in which his claims appear, Wallace Stevens, defines metaphor in such a way as to admit both similarity and difference. Metaphor, says Stevens, is the symbol for "the creation of resemblance by the imagination." But resemblance, while seeming to denote similarity, is clarified later in the essay as necessarily including difference: "If resemblance is described as a partial similarity between two dissimilar things, it complements and reinforces that which the two dissimilar things have in common. It makes it brilliant."[46] Within the space of a sentence, Stevens oscillates between emphasizing metaphor's reinforcement of similarity ("resemblance") and making clear the constitutive difference between the two terms of metaphor ("two dissimilar things"); even the term "partial similarity," which seems to underscore what is shared by the two terms, implies that there is also a great deal that is not similar.[47] Herein lies the crux of metaphor: its ability to encompass both sameness and difference at the same time.[48]

This idea is crucial to understanding metaphor (and, as we shall see, to Lee's metaphoric practice). Kenneth Burke puts it pithily: "Metaphor is a device for seeing something *in terms of* something else. It brings out the thisness of a that, or the thatness of a this" (original emphasis).[49] This gaining knowledge by analogy, by relation, marks not only metaphor but also language and thought. I. A. Richards states simply, "*Thought* is metaphoric" (original emphasis).[50]

And Nietzsche more forcefully: "The drive toward the formation of metaphors is the fundamental human drive, which one cannot for a single instance dispense with in thought, for one would thereby dispense with man himself."[51] Percy Shelley observed that "language is vitally metaphorical; that is, it marks the before unapprehended relations of things and perpetuates their apprehension. . . . "[52]

Indeed, metaphor is the form that bears the aesthetic itself.[53] It enhances reality by means of greater vividness and particularity. Thus, Lee's saying that his father's voice is "a well / of dark water, a prayer" ("The Gift," *Rose*) and his feet are "two dumb fish" ("Water," *Rose*) conveys something much more memorable than can be said without the use of metaphor.

The etymology of the word "metaphor" bears keeping in mind: it is itself a metaphor from the Greek *meta phorein*, meaning "to transfer or bear across." Thus, it holds connotations of movement across space and time. In this respect, the structure of metaphor captures well the experience of those diasporic subjects whose relationship to both the country of "origin" and the country in which they reside is marked by a gap—spatial, temporal, and linguistic—what Stuart Hall calls "an always-postponed 'arrival.'"[54] In an interview, Lee has spoken of the sense of alienation and lack of epistemological certainty many migrants feel, in relation both to a real and imagined homeland and to the new country, and the disruption of a temporal narrative: "You didn't know where you came from. You didn't know where you were going. You don't know if this had happened first, or that, or when this happened."[55] Metaphor's structure—always reaching toward but never arriving—also mirrors the structure of memory, a major obsession with Lee, and the immigrant and hyphenated poet's relationship to language, both the ancestral language from which he no longer has access and the new language, English, which he strives to speak "properly"—as well as the Anglo-American poetic tradition, Western culture (high and low), and ideas of "Americanness."

Ideas, feelings, words, images that have no precise translation from one culture to another, from childhood to adulthood, from past to present are "carried" by another idea, feeling, image that is more familiar and comprehensible to the poet and the reader. But herein lies the paradox, not contradiction, at the heart of metaphor: "What is *like* cannot be identical," as the poet Allen Grossman points out.[56] The tensions between like and unlike, near and far, together and apart, identity and difference are intrinsic to the structure of metaphor. The chiasmus at the center of metaphor constitutes both its richness and its difficulty: How does one negotiate between similarity and dissimilarity without, on the one hand, collapsing difference or, on the other, being unable to bridge the gap separating the terms?

William Blake, says David Simpson, saw analogy, not metaphor, as the "appropriate mode for the preservation of the disjunction *within* the comparison. Conventional metaphor can be equated with the Urizenic creation, and its insistence upon the solid selfhood as the nexus of perception" (original emphasis).[57] The metaphor maker, argues de Man, needs the illusion of this solid selfhood because "the figure's truth turns out to be a lie at the very moment when it asserts itself in the plenitude of its promise."[58]

But how can a "solid selfhood" exist when one's Asian American and diasporic identity—and the structure of metaphor itself— is constituted by aporia? This gap is played out on several different levels: physical (the "unassimilably alien" features of Asian Americans), cultural (not a "real" Chinese or "real" American—hence, the hyphenated term of identification), geographical (split between various real and imagined locations), linguistic (not a "native speaker"), and psychological and psychic (such as feelings of alienation and dislocatedness).

To illustrate more concretely the extratextual and literary implications of Lee's use of metaphor, let us turn to a specific poem, perhaps his most well known—the one anthologized in the *Norton*— "Persimmons," from his first book, *Rose*. The poem begins:

> In sixth grade Mrs. Walker
> slapped the back of my head
> and made me stand in the corner
> for not knowing the difference
> between *persimmon* and *precision*.
> How to choose

persimmons. This is precision.
Ripe ones are soft and brown-spotted.
Sniff the bottoms. The sweet one
will be fragrant. How to eat:
put the knife away, lay down newspaper.
Peel the skin tenderly, not to tear the meat.
Chew the skin, suck it,
and swallow. Now, eat
the meat of the fruit,
so sweet,
all of it, to the heart.[59] (original emphasis)

The first stanza provides a clear case of how the pressure to assimilate and the ever-lurking mechanisms of punishment for failure to do so find concrete manifestation in a space where the making of normative subjects and citizens is most effectively enacted—the classroom. Anxiety about language formatively marks the experience of most new immigrants in this country (Lee himself arrived in the United States at age seven, after having lived briefly in Indonesia, Hong Kong, Macau, and Japan). Yet even for those hyphenated Americans who are born here, language becomes a primary gauge by which the dominant culture determines whether one is "fully American" or not. Though speaking "good enough English" does not ensure acceptance, not speaking it undeniably writes one off.

The word "assimilation" holds specific meaning in both social and linguistic discourses. Lee has spoken directly in interviews about the violence of assimilation:

> I realized there's only one kind of transcendence, a kind of violence, because I think living in America is a violent experience, especially if you do feel like the other. And I think assimilation is a *violent* experience.[60] (original emphasis)

While Lee's Romantic desire for transcendence is ever present and his poetry itself is never overtly political, nonetheless, a strong critique of assimilation, I argue, lies barely concealed under the lyrical surface of a poem such as "Persimmons" and operates as (or more) forcefully in Lee's use of metaphor, which taps into the structure of metaphor itself, as in what is thematically dealt with in the poem.

"Predicative assimilation," writes Paul Ricoeur, consists precisely in "*making* similar, that is, semantically proximate, the terms that the metaphorical utterance brings together" (original emphasis).[61] The logic of assimilation—in this context, becoming a "full-blooded American"—also entails this "making similar," but, as David Lloyd writes in "Race Under Representation,"

> The constitution of any metaphor involves the bringing together of two elements into identity in such a manner that their differences are suppressed. Just so, the process of assimilation . . . requires that which defines the difference between the elements to remain over as a residue. . . . [T]he product of assimilation will always necessarily be in hierarchical relation to the residual, whether this be defined as, variously, the primitive, the local or the merely contingent. (72–73)

One is reminded immediately of Bhabha's definition of colonial mimicry: "the desire for a reformed recognizable Other, as *a subject of a difference that is almost the same, but not quite*" (original emphasis).[62]

Mrs. Walker is asking the young boy to make a distinction between what she seems to view as a concrete object, a fruit, and an abstract concept, precision. He is faced with a false either-or choice and is "slapped" and isolated from the class ("made to stand in the corner") when he "fails"—a false choice because while Mrs. Walker seems to extend the possibility of distinguishing or choosing, there actually is no "choice." The adult poet begins the last line of the first stanza as if he were posing the same question, "How to choose," but after the line and stanza break we see that this is not a question after all but a statement that ends with the first word in the second stanza: "persimmons."

It is in this next stanza that the adult poet firmly puts Mrs. Walker in her place. There is a turn from what appears to be an abstract semantic differentiation ("persimmon" and "precision") to a concrete and detailed description of the fruit ("Ripe ones are soft and brown-spotted . . ."). Metaphors perform not dissimilarly in their attempt to embody or make material that which is abstract by means of something more familiar. Ricoeur writes in "Metaphorical Process," "The very expression 'figure of speech' implies that in metaphor, as in the other tropes or turns, discourse assumes the nature of a body by displaying forms and traits which usually characterize the human face, man's 'figure'" (142). But unlike the distinction Mrs. Walker pedantically demands, Lee complicates the supposed binary between concrete "vehicle" and abstract "tenor" by reversing and blurring the usual "A is B" formulation. That is, instead of saying, "Precision is persimmons," where the more abstract term comes in the "A" term, he says, "This is precision," where the more abstract term is in the B position.

The indeterminacy of the "This"—does it refer to persimmons or to the act of choosing or to the line or poem itself?—further undercuts any easy either-or schematization. The forcefulness of the "This is" syntax and of the copula betrays the poet's confidence in his power to retell and to remake, but the "is" here is neither a making identical, so that differences are erased, nor a choosing. The pronoun "This" is a deictic that has no fixed referent but is dependent on the context of the utterance.[63]

It is precisely in and through language that Lee proves that "precision" and "persimmon" are not as different as Mrs. Walker thinks, that there is no clear differentiation between abstract and concrete (indeed, the little boy in linking "persimmon" and "precision" is thinking metaphorically—unlike Mrs. Walker). The precision of detail and of the slicing "c" and "s" sounds—"difference," "This," "precision"—constitutes the poet's definitive rebuke to his teacher. Notice, too, the "s" and hard "t" sounds in

> Chew the skin, suck it,
> and swallow. Now, eat
> the meat of the fruit,
> so sweet,
> all of it, to the heart.

Here the poet makes the words material by his use of internal rhyme, alliteration, and assonance. In reading these words, one devours them, makes them part of the body, in much the same way one eats the meat of the fruit. As a new immigrant, Lee would have found English words moving like strange objects in his mouth; as a poet, he creates and consumes them.

The philosophical quarrel with Mrs. Walker works not only on the level of semantics and grammar but also on the material level of syllables and phonemes. There is internal and external symmetry in the line "Persimmons. This is precision." The line is equally balanced by "persimmons" on the left and "precision" on the right, unlike the fifth line in which Mrs. Walker's demand for a distinction is unbalanced by the word "between" on the left. The layout of "s-i" and "i-s" syllables is also precisely arranged: s-i / i-s / i-s / i-s / s-i with the "i-s" and "s-i" merging together in the last word, "precision."[64] One could also read the syllables aloud as sigh-is-is-is-is-sigh. The metaphoric copula "is" thus becomes embedded and reenacted at the level of syllable and phoneme. Precision becomes performed concretely. Thus, it is in and through language that the adult poet refuses the logic that demands he divide and choose, the logic that confronts most Asian Americans.

In stanza four, Lee lists other semantic distinctions he "got . . . into trouble" for not knowing: "fight" and "fright," "wren" and "yarn." It seems fairly apparent to me why a young immigrant boy might confuse and conflate "fight" and "fright"—an act of aggression and the emotion it evokes—the subtleties of that one letter "r."[65] He posits the two terms as a chiasmus: "Fight was what I did when I was frightened, / fright was what I felt when I was fighting." Here again, the poet calls into question the notion of metaphor as a unidirectional and unproblematic trope.[66] Rather, he shows it to comprise sameness and difference crossing and intersecting in paradoxical ways. "Wren" and "yarn" bring up issues of representation itself. A "yarn," of course, can also mean a tale. And like metaphor (and language itself), the woolen yarn can create endless configurations: "a bird, a rabbit, a wee man."

The boy's mother presents a different mode of knowing from Mrs. Walker's, figural rather than literal:

My mother said every persimmon has a sun

inside, something golden, glowing,
warm as my face.

Mrs. Walker would mark as "incorrect" the figurative profusion and uncontrollability of suns in persimmons. But poetic language works precisely by such confusions and by such "misnaming," whose formal term is *catachresis*.

In the "Epistemology of Metaphor," de Man makes clear that catachresis, instead of being what John Locke calls an unnatural "abuse of language," characterizes all language (19–20). This is a fairly common deconstructive move, but here it captures the way in which any attempt to pin down what is "correct English" or what constitutes a "real" American inevitably ends up becoming an act of endless regress. It is not difficult to hear in this "unnatural"/"foreign" versus "normal"/"ordinary" dichotomy the echoes of a certain type of American jingoism—manifesting itself in the rhetoric, for example, of the unassimilably "alien" "Asiatic" or the more "benign" average-Joe discourse of American popular culture. Like the naturalization that threatens to erase difference within metaphor, the rhetoric of assimilation also threatens to produce a homogeneous "naturalized" citizen-subject. Yet at the same time, the logic of assimilation refuses a complete identity of Asian with American.

As the boy learns English and becomes "Americanized," he slowly forgets his mother's way of knowing. He also forgets the linguistic ties to his past: Chinese. What is left of the Chinese language becomes, as we see in the third stanza, a currency of exotic difference that functions as a means to traffic in nonthreatening forms of racial difference. Indeed, these little tokens of Chinese language function to defuse the threat of racial otherness even as they simultaneously mark the triumph of the speaker's assimilation into American culture and the English language:

Donna undresses, her stomach is white.
In the yard, dewy and shivering
with crickets, we lie naked,
face-up, face-down.

I teach her Chinese.
Crickets: *chiu chiu.* Dew: I've forgotten.
Naked: I've forgotten.
Ni, wo: you and me.
I part her legs,
remember to tell her
she is beautiful as the moon.

Here, the poet shows how language and erotic desire are intimately connected in the process of assimilation. The English language and Donna's white body become the means of entry into American culture. The speaker has forgotten the Chinese for certain words, "dew" and "naked," but consciously reminds himself "to tell [Donna] / she is beautiful as the moon," a phrase that happens to invoke a simile and taps self-consciously into conventional Western love-poem imagery.

One might be reminded of the idea of metaphor as translation. For Aristotle, metaphor consists in "giving the thing a name that belongs to something else."[67] Echoes of the idea of metaphor as a borrowed or "foreign" name are heard when de Man says, "It is no mere play of words that 'translate' is translated in German as '*übersetzen*' which itself translates the Greek '*meta phorein*' or metaphor."[68]

In the last few stanzas, it becomes clear that the now-adult speaker has learned his lessons all too well. When he sees his blind father after an absence, the speaker asks "how his eyes *are*, a stupid question" (added emphasis)—stupid because it serves no function but to elicit an answer he already knows, a tautology. In much the same way, to say that "a persimmon is a fleshy orange edible fruit," while technically correct, is also a useless tautology.

The father's painting of persimmons, painted while he was blind, provides a more truthful and insightful answer than semantic niceties. When the father asks the son which scroll he holds, the son answers, "*This is persimmons, Father*" (original italics). With this sentence, the poem provides the counterpart to the earlier "This is precision" and completes the answer to Mrs. Walker's question. The poem does not say, "This *painting* is *of* persimmons," but "This is persimmons." The act of painting, like the acts of poetry making and knitting, makes

material and even more vivid the concrete fruit in the act of its representation, as shown in the poem's final stanza:

> *Oh, the feel of the wolftail on the silk,*
> *the strength, the tense*
> *precision in the wrist.*
> *I painted them hundreds of times*
> *eyes closed. These I painted blind.*
> *Some things never leave a person:*
> *scent of the hair of one you love,*
> *the texture of persimmons,*
> *in your palm, the ripe weight.* (original italics)

Like his Romantic precursors, Lee himself is suspicious of the tyranny of the "making identical," a danger of metaphor. First, what
the father says is precision—"the feel of the wolftail on the silk," the
precision of the wrist—is the process, not the product, of making. A
final product, frozen in stasis, like a reified metaphor or the concept
of a "real" American or any teleological drive toward an end, forces
one to choose either-or, erasing particularities that constitute difference. Second, Lee gives his father voice in the final stanza. The "I"
here is not that of the poet but that of his father. Of course, one could
argue that in ventriloquizing the voice of his father, Lee speaks for
him, but one could also read this last stanza as an attempt to overcome the dichotomy between abstract and concrete, between self and
other. There is strength *and* precision in his holding two apparently
different and contradictory terms in tension.

While Lee's use of individual metaphors evinces an awareness
of the dangers of an unexamined deployment of metaphor—of the
making identical and ventriloquizing (which isomorphically captures
the structures and processes of assimilation)—one might criticize the
larger, and perhaps more troubling, metaphorizing "Persimmons"
enacts, both at the level of individual metaphors (such as persimmons) and at the level of the poem: that is, the transforming and
reifying of a painful childhood experience—a specific violent act of
assimilation on an immigrant Chinese American boy—into "sweet"

bites of the "poetic," like bites of persimmons, which can be consumed by the reader.

This "conversion" (or "assimilation") at the level of figurative language in this particular poem (and in others of Lee's poems) is potentially troubling for several reasons:[69] First, the turning of the specificity—more precisely, the *racial* specificity—of a traumatic scene of assimilation in an American classroom in Pennsylvania—into a more generic or dehistoricized one: here, the more exotic and "timeless" realm of "Chinese" culture, as represented by the persimmons and the boy's father. What begins as a public scene of American racial discipline (not unviolent or untraumatic) becomes transmuted into a personal instantiation of the Chinese father's and mother's essential(ized) "Chinese wisdom."[70] The poet metaphorizes Chinese culture itself into a "Chinese apple" (the persimmon).

Second, this process of reification, demonstrated by the father's painting of the persimmons, is played out at the level of representation—by metaphor's making concrete in poetic language and the father's rendering of the idea of persimmons into a painted image—so that the resulting "object" is the representation of persimmon in words or brushstrokes. In moving away from a specifically racialized episode—a teacher's traumatic disciplining of an Asian immigrant boy for his un-American "misuse" of the English language—toward a depoliticized "Chinese" scene (cultural and ethnic, not racialized) of a Chinese father painting a Chinese scroll in his home, the poet renders a painful racial (assimilationizing) encounter, so familiar to countless generations of minority and immigrant students, into an exotic "Chinese apple," a more palatable poetic product that can be "eaten" by white readers. There will be no choking on bitter critiques (of racism) here.

Let me put aside for now the implications of these larger processes of making ethnic and Asian American experience metaphorical and continue with my examination of some of the more unconventional uses of metaphor *within* Lee's poems. Though Lee himself does not view his poetry as political, his metaphoric practice may itself constitute a certain type of intervention in poetic and political discourses.

While there is no space to comprehensively detail Lee's specific metaphoric practice in both *Rose* and *City*, let me note that in his first book, metaphors appear in roughly two-thirds of the poems, most abundantly in "Always a Rose," the volume's central long poem. By contrast, in his second book, *City*, a more accomplished and ambitious collection, metaphors appear in about half the poems, though significantly in two of the most important poems in the book: "This Room and Everything in It" and the culminating poem, "The Cleaving."[71]

When speaking of "mapping" Lee's use of metaphor, I run into an immediate problem: How can one "count" metaphor? In his study of tropes in Romantic poetry, *Irony and Authority in Romantic Poetry*, David Simpson warns, "Part of the difficulty of an analysis . . . is that the term 'metaphor' asks to be considered as a determinate and monovalent signifier which, if it is thought of as a metaphor-in-use, it certainly need not be" (160). To use an example from Lee's poetry: In trying to delineate the metaphors in *Rose* in which the speaker's father explicitly appears, one notices how little of Lee's obsession with his father is captured by individual metaphors, suggesting that the father's presence does not inhere in discrete metaphoric instances.[72] The father who does appear in the metaphors is characterized by a certain mystery and inaccessibility: his voice is "a well / of dark water, a prayer" ("The Gift"). Silence attends him.

In other words, what really counts as metaphor goes beyond the deployment of identifiable tropes of fruits and flowers and hair and is constituted instead by a larger whole of intersecting parts. This observation accords with Ricoeur's assertion that "[w]hile it is true that the effect of sense is focused on the word, the production of sense is borne by the whole utterance."[73] The whole of Lee's poems, their ideas and words, become a metaphor for the poet's attempts to deal with his "homelessness" as an immigrant and as an Asian American—not just the general displacement all poets feel—and his efforts to come to terms with his two "homes": "China," a place of "origin" (but also an idea) that he has never seen and will never fully inhabit (how is "return" then possible?) and the United States.

Even those discrete metaphors in *Rose* that one can identify act to defy the usual workings of metaphor. For example, it is striking to note that while most poets use metaphor to illustrate abstract concepts with concrete images, the only truly abstract concept depicted metaphorically in *Rose* is time—the days are damp pewter ("Braiding"), summer a "white labyrinth" ("My Sleeping Loved Ones"), minutes a secret ("My Sleeping Loved Ones"), and memory is sweet ("Mnemonic"). That it is time that is metaphorized is not coincidental: Lee is obsessed with time—its passing, attempts to recapture the past through memory, and so on—in all of his books of poetry. Time works with the experiences of immigration and exile to render the past and the "home" country and language unreachable and unknowable to later generations.

The most common type of individual metaphors in *Rose* appear in the form of the speaker's attempts to capture family members and his wife (and sometimes, himself) by means of and in terms of the larger, more "eternal" (timeless, stable) world of nature or some sort of otherworldly realm: his wife is a "dark vegetable," the mole on her body a "lone planet spinning slowly," her hair a "dark / star" ("Dreaming of Hair"); his sister is an angel ("My Sleeping Loved Ones"), her body a "glimmering fish" ("Water").[74] Less frequently but also notably, the poet anthropomorphizes the world of objects, natural and human-made, translating what is nonhuman into something human: the rain is his father ("Rain Diary"), shirts go blind, shoes die of fatigue ("My Sleeping Loved Ones"). In both types of metaphorizing, the poet, rather than seeking connection to the world of the social either anchors his exilic family to the less contingent world of nature or brings distant nonhuman objects closer by making them human, emotional, and familial.

Another pattern one notices is how many metaphors are used to speak about body parts of family members—usually the father but also less frequently, his sisters and the poet's wife, Donna. Voices, hands, feet, legs, moles, brains are metaphorized into organic or natural images—fish, flames, water, vegetables, planets, flowers— all intersecting in material invocations of the poet's loved ones, dead and alive. This dwelling on family members' body parts suggests both tenderness and an anxiety around fragmentation and dissolution.

"It is worth remarking also," says Simpson, "that metaphor tends to deal in parts or single items."[75] Metaphor, like memory, is a means by which a poet tries to (re)assemble the flotsam of a lived life into some sort of recognizable intelligibility. "Somehow my life seems to me like a series of disconnected episodes that do not have anything to do with each other," said Lee in 1991; "I think that it is through memory that I am able to piece it together to make it seem like one life."[76] For immigrants and exiles, of course, this fragmentation is not merely literal and symbolic but also concrete and material: in another interview, Lee describes "refugee and immigrant life" as having "to do, of course, with old coats and rotting shoes and books falling apart and old luggage."[77] The chaotic existence of the refugee and exile is represented by broken things, the flotsam and jetsam of a destabilized existence.

Poetry becomes the space in which the various parts are reassembled in an effort to ward off the threat of dissolution, a re-membering of what was dis-membered (the family, memory, homes, possessions).[78] Poetry enables the immigrant/exilic/Asian American poet to recoup in language some of the losses ensuing from a life of wandering and to resist memory's erosions. The manner in which the poet joins/merges the two terms of these metaphors reenacts the ways in which the exile tries to anchor his life in those entities—his family, the natural world—which provide more reliable connections than those of nonfamilial humans.[79] Again, what is excluded is the hostile and threatening social world:

> No one sees his [the father's] shirts go blind,
> or knows his shoes are dying
> of fatigue. No one
> notices the population of shadows crowding his bed, or
>   his favorite
> white rose, breathless and sweating. ("My Sleeping Loved Ones")

In this passage, we breathe the closed air of the lone Chinese American family in rural Pennsylvania, the feelings of isolation, loneliness,

dislocation, fragmentation: the psychological and material consequences of the migrant conditions of many uprooted immigrants.
Nonhuman entities, both those of nature (like roses) and human-
made, are anthropomorphized. Even inanimate objects feel, and
share in, the fatigue of the immigrant experience.

But as with "Persimmons," this type of metaphorizing—so common
in *Rose*—runs the risk of reification, of both the subject and elements of
the world—what David Simpson calls the "heresy of materialism," the
"passage from illustration to apparent 'reality,' the confusion of figurative and literal."[80] And because Lee's metaphors center narrowly on
family members and nature, they seem somewhat impoverished from a
lack of connection with nonfamilial persons in the outside world.

Lee himself seems to understand the limits of his metaphoric practice in *Rose*, for in his second book, *City*, the number of metaphors
alluding to family members, body parts, and material objects has
dramatically decreased (most striking is the absence of metaphorical
descriptions of the poet's father).[81] By contrast, metaphors for two particular abstract concepts appear more frequently: death and God.[82] In
general, the poet's use of metaphor has become more mitigated, less
self-consciously "literary." In the second poem of *City*, "The Interrogation," the poet declares, "I'm through with memory" in the fifth
and sixth lines and goes on for another thirty-nine lines, to the end
of the poem, without employing a single metaphor (he repeats "I'm
through with memory" in the next-to-last line).

"This Room and Everything in It," which occurs roughly halfway through *City*, functions as a turning point in both *City* and
in Lee's metaphoric practice—a hinge marking a breakdown of
confidence in an earlier, more simplistic or imposed use of metaphor, prevalent in *Rose*.[83] The poem is also the threshold onto other
nonmetaphorical ways of knowing that finally culminate in "The
Cleaving"—the long poem that closes the volume and, in my opinion, Lee's best poem to date—in the reemergence of some discrete
metaphors but, more important, the introduction of a larger, deeper,
more complex, more subtle (less overt) deployment of metaphor, a
constellation of meaning that cannot be adequately delineated by
individual instances of metaphor.

What Lee offers in *City* are more pervasive, less identifiable metaphors that move beyond discrete images to a larger system of figurative meaning, one that provides, in the words of de Man in "Tropes (Rilke)," "another perspective" in which metaphor is not so much "defined as a substitution but as a particular type of combination" (6).[84] One can see the development of his metaphorical usage more concretely by comparing his long poem "Always a Rose" (from *Rose*) with "This Room and Everything in It" (from *City*).

In section 3 of "Always a Rose," Lee writes,

> Bend closer, let me translate my nights and days.
> Each finger is a brother or sister,
> in each thumb is smudged the deaths I'm losing count of.
> The left palm is the forsythia that never waved good-bye,
> the right is my beloved pine dying from something no one knew.
> My arms and legs are the rain in its opulence,
> my face my mother's face.
> My hair is also hers.
> . . . .
> Here are my shoulders and their winglessness,
> my spine, the arc of love.

Here, Lee's self-conscious rhetoricity manifests itself in the too-easy, almost programmatic, deployment of metaphor—each finger "translating" into a brother or sister, the left palm "the forsythia that never waved good-bye," the right "my beloved pine dying from something no one knew." The excessive rhetoric ("never," "beloved," "dying") reaches a climax with "My arms and legs are the rain in its opulence." The effortless substitution works against the intended gravity of the lines; the reader is supposed to feel tragedy and instead senses a forced "poeticity." Unlike in "Persimmons," in which the poet allows the father to speak at the end of the poem, here Lee easily assumes—and erases—his mother's identity and body: "my face my mother's face. / My hair is also hers."

"This Room and Everything in It," a poem addressed to the speaker's female lover or wife, seems to begin on the same self-conscious, almost programmatic note as section 3 of "Always a Rose" by imposing (note the use of the imperative in both) a metaphoric scheme that works spatially:

> Lie still now
> while I prepare for my future,
> certain hard days ahead,
> when I'll need what I know so clearly this moment.
>
> I am making use
> of the one thing I learned
> of all the things my father tried to teach me:
> the art of memory.
>
> I am letting this room
> and everything in it
> stand for my ideas about love
> and its difficulties.
>
> I'll let your love-cries,
> those spacious notes
> of a moment ago,
> stand for distance.
>
> Your scent,
> that scent
> of spice and a wound,
> I'll let stand for mystery.

Yet one notices a deliberateness and cautiousness here missing in "Always a Rose." The phrases "I am letting stand for," "I'll let stand for" signal the disappearance of Lee's former unselfconsciousness about the smooth deployment of metaphor ("let me translate"), the easy slide into "A is B" or "A is like/as B" ("Each finger is . . . ," "[t]he left palm is . . . ," "[m]y arms and lips are . . . ," "[m]y hair is . . . ").

In "This Room and Everything in It," no copula oils the attempts at equivalence. Only in stanzas 6 and 7 is there a brief return to unproblematized metaphor:

> Your sunken belly
> is the daily cup

of milk I drank
as a boy before morning prayer.

The sun on the face
of the wall
is God, the face
I can't see, my soul.

At first glance both these instances seem to have Christian significance and overtones, but upon closer inspection, one sees that the
usual cup of wine that is the body of Christ is replaced by a cup of
milk, and the body of Christ substituted by the female lover's body
part. The terms of the transubstantive relation are also reversed (not
"the cup of wine is . . ." but the "belly / is the . . . cup)."[85] In the
second metaphor, a "pagan" sun is metaphorized to a presumably
Christian God, whose "face / I can't see."

The poet in "This Room and Everything in It"—as in section 3
of "Always a Rose"—tries to let certain things stand for other things
in a spatial scheme. But very quickly this arrangement breaks down:

I'll close my eyes
and recall this room and everything in it:
My body is estrangement.
This desire, perfection.
Your closed eyes my extinction.
Now I've forgotten my
idea. The book
on the windowsill, riffled by wind . . .
the even-numbered pages are
the past, the odd-
numbered pages, the future.
The sun is
God, your body is milk . . .

useless, useless . . .
your cries are song, my body's not me . . .
no good . . . my idea
has evaporated . . . your hair is time, your thighs are song . . .
it had something to do

with death . . . it had something
to do with love. (original ellipses)

It is clear here that the earlier scheme of "translation" no longer
works—one is reminded again of the close tie between metaphor and
translation, as de Man noted. The self-consciously "poetic" (metaphoric) language that the poet tries to use to conjure up the beloved
Other ends up being not only inadequate but also estranging. Indeed,
the attempts at crafting and sustaining a string of poetic metaphors
break down completely. Writes Simpson: "Metaphor . . . fulfils or
fails to fulfil the mechanisms of desire"; as with metonymy, "the
protagonist is tempted to try to proceed along a chain of increasingly
resonant signifiers—hair, foot, eyes, and so on—which he might
expect to construct into a whole, into a complete presence. But this
never happens, and the pre-empting of the process of construction
produces fixation and arrested motion."[86]

Indeed, the nonmetaphoric and less precise "it had something /
to do with love" ends up being more truthful to the inadequacy of
language to "translate" the trauma and dislocatedness of the exile
than the more crafted literary attempts. The indefinite nature of the
pronoun "it" and the vague lack of specificity of the "something" capture a sense of anxious bewilderment and of forgetting, both involun-
tary and voluntary, that often attends emigration, particularly forced
emigration. In trying to say something about "something to do with
love," Lee tries to do justice to the complexity of that something without imposing his will to make metaphor. William Blake distrusted
metaphor precisely because, in Simpson's words, it "allow[s] for the
mind to establish itself as the focal point of the comparative activity.
Its selections produce re-imposed perspectives which have the features
of Urizenic solidness, plotted ratios."[87]

Timothy Yu describes what happens in "This Room and Everything
in It" as a staging of the "failure of memory . . . a moving admission of
the failure of poetry and poetic form: the speaker losing a hold on memory becomes a figure for the writer losing control over his poetic materials, as metaphors come unmoored from their referents."[88] Though I do
not disagree with this characterization, I would nuance it further to

give it greater specificity: while all poets feel anxiety about losing control over language and "poetic materials," Lee's enactment of disintegration in this poem centers specifically on the processes of metaphorizing. Furthermore, the anxieties expressed here are not just those of any poet but are rooted in, though not necessarily limited to, the concerns that afflict him as an immigrant Asian American poet specifically, despite the lack of Asian American themes or "markers" in the poem.

In "This Room and Everything in It," Lee reminds the reader of the possible pitfalls of an unexamined deployment of metaphor, especially a too-easy conflation of the two terms of the metaphor,[89] as well as the risk of the poet's speaking for the unknown Other. In the free and unexamined use of figurative language, a poet can too easily forget the irreducibility of the thisness of any person, place, or thing, "their human salience." Whereas in *Rose*, Lee compares the sound of trees to the sound of water, in *City* he proclaims instead: "But seasound differs from the sound of trees" ("Furious Versions," section 6). And in the title poem, "The City in Which I Love You," Lee's resistance to violating the integrity of what *is*—by imposing a narrative or metaphoric substitution—comes through clearly: at various points in that long poem he writes, "That woman / was not me . . . that man was not me . . . he was not me . . . they are not me . . . none of them is me . . . they are not me forever." There is something repellent about glibly asserting one can easily "identify" with others, as if all subjectivities, experiences, and beings were interchangeable.

Lee's understanding of the complexity of metaphor culminates in the central metaphor of "The Cleaving," the last poem in *City*. While a few explicit individual metaphors appear later in the poem (for example, "The soul too / is a debasement / of a text," "The soul is a corruption / and a mnemonic"), they are rare in the poem. Instead, what Lee offers is a more profound way of making metaphor by means of a larger body (or constellation) of interconnected, sometimes contradictory, ideas and feelings that cannot be collapsed into "A is B" binaries or singular instances of metaphorical meaning.

As the speaker watches the butcher at the Hon Kee grocery cutting up various roasted meats, the occasion becomes the springboard for a meditation on all sorts of identifications:

> He gossips like my grandmother, this man
> with my face, and I could stand
> amused all afternoon
> . . . .
> [H]e's delicate, narrow-
> waisted, his frame so slight a lover, some
> rough other
> might break it down
> its smooth, oily length.

While Lee begins the poem by once again invoking a family member (this time in a simile, "like my grandmother"), one notices immediately that the poet has left the kind of simple 1:1 metaphorical references and the lack of interest in other nonfamilial humans that was prevalent throughout *Rose*. For one thing, the speaker's attention to detail about this other person, who is not his father, is striking, as is the poet's inability or unwillingness to impose a simple metaphoric "ratio" onto the butcher.

The speaker observes the butcher with a blend of sympathetic curiosity, amusement, and, perhaps, a tinge of homoerotic desire. In his acts of identification, the speaker crosses multiple identity boundaries: gender, sexuality, human/nonhuman, living and dead. The lyric voice seamlessly moves from describing the butcher as a lover to analogizing him to a roast duck that a "rough other" might "break . . . down" (the language invoking rough sex, rough trade, but also the violence of hate crimes).

Two stanzas later, the speaker extends his Whitmanian empathic identification even to the nonhuman and nonliving, not a big leap given his earlier eliding of butcher and roast duck:

> Did this animal [the duck], after all, at the moment
> its neck broke,
> image the way his executioner
> shrinks from his own death?
> Is this how
> I, too, recoil from my day?

Any attempt by the reader to try to "decode" an "A is B" metaphorical scheme becomes impossible: Is the butcher the poet ("this man / with my face")? Or is the poet the butcher ("break[ing] it [the butcher and other materials for the poem] down / its smooth, oily length")? Or is the butcher the duck (and, like the duck, "shrinks from his own death")? Or is the poet the duck ("Is this how / I, too, recoil from my day")?

The poem spins into larger and larger metaphoric identifications in which the A and B terms become interchanged, intertwined, and ultimately indistinguishable: Is God the butcher (the poem is obsessed with death)? Or is the butcher God? Is the poet God ("What is it in me would / devour the world to utter it?")? Is the soul a body? ("I did not know the soul / is cleaved so that the soul might be restored")? Or is the soul a text ("The soul too / is a debasement / of a text")? Is a body a text ("All of the body's revisions end / in death")? Is eating a form of dying (What is my eating, / . . . but another / shape of going, / my immaculate expiration?")? Is dying a form of eating ("our deaths are fed / that we may continue our daily dying, / . . . As we eat we're eaten.")? Is God the text ("God is the text")? Or is the text God?

The connections between and among the A and B terms of the metaphors are inextricably intertwined and part of a larger cosmology of meaning. The traditional binary structure of metaphor is no longer adequate. If Lee invokes any binaries in the poem, it is only to invert them and/or to demonstrate their uselessness, if not their harmfulness. In "The Cleaving," Lee makes clear that "A is B" and "B is A" can (and should?) exist at the same time—without contradiction.

The term "cleaving" can aptly be used as a metaphor for the structure of metaphor itself. At the crux of metaphor is paradox, for metaphor works simultaneously in two complementary and "contradictory" realms: for example, abstract/concrete, distant/near. It makes the impossible tangible. Like metaphor, cleaving encompasses both coming together (as in "The child cleaves to his mother's breast") and breaking apart (as in "She cleaves wood with dexterity"). Lee's use of the word suggests both meanings at once throughout the poem, simultaneously identification and disidentification, similitude and dissimilitude—the very structure of assimilation. In the last stanza, the speaker states (not asks), "What then may I do / but cleave to what cleaves me." Metaphor contains within itself the key to its undoing: it is a two-way road embodying opposites, not a one-way road privileging one end point over another. The structure of metaphor encompasses like and unlike, the generalizable and the unique, the imaginative and the material, the present and the absent.

One could argue that this poetics of cleaving captures a key aspect of Asian American (poetic) subjectivity.[90] Lacking a fixed point of origin and an unproblematized relationship to language, Asian American subjects and poets are cleaved by both sides of the split/adhesion: whether a country, a poetic tradition, or a language. In very real terms, Lee—like many other diasporic subjects—faces the perils and possibilities of cleaving, in both senses of the term (his memoir is appropriately titled *The Winged Seed*). He has stated explicitly that "The Cleaving" is about "assimilation and the violence of assimilation."[91] Because of Lee's and other Asian Americans' unique interpellation as irredeemably and constitutively "alien," assimilation can never "succeed." Thus, the concept and structure of cleaving hold special force for them—not in the simplistic reductive stereotype of their being "half Asian" and "half American" but in the sense that they are split from the country of origin but still unmistakably identified with and, thus, adhered to, it. And they are cleaved from the American body and the English language—as much as they may want, and strive, to cleave to them.

The imperative to assimilate subsumes difference to similarity. David Lloyd points out in "Race Under Representation" that "[a] s the very expression 'assimilation' might suggest, racism elevates a principle of likening above that of differentiation such that its rhetorical structure is that of metaphorization" (71). Thus, the young immigrant boy in "Persimmons" is punished by his teacher for not knowing "correct" English, as any "authentic" native-born American would:

> In sixth grade Mrs. Walker
> slapped the back of my head
> and made me stand in the corner
> for not knowing the difference
> between *persimmon* and *precision*.

This idea of "not fitting" or "misnaming" characterizes the structural logic at the heart of metaphor—again, catachresis. As de Man argues in "The Epistemology of Metaphor," not only figurative language but *all* language is prone to "tropological defiguration," what Locke calls an "abuse of language" (19–20). In *An Essay Concerning Human Understanding*, Locke attacks "mixed modes" for having no equivalence in nature. This idea of metaphor as being "unnatural" accords with Aristotle's idea of metaphor as deviance, a giving of a foreign name: "Metaphor consists in giving the thing a name that belongs to something else."[92] Aristotle contrasts metaphors and "strange words" to "normal" and "ordinary" words; a statement is a riddle if made up of metaphors and a "barbarism" if made up of strange words.

Yet, even if the "foreign" immigrant boy were eventually to learn to speak "perfect English," he would still be viewed as not wholly American by many Americans. Lloyd writes,

> Like the expressions "taste" and "common sense," "assimilation" is a concept which is at once a metaphor and structured like a metaphor. But unlike taste and common sense, which embody the narrative of a movement from immediate sensation to universality, the very logic of assimilation betrays an inverse movement equally intrinsic to the process of metaphorization in general but accentuated by its status as a material practice. The constitution of any metaphor involves the bringing together of two elements into identity in such a manner that their differences are suppressed. Just so, the process of assimilation . . . requires that which defines the difference between the elements to remain over as a residue. . . . [T]he product of assimilation will always necessarily be in hierarchical relation to the residual, whether this be defined as, variously, the primitive, the local or the merely contingent.[93]

This "residue" prevents complete "Americanization." Because Asian Americans are fixedly viewed as constitutively and immutably "alien," their assimilation is, by definition, an impossibility.

Thus, Lee's metaphor of cleaving is not simply a recognition of the general existential condition of all humans in relation to language— though it is that, too—but is deeply rooted in his experiences and subjectivity as a racialized and hyphenated Asian American, as an Asian immigrant, as a diasporic Chinese person.[94] Lee recognizes this influence but, as is his wont, cannot resist the desire to universalize social and political experience into something transcendental. In a 1996 interview he says,

> I used to think that I was a guest in the language because I was
> Asian and I learned the language at the age of eight. But I see now
> that we're all guests in the language. And I think my being an immi-
> grant heightened that realization. I'm sure that it has something to
> do with my wanting to write poems. Because it's a feeling of disloca-
> tion with the thing that you love.[95]

The indefiniteness of the pronoun "it" in "I'm sure that it has some-thing to do with"—echoes of "it had something / to do with love" in "This Room and Everything in It"—and the vagueness of the "thing" suggest that Lee himself has not been able to reconcile the messiness of worldly experience with his desire to speak of the Ideal. His use of the past tense ("I used to think") and the language of epiphany and evolutionary development—"But I see now"—renders the his-torically and concretely specific forms of linguistic alienation Asian immigrants and Asian Americans are made to feel into another more "universal" "human" experience ("But I see now that we're all . . ."). At the same time, Lee is vaguely aware that the residue of specific histories persists: "I think my being an immigrant heightened that realization" (and three years later: "I've realized that there is still the culture" [96]).

I would argue that what Lee's metaphors *do* in "The Cleaving" con-stitutes an intervention that disrupts our customary ways of viewing not only metaphor but larger issues of identity and difference in the social realm, more than Lee himself is conscious of. In "The Cleav-ing" in particular, Lee brings the two disparate A and B terms into a relation that does not resemble—and is not beholden to—assimila-tion's logic of psychic and material subjugation. As the speaker in the poem views the butcher at the counter, he sees this other Chinese or Chinese Other as both a reflection and a variation of himself—both relative and stranger—and sees no logical contradiction:

> He gossips like my grandmother, this man
> with my face,
> . . . .
>
> Such a sorrowful Chinese face,
> nomad, Gobi, Northern
> . . . .
> He could be my brother, but finer,
> . . . .
> In his light-handed calligraphy
> on receipts and in his
> moodiness, he is
> a Southerner from a river-province;
> suited for scholarship, his face poised
> above an open book, he'd mumble
> his favorite passages.
> He could be my grandfather. . . .

The butcher is both a "Northern[er]" and "a Southerner," and he is variously identified with the speaker's grandmother (through a simile) and his brother and grandfather (through the "could be" of possibility). Lee seems aware of the ties and shared experiences between far-flung diasporic Chinese from various provinces, now residing in different countries: his own family's having lived in China, Indonesia, Hong Kong, Macau, Japan, Pennsylvania, and now Chicago. At this moment in the poem, the Pennsylvania-raised Chinese American poet-speaker encounters the Chinese butcher from China (and from who knows what other places) in a Chinese restaurant in Chicago.

In the poem, the language of identification ranges across metaphor, simile ("like"), the declarative ("he is"), and the conditional ("He could"), yet for the Asian American or Chinese diasporic poet, these acts of identification are not purely linguistic. They carry with them a certain historical burden and diasporic feeling of obligation to speak for all the many nameless immigrants who cannot speak for themselves, especially in English:

> Maybe it was a kind of weight that I felt. You see these immigrants
> with all this rotten luggage—what are they carrying in those things?

They're carrying history. Histories like their rotten shoes and dilapidated clothes. And in coming to this country, we are told stories to remember who we were, about things that had happened, and people we knew who had died or been imprisoned. It seemed to me that justice has something to do with remembering these people. It is justice to remember in a way that we can give memory to others.[97]

One "justice" Lee the poet has power to effect is to record those deaths, to keep them alive in historical memory, and to insist they are part of American history:

> and the standing deaths
> at the counters, in the aisles,
> the walking deaths in the streets,
> the death-far-from-home, the death-
> in-a-strange-land, these Chinatown
> deaths, these American deaths.

It is by means of his poetry that Lee confers the label "American" on those for whom that status is denied by law, by the prevailing logic that deems Asian Americans as irredeemably "alien" and constitutively non- and un-American, and/or by the impossible logic of assimilation. By his use of appositive phrases, the poet renders the Chinatown deaths into American deaths and gives full citizenship to these Chinese diasporic figures—though here, only in their lonely deaths in the land of "opportunity" and "freedom"—and "sing[s]" what the speaker calls

> this race that according to Emerson
> *managed to preserve to a hair*
> *for three or four thousand years*
> *the ugliest features in the world.* (original emphasis).

The passage Lee quotes comes from an 1824 entry in Emerson's journals (the editors note that it may have been the draft of a letter or the text of a letter Emerson had sent). In that same document, the great American Transcendentalist has no compunction in voicing his Orientalist sentiments—surprisingly virulent, even for their time, and ignorant of historical and cultural facts:

Why does the same dull current of ignoble blood creep through a
thousand generations in China without any provision for its puri-
fication, without the mixture of one drop from the fountains of
goodness & glory? . . . In our feeble vision, it would seem that the
immoveable institutions of the yellow men, [*sic*] will disappoint for
50 centuries more all expectations of a change . . . their cheerless
(because hopeless) stupidity . . . embalmed for immortality. . . . No,
they worship crockery Gods, which in Europe & America our babies
are wise enough to put in baby houses; the summit of their philosophy & science is how to make tea. . . . The closer contemplation
we condescend to bestow the more disgustful is that booby nation.
The Chinese Empire enjoys precisely a Mummy's reputation, that
of having preserved to a hair for 3 or 4,000 years the ugliest features
in the world. . . . They are not tools for other nations to use. Even
miserable Africa can say I have hewn the wood & drawn the water
to promote the wealth & civilization of other lands. But, China, rev-
erend dullness! Hoary ideot [*sic*]!, all she can say at the convocation
of nations must be—"I made the tea."[98]

Over a century and a half later, it is in poetry that Lee spars with
Emerson and tries to keep alive in writing the memory of those earlier
Chinese immigrants, who paid the harsh price of exclusion and racism in this country. At the same time he is also aware that such acts,
even if wholly sympathetic, run the risk of erasing the particularity
of others, of speaking for them. In another interview that same year,
he says,

> The imagination would be committing a criminal act if I said I
> could identify with all these people, but I know exactly what they're
> going through. I witnessed that as a child—the man lying there and
> the woman fanning his face. Now I realize that the greatest act of
> love I could commit is to give them their otherness, their absolute
> aloneness, their dignity. I don't want to go in there and muddle it up,
> to say, I'm just like them.[99]

In "The Cleaving," the speaker asks, "Was it me in the Other / I
prayed to when I prayed? . . . Was it me in the other I loved / when
I loved another?" "Metaphor . . . is necessary to creation," reminds
Simpson in *Irony and Authority*, "but risk[s] false creation, liberat-

ing the mind but threatening at the same time to establish its own extrinsic tyranny" (140).

As with love, Lee's desire to represent these others entails a sort of "consuming" of the other—in this case, other Chinese immigrants, past and present, who have paid the cost of assimilation in the United States—so as to re-present their experiences on the page:

> . . . I would eat it all
> to utter it.
> The deaths at the sinks, those bodies prepared
> for eating, I would eat . . .

This could very well be a description of the act of poetic creation itself: consuming (or reading) the world so as to write it. Elsewhere in the poem, the speaker acknowledges the dark and voracious aspect of this desire that impels the act of writing:

> I take it [a fish head] as text and evidence
> of the world's love for me,
> and I feel urged to utterance,
> urged to read the body of the world, urged
> to say it in human terms,
> my reading a kind of eating, my eating
> a kind of reading,
> my saying a diminishment, my noise
> a love-in-answer.
> What is it in me would
> devour the world to utter it?
> What is it in me will not let
> the world be, would eat
> not just this fish,
> but the one who killed it,
> the butcher who cleaned it.

The danger of metaphor, too, is this gobbling up of the other to render its difference into sameness and into a thing. Assimilation operates not dissimilarly, by engulfing the other, making difference into likeness by a process of reification. (Ricoeur gives perhaps a more

positive reading of the use of figural language: as an attempt to "g[i]
ve to discourse a quasi-bodily externalization.")[100]

At the heart of metaphor (and assimilation) lies not only paradox but
aporia—an empty space, a space not unlike the hollowness of the carp's
head that the speaker in "The Cleaving" contemplates before eating it:
"one more / articulation of a single nothing, / severally manifested."
Like memory, to whose structure it is homologous, metaphor pulls
together disparate fragments as a means of penetrating to the unknowable, the unreachable. Always coming close but never reaching the
Absolute ("God is the text"), metaphor approaches the unfamiliar by
means of the known, the strange via the familiar. Memory approaches
the once-familiar by means of the now-known (in its fragmented cobbled-together manifestations), the strange via the familiar. This issue of
the inability to arrive—of the unknowableness of the über-text—lies
at the heart of memory and metaphor (note that these spatial ideas of
arrival, the heart, are themselves metaphorical). At the center of both,
one finds a fundamental slippage, an unbridgeable gap. As Allen Grossman has written, "'Like' represents an insurmountable barrier in experience which both enables possibility and destroys possibility."[101]

But there *is* possibility. What Lee offers in his metaphor of cleaving
is not only a way of holding sameness and difference together in tension without reducing all to sameness—the making identical of metaphor and assimilation—but also the possibility of new ways of thinking
about relation and identification in both the poetic and social realms.

It is no accident that Lee chooses to identify the butcher with members of his family. But unlike the metaphors in *Rose*, which almost
always involve the poet's family members, the speaker here recognizes
nonfamily members as linked in an affective system, or rather, body:

> Brothers and sisters by blood and design,
> who sit in separate bodies of varied shapes,
> we constitute a many-membered
> body of love

Lee creates a cosmology of relation by evoking and creating linkages
of metaphoric connection, based on the idea of sibling relation

("[b]rothers and sisters") and affect (love) but not determined by "blood."[102] Unlike the workings of the traditional metaphoric relation between an abstract concept and a concrete image, Lee's vision of relationality offers a means of making connections among humans, and between humans and the larger world of nature and objects, in a manner that recognizes the individuality of these "separate bodies of varied shapes." This made world is linked by the affect of love (echoes here of the New Testament and Lee's Protestant roots).[103] The word "design" also evokes the made (designed) world of poems.

More importantly, Lee taps into a liberatory aspect of metaphor's potential: to make relations among disparate things. While the structure of metaphor always implies an impossibility of fulfilling desire—the poet can never "reach" the Beloved, his father, God, the Word, the true essence of "Chineseness" or "Americanness," or English or language—metaphor can also teach us something about making connection without erasing particularity and by holding several "antinomies" in balance. Thus, the butcher at the Hon Kee Grocery joins past and present, far and near, male and female, Chinese and non-Chinese, self and other:

> . . . the sorrow of his Shang
> dynasty face,
> African face with slit eyes. He is
> my sister, this
> beautiful Bedouin, this Shulamite,
> keeper of sabbaths, diviner
> of holy texts, this dark
> dancer, this Jew, this Asian, this one
> with the Cambodian face, Vietnamese face, this Chinese
> I daily face,
> this immigrant,
> this man with my own face.

The dangers and the potentialities inherent in metaphor are embodied in the metaphor of cleaving: the impossibility of overcoming the gap at the heart of metaphor but also the possibilities opened up in language for bringing together—not in rigid binary units but in a whole cosmology of relation—the past and the present, the familial and the nonfamilial, the human and the nonhuman, what is retained in memory and lost in time, what is neither equivalent nor utterly different. These lines offer us a vision of gender, racial, national, sexual, and bodily crossings.

Thus, Lee's use of metaphor of cleaving points to new ways of thinking about both metaphor and poetry by no longer seeing as disparate what is usually binarized: the aesthetic and the social, form and content, minority and "universal" writing, the world and the text. Furthermore, as Lee's metaphoric practice shows us, what seem like "purely literary" formal concerns, such as figures of speech, can tell us a great deal about the forms of representation beyond the text—that is, within the realm of the social and political—particularly, how racial minority subjects become constituted through formal processes, such as metaphorization, in the world.

The reception of Asian American poets and their poetry is inseparable from the interpellation and understanding of Asian Americans as racialized subjects and citizens. This question of reception is crucial (as we have seen in the Introduction and as we shall see in Chapters 3 and 5). We must change the habits of reading we bring to Asian American and all minority persons and Asian American and minority poetries if we are to learn what Lee's metaphor of cleaving has to teach us as literary critics and as Americans. No writing is more "pure" than another; no writing more "debased."

> The soul too
> is a debasement
> of a text, but, thus, it
> acquires salience, although a
> human salience, but
> inimitable, and hence, memorable.
> . . . .
> No easy thing, violence.
> One of its names? Change. . . .

While it is true that Lee suffers from a tendency to mystify his work in phenomenological terms and that the traditional lyric form itself has certain representational limits, what seems to me the major barrier to reading Asian American and minority poetry with attention to what its forms, not just its words, have to say is the ingrained reflex to shy away from thinking about what has cleaved us as a country—the division of whites and nonwhites—and what cleaves us as literary critics—binary thinking about the racial and the aesthetic. The speaker (and the poet) asks in "The Cleaving":

> What then may I do
> but cleave to what cleaves me.

This is a statement, not a question.

The "great American poet" we should look to is not Emerson—with "his transparent soul, his / soporific transcendence" and whose model of American self-reliance is "a sturdy lad from New Hampshire or Vermont"[104]—but Whitman, even with his many flaws, the Whitman of "Song of Myself":

> I take my place among you as much as among any,
> The past is the push of you, me, all, precisely the same . . . (ll.
> 1118–19)
> . . . .
> I too am not a bit tamed, I too am untranslatable . . . (l. 1333)[105]

This nation, this idea, and this poetry we call "American" is large and contains multitudes. Minority poets can be poets of the soul as well as of the body. All Americans and American poets share equally in the body politic and in the American literary tradition. As Whitman reminds us, "This is the city and I am one of the citizens" ("Song of Myself," l. 1075). We are all citizens in the city of poetry making.

THREE

Reading Too Much Into

Marilyn Chin, Translation,
and Poetry in the "Post-Race" Era

In 2008, a contretemps broke out in the Letters section of *Poetry* magazine's usually sedate, if not staid, pages. At issue was a translation by
the poet Marilyn Chin (b. 1955) of a single poem by an eighteenth-
century Vietnamese woman poet, Ho Xuan Huong, whom most
Poetry readers likely had never heard of. The anger—indeed, ferocity
and vitriol—that marked the exchange made obvious that whatever
issues were ignited, and nerves touched, went well beyond the poem
and translation in question. The battle lines drawn suggested not only
that, at the more local level, *Poetry*'s recent transition from moribund
journal of the poetry establishment to a more capacious and "diverse"
(stylistically, culturally, and racially) twenty-first-century poetry journal had not been as smooth as might appear—even with the $100
million infusion of pharmaceutical-heiress largesse[1]—but also, more
broadly, that the repressed skeletons of the 1980s culture wars (and
earlier "real" wars in Vietnam and other Asian countries) had not
been laid to rest, even in the "post-race" Obama era. The question of
the nature of translation—indeed, the very nature of poetry—was at
stake. Who has the authority to translate? Who has command of the
English language? Who has the right to write poetry?

The actors involved were not the usual suspects—this was not a
debate between, say, Dana Gioia and Charles Bernstein or Harold
Bloom and Amiri Baraka; rather, the combatants were an established
Asian American female poet and three men—a marketing and sales

director, editor, and translator—working for, or with Copper Canyon, a Pacific Northwest publisher that, if personified, would be the
equivalent of a liberal, globe-trotting, blue-state voter. The press's
diverse offerings range from mainstream poetry (for example, the
work of former US Poet Laureate W. S. Merwin) to translated poetry
by the Palestinian writer Mahmoud Darwish, contemporary Mexican
poets, and ancient Chinese poets, as well as writing by Asian American poets such as Arthur Sze and Timothy Liu.

The hostile skirmish was set off by a seemingly benign act of translation in the April 2008 issue of *Poetry* ("The Translation Issue").
Chin, a poet in her late fifties, who, like Li-Young Lee, has been
embraced by the poetry and academic establishment[2]—but who,
unlike Lee, sees herself as a "political poet"—offered her translation
of Ho Xuan Huong's modest four-line poem "Lamenting Widow":

> A woman wails, *boo hoo*, mourning her man
> Shut up, shame on you, don't cry to the hills!
> O little sister, I should have warned you
> Don't eat the meat, if it makes you cough blood![3] (original italics)

The poem was followed by a one-page "Translator's Note," in which
Chin explains the excitement she felt when she discovered Ho's
poetry. She explicitly singles out the earlier poet's skillful employment of "brilliant wit and blatant double entendre," which "tak[es]
the erotic poem to great heights." Chin makes clear that she takes this
eighteenth-century poet to be a powerful role model of female poetic
(and sexual) agency: "One could read her as a modern feminist poet,"
Chin writes (43). That Ho Xuan Huong was also a concubine does
not detract from the power of her writing but, argues Chin, may have
been a major impetus for it: "All women in the oppressive Confucian
family structure were of marginal status, but it was this oppression
that caused her to write fervently about women's issues" (43).

In the June 2008 issue of *Poetry*, one letter appeared in response
to the Chin translation: Joseph Bednarik, who identified himself as
working at Copper Canyon Press—though not revealing his position as its marketing and sales director—began by approvingly citing
the argument made by translator Eliot Weinberger (a Copper Can-

yon author), in *Nineteen Ways of Looking at Wang Wei*, for exposing oneself to multiple translations of a poem. Bednarik then proceeded to unfavorably compare Chin's translation of the Ho Xuan Huong poem to that of John Balaban, another Copper Canyon author. Bednarik specifically questioned Chin's choice of "*boo hoo*" ("[W]hich Nôm character means '*boo hoo*'?") before concluding, "I don't see how Chin's versions add depth or nuance to the work. Frankly, they read like someone noodling around in the margins of someone else's book."[4]

Chin's response followed Bednarik's letter in the same issue. It read, in full:

> The first two characters in the quatrain are onomatopoeic, mimicking the sound of a woman's crying. Therefore, "*boo-hoo*" [*sic*] is an accurate translation, both semantically and tonally. I was aiming to capture the edgy, satirical attitude so ample in Ho's work.
>
> Perhaps Joseph Bednarik is not conscious that "noodling around in the margins" is an appalling and problematic expression, fraught with demeaning sexist, racist, imperialist overtones, and born out of the very hateful stuff that Ho Xuan Huong so pointedly and wholeheartedly fought against in her poetry and in her life. All ugliness revealed, perhaps we could finally cut through his pernicious smugness and have the real discussion regarding how many Western cultural imperialists does it take to plunder Wang Wei and who, if anyone, should have the rightful claim to an Asian woman's poetry. "Noodling" could have been an unfortunate slip and not unconscious hatred; but he might as well have said "flied-licing." Perhaps Bednarik and his press believe that the white male patriarchy must forever colonize the translation of Asian poetry and that I, a dark-skinned Asian woman poet, should not be "noodling" where I don't belong. (251–52)

The structure of Chin's reply parallels that of Bednarik's critique: she starts with a particular question of translation and then moves to the larger implications of such a "mistranslation." Chin addresses head-on Bednarik's doubts about her translating skill by defending her choice of the onomatopoeic "boo hoo" on aesthetic—specifically, semantic and tonal—grounds.

In translation, of course, it is precisely in the connotative subtleties that the skill—or deficiency—of the translator and her ability in the "target language" can be most finely (and severely) judged. Semantic choices and tone are nuanced yet crucial registers. Strikingly, the term around which the disagreement flares is nondenotative: "boo hoo," an aural approximation of a bodily sound but, like all instances of onomatopoeia, one that is culturally and linguistically specific; only native speakers of a language are instantly familiar with the onomatopoeic renderings of human and nonhuman sounds. That in this particular case, the wailing sound also happens to be that of a female figure in an eighteenth-century Vietnamese woman's poem raises larger questions—for example, who has the twenty-first-century authority to render her cries intelligible to an English-speaking American audience?

Chin, following Bednarik, makes the move from the particular translation point at hand to the larger implications of her (mis)translation, but, unlike her critic, she makes explicit what she sees as the subtext of his rather generally worded two-sentence verdict.[5] Like any diligent close reader of poetry, Chin analyzes his choice of the terms "noodling" and "margins" and then directly confronts what she sees as the ideological underpinnings of his choice of language ("perhaps we could finally . . . have that real discussion"). As any careful translator would, she intensely examines his words' semantic and tonal connotations, not just their denotations. Chin pulls no punches—there is no noodling here—in giving her translation of what she thinks Bednarik *really* means in his letter.

The outcry in response to Chin's reply was immediate and vociferous: in the July–August 2008 issue, Bednarik (now fully identifying himself as "Marketing and Sales Director, Copper Canyon Press"), Michael Wiegers ("Editor, Copper Canyon Press"), the Bednarik-touted Copper Canyon translator John Balaban, and a Bengali translator/reader confront Chin. The letters contra Chin continued in the September 2008 issue, which also included letters of defense by three women writers of color—two Japanese American, Kimiko Hahn and Mitsuye Yamada, and one Native American, Joy Harjo.

The first letter published in the July–August 2008 issue is by John Balaban, the rival Ho Xuan Huong translator, who was promoted earlier by his marketing and sales director. After citing his translator credentials ("as past president of the American Literary Translator's [*sic*] Association"), Balaban opens with the same move of faux openness as Bednarik—"I believe poems can be profitably translated again and again"—before getting to the real point: "What I find awful, besides the quality of the Chin translations that appeared in *Poetry*, is her contention that she can translate Ho Xuan Huong because she can read Chinese. . . . Nôm is the old ideographic script for spoken Vietnamese; it is not Chinese."[6] He ends his letter: "Given Vietnam's troubled ancient and recent history with China, I can't figure out why Marilyn Chin thought she had some entitlement to this poetry."[7]

The lack of irony of these remarks—not to mention the vagueness and imprecision of his main evaluative adjective, "awful"—would be less striking if Balaban were not completely serious. The choice of the word "entitlement" is telling. Chin herself never uses the term (or any variant) nor does she imply that she is "entitled" to Ho Xuan Huong's poetry because of her knowledge of Chinese. Is Balaban, a white American male, any more entitled than Chin, a Chinese American female, to the poetry of an eighteenth-century Vietnamese woman poet/concubine? Given that in its history, Vietnam has had military encounters with both the Chinese and Americans, and that the twenty-year-long Vietnam War ended just thirty-three years before this encounter in the unsullied American pages of *Poetry*, one could just as easily have written, "Given Vietnam's troubled . . . recent history with [the United States], I can't figure out why [John Balaban] thought [he] had some entitlement to this poetry"—a poetry that, as Balaban himself points out, is written in an "old ideographic Vietnamese script."

What does it mean for a twenty-first-century white American man to reprimand a twenty-first-century Asian American woman for coming off as "too entitled" ("Shut up, shame on you, don't cry to the hills!")?[8] Examining the structure and logic of the argumentation in this heated exchange not only gives us insight into a particular disagreement about issues of translation and interpretation but also provides, I argue, a glimpse into the larger contestations around the place of an Asian American female poet-translator in the larger poetry world and, more broadly, the legitimacy of more "recent" and/or less institutionally entrenched American minority writing (here, Asian American) in this "post-race" age.

The logic of white men saving brown women from brown men is, of course, quite familiar.[9] It is as old as colonialism and imperialism. But here in the pages of *Poetry*, it takes a new twist: a twenty-first-century white American male translator saves a Vietnamese eighteenth-century female poet-concubine from a twenty-first-century Chinese American female poet-translator. But, as we quickly learn in the letter by Michael Wiegers, Balaban's editor at Copper Canyon Press, the old logic has not exactly disappeared:

> Apart from the translations themselves, what is troublesome about Chin's project is her contention that in translating Ho Xuan Huong she is translating from Chinese. She writes about encountering a "vocabulary that is very un-Chinese." Well, perhaps that's because, after one thousand years of domination by the Chinese, Vietnamese literati created Nôm to represent Vietnamese speech, not Chinese. Before leveling her charges of cultural imperialism, perhaps Chin might acknowledge that Ho Xuan Huong wrote in Nôm, not Chinese. . . .
>
> So my first question is: Does Marilyn Chin read either Nôm or modern Quoc-ngu Vietnamese? What are her sources for these "translations"?
>
> During my visit to Vietnam in 1998, I was granted access to the Vien Han-Nôm, the country's main institute for old script studies. Beyond the doors of the institute is a huge, anomalous hill in the alluvial plain where a Chinese army was defeated and buried in 1789. (During our own lifetime, the Chinese again tried to assimilate northern Vietnam, with a similar result.) At the site of this burial mound stands a large black marble relief inscribed in gold letters with a poem by Nguyen Hue, the general who defeated the Chinese. The first line of the poem was translated for me as "We beat you because we like to wear our hair long." In 1991, when a delegation of Chinese linguists traveling with the ISO/ Ideographic Rapporteur Group tried to read the poem, they could not. It is in Nôm. It is Vietnamese.

So my final question: how on earth does Marilyn Chin have the nerve to raise any issue of cultural insensitivity?

In other words, this brouhaha really *is* about twenty-first-century white American men saving a helpless Vietnamese eighteenth-century female poet from eighteenth-century Chinese male imperialists, who—across the gulf of time and space and gender—have become conflated with, and equivalent to, a twenty-first-century Chinese American female poet.

A closer reading of Wiegers's letter raises several issues: First, Chin, a Chinese American poet who grew up in Portland, Oregon, and now lives in San Diego is metonymically linked to China—or, more precisely, its male army—and an incursion allegedly made 219 years ago, roughly a decade after the Declaration of Independence was written. Second, Chin's authority as a translator and literary authority ("What are her sources?") is called into question, based on her dubious grasp of written ancient Nôm and modern Vietnamese. Wiegers neglects to mention that neither Balaban nor he himself ("The first line of the poem was trans-lated for me") reads Nôm[10] and that Nôm does indeed seem to be—in Balaban's foundation's website's own words—a "Chinese-like script that Vietnamese used to record their own language and its vast heritage of poetry." (Wiegers also misrepresents what Chin said in her original trans-lator's note by neglecting to mention that she herself acknowledged that "I came to understand that I was reading not Classical Chinese in its pure form, but Nôm, a Chinese-Vietnamese fusion.")

Third, the conflating of Chin and China is reemphasized by invok-ing both eighteenth-century and contemporary Chinese attempts to "assimilate" (note the verb) northern Vietnam. In making his charge, Wiegers seems to have missed the fact that more than fifty-eight thousand Americans and perhaps more than three million Vietnam-ese lost their lives in our own attempts to "assimilate" the Vietnam-ese.[11] Finally, Wiegers comes to the conclusion that since Chin/China is herself imperialist, she has no right (what "nerve") to "raise any issue of cultural insensitivity." Thus, Chin's explicit charges of racism and imperialism are neatly countered by a metonymic reading that reveals that she—like her yellow-peril "home" country, China—is the true imperialist.

Wiegers is joined by most of the other subsequent letter writers—almost all white men—in their harsh dismissal of Chin's defense,[12] which is characterized, variously, as a "tirade," "rancorous," "ad hominem," "vituperative," "uncivil," "baseless," "inflammatory," and, at best, "glib." Chin is accused not only of seeing racism where none exists but of fabricating its existence: "When there are real racism and imperialism to be found all over, it's disgraceful for a poet to try to manufacture some in the defense of her own work," writes John Poch from Lubbock, Texas, who arrogates to himself the authority and acumen to decide what is "real" racism.[13]

It is important to note that in Wiegers's letter and in many of the other letters, two large ideological fields are seamlessly conjoined: the social and political (racism, Chinese imperialism, etc.) and the linguistic (questions of translation, proficiency in a language, etc.). That Wiegers can move so easily in his argumentative logic from skepticism about Chin's knowledge of ancient Nôm to early modern Chinese military incursions to postwar Vietnamese politics and, finally, the issue of cultural sensitivity in contemporary "post-race" American culture signals that the continuity and contiguity between these ideological—aesthetic and political—realms not only goes unquestioned but is assumed and naturalized.

In reality, these two realms are connected in *all* poetry in ways that are often not recognized. Thus, my critique here of Wiegers's argumentative moves does not fault him for bringing together these two arenas but, rather, the manner in which he does so and the problematic assumptions, norms, and elisions that clearly undergird his arguments.

For example, how is it that Bednarik, Balaban, and Wiegers all easily and unproblematically equate an eighteenth-century Chinese male army, a completely unknown group entity, lost in time and space, with a twenty-first-century (Chinese) American female poet, without so much as batting an eyelash? Can one imagine the uproar that would arise if a critique of African American poet Rita Dove were to invoke an Ashanti military skirmish from more than two hundred years ago? Bednarik writes sarcastically in his second letter to the editor (in the July–August 2008 issue) about "Marilyn Chin's accusations against my Bohemian-Finnish-Slovenian XY chromosomes as a [*sic*] racist, sexist, and imperialist" (422). Bednarik finds such a move to equate a contemporary writer with his genetic makeup worthy of ridicule yet sees no irony in having done the same. Likewise, while Wiegers takes pains to point out how carefully he worked with scholars from Vietnam "to highlight the distinct cultural and historical differences between China and Vietnam—not to blur them, as Chin seems intent on doing,"[14] he himself blurs the cultural and historical differences between Chinese American and Chinese peoples.

One cannot iterate enough how common and unquestioned and problematic this conflation of Chinese and Chinese American— indeed, Asian and Asian American—is, both in the popular imaginary and in the academy. China, because of its size, long civilization, large population, and global influence, is read, in particular, as an ongoing (a)historical threat; thus, anything Chinese American is read metonymically as being "of China." And being foreign and "of China" means, of course, that one is not American (or fully American).

What are the implications of such an assumption in the linguistic realm? Obviously, given *Poetry*'s literary context and what is at stake for a poet, this question is perhaps the most crucial and sensitive of all. The letters written in opposition to Chin seem to agree on the answer: Chin is characterized as a bad writer and a bad reader of not one but two languages—she is a bad reader of Huong's poetry and Vietnamese, but also a bad reader of Bednarik's English and a bad writer of English in her translation and in her response. In this sense, she is caught in the pages of *Poetry* in a mini version of the more general no-win situation in which Asian American writers often find themselves trapped: she is not authentically Asian "enough"—in this case, she cannot read ancient Vietnamese and is not an Asian national—to be fully "Oriental" and exotic, nor is she fully American—she is not white and, as someone read as "fresh off the boat," she lacks a native relationship to the English language and, thus, the English literary tradition.

It is important at this point to note that, in her original response to Bednarik, Chin describes herself as a "dark-skinned Asian woman poet," contrasting herself with the white male translators Bednarik favors. While I might quibble with her choice of the word "Asian," it is clear that Chin does not mean to imply that as an "Asian woman," she would assent to being metonymically collapsed with a Chinese army from 1789 by a white American editor. Nor would she consider herself any less American than the white male translators Balaban and Weinberger, nor think her English any less "native" than theirs. It is this question of native—or, rather, nonnative—English proficiency that has long plagued always-already-foreign Asian Americans and, by extension, Asian American poets.

Bednarik, Balaban, and Wiegers all question Chin's authority to translate Ho Xuan Huong. While Wiegers pointedly cites the fact that the 1991 delegation of Chinese linguists—"traveling with the ISO/Ideographic Rapporteur Group"—cannot read the Vietnamese general's poem in Nôm,[15] he glides over the fact that the first line of the poem must be "translated for me." Perhaps his linguistic ignorance is understandable, given that he does not claim to be a translator of Vietnamese, but what are we to make of the fact that Balaban, too, seems to lack command of the language he faults Chin for not knowing?

A 2006 article in the *New York Times* makes clear that Balaban does not read Nôm, though he claims to speak and read modern Vietnamese.[16] In the spring of 2008, the contemporary Vietnamese American poet-translator Linh Dinh posted a critique of Balaban's *Spring Essence: The Poetry of Ho Xuan Huong*[17] on Harriet, the blog of the Poetry Foundation, which publishes *Poetry* magazine. He gives various reasons for his critique, not the least of which is the shakiness of the translator's Vietnamese: "When my wife and I heard him perform some Vietnamese poems in North Carolina [where Balaban resides] in 2004, we couldn't understand, literally, a single word."[18] The Copper Canyon triumvirate, by contrast, assumes Balaban's fluency in, if not command of, Vietnamese and Nôm and his "right" to translate Ho Xuan Huong's poetry.

More telling than Bendarik's, Balaban's, and Wiegers's indictments of Chin's Vietnamese is their strong implication that her English is also not up to par. Bednarik calls into question her choice of the colloquial "boo hoo" in her translation—significant because, as I have pointed out, colloquial English is considered more elusive than "standard English" for nonnative speakers.[19] Thus, undergirding their lines of argument against her is the unspoken charge that Chin lacks the authority to write and/or read in either the language she is translating from, Vietnamese, or the language she is translating into, English, her native tongue. Her lack of command of English encompasses not only her faulty translations but also her misreading of Bednarik's English.

Bednarik, Balaban, and Wiegers, and several other letter writers who come down hard on Chin in the pages of *Poetry*, make clear that she deserves excoriation for being a poor reader of Bednarik's letter. Her misreading of his letter in English is countered by more "accurate" readings by the respondents, beginning with Bednarik himself. He quickly corrects Chin's faulty reading of his letter by providing "proper" dictionary definitions:

> Responding to Chin's tirade against my use of the phrase "noodling around," I checked several dictionaries. *The Encarta College Dictionary* says that "noodle," as a verb, means "to improvise on an instrument in a random, meandering fashion, often in order to warm up." *Webster's* (tenth edition) says pretty much the same thing. In *The New Dictionary of American Slang* "noodling around" means "to think, esp. in a free and discursive way; indulge mental play." Finally, harkening back to the pre-Internet days, the *Dictionary of Afro-American Slang*, edited by poet Clarence Major, says: "in jazz, to play in a testy manner; also, the human head."
>
> When I consciously wrote the phrase "noodling around" I was working from some commonly understood definitions. That Chin—who describes herself as a "dark-skinned Asian woman poet"—would suggest alternate resonances makes perfect sense. She's a poet doing her job in the language. I hear her point, and thank her for it.[20]

In the next issue (September 2008) Bruce Grant from Philadelphia concurs with the jazz etymology of "noodling":

> Marilyn Chin had reason enough to be offended at Joseph Bednarik's self-serving criticism of her translations without wheeling up

the big siege engines of anti-racism, anti-sexism, and anti-imperialism. "Noodling" has nothing to do with pasta, either of the Asian or European variety, but is, rather, jazz slang, dating back to the late thirties, meaning "to improvise . . . in an informal or desultory manner."[21] (original ellipsis)

In that same issue, John Poch expresses further outrage:

> Marilyn Chin's claims of racism, sexism, and imperialism against Joseph Bednarik would be humorous if they weren't so rancorous [Letters, June 2008]. His statement that her translation seemed "like . . . noodling around in the margins" is fairly innocuous. How is his criticism sexist? Women make noodles in kitchens? How is it racist? There are Asian restaurants called "noodle shops"? (In fact, the word "noodle" comes from the German.) How is it imperialist and hateful? Who knows? And what of "margins"? Oh, the margins of the page are really the *margins* of white patriarchal poetry? (original ellipsis and emphasis; 501)

Putting aside the pedantic (if not sophomoric), tendentious, and condescending tone of these letters for the moment, one finds these responses noteworthy in several respects. First, Chin's reply is dismissed as being overly emotional ("tirade") and mean-spirited ("rancorous"), the rantings of a hysterical and angry minority woman. Second, her actions are again implicitly linked with the militaristic aggressiveness of the Chinese army from 1789: she is "wheeling up the big siege engines of anti-racism, anti-sexism, and anti-imperialism." Third, Chin is addressed as if she lacked a native understanding of English and needs to be instructed, like an ESL student, with dictionary definitions and etymologies. She obviously missed the "commonly understood definitions," Balaban points out, and Grant similarly implies that she took Bednarik's choice of the term "noodling" much too literally as "having something to do with pasta." The three letter writers take it upon themselves both to correct her misunderstanding and to translate English for her.

Fourth, both Balaban and Grant emphasize the slang nature of "noodling," derived from jazz and African American culture. Slang, like onomatopoeia, poses particular difficulty for nonnative speakers, and like connotative language, presents a challenge for translators. That Bednarik and Grant invoke African American culture is also not a particularly surprising move to those familiar with the dominant culture's tendency to construct hierarchies of minority suffering and achievement. Their comments make clear that Chin not only did not catch the commonly understood usages of proper English but does not understand black slang either. It is up to two white men to instruct her in this other "real" minority culture, which, to a certain white liberal mind, has a caché and street credibility that Asian American culture lacks.

But there is a contradiction here in the accusations being lobbed at Chin, and this is my fifth and most important point: while Bednarik and Grant criticize Chin for her inability to see beyond the literal meaning of "noodling" (having to do with pasta) to understand its rich slang meanings ("to think, esp. in a free and discursive way; indulge in mental play," "to improvise . . . in an informal or desultory manner"), all three men paradoxically find Chin most seriously guilty of having played too fast and loose with Bednarik's language, of reading between the lines. She is condemned for being a bad reader (and writer) precisely because she *reads too much into*. She is indicted for manufacturing, of imagining, racism and imperialism where none exist. Chin indulged in "mental play" and improvisation but not of the sanctioned sort, apparently.

Nowhere is this charge more clearly delineated than in Poch's insistent questioning: "How is his [Bednarik's] criticism sexist? Women make noodles in kitchens? How is it racist? There are Asian restaurants called 'noodle shops'? (In fact, the word 'noodle' comes from the German.)." He faults Chin for not taking Bednarik's "noodling" at face value—how can "noodling" be sexist or racist or imperialist when the words "noodling" and "noodle" themselves have no obvious sexist or racist or imperialist denotative or connotative meanings? As Poch points out, the etymology of the word "noodle" (= pasta) is German, not Asian, so it would be ludicrous to read anything anti-Asian in Bednarik's choice of the term.[22] In other words, Chin did not take Bednarik's words at face value—as she should have—but read them much too connotatively, finding meanings where there were none to be found.[23]

This dilemma or Catch-22 is precisely that faced by minority Americans who find themselves in the situation of calling out forms of racism that do not manifest themselves overtly (as in blatant racial slurs and/or physical violence). The difficulty with identifying and confronting racism, of course, is precisely that it often takes many disguised, nondenotative forms. Let me make clear that I am not interested in this particular episode of whether Bednarik was a "racist" in his letter or whether Chin "overreacted" in her reply, but, rather, I want to examine the structure of the rhetorical moves and the argumentative logic in a type of episode that is all too familiar in the academy and in society at large.

The plot goes something like this: A minority person/writer makes the claim that she is being treated prejudicially on the basis of her ethnicity, not her work. She is then often met by the countercharge that she is being "overly sensitive" or "reading too much into" the supposed offender's innocuous words and actions. In other words, the minority person has *misinterpreted*, misread, the other's words and/or actions. In this specific instance, Chin is found by the white male jury to be a bad reader and writer—an especially damning verdict against a poet.

Why a Catch-22? It soon becomes clear that the minority writer making a charge of racist, sexist, and/or imperialist behavior is trapped yet again in a no-win situation. As I have tried to show, she is criticized both for reading too denotatively (reading "noodling" as, literally, chow mein noodles) and for reading much too connotatively (noodling = Chinese noodles = negative Asian stereotypes = racism)—and wrongly. Poch's response is not uncommon: he takes the supposed racist word, does a literal reading of its meaning, and comes to the conclusion that, since the word is not blatantly and overtly racist, the charge of racism is false. Racism must be expressed literally (for example, in unambiguous racial epithets such as "Chink") in order to exist.[24] Poch insists that Chin show the exact link between "noodling" and its possible unsavory connotations.

Herein lies an irony. Chin is excoriated for doing precisely what good readers of poetry are supposed to do—that is, exercising her interpretive skills as a poet and a translator by thinking "in a free and discursive way" and "indulg[ing] in mental play." In Bednarik's words: "That Chin . . . would suggest alternate resonances makes perfect sense. She's a poet doing her job in the language."²⁵ Poets are supposed to read carefully, sometimes between the lines, to unpack the "alternate resonances" of words. A bad poet takes words simply at their face value.

So why, then, the angry recriminations against a poet simply doing her job? And why are these same men not equally enraged at the sassiness of Ho Xuan Huong, the eighteenth-century feminist precursor, whom Balaban, quoting Frances Fitzgerald, praises as "the brilliant bad girl of eighteenth century Vietnam"?²⁶

It turns out that not all bad girls are the same and not all readings and "alternate resonances" are equal.

To have an Asian "bad girl" poet take you to account in 2008 is quite different from idealizing an Asian bad girl poet from more than two hundred years ago who is static (not to mention dead) and compliant on the page. An Asian American woman poet who dares to mention the unutterable r-word risks incurring the wrath of even the most liberal Copper Canyon–reading multiculturalist, and even in the twenty-first-century "post-race" Obama era. As in her poetry, so in her *Poetry* response, Chin brings to the fore— "[a]ll ugliness revealed"—issues of racism, sexism, and imperialism.²⁷ But, as mentioned earlier, Chin has been critically acclaimed for her poetry. So one must ask, "Why is she raked over the coals for expressing similar sentiments in her response in *Poetry*?" What does not "translate" here?

Here is where irony enters. In her three books of poetry—*Dwarf Bamboo* (1987), *The Phoenix Gone, the Terrace Empty* (1994; hereafter, *Phoenix Gone*), *Rhapsody in Plain Yellow* (2002)—Chin is a master at deploying irony as a tool and weapon, one that is often clever and multilayered—and disguised. Irony as a rhetorical trope and a rhetorical strategy provides the poet a means of linguistic mediation that enables her—indeed, empowers her—to transmute her painful experiences as a Chinese American female, one who is marginalized in both Chinese and American cultures, into lines of poetry, into art.²⁸

Whereas Chin's accusations against Bednarik in *Poetry* may strike some (or many) as relentlessly monovocal, in her poems, I would

argue, irony—both as rhetorical trope and as a point of view[29]—
allows her to speak in multiple registers or voices simultaneously so
that her manifest statements are often "translations" of much angrier
and harsher political critiques and carry within them various semantic and emotional registers at once. The resulting poetic language is
more nuanced, contradictory, and layered than what is usually possible in nonpoetic language but, as we shall see, not without its own
risks.

Irony, which Claire Colebrook describes as "always diagnostic and
political,"[30] is a form of intervention that allows Chin to appear both
sharp-tongued and geishalike (think Ho as concubine)—not simply
"angry" and "militant"—while expressing a great deal of anger (and
sadness) about the sorts of taboo topics, such as racism, one is not
supposed to raise in polite company, even polite multiculti-philic
company. For example, one can compare the exchange in *Poetry* with
these lines from Chin's "Tonight While the Stars Are Shimmering" in
Rhapsody in Plain Yellow, published six years earlier:

> How was I saved on that boat of freedom
>   To be anointed here on the prayer mat of your love?
> . . . .
>
> I call you racist, you call me racist
>   Now we're entering forbidden territory
> I call you sexist, you call me a fool
>   And compare the canyons to breasts, anyway
> I pull your hair, you bite my nape
>   We make mad love until birdsong morning
> . . . .
>
> I take your olive branch deep within me
>   A white man's guilt, a white man's love
> Tonight while the stars are shimmering

"I call you racist, you call me racist" would not be an inaccurate characterization of the exchange between Chin and the angry white male
letter writers in *Poetry*. Yet, while Chin's straightforward expository
reply in *Poetry* invokes rancor and vitriol, this more irony-laden and

tongue-in-cheek poem—with its greater potential for miscommunication—would not likely elicit such rage. Again, why not?

On the face of it, this outcome is not logical. While any utterance must involve a certain shared language and shared context for the two parties to understand each other, irony demands even more: "[T]o read the irony you do not just have to know the context; you also have to be committed to specific beliefs and positions *within* that context [original emphasis]," writes Colebrook. "[E]ven the most 'obvious' ironies bear the possibility of not being read, and they do so precisely *because* of the contextual nature of irony" (original emphasis).[31] Therefore, one would think that irony would cause a greater problem of "translation" than straightforward denotative prose. But it is precisely irony's multivoiced nature that allows different readers to hear what they think—or want to think—they hear from the lines. For example, in the previous Chin passage, some lines speak bluntly of rhetorics (even if performative) of racism, yet others appear more submissive in tone ("How was I saved on that boat of freedom"). The parroting of a rhetoric of freedom and of Orientalist New Age sex talk might mollify those whose hackles might be raised by other more "militant" registers in the poem.

In a poem rife with irony, it is always the case that some (or even most) readers will "miss" the sharpest registers of political critique. And there's the rub.

Much of Chin's most ironic language appears in poems in which the Chinese American female speaker is having sex with a white man, as we have just seen and see again in this excerpt from her long poem "A Portrait of the Self as Nation, 1990–1991," which closes *Phoenix Gone*, her previous book of poetry:

> Now, where was I, oh yes, now I remember,
> the last time I made love, it was to *you*.
> I faintly remember your whiskers
> against my tender nape.
> You were a conquering barbarian,
> helmeted, halberded,
> beneath the gauntleted moon,

whispering Hunnish or English—
so long Oolong went the racist song,
bye-bye little chinky butterfly.
There is no cure for self-pity,
the disease is death,
ennui, disaffection,

. . . .

I loathe to admit. Yet, I shall admit it:
there was no Colonialist coercion;
sadly, we blended together well. (original italics)

Here, the Asian American female subject expresses various contradictory emotions: anger, melancholy, self-hatred, desire for the
colonizer—the emotions that often characterize the psychic states
of postcolonial or minoritized subjects. Here she is able to admit,
"There is no cure for self-pity," a statement that would have been
unthinkable in the *Poetry* magazine context. In deploying irony, an
"author presents possible voices and positions, allowing those positions to disclose their own incoherence," writes Colebrook (*Irony,*
12). Irony "relies on the force of contradiction" (166).

At first glance, it would appear that the overtly "ironic" speech in
the quoted lines are those marked by italics: these lines—themselves
quotations of a song that the speaker herself labels "racist"—clearly
come across as unambiguously problematic ("chinky"). Yet what
is one to make of an unitalicized line such as "sadly, we blended
together well"—its tone sober, even melancholic—with no obvious markers of either the ironic quoting of racist American popular
tunes or the straightforward unironic condemnation of racism, à la
Chin in *Poetry*? Yet "sadly, we blended together well" can be read
as ironic—or misread as unironic—depending on who is doing the
reading, his or her point of view, background, cultural knowledge,
context, and so on.

Indeed, in the lines "Now, where was I, oh yes, now I remember, / the last time I made love, it was to *you*," the italicized "you"
suggests that the "you" may not just be the colonialist white lover
but the reader. It is as if Chin is aware that her readers, too, could

be as oblivious as her lover is of the painful irony of her remarks. The syntax of "sadly, we blended together well" brings together two mirroring or balancing adverbs, one at the beginning of the phrase ("sadly") and the other at the end ("well"), describing two states of being that are usually seen as opposed. Irony's double-voicedness can be seen here in a contradictory state of noncontradiction ("*there was no Colonialist coercion*"). Whether the reader chooses to emphasize the "sadly" or the "well" or sees himself or herself in the "you" depends on who the "you" is.

In other words, while irony's contradictory possibilities are productive of subtle and nuanced meaning, the trope always runs the risk of being misread or only partially read. Colebrook writes, "Irony relies on a crucial feature of language as shared recognition" (*Irony*, 35–36). And, "The point of view of irony is explained socially, assuming a context of those who recognize a *said* that is other than what the speaker is saying" (original emphasis; *Irony in the Work of Philosophy*, 18–19). But what if the readers or audience do not share one's language, values, politics, and context, among other things, and do not recognize a "said" that is other than what one is saying?[32] Is shared recognition then possible?

Irony, like translation, runs the constitutive risk of being mistranslated or misread—and, I would argue, so does any discourse on race or racism, even the most straightforward, that is initiated by minority writers and persons. Thus, Chin's unironized translation of Ho Xuan Huong and her unironized "translator's note" were clearly misread, as was her expository response in *Poetry*. Her irony-laden poems have fared better with the poetry establishment—at least if measured by awards and publishing contracts—but they also demonstrate the double-edged nature of irony itself and force us to ask, "What are the benefits and costs of deploying irony?"

Since straightforward unironic discourse about race in this country is virtually impossible—given the overwhelming desire of the culture to erase or ignore histories of racial violence, the knee-jerk reactions that any discussion of race or racism seems to elicit, and the various racial and racialized subjectivities and subject positions (it is as if all the participants, occupying different racial and racialized subjectivities, spoke different languages)—perhaps the only means by which a minority writer can communicate her views on race and racism without eliciting defensiveness or hostility is by more literary and indirect modes, such as irony, parody, fantasy genres (such as science fiction), and so on. While there is always the danger of a reader's mistranslating or misreading a poem, the fact that irony allows for complexities and slippages—for reading between the lines—would seem to promise that one or some of the registers of meaning will come through to at least some of the readers. Thus, a poet could write about racism, sexism, and imperialism ironically and not be immediately slammed, as Chin was in the pages of *Poetry*, by most readers.

Ironic statements on race leave the reader several "outs": Some readers will "get" the political critique but not react defensively because of the other ambiguities in the poem (for example, the contrasting tones in the lines from "Tonight While the Stars Are Shimmering" cited earlier); others will miss the critique (the statements won't "translate"); still others may unknowingly have imbibed some of the critique—irony functioning, thus, as a sort of Trojan horse. It is precisely irony's multiple registers that allow readers to hear what they want to hear—to ignore the poet's harsher political critiques or, worse, to read the ironic voice unironically.

Yet is this pluralistic reading of Chin's poetry ultimately too easy? Is there a "choice" being made in whether one "gets" irony or not? Is a reader "choosing" to take a statement at face value, choosing to miss the more racially charged barbs that irony might entail? Is this a conscious or unconscious decision? How does societal ideology function in these "choices"? Is the act of how to read Chin's poetry the hermeneutic equivalent of choosing what one likes to eat at an ethnic food court?[33] Or—to word it more bluntly—is this pluralistic reading of Chin's poetry a cop-out?[34] There are always those readers who will take such lines as ". . . I loathe to admit. Yet, I shall admit it: / *there was no Colonialist coercion*" at face value. Colebrook writes,

> Irony has a political and ethical force. One speaks the language of colonialism and reason ironically in order to display its violence,

force and delimited viewpoint. However, this critical repetition does not only risk being unnoticed or misunderstood. It still allows the voice of colonialism to speak, even in quotation marks.[35]

Those who read the ventriloquized voice of colonialism as what the poet/speaker "intends" will be reading as literally as the Copper Canyon male letter writers in *Poetry* did Chin's reply. In turn, these men demanded that Chin read signs of racism, sexism, and imperialism literally. One could say that they asked her to read unpoetically. "Reading ironically," writes Colebrook, "is perhaps akin to reading poetically: attending not just to the reference or propositional content of words but also to what those references and propositions 'say' about our linguistic contexts" (*Irony in the Work of Philosophy*, 41). And, I would add, our social and political contexts.

At the heart of the American democratic "multicultural" experiment has been this unresolvable question of lack of shared contexts, subject positions, values, genealogies, and so on among various groups—a lack that becomes all too apparent when we try to talk about painful issues such as racism. Much does not "translate" between and among various constituencies—the "red" and "blue" voters, the Tea Party and the progressives, and a panoply of others. Who is the "we" in "We the People"? "Ironic speech," writes Colebrook, "is indirect, invoking an implicit and unstated 'they' and *effecting* a no less implicit 'we'" (original emphasis; *Irony in the Work of Philosophy*, 18).

Who are the "we" and the "they" when a poet writes a poem for a large, diverse readership, especially when that poet declares, "I am a 'woman writer of color'—my work is steeped in and is informed by feminist, multicultural, postcolonial, minority discourse—and I make no apologies for my strident, activist muse"?[36] There is always the risk—no, the certainty—that a percentage of Chin's readers will be repelled by, or not catch on to, what she is saying. There is always the risk, of course, that poetic irony will not translate, but even more so when the poet is an Asian American feminist and overtly political one. ("Do you know that . . . political poetry is shrill and rhetorical and ugly?" she asks ironically in an interview.)[37]

Marilyn Chin talks back. She refuses to be a model minority or the sort of ornamental Asian American female poet usually lauded in the media and by academics. She expresses her personal and political anger and sense of injustice at racism, sexism, and imperialism. In doing so, she knows that she runs the risk of eliciting rage, even from the most liberal multiculturalist ("O little sister, I should have warned you / Don't eat the meat, if it makes you cough blood"). Chin understands that irony is not just a speech act but a way of life and that "a way of speaking or style of language is already an existential position or point of view."[38] She takes on the risk of being misunderstood—or of being understood all too well.

FOUR

Irony's Barbarian Voices
in the Poetry of Marilyn Chin

Whereas Li-Young Lee has stated, "Art is totally ideal. Otherwise it has no function,"[1] Marilyn Chin has openly declared, "I consider myself a political poet."[2] It is clear that, for the most part, Asian American poets accepted for canonical recognition have been those who are perceived as being not overtly political, model minorities as it were (Lee in *The Norton Anthology of Poetry* and Cathy Song, winner of the first Yale Younger Poets' prize, among others). An Asian American poet who declares that "the blueprint for revolution is tattooed to my head for some reason. I can't eliminate that aspect from my being. . . . I am, at my core, a social activist in my art" is not likely to win a place for her poems in the *Norton*.[3] No "Persimmons" offered by this poet.

Nonetheless, Chin has garnered, as I said in the last chapter, a good measure of mainstream success with the literary establishment. She is published by W. W. Norton (*Rhapsody in Yellow* and her book of fiction, *Revenge of the Mooncake Vixen: A Novel*), has won several prestigious awards from foundations, and was featured on the same Bill Moyers 1995 PBS TV series, *The Language of Life*, as Li-Young Lee. I have posed the question, "Why is it that Chin's poems—which are as critical of American racism, sexism, and imperialism as are her remarks in the pages of *Poetry*—have not elicited the same sorts of violent reactions from readers as from the letter writers in *Poetry*?" and ventured an answer: Chin's pervasive use of irony in her three books of poetry mediates her ideological critiques, making them seem less overt—or, perhaps, more "missable." In other words, although Chin does not pull any punches in her poems, the multiple registers of irony in the poetic speakers' voice(s) allow some readers not to hear—or choose not to hear—the harsher registers of her political critiques.

In this chapter, I examine Chin's use of irony in greater detail—especially its relation to the idea of the "barbarian," or impure and uncultured outsider—to try to see both the potential and the limitations of this rhetorical device. As a woman writing at the nexus of two patriarchal traditions, Chin uses irony—as a trope and as a way of seeing the world—to confront the demands, assumptions, and expectations of Chinese and American cultural purists, both of whom view her as barbarian, and to make sharp critiques of racism and sexism in both American and Chinese cultures. Whereas the use of metaphor can be either conscious or unconscious, the use of irony as a figure of speech is usually motivated by authorial intention;[4] that said, there are certainly moments in Chin's poetry when she is not always in control of the ironic registers so that irony "speaks" through her. The question of where irony is located—whether in rhetorical figures of speech and speech acts or, more broadly, as a "theory of meaning" or a "way of life"[5]—is an important one.

The ironic voices in Chin's poetry are gendered and multilayered. Using a multivoiced irony allows this Chinese American female poet to mimic and dissect conflicting states of self-hatred, self-colonization, and erotic desire for the white male, even as she hits hard at forms of domination. These voices irrupt into her poems. By "irrupt," I mean irony's ability to interrupt and disrupt discourse—what Friedrich Schlegel, in defining irony, calls "permanent parabasis" (parabasis being the "interruption of a discourse by a shift in the rhetorical register"); as Paul de Man explains it, "[I]rony is everywhere, at all points the narrative can be interrupted."[6]

The female speakers of Chin's poems often occupy more than one ideological position and tonal register; their ironic voices, thus, cannot be analyzed according to the general and traditional view of the trope (admittedly, simplified here) as a binary between a stated "false" meaning and an unstated "true" message.[7] Chin's use of irony does not set up simple either-or formulations or oppositions—of "Chinese" or "American," of Chinese American female victim versus Chinese male oppressor, of Chinese American female victim versus white male oppressor, and so on. For example, there are many moments in Chin's poems in which the female speaker takes on the voice of the "colonizer," whether in viewing herself or intoning dominant ideology, as seen in the previous chapter: "How was I saved on that boat of freedom / To be anointed here on the prayer mat of your love?" ("Tonight While the Stars Are Shimmering"); "Let us drink to the fructification of America, / to the availability of all things, / to the possibility of liberty" ("Minerva Around the Swimming Hole," *Dwarf Bamboo*).

And while she takes on American stereotypes of Asian Americans (for example, the compliant "model minority") or, more specifically, stereotypes of Asian American women (either the sexually submissive and submissively sexual "lotus blossom"/"China doll" or the "hot" Suzie Wong prostitute—both eager to satisfy the white man's every desire), Chin also understands firsthand what Stuart Hall calls "the surreptitious return of desire"[8]: that is, the extent to which her and other Asian American women's psyches have been colonized so that mainstream images and desires have been internalized. Thus, even as she uses irony to mimic and undermine these stereotypes, Chin creates Chinese American female poetic speakers and fictional narrators who write frankly of their attraction to the white male colonizer (and to states of subjugation).

Like all minority Americans, Chin and her female poetic speakers have internalized both resistance to and eagerness for assimilation—epitomized by their desire for the white male body and what it represents: colonial, national, linguistic, military, and sexual power and domination. Thus, irony operates in Chin's poems as simultaneous voices—sometimes conflicting, sometimes paradoxical—interpenetrating multiple emotional and ideological registers: voices that are produced by and that manifest the violent acts of becoming "American."

As with Lee's use of metaphor, the trope of irony in Chin's poetry functions not as aesthetic embellishment (or even deconstructive "play") but as a formal manifestation whose very structure captures[9] the rivenness of subjectivity wrought by immigration, diaspora, the violence of assimilation—and as a rhetorical means to contend with the trauma of history (personal, national, and global) and, perhaps, to try to "master," this time with the agency of a poet, feelings of despair and melancholy engendered by these experiences.[10] Irony, in Luce Irigaray's words, "make[s] 'visible,' by an effect of playful repetition, what was supposed to remain invisible."[11] What may seem at first glance mainly rhetorical moves—or, worse, flourishes—can be read as much more politically significant.[12] Claire Colebrook reminds us that "[i]rony is always diagnostic and political" (*Irony*, 12).

In Chin's poems, irony's double edge slices multiple ways, undercutting notions of racial, linguistic, and cultural "authenticity"/"purity" in Chinese and American societies, both of which consider her "barbarian." Indeed, the theme of the barbarian recurs throughout Chin's three books of poetry. The term "barbarian"—and its etymological kin "barbarous," "barbarism," "barbarize," "barbarity," "barbaric"— encompasses meanings that are inseparable from issues of culture and language, as well as sexuality, particularly miscegenation.

To those "real" Chinese born and raised in China or other predominantly Chinese countries who hold essentialized notions of "Chineseness," Chin's "barbarousness" is measured proportionately as a function of the degree to which she has become "Americanized," the criteria being the (in)ability to speak Chinese and—specifically for women—assumed sexual profligacy and desire to mate with non-Chinese (that is, white) men. As a female poet writing in English in the United States, Chin poses an affront and a challenge to Confucian and patriarchal ideas in traditional Chinese thought and poetry—for example, the notion of the privileged male poet, steeped in traditional Chinese learning and culture, writing in classical Chinese.

At the same time, this binary between assimilated Chinese American and "Chinese Chinese" is not so starkly opposed as first appears: Chin, unlike most Chinese American poets,[13] has studied Chinese and has done translations from Chinese poetry.[14] She has made explicit her desire to blend Chinese and English poetic forms to produce what she calls a "fusionist aesthetics."[15] By this poetic practice, Chin revises certain customary ways of viewing what counts as Anglo-

American poetic experimentation. While fracturing syntax, erasing or deconstructing the lyric "I," and employing other such Modernist practices are considered "true" forms of "innovative" or avant-garde writing, Chin's importing of non-Western poetry techniques is not. "The 'experimentalists' have their own conventions—and I don't fit into their frame of reference," she says. "Although I see myself as an experimental poet—the 'experimentalists' or 'LANGUAGE' people will never consider me in this way."[16]

To what extent is the avant-garde coded as Western and white? And to what extent are certain kinds of experimentation, such as Chin's bringing in Chinese poetic forms, simply not considered "true" linguistic innovation because they do not tap into a Western High Modernist aesthetic? The discourse around what counts as "real" poetry often bears troubling echoes of the discourse around who counts as a "real" native speaker of English—and a "real Amer-ican"—as I have argued.

Chin appears as "barbarian" not only to those with essential-ized notions of "authentic" "Chineseness," but also to those Amer-icans with ideas of what constitutes a "full-blooded" American and a "native speaker." For a minority poet, demands for proof of cultural and linguistic authenticity weigh as heavily as notions of race and blood.

The notion of the barbarian is inseparable from ideas of who is foreign, uncivilized, uncultured, and a misuser of language—the first definition of "barbarian" (used as a noun) in the *OED* is "1. *etymologically*, A foreigner, one *whose language and customs* differ from the speaker's" (added emphasis); another meaning listed is "[a]n uncultured person, or one *who has no sympathy with literary culture*" (added emphasis).[17]

In the *OED*'s definition of the term "barbarous," characterizations of people and language are inextricable:

> 1. Of language: a. *orig.* Not Greek; *subseq.* not Greek nor Latin; *hence*, not classical or pure (Latin or Greek), abounding in "bar-barisms." b. Unpolished, *without literary culture* [added emphasis]; pertaining to an illiterate people. . . . 2. Of people: Speaking a for-eign language, foreign, outlandish; . . . 3. Uncultured, uncivilized,

unpolished; rude, rough, wild, savage. (Said of men, their manners, customs, products.) The usual opposite of *civilized* [original emphasis]. . . . 5. Like the speech of barbarians; harsh-sounding, rudely or coarsely noisy.[18]

The definition of "barbarism" primarily pertains to culture and the misuse of language:

1. a. The use of words or expressions not in accordance with the classical standard of a language, especially such as are of foreign origin; *orig.* the mixing of foreign words or phrases in Latin or Greek; *hence*, rudeness or unpolished condition of language. . . . b. A foreign or non-classical word or idiom. . . . 2. a. Barbarous social or intellectual condition; absence of culture; uncivilized ignorance and rudeness. (The proper opposite of *civilization* [original emphasis].)[19]

These definitions clearly demonstrate how inextricable ideas of the foreign and the nonnative are from judgments about language mastery and literary culture. As we saw very clearly in the confrontation between Chin and the Copper Canyon white males, a female Asian American poet—no matter how proficient she may be in English language and literature—can still be seen as foreign, alien, a Chinese from China (contemporary and premodern), and a faulty reader and speaker/writer of English. While few critics may publicly voice the question of whether Chin's English is "good enough"—the *Poetry* letter writers strongly imply it—this question often lies not far beneath the surface and may come into play, unconsciously, in judging her and other Asian American poets' work.

What is an Asian American female poet—especially a politically outspoken and bold-talking one—to do if she wants to be a "real poet"? Where is the place for her individual talent in the Anglo-American poetry tradition?

One might well understand why a Hong-Kong-born, Portland-Oregon-raised Chinese American working-class female poet, named by her father after the blonde bombshell Marilyn Monroe, might need all the irony she can muster to make her way through American society and the English-language literary world. What are the potential benefits and limitations of irony—both as a tool of self-defense and as a weapon? Some knowledge of the critical discourse on irony is helpful before we turn to Chin's poetry.

On Irony

"Despite its unwieldy complexity, irony has a frequent and common definition: saying what is contrary to what is meant," writes Claire Colebrook, perhaps the best theorist of irony writing today (*Irony*, 1). She is paraphrasing Quintilian, the first-century Roman orator who was himself looking back to ancient Greek literature. The term "irony" has its roots in the figure of the *eiron* in Greek comedy, "the underdog, weak but clever, who regularly triumphed over the stupid and boastful *alazon*," write William Van O'Connor and Ernst H. Behler in their entry on irony in the previous edition (1993) of *The New Princeton Encyclopedia of Poetry and Poetics*.[20] In an early play by Theophrast, the ironist "appears as a deceitful hypocrite pursuing his own advantage,"[21] and in Aristophanes's plays, *eironeia* "referred to lying rather than complex dissimulation."[22]

When "*eironeia*, not much later than Aristophanes, came to refer to a dissimulation that was not deceitful but clearly recognisable, and intended to be recognised, irony intersected with the political problem of meaning," writes Colebrook (*Irony*, 1). It was with Socrates that the conception of irony "considered philosophically as a mode of life"—as contrasted with the other historical conception of irony as a localized figure of speech—began and has endured, even with its many multiple detractors over time.[23] In the Greek tragedies prior to Plato, Colebrook writes, *eironeia*

> had designated deception or lying but . . . in the [Socratic] dialogues
> comes to refer to a strategy for attaining truth, a strategy that *appears* to
> accept the terms of common sense and received wisdom but ultimately
> exposes ordinary lang. [language] to be inadequate.[24] (original emphasis)

Socrates "used irony to challenge received knowledge and wisdom," writes Colebrook. He "tried to show that it is always possible that what we take to be the self-evident sense of a context or culture is far from obvious; it may be that what is being said is *not meant*. . . . Socratic irony has come to mean more than just a figure of speech and refers to a capacity to remain distant and different from what is said in general" (original emphasis; *Irony*, 2, 8).

The classical view of irony held sway, with only slight variation, until the notion of Romantic irony was introduced by Schlegel in 1797: the "consistent alternation of affirmation and negation, of exuberant emergence from oneself and self-critical retreat into oneself, of enthusiasm and skepticism."[25] The Jena theorists' view of Romantic irony is "taken up by twentieth-century theorists such as Paul de Man, Philippe Lacoue-Labarthe, and Jean-Luc Nancy," who see irony as "not limited to a figure of speech within a text but open[ing] up a point of view outside the text's own frame—parabasis," writes Colebrook.[26]

In the twentieth century, practitioners of deconstruction and New Critics alike treated the subject of irony with zeal, but while the latter viewed irony as a "reconciling power fusing the ambiguity, paradox, multiplicity, and variety of meaning in a work into the unity, wholeness, and identity which constitutes its modes of being," the former conceived of irony "in terms of a discrepancy between sign and meaning, an absence of coherence or gap among the parts of a work, and an inability to escape from a situation that has become unbearable."[27] At the same time, I would argue, both schools shared a formal emphasis on close reading and a general and equal lack of interest in the political and social implications of the trope.

As Colebrook's definition based on Quintilian demonstrates, the common more normative (and limited) notion of irony handed down in literary, rhetorical, and poetry handbooks is that of a trope or figure of speech in which "the substitution of one term for its opposite" is operative.[28] Here are two typical definitions of irony: "A statement or a point of view that is usually the opposite of what is expected"[29] and "[i]mplying a meaning opposite to the literal meaning."[30]

These are not atypical definitions in the Anglo-American tradition of criticism, in which even scholarly critical works, such as

Wayne Booth's *A Rhetoric of Irony*, that recognize the complexities of irony will, nonetheless, still tend to view it in this clear-cut and "rational" light. Booth labels irony a "direct and classic device . . . intended but covert, stable and localized."[31] Says Colebrook: "Irony, for Booth, is most often a rhetorical figure or trope within an otherwise stable context of human sense and understanding. . . . For Booth, irony assumes, rather than disrupts, a common ground" (*Irony*, 44).

Colebrook groups philosophers such as John Searle and literary critics such as Booth and D. C. Muecke in the category of those who "see irony as a rhetorical figure that is ultimately recognised because there is something like shared human understanding. Socrates' irony would, or should, be a rhetorical move in order to reinforce truth and consensus" (*Irony*, 44).

As noted earlier, there is a countertradition to this view of irony as stable, localized, and structured relatively unambiguously, another line of thinking that begins with Schlegel—his work, says de Man, is "where the problem [of irony] really gets worked out"[32]—who sees ironic meaning not as an either-or binary of clean and clear-cut opposites but as an interaction between the two (or more) meanings implicit in ironic discourse. Colebrook describes this countergroup (in which she includes Kierkegaard and the literary critic Linda Hutcheon) as encompassing those who

> see irony as a way of life, embodied in the figure of Socrates who refused to present virtue and the good life as a fixed ideal that could be known. Irony—the continual questioning or a distance from fixed norms—is the possibility of politics as *praxis*: as engaged activity achieved through dynamic speech and collective participation. . . . Those who celebrate the destabilising force of irony, by contrast, insist that politics is the rejection, contestation or disruption of shared norms. (*Irony*, 44–45)

This "destabilized" view of irony takes into account the messiness and interpenetrability of the two terms of the ironic "hinge," as well as the political/social context of ironic discourse, and raises the question of irony's reception. This view of irony as a means to contest or disrupt shared norms, rather than the more "stable" one espoused by Booth, Searle, et al., illuminates the various ways in which Chin deploys—and works through—irony in her poetry. The voices in her poetry are not simply sarcastically mimicking those of the "oppressor" while asking us to decode the "true" or "real" voice of a Chinese American woman who stands outside of, and is untouched by, colonialism's and racism's contaminations. On the contrary, Chin is fully aware of the degree to which she is implicated in the voices she takes on. Irony is never rational or controllable, reminds Schlegel, for whom it is "the simultaneous presence of *two* meanings between which it is not possible to decide" (original emphasis).[33]

For Schlegel, says Georgia Albert,

> [t]he two "sides" are unable to coexist peacefully: Schlegel speaks, in different contexts, of their evocation of an "indissoluble antagonism" (*Lyceum* Fragment 108) and of the "continual self-creating interchange of two conflicting thoughts" (*Athenäum* Fragment 121, *KFSA* 2:184; *Fragments*, 33). The relation between the two "sides" of irony is by necessity a warlike one: they can only exist at each other's expense, since each of them is the negation and thus the annihilation of the other.[34]

Hutcheon, in *Irony's Edge*, agrees with the idea of simultaneity and undecidability between the two "sides"—"ironic meaning as something in flux, and not fixed . . . a kind of simultaneous perception of more than one meaning"—but would likely disagree with the "warlike" characterization of irony's structure (60). Her view is more positive and inclusive, positing a third meaning that results from the interaction between the two "sides": "[B]oth the said and the unsaid together make up that third meaning, and I want to argue that *this* is what should more accurately be called the 'ironic' meaning" (original emphasis; 60).

Kenneth Burke, in *A Grammar of Motives*, opens up irony to include multiple (more than two) perspectives:

> Irony arises when one tries, by the interaction of terms upon one another, to produce a *development* which uses all the terms. Hence, from the standpoint of this total form (this "perspective of perspec-

tives"), none of the participating "sub-perspectives" can be treated as either precisely right or precisely wrong. . . . [T]he dialectic of this participation . . . requires that all the sub-certainties be considered as neither true nor false, but *contributory*.[35] (original emphasis)

Despite the minor differences in their theories, Schlegel, Hutcheon, and Burke each offers a view of irony that sees both the spoken and unspoken meanings of irony as contributing to the overall ironic meaning. This rejection of the reductive either-or formulation of irony holds particular implications for the interpretation of Asian American poetry.

Historically, the clichéd model of Asian Americans as having dual selves and dual allegiances—what Frank Chin calls "[t]his myth of being either/or and the equally goofy concept of the dual personal-ity"[36]—has not only caricatured them but also marked them as per-niciously unknowable ("inscrutable") and untrustworthy (traitorous). Even in this day of diasporic *jouissance*, the dangers of simple either-or formulations about Asian American identity and literature have not been made obsolete, as one can glean from reading reviews of Asian American writing.

The deployment of irony has never been separate from the notion of the political: "[W]hy, from its emergence in Ancient Greece to the present, has irony been perceived as a political problem?" asks Colebrook (*Irony*, 16). Like Claire Colebrook, Linda Hutcheon is a contemporary theorist who recognizes the larger political and social implications of irony. She writes in *Irony's Edge*:

> Given th[e] vast amount of previous work on the general topic
> of irony, my choice has been to look at what might be called the
> "scene" of irony: that is, to treat it not as an isolated trope to be
> analyzed by formalist means but as a political issue, in the broadest
> sense of the word. (2)

> Because irony, as defined in this study, happens in something called
> "discourse," its semantic and syntactic dimensions cannot be con-
> sidered separately from the social, historical and cultural aspects of
> its contexts of deployment and attribution. Issues of authority and
> power are encoded in that notion of "discourse" today in much

the same way that, in earlier times, they were encoded in the word "rhetoric." . . . Since irony involves social interaction, there is no reason for it to be less implicated in questions of hierarchy and power (in terms of either maintenance or subversion) than any other form of discourse. (17, 40)

Hutcheon points out that irony has been used equally by conservatives to preserve the status quo and by those in the margins wishing to overturn the powers-that-be. Thus, she argues, irony's nature is "transideological" and "there is no *necessary* relationship between irony and radical politics or even radical formal innovation" (original emphasis; 15, 10). This view of irony as transideological imbues Hutcheon's discussion of irony's different functions—for example, when she speaks of its "oppositional function":

For those positioned *within* a dominant ideology, such a contesting might be seen as abusive or threatening; for those marginalized and working to undo that dominance, it might be **subversive** or **transgressive** in the newer, positive senses that those words have taken on in recent writing about gender, race, class, and sexuality. (original boldface and italics; 52)

Yet Hutcheon also notes almost immediately that "Freud had argued that ironic modes such as parody, travesty, and caricature are always, despite their seemingly innocent humor, actually 'directed against people and objects which *lay claim to authority and respect*'" (added emphasis; 53).[37] That said, while Hutcheon is correct in describing irony as transideological, her view sometimes runs the danger of diluting irony into something only contingently political or, at worst, even depoliticized or apolitical. As one reviewer writes, "[Hutcheon's] emphasis on individuals and their particular matrices of discursive communities makes any irony seem more accidental than political."[38]

Of course, irony, like parody, can be used by anyone and any side of an ideological battle. Even so, it is not hard to understand why a Chinese American female poet from the working class might be particularly drawn to and find power in the use of irony—"the mode of the unsaid, the unheard, the unseen"[39]—as she contends with her position as a minority woman and a minority poet in America. Both

Chinese and American cultures, for different reasons, expect—indeed demand—that she be obliging, voiceless, and invisible. As Hutcheon writes, "[I]rony can function for the passive aggressive personality, but it also works as the undermining-from-within of the politically repressed," and, in the words of Michael M. J. Fischer, as a "survival skill, a tool for acknowledging complexity, a means of exposing or subverting oppressive hegemonic ideologies."[40]

The various ways in which irony suggests other modes of discourse, such as imitation, parody, sarcasm, and qualities such as clever wit and indirection, call to mind Homi Bhabha's definition of colonial mimicry as "mimicry [that] represents an *ironic* compromise" (original emphasis).[41] But whose ironic compromise? The colonizers' or the colonized's? While technically not colonial subjects, minorities in the United States face strictures of assimilation that demand as much adherence to regulative norms as colonialism's imperatives (it is also debatable whether racism is "worse" in actual colonies, such as India under British rule, or in so-called democratic countries with a history of white settler colonialism, genocide, and chattel slavery). The voice or voices that have been forced to parrot, mimic, and imbibe dominant discourses break through in Chin's poetry as aural manifestations of this internal(ized) colonization.

Mimicking colonial and assimilative norms and ideals can function not only as a defense mechanism but also as a disguised and effective mode of subversion from "within." Self-deprecation from a member of a marginalized minority within a hegemonic national ideology and body can be both a defensive and an offensive strategy. The roots of the word "irony" suggest both possibilities: "The *eiron*, who gave irony its (bad) name, was indeed a self-deprecating figure, appearing less than he (or, rather less commonly, she) was, but sometimes this was interpreted as a deliberate attempt to render oneself invulnerable."[42]

Because the ironist takes on the voice of the dominant discourse, which often has great "absorptive capacity,"[43] she or he in some way appropriates the power of that discourse.[44] With irony, it is always difficult to separate the overlapping possibilities of humble distancing, tactics of deception, desire for revenge, and so on. Irony also balances on a fine line between anger and despair: it is always threatening to tip over into unbridled venom or utter melancholy. "Sometimes irony can indeed be interpreted as a withdrawal of affect; sometimes, however, there is a deliberate engaging of emotion," writes Hutcheon (*Irony's Edge*, 15). Irony can sometimes involve both actions simultaneously: for example, a seeming lack of affect as a cover for rage.

The would-be user of irony is, as Burke points out, never free of potential temptations or entrapments.[45] And because irony is a dialectic that involves both writer and reader, the audience for ironic discourse is also drawn into the risks (and pleasures) of irony.

A closer look at Chin's poetry will more specifically illuminate the issues a theoretical discussion of irony brings forth. In a 1995 interview with Bill Moyers, Chin said:

> There's a doubleness to nearly all my work, to how I feel about things, and perhaps especially about assimilation. As I've said, my family's past is irretrievable, but assimilation *must* happen. There's *no way* I can force my children to speak Chinese. There's *no way* that the pure yellow seed, as my grandmother called it, will continue. . . . The Chinese want to keep the blood pure—my grandmother used to sit on the porch with a broom and try to sweep away the white boys from dating us—but assimilation is inescapable. . . . Just as I think it's impossible to keep Chineseness pure, I think it's also impossible to keep whiteness pure. I think *everything* must merge, and I'm willing to have it merge within me, in my poetry.[46] (original emphasis)

Her statements reveal many of the major concerns in her poetry and how irony's structure captures these "bifurcated" issues:[47] a sense of dislocation from both China and the (Chinese) past and the United States and American culture; the relationship to a "pure" "Chineseness" or whiteness; hunger for assimilation and the American Dream, particularly as mediated through miscegenation with white men ("*everything* must merge, and I'm willing to have it merge within me"); and the desire to blend two (or more) ways of being and perceiving in her poetry.

These various topoi bleed into one another, not unlike the "subperspectives" Burke speaks of in his discussion of irony. Thus, being dislocated from a (Chinese) past involves the poet's broken relation to a "pure" Chineseness and the perception by "real" Chinese that she is a barbarian who has tainted her blood with that of white Americans and who also cannot speak Chinese fluently. At the same time, any easy assimilation into American culture is thwarted by those Americans who see her as a barbaric "Oriental"—neither a "pure-blooded American" nor a "native speaker." These various difficulties are mediated by issues of language: an Asian American poet is viewed deficient until proven otherwise in her mastery of either her "familial" Asian language or English.

"An Essay on Assimilation"

My discussion of Chin's poetry centers on her use of irony as a means and a strategy to have her voice heard in the English poetic tradition and in the American polis, despite the social, political, and ideological forces arrayed to silence, ignore, and marginalize her as a Chinese American female poet. In her three books of poetry, Chin grapples with questions concerning assimilation, miscegenation, the psychic fallout from becoming "American" and—always, even if not always stated—the central question of poetry and language, especially the English language, in whose poetic tradition she strives to make a place, a name, and a home for herself.

I begin by examining in detail one poem from her first volume from 1987, *Dwarf Bamboo*—"Exile's Letter (*Or: An Essay on Assimilation*)," a poem that engages with these various interlocking issues—before moving on to the poems in *The Phoenix Gone, the Terrace Empty* (1994), a book that is more realistic (or bitter) about the costs and failure of assimilation, and then to *Rhapsody in Plain Yellow* (2002), whose poems, while still ironic, are even more imbued with melancholy.

Here is the complete text of "Exile's Letter,"[48] which starts with an epigraph "from a distant cousin, circa 1964":

> We are in Louisiana now
> planting soy for an aristocrat

with a French surname,
I think, Prevert; and no,
he's not what his name suggests,
but rather, a stoic, truthful man,
a professed de Gaulian
devoted to Mother France
and understands, so he says,
the plight of the races.
Too bad that his wife, mad
and dying of cancer,
has offered him no children,
an unjust retribution
for a man so sure of his creed.
One cool summer evening,
and the field alight with flies,
she came to us, whispering
"There were dogs here
who vanished in the deep of night,
prized setters and pointers,
well-groomed and with papers.
I don't believe you have erred
and have eaten ours as your own."
Grandmother touched her arm.
"Let us speak the truth, Madame,
it was *your* dogs, remember,
who crossed the fence,
who delighted in our cabbage."
The woman nodded and cried,
"Oh my little children,"
then, drove off into the sunset
in her station wagon filled
with seed for fodder.
"The dying are not unwise,
even the most dessicated [*sic*] cactus
issues a flower before death."
Grandmother said this, gazing
at the vast, cultivated wasteland.
Life goes on, Mei Ling,

Even I've bloomed lovelier, I think,
resembling you a little,
but rounder where profitable.
And behind that briared fence
the boys are watching, even now,
the white boys. (original emphasis; 42–43)

Chin's poem resounds with multiple voices and ironic manifestations, which are not easy to pin down. In *Irony's Edge*, Hutcheon delineates between "signals" of irony that function meta-ironically—that is, that "do not so much constitute irony in themselves as signal the possibility of ironic attribution" (154), such as graphic punctuation signs and typographical markers—and those that function "structurally" in five sorts of manifestations: changes of register, exaggeration/understatement, contradiction/incongruity, literalization/simplification, and repetition/echoic mention (156). Chin employs variations of all five in "Exile's Letter," an "Essay on Assimilation."

The speaker of the poem, Mei Ling's (Marilyn's) cousin, whether consciously or not, documents the subtle processes of assimilation. She begins matter-of-factly—"We are in Louisiana now / planting soy for an aristocrat / with a French surname"—but for most readers, the situation of a Chinese family planting soy, a traditionally Asian crop, in Louisiana might strike them as strange or "ironic."[49]

The hyperbolic quality of "aristocrat" is more truly ironic: we sense that this man with a French name is probably no more than a Cajun farmer in the backwaters of Louisiana and perhaps has tried to pass himself off as aristocracy to these Chinese immigrants. The cousin herself seems to have fallen for the trick—for example, one hears in the cousin's voice her slight rebuke to what she imagines will be her cousin Mei-ling's unsophisticated misreading of the French name "Prevert":

    and no,
he's not what his name suggests,
but rather, a stoic, truthful man,
a professed de Gaulian
devoted to Mother France

and understands, so he says,
the plight of the races.

Here she seems to take on the voice of the dominant order. Yet the
cousin's ventriloquizing of the "aristocrat" Prevert's voice ("devoted to
Mother France / and understand[ing] . . . / the plight of the races") is
undercut, whether consciously or not, by her "professed" and "so he
says." We also hear, whether she does or not, the implicit condescen-
sion and racism in the de Gaulian's phrase "the plight of the races."

What goes unspoken but resounds in these first few lines is the
material reality of the differing receptions various immigrant groups
have experienced in this country. As Ronald Takaki writes, "Louisiana and Mississippi planters imported Chinese laborers and pitted
them against black workers during the 1870s. They praised the workers from Asia for outproducing blacks in per-worker competition, and
used the Chinese to 'regulate' the detestable system of black labor.[50]
A southern governor frankly explained: 'Undoubtedly the underlying motive for this effort to bring in Chinese laborers was to punish
the negro for having abandoned the control of his old master, and to
regulate the conditions of his employment and the scale of wages to
be paid to him.'"[51] Here in Chin's poem, Chinese immigrants also
end up displacing fellow black laborers to toil for a fellow immigrant
who—because he is white and French (what passes as an "aristocrat"
in this country)—has garnered social and economic acceptance, having much more easily become upwardly mobile, and feels no hesitation in exploiting racially minoritized newcomers in turn.

One can read the cousin's "Too bad" as either the assimilated subject's "straight" comment on the plight of a confident white man ("an
unjust retribution / for a man so sure of his creed") or as the sarcastic
happily vengeful rebuff of a more knowing subject. The difficulty in
pinning down the irony in this poem occurs at multiple levels: at the
level of the speaker's speech and at the level of the poet's writing of
the narrator's voice. After all, it is the grown "Mei Ling," who bears
the same Chinese name as that of the politicized poet Marilyn Chin,
who retrospectively "reads" the 1964 letter of her in-the-process-of-
becoming-assimilated cousin. In the act of writing, in what the poet

chooses to present and represent, Chin introduces irony as a form of indirect social commentary on the American situation the speaker's cousin writes about, as well as on the Preverts and the cousin herself. Schlegel's "permanent parabasis," Hutcheon's "simultaneous perception of more than one meaning," and Burke's multiple sub-perspectives all come into play in the voice of the Chinese American girl who is in the process of either being assimilated into dominant ideologies and mythologies or coming to political awareness of the disjunctions between the American Dream and reality. Mei Ling and her cousin represent two different ideological perspectives within what is usually seen as a monotonously homogeneous "Asian American" identity. Thus, Chin punctures the idea of the monolithic Oriental and the unindividuated Asian "horde" by means of these multiple (and multiply ironic) voices rather than by direct statement.

Interestingly, Prevert's wife expresses her racist assumptions and accusations under the thin disguise of irony, too, using indirection to indict:

> "There were dogs here
> who vanished in the deep of night,
> prized setters and pointers,
> well-groomed and with papers.
> I don't believe you have erred
> and have eaten ours as your own."

Here the poet "allows" Madame Prevert to speak in her "own" voice in the poem, and as the Frenchwoman does so, she reveals the sorts of binary structures and binary thinking that Chin's irony complicates. Madame Prevert's use of ironic sarcasm bifurcates neatly between a stated meaning—"I don't believe you have erred"—worded in the negative, which is exactly the opposite of her "true" meaning: "I do believe you have eaten our dogs."[52]

Equally accusatory is her clear-cut designation of "ours" and "your": the pronouns echo the "us versus them" rhetoric of American chauvinism, both domestic and international. The phrase "your own" is also ironically biting, playing on the double meaning of "own," as it implicates the Chinese family for stealing, for taking something that they do not own as their own. Though Madame Prevert herself is foreign, the fact that she is white and European and of a higher class enables her to employ irony primarily as a superior expression of social cattiness (and patronizing passive-aggressiveness). Unlike Chin and other minority subjects, Madame Prevert, in her use of irony, does not need to self-defensively negotiate various registers of discourse; instead, she can assert a stable form of irony that assumes a certain superiority and imposes its binary on other inferior others. For her, irony is offensive, not defensive. Her voice—ventriloquized by Chin in the poem—echoes the dominant order's stereotypes of Chinese as thieving, barbaric dogeaters (with less of a "pedigree" and legal right to be there than the "well-groomed" setters and pointers "with papers").

It is the Chinese grandmother who exposes and confronts the Frenchwoman's double-speak by speaking "straight":

> "Let us speak the truth, Madame,
> it was *your* dogs, remember,
> who crossed the fence,
> who delighted in our cabbage."

She turns the accusatory pronouns back onto Madame Prevert—"*your* dogs"—while at the same time giving those dogs a quasi-human agency ("who delighted in our cabbage"). Those with a knowledge of European semi-imperialism in nineteenth- and early twentieth-century China might well read another level of meaning and irony in this reversal of guilt, what John King Fairbank described as "the oft-mentioned (but never photographed?) sign at the Public Garden on the Shanghai bund (waterfront): 'No Dogs or Chinese Allowed.'"[53] In the end, the grandmother evades answering Madame Prevert's question.

The Frenchwoman's condescending cry, "Oh my little children," signifies that she knows she has been outwitted and betrays her "hurt" that those poor little Asians—who, in her mind, she has done so much to help—have now turned on her like unfeeling ingrates. She drives off "into the sunset," like a fading cowboy, in her "station wagon filled / with seed for fodder." The implied idea of a dying American Dream or a dying West (Madame Prevert is childless) is reinforced by the grandmother's proverblike comment:

> "The dying are not unwise,
> even the most dessicated [*sic*] cactus
> issues a flower before death."
> Grandmother said this, gazing
> at the vast, cultivated wasteland.

But irony comes into play here, too, for the "dessicated cactus" could just as well refer to those last "real" Chinese whose "pure yellow seed" are also going to fodder, to "waste," Chinese American offspring who will not produce more "pure yellow seed" of their own. Thus, Madame Prevert's and the grandmother's shared desire to preserve the "pure seed" of what is "truly" American (white) and what is "truly" Chinese—both based on fictions of blood and biological descent—is ultimately doomed. The poem yokes the two women in its political critique, even if the attitude of the poetic speaker is much more sympathetic toward the grandmother.

The oxymoronic description of America—"cultivated waste-land"[54]—belies the immigrant's mixed feelings about this new country, what Chin elsewhere calls "the tundra / Of the logical" ("We Are Americans Now, We Live in the Tundra," *Dwarf Bamboo*) with a "gold coin at the horizon" ("A Chinaman's Chance," *Dwarf Bamboo*). The idea of vast plains, tundras, calls to mind the depopulated (of Indians, bison, trees) American West and the far reaches of China's frontier, where the non-Han "barbarians" roamed. Here, the grandmother speaks in the voice of a Chinese from China, as someone who sees the United States as a barbarian land.

These "barbarians" take on identifiable form in the last few lines of "Exile's Letter":

> Life goes on, Mei Ling,
> Even I've bloomed lovelier, I think,
> resembling you a little,
> but rounder where profitable.
> And behind that briared fence
> the boys are watching, even now,
> the white boys.

Here, the poetic voice is not that of the poet but the voice of Mei Ling's (Marilyn's) cousin. Are we to mistrust her point of view?[55] Are we to read her words ironically? Is her "Life goes on" a flip American truism? Or something more disquieting? The Chinese American girl has begun to realize that her blossoming into adult sexuality can be "profitable," in terms of both sexual and economic payoff, to the "white boys" watching behind the briared fence.[56] She understands that her Asian female sexuality can be used as a means of entry into certain privileged domains of power usually barred to nonwhites (though provisionally and conditionally accessible, in limited ways, to assimilated minority subjects). The female sexual body becomes the material vehicle for border crossings and upward mobility.[57] The speaker's "even now" suggests the continuing and continual presence of the white male gaze—and of the inevitability of assimilation.

The Barbarian

The figure of the barbarian "behind that briared fence" looms large in *The Phoenix Gone, the Terrace Empty* (whose title comes from a Li Bo poem[58]), most explicitly in a pair of poems—"The Barbarians Are Coming" and "Barbarian Suite"—in the first section of the volume, "Exile's Letter," as well as in a few poems in *Rhapsody in Plain Yellow*—especially "Bold Beauty" and "Where We Live Now (Vol. 3, #4)." The idea of the "barbarian," one of the major figures in Chin's poetry, offers a means of discussing the complex, intermingled issues of racial, cultural, and sexual "purity" and social, cultural, and linguistic assimilation.

First, some background: In the long tradition of classical Chinese poetry, one type of recurring poem is that of the exile who has been forced to live on the frontiers among "barbarians," or non-Han Chinese. Men were sent there either as soldiers or as a means of punishment; women could be married off to "barbarian" generals as a means to ward off invasion, consolidate territory, and form political alliances.[59] China had long been plagued by invaders from the north and west—hence, the building of the Great Wall—but in its own self-mythologizing has often glossed over the fact that its history is far from monolithic ("pure" Han) and unbroken. China has in fact been ruled for long periods of times by "barbarians"—most notably the Mongols (Yuan dynasty, 1271–1368) and the Manchus (Qing dynasty, 1644–1911), and had been subjected to a long period of Western domination from the nineteenth century until only very recently.

Although writing poems was essential for a man's classical education, this activity was unavailable to most women, for whom literacy was a rare privilege in the premodern period (as it was for most of China's population). Whatever poems were written by women in earlier centuries mostly did not survive. One whose did was Ts'ai Yen (162?–239?), considered the "first great woman poet in Chinese history."[60] A widow, she was captured by the Huns around 195 and "taken to the North, where she became the concubine of a Hunnish chieftain and bore him two sons"; many years later she was ransomed and married to a Han officer serving her father's friend, a warlord. Her two Hun sons were left behind. Ts'ai Yen wrote "18 Verses Sung to a Tatar Reed Whistle" (ca. 200) about the sorrows of exile and of leaving her sons to return to the Chinese capital, Chang An (now Xi'An):

A Tatar chief forced me to become his wife,
And took me far away to Heaven's edge.
Ten thousand clouds and mountains
Bar my road home,
And whirlwinds of dust and sand
Blow for a thousand miles.
Men here are as savage as giant vipers,
And strut about in armor, snapping their bows.
As I sing the second stanza I almost break the lutestrings.
Will broken, heart broken, I sing to myself. (section 2)

The seventeenth stanza. My heart aches, my tears fall.
Mountain passes rise before us, the way is hard.
Before I missed my homeland
So much my heart was disordered.
Now I think again and again, over and over,
Of the sons I have lost
. . . .

I will never know them again
Once I have entered Chang An. (section 17)[61]

This poem pertains to my discussion of Chin for three reasons:
First, it is one of the few poems written by a Chinese woman exile.
Later male poets more commonly took on a stylized female voice
as a means to express what had hitherto been closed to them. The
"feminine" voice, writes Stephen Owen, was "felt to be a language
of sensibility, with the capacity to express feeling more perfectly than
the symmetrical regularity of classical poetry."[62] This voice should
not be unfamiliar to Western readers of Pound's famous translation
of a Tang dynasty (618–907) poem by Li Bo, "The River Merchant's
Wife: A Letter," written in the persona of a wife awaiting her husband's return from far away. Second, "18 Verses Sung to a Tatar Reed
Whistle" gives a flavor of the earnest and mournful tone of a classical
"woman's poem" that Chin both alludes to and ironizes—not at the
expense of the female voice but as a means of empowering the female
speaker. Third, Ts'ai Yen can also be cast as both a poet and a heroine, as Maxine Hong Kingston does in "A Song for a Barbarian Reed
Pipe," the last section of her *Woman Warrior* (she chooses the story of
Ts'ai Yen to end the book).[63]

Like Kingston, Chin sees Ts'ai Yen as a brave "woman warrior"
and devotes an entire poem, "Bold Beauty," in *Rhapsody in Plain
Yellow* (52) to her. For both Chinese American women writers, Ts'ai
Yen represents a potentially powerful role model, whose historical
situation as a literal bodily "translator" between two cultures (one
"civilized," one "barbaric") is analogous to that of modern-day
Chinese American women, who also negotiate two cultures and
whose bodies are equally contested and traded. Ts'ai Yen acts in
what some may see as the manner of a prototypical male hero to
save her family and her homeland: "Our heroine turns over and
slits the throat of her beloved. / She would avenge her family, her
sovereignty, her dead" ("Bold Beauty," from *Rhapsody in Plain Yellow*). Chin clearly identifies with her as a poet (as she later does with
Ho Xuan Huong): "She who survives to tell the tale shall hold the
power" ("Bold Beauty"). Using the figure of Ts'ai Yen as an aveng-

ing woman and poet—both filial Han daughter and "barbarian" wife—Chin and Kingston deconstruct the easy binary of "barbarian" and "civilized." Chin's poetry also calls into question essentialist notions of Chinese and American poetic traditions.

The idea of (the) barbarian touches upon many issues critical to Chin's work, issues usually framed as either-or binaries that she uses irony to debunk: cultural, linguistic, and racial purity or authenticity from essentializing discourses of Chineseness, Americanness, whiteness; the imperative to assimilate (that is, pass as white) or, alternatively, the imperative to ensure that the "pure yellow seed," as her grandmother called it, will continue; her own fear that she has become "barbarian" and will forget her Chinese past.

In her poems Chin invokes the idea of the barbarian in three main ways: in the situation of the Han Chinese exile living far from home among "barbarians" (non-Han Chinese) on the loess, prairie, and frontier—and, by extension, the American tundra; in the fear of "barbarian" invasions felt by both Chinese and Americans; and in the figure of the Chinese American, who is viewed as barbarian by certain Americans and as becoming-barbarian by some Chinese.

In *Phoenix Gone*, two poems explicitly use the word "barbarian" in their title: "The Barbarians Are Coming" and "Barbarian Suite." Here is "The Barbarians Are Coming" in its entirety:

War chariots thunder, horses neigh, *the barbarians are coming.*
What are we waiting for, young nubile women pointing at the wall,
    the barbarians are coming.
They have heard about a weakened link in the wall. So, the *barbarians
    have ears among us.*
So deceive yourself with illusions: you are only one woman, holding one
    broken brick in the wall.
So deceive yourself with illusions: as if you matter, that brick and that
    wall.
The barbarians are coming: they have red beards or beardless with a top
    knot.

The barbarians are coming: they are your fathers, brothers, teachers,
  lovers; and they are clearly an other.
The barbarians are coming:
        If you call me a horse, I must be a horse.
        If you call me a bison, I am equally guilty.

When a thing is true and is correctly described, one doubles the blame by
  not admitting it: so, Chuangtzu, himself, was a barbarian king!
Horse, horse, bison, bison, *the barbarians are coming*—
and how they love to come.
The smells of the great frontier exult in them. (original italics)[64]

Because irony is registered in so many different and subtle ways (italicization, repetition, understatement, overstatement, ventriloquism,
and so on), pinning it down with certainty is often difficult. "The
Barbarians Are Coming" clearly illustrates Schlegel's idea of irony as
parabasis, Burke's idea of "sub-perspectives," Hutcheon's "simultaneous perception of more than one meaning," and Colebrook's idea of
irony as a broader "theory of meaning" and/or a "way of life." And
like Bakhtin's "heteroglossic" novelistic discourse, irony in this poem
is always slippery and multivoiced.

The italicization and overrepetition of the phrase "the barbarians are coming" signals fear and anxiety—Chin ironically ven-
triloquizes both the Han Chinese's fear of the northern invaders
(and of white American men coming to take their Chinese American daughters) and American popular yellow-peril rhetoric—as
well as desire (the sexual pun of "coming"). At the same time, the
slightly hysterical rhythm, syntax, and italicization of the phrase
echo Chicken Little's "the sky is falling!" and serve to undercut or
belittle the hysteria. Thus, the poem both sets up the fear—the repetition suggests the rumbling threat of horse hooves and the pervasive presence of these "marauders"—and desire, while also undercutting them at every turn (for example, the blasé tone of "what
are we waiting for, young nubile women . . ."), allowing for Hutcheon's "simultaneous perception of more than one meaning." Irony
enables the Chinese/Chinese American woman, who is expected by
the patriarchal powers-that-be to mouth their xenophobic lines, to

subvert the stated meaning of the lines, allowing multiple meanings and voices to break through.

The war imagery of the poem, especially of the first line, recalls both American yellow-peril rhetoric (the Chinese "invasion") and the old Chinese fear of northern invaders breaching the Great Wall. But unlike in Ts'ai Yen's poem, the woman speaker here is not intimidated by the military maneuvers. Compare Ts'ai Yen's tone:

> Men here are as savage as giant vipers,
> And strut about in armor, snapping their bows.
> As I sing the second stanza I almost break the lutestrings.
> Will broken, heart broken, I sing to myself.

Chin's female speaker, by contrast, mocks male militaristic fears and almost celebrates the possibility of barbarians coming to take her: "The smells of the great frontier exult in them." (Her tone sounds more like Ho Xuan Huong's than Ts'ai Yen's.) Like those foreigners who threaten to breach the wall or border at any moment, the various ironic voices in "The Barbarians Are Coming" irrupt into the fabric of the poem, not unlike the "disruption of narrative illusion, the *aparté*, the aside to the audience," writes de Man, "by means of which the illusion of the fiction is broken"—or parabasis.[65]

"The Barbarians Are Coming" is saturated with sexual innuendos and puns: the "young nubile women," the weakened hole in the wall, women equated with horses who are ridden, the barbarians who "love to come." The fear—and attraction—of miscegenation cuts many ways. Here, again, Burke's idea of multiple subperspectives is useful: the speaker's voice can be identified with either a Chinese woman (or women: the first-person pronoun shifts from plural to singular in the course of the poem) who fears—and desires—the barbarian non-Han men (Mongols, white Americans), or a Chinese American woman who fears—and desires—either white men or Chinese men: "they have red beards or beardless with a top knot";[66] "your fathers, brothers, teachers, lovers; and they are clearly an other." A third possibility, though slightly less plausible, is that the speaker could be speaking from the point of view of a white American woman who fears and desires the "beardless" foreign (Asian?) men with top knots.[67]

The identity of the "you" shifts throughout the lines and functions, variously, as a stand-in for the "I" ("you are only one woman"), the barbarian male other ("If you call me a horse, I must be a horse"), or the "I" as seen from the misogynistic point of view of the male other and internalized by the speaker ("as if you matter").

Chin's ironic discourse reverberates not only with the anxieties of the speaker(s) but also with the general discourse of fear around them. American yellow-peril discourse constantly invokes the specter of "Asiatic" hordes (and in the early twentieth century, the West Coast hysteria that lascivious "Asiatic" men—such as Filipino farmworkers in California—were taking white women away and sexually violating them[68]). Strict Confucian regimes also impose onerous sexual codes on their women: the loss of "Chineseness" by means of miscegenation—red-bearded white men taking Chinese daughters away—almost always implicates the woman for being "whoreish."

At the same time, sexual desire is also felt insistently throughout the poem—not just that of the male marauders but also, shockingly perhaps, that of the Chinese (American) female speaker(s). This desire manifests itself both thematically and formally in the insistent rhythms, in the language ("The smells of the great frontier exult in them"), in the Chinese (American) woman's identification with the horses who are ridden ("If you call me a horse, I must be a horse"[69]).

The identity of the female speaker is not easily ascertained because the poem oscillates between first-person plural; second-person singular and, possibly, plural; and first-person singular voices. What rings clear is that the female body serves as the vehicle through and over which the "pure" culture of the center must mediate the "barbaric" margins. The slightly comic sarcastic second line ("What are we waiting for, young nubile women pointing at the wall") shows the women looking at themselves from both the first-person plural perspective ("What are we waiting for") and the third-person perspective ("young nubile women")—or, rather, the third-person perspective that has been internalized, mockingly or not, into the first-person: "young [and] nubile" is how the men of their own blood and the "barbarians" view them. The women are property to be protected and to be taken away. They are also seen as potential sexual, racial, and national traitors or Malinche figures: "So, the *barbarians have ears among us.*"

Inevitably, these Chinese and Chinese American women have internalized a misogynistic (a more positive adjective would be "self-deprecating") and patriarchal point of view: "you are only one woman," "as if you matter." While they are bodies/objects to be traded among different men, they are also weighted with the heavy responsibility of shoring up national boundaries—their bodies expected to prevent the walls from being breached but also to be available to be penetrated at will.

In lines 4 and 5 of "The Barbarians Are Coming," the speaker's attempts to kid herself with "illusions" about her importance in holding back the hordes only serve to highlight the anxiety and guilt she harbors about allowing the "barbarians" to penetrate her and reach her people:

> So deceive yourself with illusions: you are only one woman, holding one
> broken brick in the wall.
> So deceive yourself with illusions: as if you matter, that brick and that
> wall.

Unspoken but understood are the accusations of failure by her people: "as if you matter, that brick and that wall." In this phrase, "you" and "brick" and "wall" are made grammatically equivalent if "that brick and that wall" are read as appositive modifiers of "you." The female body is linked to things inanimate and inhuman—both are ultimately futile: neither the brick nor the wall nor her body will prevent penetration and intermixing from eventually happening (one might also read the brick and the wall as being slightly personified, addressed apostrophically as "you").

The italicized and unitalicized halves of sentences in "The Barbarians Are Coming" serve to echo and counterpoint each other: It soon becomes clear that any easy binaries become difficult to sustain. For example, the two halves of the first line seem to reinforce each other and stay in the same rhetorical register, but from the second line on, there is no consistent pattern. One would tend to read line 6 "straight"—"*The barbarians are coming*: they have red beards or beardless with a top knot"—yet line 7 repeats the italicized phrase but with a different ending: "*The barbarians are coming*: they are your fathers, brothers, teachers, lovers; and they are clearly an other." This last voice, which punctures the xenophobic first half of the line, is certainly not the same as the voice in the second half of line 6. The very line itself mirrors irony's form only to collapse it: the two sides of the binary, self and other, native and foreigner, cannot be clearly distinguished. The barbarian is shown to be internal to the home and to the homeland/nation. There is fear *and* attraction. What is "native" or joined by blood can turn out to be "an other," a barbarian"—and vice versa. The threat of miscegenation (and incest) is found all along in the most domestic of spaces, one's home(land),[70] which is supposed to be protected by "that brick and that wall."

The voice in the second half of line 8 is different still: "*The barbarians are coming*: / If you call me a horse, I must be a horse. / If you call me a bison, I am equally guilty." Here, the female speaker seems to take on the passive obedient voice of the Asian American woman—"I'll be whatever you want me to be"—but, again, irony undercuts the sincerity of her remarks in the exaggeratedly submissive word choice ("must be," "equally guilty"). She is called one breed of animal by one group, another breed by the other. Horses in China were associated with the northern and western barbarians, who were skilled horsemen; bison, an indigenous American animal, are associated with Native American "barbarians." Thus, the line suggests that the female speaker is considered "barbarian" by both the Chinese and the Americans. The irony that saturates her seemingly submissive accession to these animalistic designations suggests that she is much more resistant to being "ridden" than she might appear.

The rhetorical register shifts once again in the next stanza, which quotes one of China's great philosophers, Chuang Tzu, himself a master of paradox—"When a thing is true and is correctly described, one doubles the blame by not admitting it"—but the first line ends with a conclusion that would appall Chinese purists and nationalists: "so, Chuangtzu, himself, was a barbarian king!"

The end of the poem seems both a resignation to conquest ("Horse, horse, bison, bison, *the barbarians are coming*") and an exuberant sexual release ("and how they love to come. / The smells of the great frontier exult in them"). Chin herself has said, "So much of my poetry is about assimilation—about fearing it and loathing it but also celebrating the wonderful magic of it."[71] This fear and loathing and celebratory desire structure the Asian American woman's subjectivity and her desires for whiteness (and white recognition for her as a subject, citizen, and as a poet). In speaking of Frantz Fanon's recognition of the internalization of the self-as-other, Stuart Hall writes, "And in the doubling, fear and desire double for one another and play across the structures of otherness, complicating its politics."[72]

Miscegenation and Assimilation

From the founding of the United States, Americans have been obsessed with race and sex (and money)—or more accurately, sex-in-race and race-in-sex, loathing and desire; thus, it is not surprising that the question of what constitutes a "red-blooded American" has been mediated through these two issues as well. For Chin, as for the Chinese American female speakers of her poems, assimilating as an Asian American woman is inextricably entangled with her coupling with white men. For many of the Chinese father figures in Chin's poems, assimilation is enacted through the bodies of white women, both movie images (Marilyn Monroe) and flesh-and-blood ones— "He abandoned her [his Chinese wife] for a blonde," says the speaker of her father in "Chinese Quatrains (The Woman in Tomb 44)" from *Rhapsody in Plain Yellow*—and through the belief in capitalism and American myths of progress and success.

A great number of Chin's poems deal with her anxiety about dating white men, losing her "Chineseness," but also her desire for them— what Stuart Hall calls "the deep ambivalence of identification and desire."[73] Miscegenation offers the possibility of full American citizenship—"*Better dance //* With the one named Rochester / who likes your kind. / Let us dub him / 'the point of entry'" (original italics, "A Break in the Rain," *Phoenix Gone*)—and access to the American Dream— "no need to struggle, he would take her away / on his white, white steed and panniers of riches" ("Bold Beauty," *Rhapsody in Plain Yellow*)—but also various dangers: the censure of her Chinese family, the loss of Chinese culture, and the fear of playing into the hands of white men with preconceived notions of a submissive, sexual China doll.

For Chin, these men take many forms: the "American Joes," with a penchant for mail-order brides and Suzie Wongs, the fantasies of countless GIs in strip bars across Southeast Asia—"the girl with the queue-rope of black hair, / The girl who brings you Blue Nun and souvenirs // Made in Hong Kong, small bright thingamajigs / That snake from your pelvis to your heart, rigged // With bedroom accoutrement" ("A Dream in the Life of American Joe," *Dwarf Bamboo*)—but also young hip punks:

> Amerigo has his finger on the pulse of China.
> He, Amerigo, is dressed profoundly punk:
> Mohawk-pate, spiked dog collar, black leather thighs.
> She, China, freshly hennaed and boaed, is intrigued
> with the new diaspora and the sexual freedom
> called *bondage*. "Isn't *bondage*, therefore,
> a *kind* of freedom?" she asks, wanly.
> (original emphasis; "Composed near the Bay Bridge," *Phoenix Gone*)

But as these last lines indicate, the Chinese American woman can relish her sexual freedom in complicated and not fully understood ways that rationalize her bondage to Amerigo/America.

When Chin says, "So much of my poetry is about assimilation— about fearing it and loathing it but also celebrating the wonderful magic of it,"[74] that "wonderful magic" includes interracial sexual excitement.[75] The Chinese American female speaker in the poem "I Confess . . ." (*Dwarf Bamboo*) sees no necessary contradiction between filial piety and sexual independence, or so she says—with irony:

> "Dear Mentors:
> one day I am filial
> monkey, practicing reading

and writing. Next day
I wear ink
eyeliner, open up
Mandarin frocks for the boys." ("I Confess . . . ," *Dwarf Bamboo*)

The ironic implications of the lines indicate that she is aware of the roles she plays ("I am filial / monkey, practicing reading / and writing") and her own complicity in Orientalizing herself by opening up her "Mandarin frocks for the boys."

Sexual desire has an engine of its own, "this greedy body / in search of its destiny" ("Minerva Around the Swimming Hole," *Dwarf Bamboo*) so that with Roberto, "I forget what race I am, what sex I am" ("Art Is What Humans Leave Behind, Roberto," *Dwarf Bamboo*). In her prose piece, "Happiness: A Manifesto," originally published in 1995,[76] Chin explores all the dazzling dimensions of sexual desire for a white man, a desire that exists despite her "usual dyed-in-the-wool diatribe against male domination":

His beauty, his male beauty, is a feeling that I know; it is not anything that I could sum up, pontificate on, illuminate via a terse and explosive gender discussion with my radical women friends: on our "mindful" level, in the great dialectic of things, he shall always be the hegemonist/oppressor/invader. The imperialist other who keeps us dissatisfied and yearning. (55)

Yet when she "cross[es] his threshold, I kick off my sensible shoes, slither into my silky, sequined skin, lie back like some self-appointed goddess" (56). During the day, when she puts on "that postcolonial/ scruffy tweed jacket" and goes to the "local Southern California state university to teach Introduction to American Ethnic Literature . . . I shall represent all the oppressed female intellectuals of the Third World. I shall begin each day by reminding these spoiled blond surfing children that their forefathers were slave owners, their grandfathers were Chinamen killers, their fathers were patriarchal pigs . . . their boyfriends were possible rapists" (56).

What does it mean for this self-declared Asian American feminist, the "radical" or "militant" bane of the Copper Canyon and *Poetry* letter-writing crowd, to take on the voice of someone who openly mocks "gender discussion[s] with my radical women friends," classes such as "Introduction to American Ethnic Literature,"[77] and the discourse of "oppressed female intellectuals of the Third World"? What does it mean for the Chinese American speaker to use racially pejorative terms such as "Chinamen"? How is irony at work in these lines? Or is it?

With her white lover, says the narrator, "[g]ender studies were now rendered moot or just the name of some dusty journal printed in Indiana":

> [H]e was biting my ear, uttering the most salacious dreams in
> all of the Western empire. In my tenth orifice, we traveled the
> world. . . . Oohh the tundras, the prairies. . . . How he plowed me
> backward and forward and forward, until I couldn't remember my
> race, my color, my destiny. . . . My post-colonial position at the world
> in this moment was supine. . . . We stayed attached, cock and cunt,
> two multi-limbed creatures, fucking for dear life. (58–59)

There seems to be no conflicted ambiguity to this sexual hunger, though there is obvious ironic humor in the description ("My post-colonial position . . . was supine").

What Chin demonstrates in "Happiness: A Manifesto" is that irony works not in the simple Quintilianesque or Boothian sense of substituting a term for its opposite in a stable manner but as multiple conflicting voices irrupting into and disrupting the text—the "permanent parabasis" that reveals in the acts of rupturing the various paradoxical internalized ideologies, discourses, and rhetorics at work in the poem and in the psyche and sexual desires of this particular Asian American woman poet and persona. When the speaker says, "His beauty, his male beauty, is a feeling that I know," she means it.[78]

(Male) sexual freedom is, of course, one of the myths of the American Dream. Chin has said, "I see myself and my identity as nonstatic. I see myself as a frontier, and I see my limits as limitless."[79] While she may see her own sexual desire as limitless as a man's, Chin, as well as anyone, knows the costs of these myths, especially for women of color. The reality is that she is the ground to be "plowed backward and forward" by the white imperial conqueror (cum–white American "liberator").

Another American myth is that sex is purely personal or "individual"—"*I couldn't remember my race, my color*" (antimiscegenation laws, lynchings, and so on fly out the window). Yet reality proves time and time again that sex is never purely just "cock and cunt" in the privacy of one's domestic space. For the unreliable Chinese immigrant fathers in Chin's poems, as for her own father, the idea of the American Dream involves both white women and economic success: "*My father's dream is my dream: / fast cars and California gold; / the singles bar is my watering hole*" (original italics; "Art Wong Is Alive and Ill and Struggling in Oakland California," *Dwarf Bamboo*). "Fast" cars are, of course, a symbol of American upward mobility and sexual freedom. This immigrant from Hong Kong, a British colony, is "obsessed with a bombshell blonde" (Marilyn Monroe) and names his daughter after her by transliterating Mei Ling to Marilyn ("How I Got That Name," *Phoenix Gone*). In "Where We Live Now (II)" in *Dwarf Bamboo*, the speaker tells of her father's infidelity with a white woman:

> He, too, sends a photograph
> of himself and an unnamed woman.
>
> Notice the cryptic message,
> "business as busy as usual,
> and the woman is only temporary."
>
> Such a typical American story,
> but it wouldn't hurt to recognize—
> she was white and very beautiful.

The "typical American story" links business and business as usual with a "white and very beautiful" woman. The understatement of "but it wouldn't hurt to recognize" masks deep sorrow and hurt.

"[M]any argue that ironists only *appear* cool and restrained on the surface as a way to mask actual hostility and emotional involvement," writes Hutcheon (original emphasis; *Irony's Edge*, 41). One of irony's functions is to mediate sorrow and rage. Because of irony's unstable nature, expressions of humor and sarcasm often vibrate and oscillate toward feelings of deep bitterness, revenge, resignation, and sadness. Seeming self-deprecation might mask anger and aggressive impulses. Chin knows well the demands implicit in the "model minority" stereotype and the gender expectations imposed by Chinese and American cultures that women be seen and not heard. In this latter regard, the Asian American female speaker in "Where We Live Now (II)" and the "unnamed" "only temporary" white mistress of her father are linked as victims of patriarchy and sexism.

In her 1995 interview with Moyers, Chin explains the (auto)biographical facts around her father's infidelity when she was seven years old, shortly after the family had arrived in the United States:

> My father had a white lover and he was on the phone with her in an adjoining room while my mother, who couldn't speak English, was in the living room sewing and not understanding anything about what was going on. That was a very damaging experience for me as a child and it's been painful ever since. I try to resolve that experience in my poetry. All my love poems work on the personal level, but they also work on this familial level, in which over and over again I try to speak to my father and to resolve what was unresolvable—to ask him why he left us and why he left us for a white woman. And once again in my poems the white woman works on the personal level in that, indeed, "she's" what fragmented our family. The white woman is also symbolic of the American dream and of what happens to the immigrant family—in this case, the Chinese family—upon reaching these shores.
>
> This is the fragmentation that I write about over and over again, hoping to resolve the pain, hoping to speak through my mother's suffering, hoping to be a conduit for her voice and for the voices of other Asian women. (75)

Two important points emerge from this account: first, the personal is never purely the personal or even the familial but is always also social and ideological, and historical; second, becoming "American" necessitates a painful assimilative process in which the threefold nexus of race, sex, and language is violently brought to bear upon the "alien." In Chin's case, assimilation's negative associations become linked in the Chinese American girl's imaginary with her father's desire for white women. The cost of her father's pursuit of the American Dream is the cruelty toward and suffering of the Chinese immigrant non-English-speaking wife/mother. "[T]he fact that my mother cannot be happy in this new country shall haunt me forever and shall haunt my poetry forever," says Chin to Moyers (78).

Indeed, Chin is always aware of the psychic and material costs of assimilation—both to herself and to other Asian women, like her mother, who do not have the language or skills to survive the brutal processes of emigration, alienation, and assimilation. In *Phoenix Gone*, Chin writes a series of poems to Asian women who paid the highest psychic costs: mental illness and suicide. In her "Elegy for Chloe Nguyen" and in the eight poems that comprise the section "Homage to Diana Toy,"[80] Chin explores the broken promises of the American Dream: "the fifty paltry stars / that amount to a little more / than sensible graphics / and fine accounting" ("First Lessons, Redux").

Thus, Chin's use of irony as a means to navigate the power dynamics of sexual relations with white men is refracted or triangulated through her acute awareness that she is always competing with white women, the American ideal of female desirability, for both her Chinese father's and society's recognition, and that there is always the danger of being psychically destroyed in such a high-stakes sexual and racial "battle royal." The ironic voices in Chin's poems are rife with intersecting, often conflicting emotions—desire, belligerence ("If this doesn't please you, too bad, it's all I have" ["Summer Love," *Phoenix Gone*]), melancholy—in other words, both self-conscious and unconscious internalization of racist and colonialist ideas about "Oriental dolls" and ideological notions of white female beauty but also a hunger to "conquer" white men sexually with the same zeal her father pursued white women and to empower herself with the same sexual—and textual—freedom men arrogate to themselves.

"Home is the grandest illusion," says the female speaker in "Where We Live Now (Vol. 3, #4)" (*Rhapsody in Plain Yellow*)—home meaning both the familial domestic home and the "homeland" (whether China or the United States). But there is another "home" that promises more possibility. In the dedicatory poem to her mother, "Prelude," in *Phoenix Gone*, Chin ends the poem with these lines: "And we shall always live / in this poetry that you love." This poetry is presumably in Chinese (her mother did not speak English), but Chin's own poems in English can also be read as attempts to find a "home" for herself and for her mother and other Asian women whose voices have not been heard, whose names have been lost. But finding a place for an Asian American woman in the English poetic tradition can prove to be as difficult as finding one in the American homeland.

Tradition and the Individual Chinese American Talent

In *Rhapsody in Plain Yellow* Chin overtly conjoins the mastering of English-language poetry with the sexual seduction of men so that there is no doubt in the reader's mind that "becoming American" happens by means of sexual, linguistic, and cultural coupling(s). In "So, You Fucked John Donne," the speaker says,

> So, you fucked John Donne.
> Wasn't very nice of you.
> He was betrothed to God, you know,
> a diet of worms for you!
>
> So, you fucked John Keats.
> He's got the sickness, you know.
> You *took precautions*, you say.
> So, you fucked him anyway.
>
> John Donne, John Keats,
> John Guevara, John Wong,
> John Kennedy, Johnny John-John.
> The beautiful, the wreckless, the strong.
>
> *Poor thang*, you had no self-worth then,
> you fucked them all for a song. (original italics)

Here, the speaker—who may be addressing another as "you" or using the second-person pronoun as a stand-in for "I"—casts the female figure in an ambiguous sexual role, the valence of which largely depends on how one reads "[p]oor thang" (a very American colloquialism).[81] If read "straight," the phrase renders her a woman of "no self-worth" who has fucked either a poet that is so ideal he is "betrothed to God" or a poet who is the prototypically sickly Romantic poet; if read ironically, "[p]oor thang" endows her with sexual agency—she takes on the role of sexual conqueress who fucks not only Donne and Keats but, in a show of exuberant promiscuity, all types of men: Latino and Chinese, JFK, and "Johnny John-John" (JFK Jr. or any "john").

By means of not only referential meaning (Donne and Keats) but also traditional rhyme and irony, Chin simultaneously takes on the stereotype of the Asian sexual object—working with and against it—and the idea of the unviolability of the poetic canon and inserts herself in the English poetic tradition. Like "[p]oor thang," the phrase "fucked them all for a song," colloquial but less slangy, is a pivotal one in deciding (ironic) meaning in both the sexual and poetic registers: again, is she a low-grade prostitute or a conquering female/poet "entitled" to her desires? "For a song" suggests she is both—she fucks canonical dead white male poets for a mere trifle, but she also fucks for, and in the service of, poetry (song = lyric).

Later, in the eponymous poem of *Rhapsody in Plain Yellow* (the last and best in the volume, dedicated to Chin's late lover, Charles), poetry and sex are again commingled:

> Say: there is poetry in his body, poetry
>   in his body, yes, say:
> this dead love, this dead love
>   this dead, dead love, this lovely death,
> this white percale, white of hell, of heavenly shale.
>   Centerfolia . . . say: kiss her sweet lips.
> Say: what rhymes with "flower":
>   "bower," "shower," "power"?
> I am that yellow girl, that famished yellow girl
>   from the first world.
> Say: I don't give a shit about nothing
>   'xcept my cat, your cock and poetry.
> Say: a refuge between sleeping and dying.
>   Say: to Maui   to Maui   to Maui
> Creeps in his petty pompadour. (original ellipsis)

The speaker parodies the famous lines from *Macbeth* ("Tomorrow, and tomorrow, and tomorrow . . .") and takes a swipe at Romantic poetry ("bower"); later in the poem, she does the same with Ginsberg's "Howl" and Keats's "Ode on a Grecian Urn" and also invokes Kafka,

Hélène Cixous, and Camus. Is the parodying here mimicry or slavish imitation, commanded by the imperative "Say"? Or is Chin rebelling against the English poetic tradition and its imperatives? "Say" can also mean "for example" or can be used in American slapstick to inject a tone of sarcasm ("Say!"—as in the Three Stooges routines). "Say" also appears famously in "The Star-Spangled Banner": "Oh, say can you see . . . / Oh, say does that star-spangled banner yet wave . . . ").

"Rhapsody in Plain Yellow" begins with this line, forming its own stanza:

Say: 言

The next stanza begins:

> I love you, I love you, I love you, no matter
>   your race, your sex, your color. Say:

The poem begins by signaling that Chin is coming out of two linguistic and poetic traditions, before moving seamlessly, as we have seen so often, from the world of language and poetry to the topic of sex, again racialized—or, rather, universalized ("no matter / your race, your sex, your color"). In saying "I don't give a shit about nothing / 'cept my cat, your cock and poetry," the speaker conflates poetry, the (dead) white male lover, and sex. The dead love is both "Charles" and a white poetic tradition: "your cock and poetry." In using colloquial ungrammatical English, the speaker refuses "proper English" (by use of a double negative) while, at the same time, demonstrating, in her unselfconscious use of slangy (and sexual) diction and earthy Anglo-Saxon expletives, that she is a "native speaker."

The speaker of "Rhapsody in Plain Yellow" is "that yellow girl, that famished yellow girl / from the first world" (contrary to the common American stereotype that Chinese Americans are "fresh off the boat" and fluent in Chinese, Chin makes clear here that the speaker comes from the "first world," not the third). As in "The Barbarians Are Coming," the speaker is acutely aware that she is the product of two patriarchal cultures, Western ("John Donne, John Keats / . . . John Kennedy") and Chinese ("John Wong").

Chin the poet is also painfully aware that she is seen as a latecomer and outsider to two great and long poetic traditions: Chinese and English. The note accompanying the poem explains that its form "mocks the *fu* form, characterized by long, poetic exposition." So Shakespeare and Keats and Ginsberg mingle in a mock-*fu* form. Though there is not enough room in this book to fully analyze Chin's experimentation with Chinese poetic forms in English-language poetry—experimentation that, as noted earlier, does not "count" as "experimental" in the contemporary poetry avant-garde (dominated by Language and conceptual poets)—I do want to briefly discuss how the use of the first-person pronoun (the lyric "I") functions differently for Chin than for most white poets, lyric or avant-garde, and how this pronoun usage is influenced by the Chinese poetic tradition.

In a 1989 interview with Maxine Hong Kingston, Chin says, "I always think back to the T'ang Dynasty when I write poetry. I feel that I am very much a part of that Chinese tradition. I don't want to be cut off from it. That's why I studied classical Chinese. I feel it's very, very important."[82] And a few years later, she states, "[W]hen I talk about myself the 'I' is always personal and also always representative of other Chinese Americans like myself."[83]

On the surface, Chin's female speakers may resemble those of other white female lyric poets—for example, the expression of Asian women's psychic suffering in her poetry may remind one of similar renderings of female psychic distress by confessional poets—but the difference, I would argue, is that Chin does not feel she has the "luxury" or desire to limit her focus to the private or personal "I." So much of her psychic pain and that of women like her mother and Diana Toy find their roots in the traumas of emigration, racism, assimilation, and sexism. Admittedly, white women poets do often invoke larger social issues of sexism—and the "I" in confessional poetry is often a persona—nonetheless, "racially unmarked" female poets have more leeway, and choice, to be solely concerned with the individual and the personal if they should so choose.[84]

Chin's seeing herself as deeply connected to a larger group beyond a purely personal "I" also extends to how she sees her poems in relation to poetic tradition(s), and not just the English one. Chin borrows Chinese poetic techniques and form and experiments with them in the English language. By bringing in such models, she necessarily imports a different perspective, embedded in the ghostly linguistic structures that underpin these poetic forms, even if the language is no longer Chinese.

Perhaps the most pertinent hallmark distinguishing Chinese poetry from English-language poetry for this discussion is what the scholar of Chinese literature James J. Y. Liu calls "omissions of the subject." Such an omission

> allows the poet not to intrude his own personality upon the scene, for the missing subject can be readily identified with anyone, whether the reader or some imaginary person. Consequently, Chinese poetry often has an impersonal and universal quality, compared with which much Western poetry appears egocentric and earth-bound.[85]

While I take issue with Liu's praise of the "universal"—in a racially diverse (and riven) nation such as the United States, not all poetry is created equal; thus, a reader is not likely to automatically identify (with) the speaker of a poem written by a Chinese American female poet as a "universal" subject,[86] "readily identified with anyone"—his point about the fluidity of the subject (by omission of a lyric "I") is important. Indeed, these grammatical differences imply different worldviews or perspectives.

In "Syntax and Horizon of Representation in Classical Chinese and Modern American Poetry," the comparative literature critic Wai-lim Yip describes how

> the classical Chinese language, as it is used in poetry, is free from syntactical rigidities—having no articles, personal pronouns, verb declensions, or connective elements such as prepositions and conjunctions and being indeterminate in parts of speech. (29)

Liu, in "Some Grammatical Aspects of the Language of Poetry," writes that "the greater freedom from grammatical restrictions enjoyed by Chinese bestows on it certain advantages over English as a medium for poetry. . . . Chinese grammar is fluid, not architectural" (39, 46). Like Yip, he cites various differences between Chinese and English poetic syntax: no requirement of any indication of number; absence of tense; "frequent" omission of the subject of a verb; omissions "[s]ometimes even [of] verbs"; inversion (for example, a verb preceding its subject);

fluidity of parts of speech (such as using nouns verbally).[87] Many of these syntactical deviations occur in English-language poetry, but, unlike in Chinese poetry, they are precisely noticed as "deviations."

Yip analogizes the differences in Chinese and English poetic perspective to differences in perspective in Chinese and Western painting:

> We can explain the predicative activities and habits of mind in Indo-European languages by the Western concept of perspective. . . . [O]bjects are seen from a fixed location by one individual looking toward a fixed direction. But in almost all Chinese landscape paintings, we see scenes not only from the front but also from the rear; not one moment from one specific perspective but many moments from many viewpoints.[88]

While Yip's view holds more for more traditional English poetic forms, the point is, nonetheless, well taken. In Chinese painting and poetry, even in its most traditional forms—rather, precisely in its most traditional forms (classical poetry)—spatial and temporal incongruities are held in tension. As with Burke's concept of irony, "multiple perspectives" inhere.

The use of multiple perspectives in many of Chin's poems is often tied to, as I have noted, her use of pronouns. For example, pronouns can, and do, shift from first person to second or third person; a first-person perspective can be voiced by a second-person pronoun; or multiple perspectives and different subject positions can be voiced by the same pronoun—say, the speakerly "I"—as we see in "Rhapsody in Plain Yellow," where we get lines such as these: "Say: Chinawoman, I am a contradiction in terms: / I embody frugality and ecstasy," but also "Say: I am dismayed by your cloying promiscuousness / and fawning attitude." And what about

> Say: I am a very small boy, a very small boy,
>   I am a teeny weeny little boy
> who yearns to be punished.
>   Say, I can't live without you

Here, we see variously the perspective of an exuberant Whitmanian "Chinawoman," that of a censorious outsider (or is it an internalized self-hating voice—or both?), that of a boy—or a man indulging in sadomasochistic sex play. And whose voice says, "Say, I can't live without you"? The Chinese American woman? The white man?

Perspective is also important to who "gets" irony, for irony is wholly dependent on the reader or group that interprets (or fails to interpret) it. When Chin writes "Sir, Master, Dominatrix" ("Portrait of the Self as Nation," *Phoenix Gone*), one can see how different interpretive communities might read it ironically or "straight." And the divisions do not necessarily fall along racial (or gender) lines. Hutcheon writes in *Irony's Edge*, "[T]here is a great diversity of speech within even a single speech community," adding that "we all belong to many overlapping (and sometimes even conflicting) communities or collectives" (89, 92).

What is fiercely clear throughout Chin's poems—and in the poems of all the poets discussed in this book—is that writing poetry, English-language poetry, represents one means (real or imagined) for the Asian American poet to wrest some form of agency in the face of overpowering linguistic dominance, canonical poetic traditions, assimilative pressures in American society, and the cultural logic that dictates that "English-language poetry" and "Asian American" are mutually exclusive terms. "Bold Beauty," the poem about Ts'ai Yen, ends with this line: "She who survives to tell the tale shall hold the power."

In "Rhapsody in Plain Yellow," the female speaker addresses a "you":

And you, relentless Sinophile,
    holding my long hair, my frayed dreams.

My turn to objectify you.
    I, the lunatic, the lover, the poet,
the face of an orphan static with flies,
    the scourge of the old world,
which reminds us—it ain't all randy dandy
    in the new kingdom.

The speaker is the "scourge of the old world," a phrase that could mean she is a scourge to the Chinese in China, but she also an old-world scourge in the "new kingdom": "kingdom" links the empire in the New World, the United States, with the old "Middle Kingdom." She is considered a "scourge" in both.

Is there one "you" in this section or many? If the latter, does "you" signify different people at different points or different people simultaneously? Is "you" her dead white male lover (the "relentless Sinophile")? Is he the "you" referred to in "My turn to objectify you"? Or is the "you" also referring to the speaker herself ("I, the lunatic, the lover, the poet")? Or possibly even the reader? Or all three at once?

When a Chinese American female speaker baldly declares, "My turn to objectify you," she is making a political statement in both the societal and poetic arenas. It is the "turn" of the Oriental sex object and the Third World object of white liberal pity (an "orphan static with flies") to talk back—she/they are given voice by the poet. And it is the Asian American woman poet's turn to write back, to assume her agency and her place in the empire of poetry. The poet-speaker's sassy turn to the American colloquial—"it ain't all randy dandy / in the new kingdom"—signals her purchase on authentic "American" speech.

Three stanzas earlier, the speaker asks,

> With whose tongue were we born?
> The language of the masters is the language of the aggressors.
>   We've studied their cadence carefully—
> enrolled in a class to *improve our accent.*
>   Meanwhile, they hover over, waiting for us to stumble . . .
> to drop an article, mispronounce an R.
>   Say: softly, softly, the silent gunboats glide.
> O onerous sibilants, O onomatopoetic glibness. (original emphasis)

Note the pronouns again: Who is the "we"? All minority poets and "nonnative" speakers? Chin wrenches the "us versus them" rhetoric of US nativist discourses and of US mythology ("We, Americans") and turns it back on itself. Who is the "they"? The "they" remind us of the Copper Canyon men "hover[ing] over" Chin, "waiting for [her] to stumble . . . / to drop an article, mispronounce an R." "O onomatopoetic glibness" ironically foreshadows their denigration of Chin's choice of "boo hoo" in her translation. The gunboats glide silently, "onerous sibilants." Chin signals her understanding of the inseparability of imperial military ambitions—both the West in China and the United States abroad—and the cultural offshoots and enablers of empire: the domination of English as a language and of English literature as a canonical literature that violently excludes nonnative speakers and sets strict rules (of exclusion and exclusivity) for those who might want to enter the kingdom of poetry. No riffraff allowed.

But while she writes, Chin also knows that poetry can be a "vast orphanage" ("How Deep Is the River of God," *Rhapsody in Plain Yellow*) for those like Chin who have no forebears or parents in this language or tradition:

> *The poet guards the conscience of society*—no, you're wrong.
> She stands lonely on that hillock observing the pastures.
> The world scoffs back with bog and terror.
> Fake paradise, imported palmettos
> (original italics; "Summer Sonatina," *Rhapsody in Plain Yellow*)

Who makes the italicized declaration? And who counters its veracity? Is the "she" the poet here? Or is the poet the "universal" "racially unmarked" poet invoked by the mocking references to "[f]ake paradise" (Dante) and "imported palmettos" (Stevens). The fake paradise and imported palmettos also refer to the Disneyland ("the Happiest Place on Earth") qualities of American culture and of the American Dream. Again, the English poetic tradition and normative American culture leave the "she . . . lonely on that hillock observing the pastures" (one is reminded of the "vast, cultivated wasteland" in "Exile's Letter").

Yet in the midst of bleakness, reminds Paul Celan, "[o]nly one thing remain[s] reachable, close and secure amid all losses: language. Yes, language."[89] Indeed, in "Rhapsody in Plain Yellow," the speaker at moments *becomes* language:

> Say: down blue margins
> My inky love runs. Tearfully,
>   tearfully, the pearl concubine runs.

The "pearl concubine" is the Asian prostitute, the geisha, the concubine, Suzie Wong, Ho Xuan Huong, Ts'ai Yen, Marilyn Chin—"I, the lunatic, the lover, the poet"—the Asian American female poet. "[B]lue" connotes both pornographic and melancholic. The poet has become the ink, has become the poem.

And again later in "Rhapsody in Plain Yellow":

Say: I am the sentence which shall at last elude her.

The "I" has become language and the "I" has split from the "her" (is "her" the female poetic speaker or her mother?). As a Chinese American woman poet writing in the last decades of the twentieth century and the beginning of the twenty-first, Marilyn Chin is acutely aware of the history of those, like her mother, who came before her and suffered in the "fantastical diaspora of tears" ("Rhapsody in Plain Yellow")— those who were denied full recognition as Americans—and denied the possibility of being or becoming fully expressive speaking and writing subjects in the English language.

While she herself could have chosen to more easily assimilate and have a better shot at the *Norton Anthology of Poetry*, Chin opts instead to write explicitly political poetry and to risk being rebuffed by asserting her right to a foothold in two (patriarchal) poetic traditions that do not want to grant her entry. She uses Chinese and English poetic forms in the English language, language that she wields with the cutting force of irony—irony not as mere technique but as worldview—to express the politicized and multiple perspectives of a twenty-first-century Chinese American female poet who belongs in the American body, political and poetic, as much as anyone else.

In so doing, Chin offers new perspectives on English poetry, particularly the lyric and what constitutes the lyric subject, and shows us how irony can unleash the multitudinous voices of American subjectivity and the possibilities inherent in our own histories. In the words of James Baldwin: "American history is longer, larger, more various, more beautiful and more terrible than anything anyone has ever said about it."[90]

FIVE

Undercover Asian

*John Yau and the Politics of Ethnic Identification
and Self-Identification*

Film noir, Jasper Johns, Peter Lorre, Anna May Wong, Eugene Dela-croix, Boris Karloff, Dashiell Hammett, X-rated movies, German Expressionist writers: upon encountering the poetry of John Yau (b. 1950), many readers find their expectations and preconceptions about Asian American writing unsettled. Not only the paucity of the "usual (signifying) suspects" but also his experimental style, prolific output—more than a dozen volumes of poetry, two books of short stories, numerous art monographs, countless art reviews, and contributions to artists' catalogues[1]—and his choice of career as an art critic give Yau a distinct profile in the field of Asian American poetry, and, indeed, contemporary American literature.

Unlike the work of either Li-Young Lee or Marilyn Chin, Yau's work taps more explicitly into avant-garde American and European traditions. Its forms immediately strike the reader as less readily comprehensible and more overtly "experimental." The reader is thrown off by the lack of explicit ethnic markers, the absence of an unprob-lematic autobiographical "I" or a clearly delineated political voice, the treatment of issues of subjectivity and race by means of mirrors, as it were, rather than straight on. What is a reading public that typi-cally expects the speaker[2] of Asian American poems to be writing about themes of family and an Asian past to make of a narrator who says, "Could I use 'beloved' when I didn't love them [his parents] and hardly knew them?"[3] Or of Yau's observation that "the mind's capacity to remember can interfere with the body's ability to experience, that this is the polar situation which must be avoided"?[4]

That said, Yau's poetry, even as it is infused (as any individual poet's work is) by its own sensibility and forms of being, also formally manifests the effects of Yau's social, political, and cultural interpellations and negotiations as a racialized minority American subject and writer. Just as important as these influences, of course, are Yau's early exposure to visual art, his intense engagement with the art world, his having studied with poet Robert Kelly at Bard, and other such artistic influences. As Gerald Bruns writes in his introduction to the volume *Readings in Russian Poetics*, "What counts as art is local or internal to the social space in which it is created (the formalism of Moscow is not that of St. Petersburg)."[5]

Thus, Yau, raised in Brookline, Massachusetts, by Shanghainese parents, was exposed to different sorts of social and aesthetic stimuli than Lee, raised in western Pennsylvania, the son of an educated Presbyterian minister, or Chin, raised in Portland, Oregon, the daughter of working-class, Cantonese-speaking restaurant owners. But all three were similarly interpellated in American society as "the Other—the chink."[6] There is no contradiction in claiming that, while Yau's poetry is not the same Asian American literary writing as Lee's and Chin's— nor, despite their having shared certain similar racial experiences, is his handling of such issues as assimilation, history, racism, linguistic displacement the same as theirs—the three poets' having been racially interpellated as "Oriental" in the twentieth-century United States is a significant fact in the formation of their poetic subjectivity.

Even to bring race or racial interpellation to bear on experimental writing is to risk being accused of "sneaking" racial essence and "experiential content" in through the back door. In the words of Warren Liu,

> Recognizing that earlier formations of Asian American literature were premised on notions of authenticity, representative-ness, and identity that formed exclusionary and, at times, one-dimensional constructs of literary representations as "essentialized" objects, contemporary critics of Asian American literature are now engaged in an effort to find new conceptualizations through which the "Asian" might re-appear.[7]

As troubling as these critics' "conscription" of what Liu calls "Asian American experimental literature" into "a reformed canon of Asian American work" (10) is their parallel critical attempt to "read the experimental as experiential," to subsume "the experimental charge of their [Asian American experimental writers'] work . . . by the disciplinary necessity for a (veiled) stable object of study" (7). These critics—he cites Jeannie Chiu, Timothy Yu, Zhou Xiaojing, and Laura Kang as examples—"accept the premise that ethnicity is best imagined as a readable, recognizable, and re-writeable condition, even if that condition is, in material terms, diffuse, obtuse, and unstable" (9). The term and category "Asian American," argues Liu, is as "uncontainable" as the category "experimental" (5).

This is subtle thinking about the term "Asian American experimental literature." I share Liu's concerns about the dangers of such general homogenizing categories as "Asian American" and "experimental"; his criticisms about the content-driven readings of Asian American literature, especially experimental work, by Asian American and non–Asian American critics alike; his resistance to critical attempts to "'translate,' so to speak, the experimental, so that it more transparently represents the experience of the ethnic subject's authorship," to posit "a positivistic correlation between literary text and subjective singularity" (9); and his advocacy of a "reading of difficulty that leaves certain things difficult" (8). That there are critics of Liu's caliber having this conversation about Asian American experimental texts and the dozen or so critical writings on this work is an encouraging sign of critical dialogues to come.

Nonetheless, while I fully understand this concern about the possible critical "over-simplification of both sides of the world/text equation" and the "overlook[ing of] the multiple, unanchored interpretive possibilities offered by these nonnarrative and textually unmoored figurations" (9), I would also urge, as I do throughout this book, that the institutional and political contexts that surround Asian American experimental poetry in the academy be kept in mind at all times. While it is certainly necessary to question the handful of Asian American critics who might try to bring the "experiential" in dialogue with the "experimental"—as if the experiential were not already part of the experimental—in an oversimplifying manner, one must not forget or fail to interrogate the larger structures and authority/authorizing figures that have the power—a power that does not go unwielded—to exclude and occlude this body of work (Asian American experimental poetry and Asian American literature in general).

Is there the danger that Asian American critics might read experimental writing by minority writers in reductive ways? Yes. This is true of all critics when approaching experimental writing: there is a strong desire to, in Liu's words, "tame" the "stubbornly unruly text" (2). As Charles Bernstein says of most critical work on Gertrude Stein, "Stein criticism is haunted by the ghost of explanation."[8] But to assert the "impossibility of claiming an unproblematic correlation between ethnic subjectivity and textual object," as Liu does (123), is not equivalent to saying that one can (or should) then make *no* claims at all about possible links.

Again, what is the larger picture? And where does power lie? To use a historical analogy: in focusing on the internecine battles between Booker T. Washington and W. E. B. Du Bois during the Jim Crow era or between Martin Luther King Jr. and Malcolm X in the 1960s, one can sometimes be made to forget, even if temporarily, the larger and more brutal powers and structures at work—both materially and ideologically.

In other words, by placing the onus on the very few Asian American critics of Asian American poetry for producing oversimplifying work on experimental Asian American writing, Liu allows to drop out of his range of vision the prevailing structural and ideological formations in American society—shored up, as Edward Said reminds us, by humanistic discourses—which hegemonically render and represent American minority subjectivities and writing in reductive and reified terms. To forget this fact is to depoliticize one's criticism and to practice an "expertise . . . based upon noninterference" (*WTC*, 2).

To recognize that certain shared social and racial experiences can and do infuse subjectivities, poetic and otherwise, is not to deny the individuality of each poetic act but to affirm, as Said emphasizes, that texts "are nevertheless a part of the social world, human life, and of course, the historical moments in which they are located and interpreted" (4). The personal, aesthetic, social, and political simultaneously coexist (and constantly oscillate) within all poets—and poems. In the particular case of John Yau, the complex and vexed polyvocal nature of his poetic subjectivity and poems reflect not only his being seen—or not seen, as the case may be—as "Asian" but also his difficult process of becoming "Asian American," particularly an Asian American poet, to himself and in the eyes of the critics. At the same time, one senses that Yau has never been fully comfortable with the label "Asian American," even as it has served him well. As Liu notes, Yau's work (and that of the other Asian American experimental poets, such as Theresa Hak Kyung Cha, Myung Mi Kim, and Mei-mei Berssenbrugge) "resist[s], in various ways, the kinds of literary operations that might allow readers and critics an access to a notion of subjectivity that is reflectively ethnic" (7).[9]

For decades, Yau never quite fit any poetry category—Language, avant-garde, cultural nationalist, ethnic, postmodernist, conceptual, among others—and, to some extent, still does not. After years of being identified with, and as a student of, John Ashbery and as one of several second-generation New York School poets, Yau has only in the last decade or so garnered formal recognition as an important contemporary poet—to a not insignificant extent, I would argue, because a small number of Asian American scholars[10] have written on him and argued for his importance as a major Asian American and American poet. It is quite certain that, without the institutionalization of Asian American studies in the 1990s, Yau would be much less visible in the poetry world than he is today.

In this chapter, I examine the fraught path that has led to the now commonplace categorization and interpellation of Yau as an "Asian American poet." First, I discuss Yau's reception by white critics in his early to midcareer by focusing on an intensely acrimonious exchange between Yau and the poet-translator Eliot Weinberger in the pages of *American Poetry Review* in 1994, which raised the question of his self-identification and his "genuineness" as an "Asian American" poet. The confrontation touched enough nerves for numerous poets and critics to take sides; while predating the Marilyn Chin-Copper Canyon face-off by fourteen years, the Yau-Weinberger confrontation underscores the feeling of "*plus ça change . . .*" about the American poetry world, its inability to deal head-on and honestly with issues of race,[11] and its largely misinformed perception and reception of Asian American poets and poetry.

Second, I test the strength of Weinberger's and other critics' assertion that Yau was neither a "real" nor a self-identified minority or "Asian" by examining specific poems in Yau's oeuvre, from his first book, *Crossing Canal Street* (1976), to those in *Radiant Silhouette: New and Selected Work 1974–1988* (1989),[12] a volume that appears right before his inclusion in various Asian American literary anthologies in the early 1990s and his official acceptance as an "Asian American poet." Not long after, Yau's work started to gain wider recognition by critics in the larger (white) world of contemporary poetry. One sign of the shift in Yau's career around that time is that after years of being published by the small independent press Black Sparrow, Yau chose to go with Penguin Books for his *Borrowed Love Poems*, which appeared in 2002 (a subsequent volume, *Paradiso Diaspora*, was also published by Penguin in 2006).[13]

Though he became viewed early in his career as one of the second-generation poets of the New York School, Yau has, in various interviews throughout the years, consistently characterized what he sees as the invisibility of his work in various poetry circles in the late 1970s and the 1980s—the period before he was included in anthologies of Asian American writing.[14] In 1993, when I interviewed him in New York City, he told me, "There was literally nobody sympathetic to me. Nobody. They couldn't see what I was getting at."[15] At the same time, Asian American writers—many of whom, like the men who comprised the editorial collective of the 1974 anthology of Asian American writing *Aiiieeeee!* (Frank Chin, Jeffery Paul Chan, Lawson Fusao Inada, Shawn Wong), had cultural nationalist leanings—rejected his work, according to Yau, because they thought it was "not Asian enough." Thus, "there was this feeling 'Well, who am I related to or identified with?' I'm identified with the New York School but I don't feel a part of it" (personal interview).

Eight years later, in an interview with *Verse* magazine's Matthew Rohrer, Yau spoke similarly:

[A]ll three [early poetry books: *Sometimes, Broken Off by the Music,
The Sleepless Night of Eugene Delacroix*[16]] came out within a year
[1980–81]. And as far as I could tell nothing happened. I didn't get
asked to read anywhere, nobody sent me requests to publish my
poems. I felt kind of invisible.[17] And I just thought maybe that was
the way it was. But I also think it was because at that point I didn't
really fit in. I wasn't really connected. By then I felt like I was somewhat disconnected to the New York School, and at the same time I
wasn't connected to the Language poets, who were kind of around
the same age I was. I wasn't really connected to anybody. I got some
letters from the Asian-American poets on the West coast [*sic*], and
then they decided they didn't like my work, so I felt disconnected
from them. And then in a way the disconnection became useful,
actually. Because then I decided maybe it was better not to belong to
any group. Not to be connected to any scene. And so I kind of just
stayed on my own.[18]

Yau's awareness of his status in the poetry world is marked by
his retrospective characterization of that time period: "[A]t that
point I didn't really fit in." Although in hindsight he frames his
marginalization as being partly a matter of choice and disavows
the desire to belong to any group or "scene," it was Yau's being
identified with John Ashbery, his former teacher who selected
Yau's *Corpse and Mirror* (1983) as a National Poetry Series selection,[19] that first brought him notice in the New York City poetry
world—as his institutional recognition by Asian American academics a decade or so later was to give him a firmer place in the
larger literary world.

Yau speaks of the association with Ashbery as having been "both
beneficial to me and worked against me" (personal interview). He
tells Rohrer that his break with the New York School poets came
about as a result of his not being "confessional" enough for them:

"I do this/I do that." Well, in a way I didn't accept their ideology.
The Asian-Americans, or the poets associated with the New York
School, or the Language poets, each had a kind of overt or covert
ideology and I didn't really accept any of them. So in a way it made
sense that I didn't connect with them.[20]

The Ashbery connection and the perception that his work did not fit narrow definitions of "ethnic poetry" meant that, until the early 1990s, both mainstream and experimental poetry critics neglected Yau's subject position and history as an Asian American (writer) when reviewing his work.

Yau himself felt that Richard Elman's 1983 review of *Corpse and Mirror* in the *New York Times Book Review*[21] was "racist" for this oversight—particularly inexplicable given Yau's photo on the back cover (personal interview). In a 1997 review of his poetry volume *Forbidden Entries*, Marjorie Perloff alluded to his earlier book of poems *Sometimes* (1979) and commented, "[T]here was no indication, at this stage of Yau's career, that the poet is in fact Chinese-American,"[22] a baffling statement given Yau's photo on the back cover; the poems titled "Marco Polo," "From the Chinese," "Chinese Villanelle"; the autobiographical poem "Their Shadows," which is about his grandparents; and the numerous poems about New York City Chinatown in his first book, *Crossing Canal Street* (whose title provides a clue to the perceptive reader: Canal Street demarcates the boundary between New York City's Chinatown and the overwhelmingly white world of the SoHo art district). It was as if an experimental Asian American poet were such a contradiction in terms that white critics, both mainstream and avant-garde, could not register the fact.

Being part of no group—by necessity or by choice—can sometimes look suspiciously like trying to be all things to all groups. The bitter, heated 1994 exchange between Yau and Eliot Weinberger in the pages of *American Poetry Review* ignited charges and countercharges of white liberal racism, career opportunism, ethnic posing, disingenuous denials, and self-loathing. The truths of Yau's relationship to his ethnicity and his career trajectory, of course, lie somewhere between the accusations and denials, truths as complex and contradictory as those constituting any Asian American or minority (or white) subject/poet.

"*Je un autre*, wrote Rimbaud [original italics]," cites Yau, misquoting the French poet's "Je est un autre" in his 1994 essay "Between the Forest and Its Trees." "I am the Other—the chink, the lazy son, the surrealist, the uptight East Coast Banana, the poet who is too postmodern for the modernists and too modern for the postmodernists. You have your labels, their falsifying categories, but I have words. I—the I writes—will not be spoken for."[23] In Rimbaud's original phrase, the first-person pronoun is disjunctively given a third-person verb. The "I" becomes an Other: from first-person subject to third-person object. Tellingly, in Yau's misquote, the copula (which renders being, whether first person or third person) drops out altogether—an apt analogue, even if unintentional, to the invisibility and nonexistence of Asian Americans in the public and cultural imagination and spheres.

Later in the same essay, Yau asks, "Might it not be possible that the self is made up of many selves, incomplete and fragmented?" (41). In his poetry, Yau often chooses to tap into these fragmented multiple selves through formal, rather than solely thematic, means: by use of repetition, circularity, narrative fragmentation, parataxis, interruption, substitution (of letter and/or word), framing issues, and various other techniques, but perhaps none is used more—or more effectively—than parody.

As evidenced by the somewhat defensive tone of Yau's list—"the chink, the lazy son," and so on—a Chinese American poet acknowledging these "many selves" on the explicit thematic level runs the risk of being called, variously, an ethnic opportunist, "militant," self-hater, or a yellow Uncle Tom (Charlie Chan).

Ethnic Identification and Self-Identification: Weinberger Versus Yau

In 1994, in the pages of *American Poetry Review* (*APR*), critic and translator Eliot Weinberger accused Yau of "creat[ing] a remarkable new persona for himself: that of the angry outsider 'person of color.'"[24] Weinberger was writing in response to Yau's negative review in *APR* of his 1993 anthology *American Poetry Since 1950: Innovators and Outsiders* two months prior.[25] In that piece, "Neither Us nor Them," Yau criticizes Weinberger for the "logic and didactic reasoning he uses to bring them [the poets] together in a single volume"—namely, Weinberger's criteria that the poets be born before the end of World War II and have published work of importance after 1950—primarily because those criteria allowed Weinberger, argues Yau, to justify which poets, or which types of poets, to exclude:

> Weinberger's need to construct hierarchies and either/or constructs prevents him from responding to the changing complexity of post-war American poetry, its various traditions.[26]
>
> *American Poetry Since 1950: Innovators & Outsiders* begins with William Carlos Williams (1883–1963) and ends with Michael Palmer (b. 1943). There are thirty-five poets in all, five of whom are women. Denise Levertov (b. 1923) and Susan Howe (b. 1937) are the only women among the nineteen active poets Weinberger has judged important enough to include. Langston Hughes (1902–1967) and Amiri Baraka (Leroi [*sic*] Jones) (b. 1934) are the only African-American poets. As to other *Others*, forget it. Weinberger has clear reasons for this: "The demographic complexity of the United States is reflected in the work itself, rather than the police-blotter profiles of the poets." I suppose "police-blotter" is supposed to throw a scare into anyone who might wish to look deeper, who might even begin to question Weinberger's assumptions: "Those who count heads according to gender and race should first consider how many poets genuinely qualify within these chronological limits." (original emphasis; 45–46)

In the Letters section, Weinberger and five of his supporters—Esther Allen, Forrest Gander, David Hinton, Roberto Tejada, and Cecilia Vicuña—respond to Yau's accusations by lambasting him for his "nervous breakdown in print," his "rant," "crazed invective," "sick race-mongering," "repellent race-baiting," "idiotic conclusions," and "opportunism."[27] These terms sound uncannily like those to be used against Chin in the pages of *Poetry* fourteen years later, when she, too, dared to bring up the issue of racism in the American poetry world.

Weinberger's use of the adverb "genuinely," quoted by Yau, reveals that the ability to decide who "genuinely qualify" as poets worthy of anthologization as "real" poets is something that those who "count heads according to gender and race" lack. One hears echoes of the anti-"identity politics" stance of Perloff, Gourgouris, Izenberg, et al. in the *PMLA*'s "New Lyric" forum and the defense of the "merely literary" but also the rhetoric and ideology of the Copper Canyon and *Poetry* letter-writing groups who arrogate to themselves the right and the acumen to decide who is the "genuine" translator of Asian poetry.

The *plus ça change* nature of these controversies, while perhaps not surprising, is, at first glance, noteworthy given the differing aesthetic allegiances at work:[28] Weinberger and most of his defenders in *APR*, unlike the Copper Canyon crew in *Poetry*, are poets (including nonwhite ones) and poetry translators from quasi-avant-garde circles (more experimental than Copper Canyon and *Poetry* poets). That said, the similarities between the Copper Canyon crew and the Weinberger cluster are not merely coincidental or juxtapositional: Weinberger, of course, is precisely the translator Joseph Bednarik, Copper Canyon's marketing and sales director, cites in his critique of Marilyn Chin's translation of the Ho Xuan Huong poem a decade and a half later in *Poetry*. It turns out, too, that of the six *APR* letter writers writing in defense of Weinberger against Yau (including Weinberger himself), three are white translators of either Latin American (Weinberger and Allen) or Asian literature (Weinberger and Hinton), and both Hinton and Weinberger publish or have published with Copper Canyon. Thus, Weinberger and Hinton share with Balaban not only a publisher but the mantle of being a white (male) translator, linguistic and cultural, of Asian poets.

Weinberger and Allen are also the co-translators of the work of the Chilean poet Cecilia Vicuña, who writes in defense of Weinberger in the same issue of *APR*. In a by-now-familiar move, Weinberger bolsters his case against the "fake" minority poet, the Asian American Yau, by bringing in two Latino/a poets, who are presumably "real" ethnics: Vicuña and Roberto Tejada. In other words, of the six writers who go up against Yau, two are ethnic minorities, and three are white translators of nonwhite Others.

Thus, perhaps not surprisingly, Weinberger, like Balaban, cites his own "multicultural" credentials—and discredits Yau's—as a means to defend his accusation that Yau has expediently taken on the "remarkable new persona" of "angry outsider 'person of color'":

[Yau] has probably never written a topical social-protest poem in his adult life. . . .

Thus, in the climate of these times because of the skins we were born into, John can feel free to claim that I "refuse to address" pluralism and multiculturalism, knowing full well that this has been my entire life. I spent years studying Chinese— which John barely speaks and cannot read—and have written extensively on Chinese poetry. (The one time John had to write on it . . . he quoted me.) . . . John has never, before this, written on any minority writers. I got a prize from PEN for my "work as a whole in promoting Hispanic literature in the U.S." My latest book is largely about Asia and Latin America. John's latest book is on Andy Warhol. . . . This is demagoguery, pure and simple— coming from a man who has never publicly, before this, shown any interest in black writers at all. I will not dignify his scum-bag race-baiting with a point-by-point response, or a defensive white liberal list of the things I've written and the publishing projects I've been involved with. (43)

But a "defensive white liberal" list is precisely what Weinberger spends most of his letter enumerating. This same type of white liberal multicultural defense would be voiced by several of the letter writers against Marilyn Chin in 2008: Weinberger's "I spent years studying Chinese" echoes John Balaban's claim of insider access to Vietnamese culture; Weinberger's charge of Yau's "race-baiting" (especially ironic given his own unexamined use of "police-blotter profile") was almost identical to the accusations, both spoken and unspoken, made by the angry letter writers in *Poetry*. And there are other similarities between the logics of the argumentation in these two fracases: Weinberger's faulting of Yau for having "never publicly, before this, shown any interest in black writers at all" has not a little in common with the *Poetry* letter writers' taking Marilyn Chin to task for supposedly not knowing the African American slang meanings of "noodling." In both cases, a white liberal pits a "real" minority (African American) against a "fake" minority (Asian American) so as to discredit the "fake" minority and to make the white liberal look unracist and multicultural—and virtuous.

Weinberger's remark about "the climate of these times" prefigures Perloff's and Gourgouris's characterization of the same contemporary postlapsarian period of "identity politics" fourteen years later (the "fall" obviously took place after the civil rights movements and Third World Strike of the 1960s and continues until the current moment, a period of over fifty years). What is breathtaking in Weinberger's sentence is his causal logic: "Thus, in the climate of these times *because* of the skins we were born into, John can feel free to claim that I 'refuse to address' pluralism and multiculturalism" (added emphasis). Yau rightly responds, "One's color is neither something you can put on and take off, like a coat, nor an ideology you announce one moment and ignore at another."[29] He also calls out Weinberger for not addressing the substantive points he made in his review: "Mr. Weinberger makes many points, but he fails to address the primary and simple issue I raised in my essay." Aldon Nielsen, one of the few critics of avant-garde poetry who focuses on issues of race, agrees; in his 1997 book on African American experimental poetry, *Black Chant: Languages of African-American Postmodernism*, he points out that "[Weinberger's] only real response to Yau's central charge is to deny it."[30]

The heatedness of the accusations and counteraccusations—of racial opportunism, of veiled white liberal racism—gives some indication that whatever raw nerves were being touched had less to do with feelings of anger toward the attacker than feelings about oneself (note how frequently the pronouns "I" and "my" appear in even the brief excerpt of Weinberger's letter cited). Nevertheless, a reader might still be left wondering, "So how accurate is Weinberger's charge that *John knows he is lying* (original italics)?" Was Yau, up until the early 1990s, a whitewashed avant-garde poet running with the New York School and SoHo artists—an "uptight East Coast Banana"? Or has he always been, as he claims, interested in issues of autobiography and racial identity—"I've thought of myself as a poet who wanted to write about things 'autobiographical' but am always trying to figure out how to do it"[31]—yet chose to deal with these issues in less overt (less thematized) fashion?

The truth, of course, is not so simple and clear-cut, as nothing about race and racial identity in the United States is. Yes, one could make the case that in the first ten years of his career, Yau did seem less than eager to identify with other Asian American writers—whether a result of, as he claims, aesthetic and/or ideological differences or his own feelings of denial/self-hatred (most likely a combination of those feelings and others).[32] Yet whatever the lack of Yau's public identification as a Chinese American poet, both Weinberger and Perloff are mistaken when they imply that ethnic identity has somehow never concerned Yau and that he "took it on" only late in his career and for purely opportunistic reasons. As the Asian American critic George Uba says, "His identity formation involves the dissolving of the more apparent evidences of the 'ethnic' but not a denial that such evidences, on some level, persist."[33]

In various interviews, Yau's own statements about his Chinese American background and identity are often modulated by the conversation's context and who is doing the questioning. In his interview with the editor of *Talisman: A Journal of Contemporary Poetry and Poetics*, Edward Foster, who ran a special issue on Yau in 1990, Yau alludes to his being Chinese American in this manner:

> You know, who you are is simply an accident of birth. You know, you're born through this thing you didn't decide on, but then you're imprinted in all sorts of ways. A Boston Brahmin or a first-generation child of an immigrant. You can make a bigger case about that, or you can try to use it without making a giant case about it. You know, it doesn't entitle you to anything. It just simply is what happened. And I don't want to deal with the accident of my birth as a right or entitlement. But I don't want to ignore it either, and so it becomes to me an interesting dilemma: how do I deal with it? How do I write about it?[34]

One might ask what the "thing" is in "you're born through this thing you didn't decide on." The phrase "Boston Brahmin" might refer to Robert Lowell, another Boston poet but one who would be perceived and received very differently in the literary world and in the English poetic tradition than Yau, a "first-generation child of an immigrant."

In that same interview, Yau names writers who influenced him, some of whose poetry he imitated: Ezra Pound, Harry Matthews, Raymond Roussel, John Gould Fletcher, H. D., T. E. Hulme, John Ashbery, Clark Coolidge, Michael Palmer, Barbara Guest, Jack Spicer, Laura Riding, John Weiners, the Beats, Robert Creeley—predominantly white writers from what one experimental poetry anthology dubs "the other side of the century" (that is, that avant-garde poetic tradition running counter to the genealogy posited by *The Norton Anthology of Modern Poetry*). Yau also mentions to Foster that he was reading Yukio Mishima in high school but does not go into detail about the significance of this fact. By contrast, in his interview with me in 1993, he told me that, because he was "definitely looking" for Asian American role models while growing up in Brookline, he looked to Mishima and the artist Isamu Noguchi.[35]

Yau's having grown up Chinese American in suburban Boston and having been exposed as a boy to the art museums in Boston by his mother, among a myriad of other social and aesthetic influences, are not incidental to his work (and I do not just mean thematically incidental). Are there ways in which his experiences and subjectivity as a minority American (specifically, Chinese American) operate "covertly" in his poems, not unlike the movements of the undercover Genghis Chan? Was Yau an undercover Asian, a covert radical, an inscrutable Oriental enigma, an actor in yellowface, a banana?

Let us examine the trajectory of his career, particularly the books preceding the appearance of the clearly ethnically marked Genghis Chan[36] and before Yau became an "Asian American poet."

The First Seven Books

A quick glance at Yau's first seven books—*Crossing Canal Street* (1976); *The Reading of An Ever-Changing Tale* (1977); *Sometimes* (1979); *The Sleepless Night of Eugene Delacroix* (1980), a collection of prose pieces; *Notarikon* (1981), which was subsequently incorporated into *Broken Off by the Music* (1981); *Corpse and Mirror* (1983)[37]—reveals that, even from the beginning, Yau's poems formally manifest the uneasy negotiation, if not outright battle, between his aesthetic drives and his experiences of being interpellated as "the chink, . . . the uptight East Coast Banana."[38] His books yield plenty of contradictory layers— traces of the "self [that] is made up of many selves, incomplete and fragmented."[39]

The chapbook *Crossing Canal Street* inaugurates the representation of this fragmented self: Canal Street separates Chinatown from SoHo, the art gallery district in Manhattan, functioning as both a literal and a metaphorical marker of two "sites" of Yau's identity (white/downtown/artsy and Chinese/Chinese American). Of the thirteen poems in the book, seven deal explicitly with Chinese or Chinese American themes, with titles such as "Suggested by a Chinese Woman Eating Alone on Mott Street," "An Old Chinese Gentleman Drops In to See His Cronies in a Coffeeshop (Mott Street)," and "Kuo Min Tang Chinese Nationalist Party."

As is evident from the titles, the poems suggest classical Chinese poetry, not only in their content but also in their forms. However, unlike the poems of Marilyn Chin, Yau's do not read as direct imitations of Tu Fu or Li Bai but as imitations of Poundian imitations (filtered through Ernest Fenollosa) of classical Chinese poetry. Indeed, in *Crossing Canal Street*, Yau observes these old Chinese men and women from a Poundian Imagist perspective that is both distanced and somewhat coy. He is not a "native informant" of Asian culture— as so many reviewers assume is the case with Asian American writers[40]—but a Chinese American poet who comes to his "Chineseness" to a not inconsiderable extent textually: that is, via Pound in English-language poems, not Chinese ones. In his interview with Edward Foster, Yau said, "Pound's Chinese poems were very, very meaningful to me then. I just read them over and over again. For me, they were about being Chinese, about some kind of identity" (43).[41] This statement acknowledges that for Yau, as for many Asian Americans, the formation of an ethnic identity and perceptions of Asian culture was and is largely determined by white (high and low) culture's refracted depictions.[42] In this light, T. S. Eliot's unironic declaration that "Pound is the inventor of Chinese poetry for our time"[43] might be extended to include "inventor of Chinese American poetic subjectivity," especially for those poets coming of age in the decades before the Third World Strike and Yellow Power movements of the 1960s and 1970s.

The poems in *Crossing Canal Street* first appear to be imitations of classical Chinese poetry,[44] but upon closer inspection reveal themselves to be more akin to those Pound poems and translations that use the so-called pictographic Chinese style Pound praised so highly—

Yau's images seem rendered in Pound's Imagist style. There is no indication in the poems that they were written by a Chinese American
poet: the poems are suffused with Orientalist references and images
(such as "brocade pearl silk" in "Suggested by a Waitress In YEE'S").
Two of the poems refer to the Chinese detective main character Judge
Dee, from a popular series of novels by the Dutch Orientalist scholar
Robert van Gulik published in the 1950s and 1960s.[45] The main clue
that the author is "Oriental" is found in the chapbook's exotifying
preface—written by Robert Kelly, Yau's teacher at Bard College—
who refers to the New England Yau as a "far kin" of the "Crimean
Tatars" (rumblings of Genghis Khan).

It is perhaps inevitable that a young Chinese American poet would
imitate the style of a major white poet (after all, these are his dominant poetic influences), but what is discomfiting in *Crossing Canal
Street* is the distance and disdain—at moments, disgust—with which
Yau observes the inhabitants of Chinatown. In his portrayals, Chinese men and women and their body parts are likened to animals and
objects: an egg, moon, bird of prey ("Suggested by a Chinese Woman
Eating Alone on Mott Street"); sides of meat, pigeons, locusts ("Suggested by Men at the Lunch Counter [Mott St.]"); almond petals,
black drops of oil ("The Waiter"); dried fruit ("An Old Chinese Gentleman Drops In to See His Cronies in a Coffeeshop [Mott Street]");
pigeons, squirrels, and vultures ("A Recent Saturday Night").[46] The
speaker is an ethnographic observer who, like all ethnographers,
brings his racial prejudices and revulsions to the table.

It is important to note the total absence of the poetic "I" of the
speaker (though "we" and "our" are used) in the chapbook. The only
use of "I" appears in the dramatic monologues of "The Waiter" or
Judge Dee—a "Chinese" character, like Charlie Chan, created by a
white author. In the place of the poetic first person are a lot of third-
person pronouns: "she," "her," "his," "they." This is ethnographic
observation by a Chinese American poet whose notion of his own
subjectivity is mediated by and filtered through Imagist verse and
Orientalist detective novels. The only moment in the collection in
which the speaker seems to be described directly is in the poem "The
Waiter": "he [the waiter] is paid to watch you eat." Here, he uses the

second-person pronoun to describe himself. Thus, the speaker's subjectivity is split: he is an observer of himself as an Other, a "you," though not completely a third-person object.[47]

At this early stage, one sees little evidence of Yau's characteristic parodic distance from his subject matter. These imitations lack parody's critical edge or what Bakhtin describes as parody's "nature": "transpos[ing] the values of the parodied style."[48] Yau has yet to learn what he admonishes (Asian American) readers and himself for eighteen years later: "You are spoken for when you learn to mimic your master's voice, when you accept the limits of his or her poems as if they were your own."[49]

Perhaps not unintentionally, Yau includes no overt ethnic signifiers in his second book, *The Reading of an Ever-Changing Tale* (1977), but the effects of his subject position ("the accident of my birth") and subjectivity might be read as revealing themselves in a poem title ("The Yellow Window") and in certain lines: "They were imposters / 'But so are you'" ("The Loop") and "[c]ertain colors got lodged under / the fingernails before their names / came to grace our speech" ("The Reading of an Ever-Changing Tale," 1–3). The voice in *The Reading of an Ever-Changing Tale* is more wry, knowing, and cynical than that in *Crossing Canal Street*—all of Yau's books to come will include variations of this ironic/parodic voice, one in which the self steps outside the self and provides commentary on itself—the "I" splitting into both subject and object.

In Yau's next book of poems, *Sometimes* (1979), a more accomplished volume than his previous two (though it includes some poems from the appropriately named *The Reading of an Ever-Changing Tale*), ethnic signifiers are suggested by the section and poem title "Marco Polo," a stray line ("As an ancient Chinese poet wrote . . ."—from "Shimmering Pediment"), and in particular three poems in the last section: "Their Shadows," an autobiographical poem about his Chinese paternal grandfather and English paternal grandmother; and two imitations of classical Chinese poems, "From the Chinese" and "Chinese Villanelle."

It is in *Sometimes* that Yau first publishes his overtly experimental combinatory poems (with puns and letter and word substitutions)—what Edward Foster calls "word salad" poems—which are by now, a trademark of his poetry. Here is "Ten Songs" in its entirety:

> Trying to find a way to say something that would make it
>   make its sense
> Trying to find a way to weigh something that would make
>   its own lense
> Finding it trying to say something they would
>   make a lense of
> Finding the saying of something weighing the sense
>   of it trying
> Making the trying something that would find its sense
> Sensing the making trying to find something it says
> Saying the finding is there to find is making it make sense
> Making it make sense is finding something to say
> Something to say is finding a lense to sense the making
> Something making the making something something else

In the interview with Foster, Yau explains that he started writing these types of poems in the mid-1970s, having been directly influenced by the artist Richard Artschwager's drawings (and indirectly influenced by the Oulipo writers Raymond Roussel and Harry Mathews):[50]

> At a certain point I realized my poems were so dependent on the visual image that I wanted to react against that. . . . And so I thought, why not just use words as physical things in some way, literally cut them up and play around with them. (43–44)

The form of "Ten Songs" embodies the act of the poet's "[t]rying to find a way to say something that would make it make its sense" (line 1). At the same time, there is no "I" in the poem who might be the agent of the trying to make sense; instead, there are only the third-person "it" and "they." The erasing, or deconstructing, of a traditional lyric "I" ("the single modulating voice that names itself and others in an easily consumable narrative—writing in a language that is transparent, a window overlooking a world we all have in common"[51]) would become a hallmark in Yau's poems.

Though most white critics have read this erasure of the subject as a generic postmodern move, Yau, in an interview with the Asian American Writers' Workshop's Eileen Tabios, says that the social and ethnic context of his family upbringing, as much as the eccentricities particular to any family, "shows up in my poetry as me being slightly disenfranchised, isolated, trying to communicate, and thinking communication is largely impossible."[52] He also makes clear in the same interview that his desire to get away from a certain confessional autobiographical "I" in general had much to do with growing up Chinese American:

> [A]lmost from the beginning I wanted to get away from that "I." It was something I associated with Robert Lowell and Sylvia Plath: the "I" as victim. There seemed to be something wrong with it, something privileged. . . . O'Hara believed his life was immensely interesting. . . . But I didn't see my life as that immensely interesting. . . . Maybe it's part of being Asian American, that is, that my family spent hours talking about the importance of family versus the individual. (386)

The absence of a poetic "I" in "Ten Songs" can be read in various contradictory ways: as a means to escape the fiction of the lyric "I," the privileged "I" of confessional poetry;[53] as an admission of poetic impotence (a lack of agency, not unlike what many minority poets experience in relation to the English poetic tradition); as a form of liberation: the "I" is no longer the one being judged for not saying something that "makes sense" or not speaking English like a native speaker. The desire to "make sense" is expressed in terms of language itself, not of the poet as agent. The fact that Yau does not say, "*I* am trying to find a way to say something that would make sense," but instead, "Trying to find a way to say something that would make it make *its* sense" (added emphasis) transfers agency from the poet to the "it"—language, the words themselves. Thus, if the "something" cannot be said in a way that makes sense, it is the fault of some abstract and vague "it," not the poetic "I" (or the poet).

The poem walks a fine line between enacting an arduous attempt to find or say something that "makes sense" and seeming nonsensical (indeed, there is an almost sped-up slapstick manner to the poem as one moves through the lines). Here, Yau destabilizes the terms of what "makes sense." Certainly, the trying to "make sense"—whether speaking or understanding—is a condition many immigrants face with a foreign language. In the United States, where the push for monolingualism and an official national language ("English Only") is especially strong, language is a "lense" used to judge one's fitness as an American. Asian Americans, even those who are native speakers, are often assumed not to be able to "make sense" of English—as demonstrated by the chop-suey broken English that generations of Asian American actors, usually totally fluent in English, have been forced to spout in countless Hollywood films (such as Roman Polanski's *Chinatown*) up until the present day.

The poem also implicitly mocks conventional "logical" narrative approaches to "find[ing] a way to say something" that would "make sense" and the assumption that words arranged in an orderly linear manner actually do make sense.[54] Indeed, the sentences in "Ten Songs" never become total nonsense: syntax is kept intact, though semantic meaning and grammar have been torqued. The collage effect[55] gives materiality to the words ("Trying to find a way to weigh something"), pulling the reader away from a focus on the semantic content and a desire for narrative meaning. The poem gives the sense that individual words have been cut out and re-glued in different sentences. Words are material things, not just abstract "somethings." The "making" and the "finding" are as important as—or more important than—the trying to make sense.

The work of visual artists gave Yau not only the idea for the cut-up poem but also a way to think about the "I" in poetry. Tabios asks him, "Can one ever lose the 'I'?" Yau replies,

> No. But you can shift it to a different plane and that "I" then has its own or different meaning from the one associated with "You." I think of abstract expressionism where the "I" is the subject versus minimalism where the "I" is the object. Is there an "I" that is both object and subject, an "I" seen in different profiles.[56]

Yau makes clear that the "I" has not been totally erased. For the Chinese American poet there is no such privilege of simply erasing the

subject nor his racialized subjectivity; "[o]ne's color is neither something you can put on and take off, like a coat," as Yau reminded Eliot
Weinberger.[57] Indeed, in the poem's and the poet's and the speaker's
strenuous efforts to make sense—the entire poem itself is an enactment of the "trying" (there are ten songs, not one)—one feels the
burden of the desire to understand and to be understood.

This striving to make sense and to be made sense of would hold a
particular (not unpainful) resonance for an Asian American. There
is not a single marker of anything "Asian" in "Ten Songs," yet the
speaker's and the poet's attempts to be understood in language (English) cannot be wholly delinked, I would argue, from Yau's experiences as an Asian American, viewed as an outsider both to the English
poetic and to the Western artistic traditions. The different attempts
to recombine words in "Ten Songs" suggest the efforts of someone
trying to break the combination of a lock or a code. In combining
words in seemingly nonsensical ways, Yau is both willing to risk
sounding like he is writing "chop-suey" broken English and leveling
an arbitrary (or rigged?) playing field by demonstrating how language
can be broken down into material units, which can be recombined
in random ways so that the difference between "proper English" and
"broken" English becomes blurred and ambiguous.[58]

It is in his volumes of prose, not poetry, that Yau begins to write
pieces that are much more explicitly autobiographical—and racially
marked. Yau's fourth book, *The Sleepless Night of Eugene Delacroix*
(1980), like his two later volumes of prose, *Hawaiian Cowboys* (1995)
and *My Symptoms* (1998), displays an unflinching honesty about a Chinese American family and about issues concerning American history,
society, and race. While one cannot assume that the speaker is necessarily the author, the details in these prose pieces echo to a great extent
what Yau has said about his parents in various interviews. Timothy Yu
writes that narrative "figures heavily in Yau's work,"[59] a description that
I would say holds true more for his prose pieces than for his poems.

Two pieces in *Sleepless Night* offer portraits of Chinese parents: "Electric Drills" (23–25) and "Toy Trucks and Fried Rice" (33–36).[60] The
latter, a description of the "Chinese Benevolent Association's Annual
Christmas Party," provides an explicit portrayal of the poetic speaker's

parents, their background, and the poetic speaker's relationship to his ethnicity:

> He had come to the party with his parents. He had been told ever since he could remember that he was Chinese. He had never lived in Chinatown and he couldn't speak Chinese. . . . His mother was from Shanghai and spoke the dialect common to that area, and known as Shanghainese. The people at the party . . . spoke Cantonese and were, according to his mother, only farmers anyway. (34)

> He sat in a metal folding chair and listened to a language neither he nor his parents could understand. (36)

Here, Yau deconstructs the notion of an authentic homogeneous "Chineseness," fracturing it along various lines—dialect, class, and culture. Even the food served at the party is "mediocre Chinese restaurant food," probably the kind of "fake" or Americanized Chinese food served at Chinese restaurants in the United States in the 1950s and 1960s; thus, the fried rice is a simulacrum, like the toy trucks. The Chinese American boy is also a simulacrum of a "real" Chinese boy: his relationship to "Chineseness" takes the form of negation ("He had never lived in Chinatown and he couldn't speak Chinese") and of secondhandedness ("He had come to the party with his parents." "He had been told ever since he could remember that he was Chinese").

While the Chinese American boy who is the protagonist of the piece (he is referred to in the third person only) is perhaps understandably not "really Chinese," the story reveals that the boy's parents, who are from China, are not "truly" Chinese either. The father's mother (like Yau's paternal grandmother) is an "English Catholic," and neither parent speaks the Chinese dialect spoken at the party (Cantonese). The boy's parents are (or fancy themselves to be) of a higher class and do not fit the stereotype of what was considered "Chinese" in midcentury America: Cantonese-speaking working-class restaurant workers in Chinatown. But the Chinese at the party also turn out not to be all that "real" either: the women wear "beehived" Western hair-dos, and the men have fake (gold) teeth. Everything is like the "bright embroidered satin, a kind of tinsel" (36)—not what it seems (not unlike the dreams of "Gold Mountain" and the American Dream).

In his interview with Rohrer, Yau speaks about not having been raised in a "traditional" Chinese American family:

> The furthest thing from it. Even though my parents spoke Chinese, they spoke a certain dialect, and they would point out that it was a dialect nobody else spoke in America, because they were from Shanghai and most Chinese in America at that time were from Canton. So of course they couldn't fit in. They thought of most Chinese in America as the country mice. And they were sophisticates from the city. They were interested in bringing me to concerts, and art. (187)

Here, we can see not only the opposition between lower-class Cantonese-speaking Chinese and more "sophisticated" Shanghainese-speaking Westernized Chinese—but also the isolation and negation of being the only Chinese family speaking a dialect of Chinese "nobody else spoke in America." (To speak a dialect no one else speaks, including one's "compatriots," in a foreign country is to be unheard, to be close to linguistic extinction, to almost not exist at all.) A certain opposition is also set up between Chineseness of an earthy "truer" sort and the artsiness of Yau's parents that is read as a dilution of "Chineseness." In "Toy Trucks," the speaker relates, "He had never asked his father if he felt like he were Chinese" (34). Note the use of the conditional ("if") and the subjunctive ("he were"). Chineseness is presented here as not something in the blood or "real" but something one either "feels like" or not.

"Chineseness" of a monolithic sort is also imposed upon "Oriental" immigrants and their children in the United States as they are forcefully and racially interpellated within American society. In "Toy Trucks and Fried Rice," the speaker's parents see themselves as differentiated from, and superior to, the Cantonese "farmers"; his mother explains that "[t]he differences were more than just that of language and economics, urban and rural. His mother reminded him that his grandfather was taller than anyone in this room, as were most people from Shanghai" (34). Yet, the speaker notes, "His mother, however, was only a little over five feet tall, and in this way was indistinguishable from most of the women in the room" (34). In this American society, in which whiteness is privileged, fine-grained differences of class, region, dialect, education, physical characteristics, taste, culture, which may be important in China, are negated: all these various Chinese immigrants, whatever their differences, become indistinguishable—looking "all alike" as Orientals, gooks, Chinks, Chinese. Thus, the pathos the reader feels in recognizing the futility of the mother's strenuous efforts to make these distinctions legible to her son.

Like Li-Young Lee's family, Yau's parents were scarred by the traumas of emigration and political turmoil in Asia, but unlike Lee, Yau does not—is unable to—romanticize his family (or memory). He recalls:

> My family was dysfunctional, traumatized by the Second World War and by having to emigrate to American [*sic*] in 1949, penniless and largely without friends. They had to start over, but they could not let go of the past, about which they were unrealistic. So I didn't believe in the family, but I also didn't believe in the "I"—particularly the "I" as victim.[61]

While Yau affects an unemotional tone here, the syntax of the first sentence conjunctively equates World War II and emigration to the United States as being equally traumatic (the typo is telling: "emigrat[ing] to American"—that is, becoming American—is equally distressing). Thus, the form of Yau's language undermines the usual ethnic narrative claims of Asian immigrants' finding freedom and safety in the "land of opportunity." And though Yau would recoil from the sort of Romantic poetic language Li-Young Lee uses in his poetry, both he and Lee speak about their parents' not being able to "let go of the past." Yau characterizes this inability as a failure to be "realistic" (in other words, they were not as pragmatic as the hard-bitten white American heroes of Yau's admired film noir or of countless Horatio Alger stories and American myths. Americans and American history are, of course, all about "letting go" of the past).

As in many of Yau's poems, the issue of the "I"—and of pronouns in general—figures importantly in "Toy Trucks."[62] While the piece has the seemingly conventional narrative style (autobiographical, mimetically descriptive) and theme (a remembrance of a childhood "ethnic" experience) of much ethnic writing, "Toy Trucks" refuses any easy access to family, nostalgia, Chinese culture, or memory. The second line reads, "It was, if anything, for their children." The antecedent for the "It" seems to be the "Chinese Benevolent Association's Annual Christmas Party," but the "if anything" suggests that there is no "real" there there (not that some "real" could exist).

What does come crashing into the poet's remembrance of this childhood scene is history, American history:

> There was another reason for not asking his father [if he felt like he were Chinese]. The one thing his father talked about, besides the war, was American history. Every week his father went to the public library and brought home old diaries, documents and studies about the American Indians, especially the Sioux, Apaches and Seminoles. They were the fighters his father told him. His father also told him the Indians were the only true Americans, and everyone else was a fake. (34)

Here, the father identifies Native Americans as the "fighters" and "the only true Americans," countering a hegemonic view of history in which Native Americans and other minorities are inferior, subordinated, and powerless. This claim undercuts the usual whitewashed notions of Anglo-Europeans' having an intrinsic claim to being "real" Americans.[63] Everyone was a "fake" American, including—or most especially—white Americans.

Though the father explicitly says that Native Americans alone are the "only true Americans"—thus excluding Asians, blacks, and other minorities in the "they"—it is clear that both the father and the speaker identify with Native Americans in the heroic third-person pronoun "they" (here, Yau détourns the vilified pronoun, usually invoked in jingoistic "us versus them" phrases) who are the only "fighters" and the only "true Americans." That said, the undecidability and ambiguity of whether Asian Americans are included or excluded from the "they" perfectly captures the ambivalent psychic identifications faced by many minority Americans who, as James Baldwin has described, wanted to identify with the cowboys against the Indians but then were made to know, with a shock, that they were neither seen as heroic cowboys nor included in the "we, Americans":

> It comes as a great shock around the age of 5, 6 or 7 to discover that the flag to which you have pledged allegiance, along with everybody else, has not pledged allegiance to you. It comes as a great shock to see Gary Cooper killing off the Indians and, although you are root-ing for Gary Cooper, that the Indians are you.[64]

Asian Americans, who are often read as "honorary whites" or not "real minorities" and as constitutively foreign and non- and un-American, cannot but have internalized modes of ambivalence—some shared with other minority children, as Baldwin details, and some particular to their being "Oriental."

While "Toy Trucks and Fried Rice" dismantles the notion of an authentic "Chineseness" and a "true" or "real" "Americanness," it does so with the nuanced recognition that the two terms of the title, toy trucks and fried rice—like the two parts of "Chinese Ameri-can"—cannot be made commensurate. Nor are they necessarily or completely binarily opposed for Chinese Americans. Neither of the two terms of the dyad is a "true" or "real" thing or essence. Just as a toy truck is a plastic representation of a generic "real truck" and Americanized fried rice a version of "real" Chinese fried rice, so nei-ther "Chinese" nor "American" names a "true" or "real" thing. They are placeholders—they conjure in American minds some "true" or "real" essences that do not exist.

But to deessentialize these terms is not to say that the category "Chinese American" does not exist in historical time and in the United States, nor it is to say that these signifiers do not have power-ful ideological charges and material effects. While there is not one designatable or stable "Chinese American" identity, there *is* the real-ity of what it means to grow up racially marked as "Asian" in the United States—in other words, as someone whose very subjectivity is structured by someone else's hegemonic ideas of what "Chinese" and

"American" are. As Bakhtin writes, "The ideological becoming of a human being . . . is the process of selectively assimilating the words of others"[65]—and, as the case may be, being assimilated by others.

Thus, while Yau is properly skeptical of the "I," he also cannot fully let it go because his very subjectivity as a poet is a function of history that cannot be wished away or made metaphorical or completely abstract—the very material and daily pressures of this history are felt too strongly—even as the poet pushes the limits of formal experimentation. As Yu points out, "[I]t's clear that Yau's shift of focus from the self to writing is not as radical as the Language poets' interest in 'language itself.' . . . 'Toy Trucks' also helps explain why simply bracketing 'history' or 'content,' as much Language poetry does, is not an option for Yau. . . . History is inescapable."[66]

In an interview with Eileen Tabios, Yau says his efforts to express his subjectivity in a manner that neither denied subjectivity nor rendered it solipsistic was influenced by reading certain poets, such as Ashbery, O'Hara, and Weiners, "who were gay but used an 'I' that's not necessarily gay."[67] While gay white male poets clearly retain privilege as white men, their sexual minoritization makes it difficult for them to occupy a poet's normative (heteronormative) speaking subject position (in confessional poetry, often an avowedly womanizing one—as with Robert Lowell and John Berryman).[68] It is clear that for minorities, whether racial or sexual, the option of simply erasing the "I" or trying to occupy an abstract universal subject position is not a viable option. Yau clearly wants to retain an "I" but not the normative one of what some call official verse culture.[69]

In *Broken Off by the Music* (1981), his sixth book, Yau's style becomes much more experimental. Many of the poems feel surreal. The middle section, "Late Night Movies," comprises his first series of punning letter- and word-substitution/combination poems begun in *Sometimes*; this four-poem series prefigures in theme and style his later Genghis Chan and "Hollywood Asians" series. *Broken Off by the Music* contains virtually no signs of ethnicity (only the title of one poem, "Shanghai Shenanigans"), leading one to conjecture that, at this stage in his career, there is an inverse correlation between formal experimentation and his ability to write about race or ethnicity (though, as I demonstrated in my reading of "Ten Songs," the influence of this racialized history makes itself felt at the level of form, even in those poems lacking overt ethnic "content").

At this historical moment of the nation and of the American poetry world—in the late 1970s and very early 1980s, before the canon wars and before "multiculturalism" came into vogue—the silent message seemed to be that joining the avant-garde poetry "camp," or any poetry camp, from which most minority poets were or felt excluded, precluded one from talking about ethnicity. One is reminded of Yau's recollection of his first becoming aware of the New York art world:

> I remember I started reading *Art in America*, *Artforum*, and *Art News* when I was in Boston University. And I remember thinking when I was young that I could never write for *Artforum* because I didn't understand what anybody said in that magazine. It seemed to be speaking to an incredibly intelligent audience, and I wasn't part of it.[70]

While it is true that many people feel excluded from the rarified New York art world, it is equally true that that world—like the avant-garde literary world—is overwhelmingly white (and largely upper-middle and upper class[71]). Indeed, what is unspoken but implied is that the very idea of the "avant-garde" or "great art" is coded as white, educated, and wealthy. These are coteries not likely to consider a son of Chinese immigrants for membership.

Yau's awareness of this exclusivity is made explicit when he repeatedly emphasizes Andy Warhol's outsider son-of-immigrants status in his book *In the Realm of Appearances: The Art of Andy Warhol*: "Whereas by the 1960s Wyeth's family was considered an American institution, and was celebrated in the press, Warhol's family were impoverished immigrants. His father was a coal miner and his mother a housewife; neither of them ever spoke English with ease."[72] Yau underscores Warhol's immigrant background and the fact that his parents never spoke English "with ease"—details that other art critics tend to gloss over—by contrasting the Warholas with that representative "all-American" family of artists, the Wyeths, whose popular illustrations (by N. C., the father) and their iconic painting of a wist-ful lost American (WASP) landscape and mood, *Christina's World* (by Andrew, the son), epitomize a wholesome (and whole) sense of social and artistic identity.

Even the language Yau uses to describe Warhol's art career directly partakes of the language of discourses of race and ethnicity:

> In each phase of his career Warhol was an assimilationist, some-one who did what he thought would get him accepted by those he believed were more successful or, if not that, more wealthy and more powerful than he. He was good at targeting his market. He was someone who couldn't forget that he was the son of immigrants and had to prove himself. This need was the job he never knew how to leave. (64)

> [H]e hated the fact that he was an outsider. (77)

> The language Warhol would in his lifetime master, the one his par-ents never learned to express, is one that tries to disguise its rage and obsequiousness. It is the language of someone who is desperate to belong. (126)

Here, Yau understands that fitting into the world of high culture necessitates that an outsider, racial and/or class-based, master a "language" in order to "assimilate." One feels the intensity of Yau's emotional identification with Warhol—the feelings of "rage and obsequiousness, the "hat[red]" of his outsider status, the "desperat[ion] to belong"—even as the Chinese American poet judges the Lemko (now Slovakian) Pop artist harshly: "The young-est son of a poor working-class family, Warhol desperately wanted to gain admittance to bourgeois society" (97). Yau seems to be sub-limating his own self-loathing about his racial outsiderliness into an indictment of Warhol's desperate class strivings. Both he and War-hol hungered to belong and make it in the art world. Thus, even in art criticism that reveals nothing overtly "ethnic" or autobiographi-cal, Yau's experiences and position as a racially marked subject make themselves felt, albeit indirectly.

Corpse and Mirror

Yau gained a measure of wider visibility in the poetry world when, in 1983, his *Corpse and Mirror* was chosen by John Ashbery as one of the National Poetry Series prizewinners and was published by Holt, Rinehart Winston. On the front of the book, a black-and-white reproduction of Jasper Johns's rather stark diptych painting *Corpse and Mirror*[73] fills the center of the mostly black cover; on the back, a photo of a black-clad Yau sitting next to a "primitive" African carved mask[74] appears beside a bio blurb informing the reader that Yau "presently lives in Manhattan . . . [and] his art reviews and essays have been published in *Art in America, Artforum, Artsmagazine* [*sic*], *Portfolio,* and *Vogue.*" He had arrived—or so it seemed. (Yau had followed in Ashbery's footsteps as an art critic. Johns was in fact one of the painters Warhol desperately envied for belonging to the "real" art world while Warhol himself toiled as a commercial illustrator.) Yau's *Corpse and Mirror,* a mixture of poetry and prose pieces, includes selections from three previous volumes (*The Reading of an Ever-Changing Tale, Notarikon,* and *Broken Off by the Music*) and shows Yau's talents to their advantage.

There is a maturity and haunting seriousness to the writing in *Corpse and Mirror*—images of death and disembodiment float above desolate de Chirico-like landscapes suspended in a surreal (and unreal) sense of time; the speaker is often figured as an outsider, solitary. *Corpse and Mirror* maintains a balance between pieces that address autobiography and questions of ethnicity directly and those that treat Yau's experiences as an Asian American subject in more transmuted form.

For example, in section 3 of the book, "Variations on Corpse and Mirror," "Missing Pages," a fablelike tale about a tourist island whose "jeweled towers" rise from the bay, ends with a local host explaining to the tourists how the legend of the towers comes about:

> Anyone can add whatever they like to the story, or take some chunk
> of it away, if, in their opinion, it impedes the narrative flow. At
> the beginning of summer (or the tourist season) the story, by then
> refined into its smoothest chapters, is written down by the mayor.
> A vote is taken by the council. If it passes approval, which it always

does after a few revisions are made, the story is sealed away in a
vault.

In the fall, when school begins, the children of the island are
taught the story in their classes. It becomes the basis for the entire
curriculum: literature, mathematics, even biology and the other
natural sciences. In this way the children learn what must be forgotten, if they are to continue sleeping in their whitewashed cottages by
the sea. (34)

The parable- or fable-like style of the writing suggests a "timeless"
ahistorical quality to what is being narrated. But, like the official history of Native Americans that the father tells his son about in "Toy
Trucks," this is the normative and normativized state-approved version "sealed away in a vault" and then taught to the children in their
classes, the hegemonic version that "becomes the basis for the entire
curriculum." Only by learning this story—made to seem smooth and
"natural" and inevitable by the enforced erasure or forgetting of the
earlier human-made and contingent prehistory of the story and by
eliminating chunks that might impede "the narrative flow"—can the
children "continue sleeping in their whitewashed cottages." "Whitewashed" echoes the implied description by the father in "Toy Trucks
and Fried Rice" of the official version of US history.

And while the prevailing opinion is that "[a]nyone can add whatever they like to the story," the open question remains: Who decides
when the story has been refined "into its smoothest chapters" and
who comprises the "council" that decides when "the story is [to be]
sealed away in a vault" (note the passive voice here, the voice of laws)?
In this faux democracy, votes are taken but it is clear that the story is
"always" passed by the council.

Throughout these two paragraphs, the frequently used indefinite
pronoun "it" seems to refer to the "story," but in the first sentence "it"
could refer back to the "chunk" that "impedes the narrative flow."
What is the "it" that "impedes the narrative flow"? A part of the story
or the whole of the story? What is "missing"? The end of "Missing
Pages" contains another ambiguous pronoun, "what." The lack of
clarity about the antecedent of "what" and the juxtaposition of the
conditional phrase "if they are to continue sleeping in their white-

washed cottages" right after the word "forgotten" result in variant, possibly contradictory, readings of the ending.

The normal reading of the syntax suggests that, in order to keep sleeping peacefully in their "whitewashed" (one might read assimilated, Americanized) homes, the children learn "what must be forgotten"—that is, they must eventually forget the official version they have learned. Here, the "modal auxiliary "must" gives a sense of both certainty and obligation (and though not an imperative, lends an imperative feeling). Again, who is the authorizing power that dictates what "must be forgotten"? The phrase also implies a temporal future (they have learned the story, but in the future they will have to forget it). This reading equates the "what" with the official story that the children have learned—the "basis for the entire curriculum"—but it is an interpretation that perhaps calls into question my earlier reading that what must be forgotten are the missing bits of the official "whitewashed" story.

A second interpretation would be that what the children learn is not so much or not only the story but the necessity (or process?) of historical erasure: the story that they are learning embodies within itself "what must be forgotten" (for example, that Indians were heroic). In this reading, "what must be" refers to the past, not the future—what has already been erased (the "missing pages"). This version accords with the idea that in order to continue sleeping in a false state of peacefulness, the children must learn the state-approved story in which all the bits that are not smooth have necessarily been whittled away or excluded. This is the version of history one gets in most classrooms—the one Yau's father rails against.

But how can children learn "what must be forgotten" if it has already been forgotten?

There is a third reading: the phrase "what must be forgotten" might signal a change in voice, a shift in tonal register from the rest of the sentence—more specifically, an authorial intrusion. This second voice is an example of what Bakhtin calls, in "Discourse in the Novel," a "hybrid construction": "an utterance that belongs, by its grammatical (syntactic) and compositional markers, to a single speaker, but that actually contains mixed within it two utterances, two speech manners, two styles, two 'languages,' two semantic and axiological belief systems" (304). In this reading, the children must learn these (national) stories in order to continue sleeping in their whitewashed cottages, but, as the more prescient speaker reminds us—in a voice that ruptures the univocal fabric of the fable's language—it is crucial that these stories "be forgotten." Here, "must" can be read more as an (imperative) warning to those who might become sucked in and assimilated.

Thus, "Missing Pages" parodies myths of national history and democratic decision making, as well as "timeless" fables that purport to teach a lesson. Yau rips off the ideological mask to show that the bases of these legends are not founded in "dream[s] from heaven" but made by men "in daylight and desire" (33).

In the last two sections of *Corpse and Mirror* ("The Lost Colony" and "Carp and Goldfish"), markers of "Chineseness" become increasingly overt. In section 5, "The Lost Colony," three previously published poems—"Chinese Villanelle," "Three Poems for Li Shang-yin," and "Shanghai Shenanigans"—allude in their themes to classical Chinese poetry, but their tone is modern-American slangy (as suggested by "shenanigans"). Yau has left behind the imitations of Pound's Orientalized *Cathay* poems from his first book. Though there is nothing explicitly autobiographical in these poems, the appearance of an "I" in all three poems and the explicitly "Chinese" poem titles hint that he has left the "racially unmarked" and "timeless" world of "Missing Pages."

Indeed, in section 6 of *Corpse and Mirror*, titled "Carp and Gold-fish," Yau takes up once more the topic of his parents and his childhood—begun in "Electric Drills" and "Toy Trucks and Fried Rice" (*Sleepless Night*)—in "Two Kinds of Story-Telling," "After the War (I)," "After the War (II)," "After the War (III)," "After the War (IV)," "Two Kinds of Language," and "Carp and Goldfish." Perhaps it is not coincidental that these pieces show some of Yau's most powerful writing during the first half of his career—it is as if, freed from the ahistorical, somewhat abstracted atmosphere of the volume's other poems, he is finally able not only to talk more freely about history, both personal and national, but also to begin to question head-on the official stories one is told.

Yau explains how he came to write the poem "Carp and Goldfish," whose title he "heard in [his] head as a pun on 'Corpse and Mirror'":

> [T]his pun encouraged me to think of a way out of the "Corpse and Mirror" poems, because I didn't like the time in those poems, the mythical time—it seemed too removed or remote to be actual. And I had this memory of something that happened to me as a child that I . . . [original ellipses] was trying to figure out a way to write about, and I kept circling it. . . . And so one thing led to another, and I thought, could I make a diptych out of this piece of prose? Could I get an echo going back and forth between two narratives? . . . I didn't want to focus on one event but to bounce it off something else without diminishing it. . . . Maybe I was reacting against, you know, having grown up and having read Robert Lowell and disliking the subjective excesses of his work. So the question became, how do you use autobiography?[75]

Yau returns to this question of how to keep the "I" but "shift it to a different plane."[76] To turn to the autobiographical is not, in Yau's case, to turn confessional or even personal; it is a turn toward history (the "actual"), not away from it. The privilege of writing self-indulgently about one's personal problems (as Lowell does, Yau implies) assumes that one's own experience is interesting or generalizable in some way—a "universal" privilege denied to writers of color in this country. But completely erasing the subject (and the subjectivity) that exists in history is not an option. Thus, Yau struggles in *Corpse and Mirror* and in much of his poetry to find a way to deal with his own history (and that of other "others") as it intersects with larger social and political histories, without either resorting to prescribed autobiographical (narrative) modes or completely eliminating the "I."

Yau's concern with the autobiographical in *Corpse and Mirror*, published in 1983, coincides with, and may have been influenced by, a similar turn in the career of Jasper Johns. In *The United States of Jasper Johns*, Yau writes about Johns's *Racing Thoughts* paintings of 1983 and 1984:

> Since Johns has spent much of his career deliberately refusing to make any overt autobiographical references, the changes he made

in the early 1980s must be regarded as significant. . . . However, the subject was the artist's life rather than personal memories. After all, memory, as Johns' *Flag* made clear, is not to be trusted; it interferes with one's experience of reality. (103)

One usually thinks of the substance of a life as being synonymous with personal memories. Yau implies here that a life is separate from, and much more than, what is personal and subjective—a life has its own reality separate from one's experience of it. As we saw in "Toy Trucks and Fried Rice," Yau uses materials from his own life without turning them simply into "personal memories": at no point does he attempt to retroactively interpret or comment sentimentally on these childhood incidents. Like his hero Johns, who "knew that he could not succumb to the power of memory and personal associations, that he had to be as rigorous in his examination of his thoughts as he was of the flag" (*USJJ*, 90), Yau refuses nostalgia; like Johns, he, too, must "ensure that any reference to the past is connected to the present. . . . Otherwise the paintings will seem nostalgic in their intent" (107).[77] Nostalgia can operate on both the personal and national levels (the flag, of course, is the ultimate symbol of a nation-state). Yau must be as "rigorous" in his examination of national myths and narratives as Johns is in his examination of the "stars and stripes," which the painter reduces to another painterly surface, a flat pictorial representation.

Yau's description of the work of Johns could aptly be applied to his own: "Johns makes a sculpture that is neither an expression of the 'I' nor a pure work of art."[78] In "Between the Forest and Its Trees," Yau asks, "Might not this I be a false mirror?" (38). Mirrors are a recurrent image in Yau's work—but his mirrors do not reflect clearly and straightforwardly; they distort and refract the subject in much the same way that language does.

The diptych, the form of Johns's *Corpse and Mirror*, provides a means to "get an echo going back and forth," to refract between different versions of the "I" and between different versions of a "story." Unlike a heterosexual white male poet, such as Robert Lowell, who can occupy the position of the supposedly "racially unmarked" "universal," Yau and Johns, as racially and sexually minoritized others, have been forced to call into question univocal and normative narratives and myths. Their "I" has never not been refracted, doubled, falsely mirrored.

Yau uses the diptych form in four of the twelve poems in the last section of *Corpse and Mirror*. "Carp and Goldfish," the last poem in the book, is comprised of two counterpointed sections. The first tells a fablelike story of a five-year-old prince in old China, who watches the carp in a garden pond while the narrator presages the fall of the kingdom: the prince eventually gets sick, the fish are forgotten ("[i]n the pond, the carp are still listening, unable to hear their names drift over the kingdom"), the "countryside succumbs to disease and terror," and "[s]ucceeding reigns of tyrants" bury the pond (84). The tone of the piece sounds vaguely mythical, like the tone of a fairy tale or a parable, and vaguely "Chinese" in its references to "clouds [that] turn into dragons," the "moon trembl[ing] against the sky," and "mulberry branches." The first three sentences give an idea of this flavor:

> Some fish we peel back, leaving only the bones. Others devour us, leaving only the stories. This one begins in a garden in China, where a young prince is sitting alone on a bench beside a turquoise pond. (84)

As in some of Yau's earlier poems, there is a vague, undecidable quality to the pronouns: "some," "[o]thers," "[t]his one." Again, questions are raised: What are the antecedents of these pronouns? "Some fish"—which ones? Does "[o]thers" refer to other fish or to other people? Are the "[o]thers" different from the "[s]ome"? Does "[t]his one" refer to a fish or to a story or both? The first half of "Carp and Goldfish" ends:

> Succeeding reigns of tyrants—their names twisting through history like snakes—bury the pond beneath their own interpretation of heaven's grandeur. Meanwhile, the carp burrow into a book by someone whose ability to remember facts circumscribes his desire to tell stories. (84).

As in "Missing Pages," the poet seems concerned with names, stories, history, "facts." The tyrants bury the pond beneath their "own interpretation[s]." Does the pond represent "reality" or history? Is the

pond similar to what "must be forgotten"? What do the fish represent? They both "devour us" so that our bones are left as stories and
are devoured by us. Who is included in the "we" and "us" and "our"?
The fish are also the forgotten ones buried by "[s]ucceeding reigns of
tyrants" "unable to hear their names" (whose names?). Are these fish
the same as the carp that "burrow into a book by someone whose
ability to remember facts circumscribes his desire to tell stories" (note
the double meaning of "stories": tales and lies)? Who is the "someone"
(again, a pronoun with an unclear antecedent)? What is the relation
between the snakelike names that "twist through history" and the carp
that "burrow into a book"?

The second half of the diptych is set in modern times, in the United
States, presumably: a young boy decides, while his father sleeps nearby,
to make his new goldfish feel "comfortable in their new home" (85).
Remembering "the way the ocean rocked endlessly the day his parents
took him to the beach" (85), the boy places the fishbowl on the back
of his toy dump truck, sloshes the truck back and forth to mimic the
waves of the ocean, and finally decides to add salt to their bowl, to
make the water seem more like seawater. It is this final act, of course,
that kills them. Yau does not narrate the goldfish's death but strongly
implies it. "Carp and Goldfish" ends:

> One teaspoon, a little more rocking, and they would soon be asleep.
> His arm was tired, but he continued to push the truck back and forth
> in the darkened room. He knew he could not stop until they were
> resting, comfortable in their new home. (85)

"Home," of course, is ironic. Though the boy means well, he sends the
fish to their final home, their death. Because he liked the ocean, he
assumes the goldfish will like the ocean. But goldfish (and carp) are
freshwater fish.

The history of goldfish is relevant here: they are native to China,
where they were first domesticated centuries ago from the wild form,
a carplike fish, more than a thousand years ago.[79] Thus, the carp and
the goldfish in the two halves of the diptych are related (biologically,
homologically, and symbolically—both figure as symbols of prosperity
in Chinese culture), but, with the passage of time and dissimilar envi-

ronments, they have become differentiated (in this case, miniaturized, made ornamental).

Unlike the boy prince in China in the first half of "Carp and Gold-fish," the modern-day boy in the second half is racially "unmarked": Does he represent Yau as a boy (is this an autobiographical memory, as Yau suggests in his interview with Foster: "I had this memory of something that happened to me as a child") or someone else? If the boy is Chinese American, how is he related to the Chinese boy prince? Both boys end up not treating their fish well but for very different reasons: the prince because he has fallen sick and neglects them, the modern-day boy because he actively kills them (though he does not mean to).

Or is the boy not Chinese American (or a very assimilated Chinese American) who kills the "Chinese" fish? Some lines suggest this interpretation:

> To the young boy standing in front of the large glass tanks . . . all
> the goldfish looked more or less the same. It was only after he stared
> into one tank for a long time that he saw any difference among them.
> (84–85)

> He lay on his stomach on the floor and stared intently at the fish. Back
> and forth they swam, unconcerned with their intruder. They looked as
> if the only thought on their minds was escape. It was difficult to name
> creatures so alien and indifferent, and he had not been able to find any
> that he liked. (85)

The view of the Chinese fish as "look[ing] more or less the same" echoes the "all Asians look alike" attitude of many Americans, as does the characterization of the fish as being "so alien." Like the two halves of Johns's *Corpse and Mirror*, the two halves of "Carp and Goldfish" are versions of each another—similar but not identical.

How are the two halves of "Carp and Goldfish" related? What are they saying to each other? Is the modern-day boy "related" to the Chinese boy prince in the same way that the goldfish is a distant kin of the Chinese carp? But if the boy is Chinese American, what is Yau saying by depicting him ("their intruder") as murderously imposing his will—what he thinks they will like or want—on the "Chinese" fish? I think that clues lie in the diptych form, which allows the two stories both to echo and to comment upon each other.

One would do well to look again at Johns's *Corpse and Mirror*. Some viewers might read Johns's diptych as follows: the left side constitutes a "good" or "true" representation, and the right side an inferior or "debased" one (because revised, draftlike, smudged). But to read the painting in this way is not to look carefully, to allow assumptions and customary habits about visual representation and what is a "real" (or "pure") or "good" art object and what is a "fake" (or sullied) or "bad" one.

If we make this distinction between the two halves of Johns's diptych, the painting itself—and Johns's title—brings us up short. If the title is *Corpse and Mirror*, why is the undefaced left side of the painting aligned with the "corpse" of the title (not exactly one's idea of something pure and good)? And what does it mean for the left half to be a "real" or "true" representation of something abstract? There is nothing mimetically depicted here. Indeed, the cross-hatched black marks look like magnified, slightly disturbing, brushstrokes. All there is is representation.

Then one begins to realize that, in highlighting the "made-ness" of the painting by means of these magnified brushstrokes, Johns has made the left-hand side echo the right-hand side: both reveal the process that goes into the making of the paintings. The right half makes glaringly apparent the materiality of both a "finished" painting (what the left side supposedly depicts) and the act of painting. The hand of the painter is evident everywhere in the right half: the crossings out, erasures, smudges reveal what could be tentative first attempts, later revisions, intentional erasures, unintentional smudging, and/or damage. The "mirror" half brings out the materiality of the painting process and the artwork itself—in the smudged paint, the "burn mark" of a household iron, and so forth. Thus, Johns brings the world of abstract visual representation and the material world of history together and deconstructs the idea of a good or finished or pure art form versus a bad or incomplete or debased one.

In other words, to see beyond an initial impression of the painting and the usual assumptions about what a piece of visual art is or must be, one needs to look much more closely, beyond the "theme" of the painting—admittedly, easier to do with a piece of abstract visual art than with written representation, which uses the means of everyday communication—and really *see* what the concrete formal particularities of the painting do and say.

Likewise, with Yau's "Carp and Goldfish," one must look beyond a superficial reading of both Yau's writing and one's usual assumptions about what is "Chinese" and what is "American." It would be easy to read the second half of the piece as simply a largely identical mirror of the first (little boy, fish, fish die) or a binary opposite (poor Chinese prince cannot save his fish because he is sick; cruel little American boy kills his) or a "debased" version (boy prince in China is the "real" Chinese and the little boy in the United States a "fake" version: Chinese American).

As with the Johns painting, the diptych form is used not to structure the two halves as simply mirror reflections or "good" or "bad" versions of each other. Thus, just as the right-hand side of Johns's *Corpse and Mirror* shows the process of making and the materiality of the painting—the painting's place in history—so Yau's second half depicts a Chinese American boy who himself bears the marks of history. He is neither "purely" Chinese nor "purely" American—as if these things existed—nor is he a sullied or secondary version of a "real" Chinese boy.

The boy is himself American and has been formed by (and also internalized) the racial logics of this country. Whether one views the goldfish as standing in for what is Chinese—goldfish are originally from China—or Chinese American—the goldfish may be descended from Chinese carp but have changed over time, and the ones in the story are living in the United States—what is clear is that the boy imposes upon the fish a logic of who he thinks they are (saltwater fish, which they are not) and his own idea of what their "home" is (the ocean). He sees them with the same American eyes: as "alien" and as "look[ing] more or less the same" (not unlike the judgment of the Chinese American boy about the Chinese people at the Christmas party in "Toy Trucks and Fried Rice").[80]

This murderous logic of home ("go back where you came from") and not truly seeing what Others are echo a dominant and prevailing American view of what "we" think "those" Chinese and Chinese Americans are: alien, nondifferentiable, non-American, tied to some putative "home" (China), yet not really a "real" Chinese (like the carp in the palace pond, the boy prince in China). A Chinese American can no more "go back" to someone else's idea of his home (China) than the goldfish can live in the ocean. For Chinese Americans, as for the "domesticated" goldfish, this notion of return is "both an impossibility and a repressive illusion."[81] One reason the boy is able to arrogate to himself the task of doing what is best for the fish is that he distances himself from them, viewing them as utterly "alien and indifferent" ("he had not been able to find any that he liked").

Nor is someone else's idea of how they should acclimate to their "new home" benign when it is forcibly imposed. Even though meant to be benevolent, the boy's efforts to make the goldfish feel "at home"—to assimilate them to their fishbowl and then put them on the back of an American toy truck—necessitate his imposing his vision of what he thinks they like, based on what he himself likes, in an act of (mis) identification that not only does not acknowledge or respect the fully dimensional singularity and *being* of the fish but kills them. "You have your labels, their falsifying categories, but I have words. I—the I writes—will not be spoken for," says Yau.[82]

Thus, to make the claim, as Weinberger and Perloff do, that Yau is not "Chinese" or "really Chinese" or a "real Chinese" or a "real" minority is, I would argue, to arrogate to themselves the knowledge and the power to decide who is "Chinese" or a "real" minority or a "real" poet and who is not—and to be blind to that power (and privilege). Both Weinberger and Perloff reveal assumptions and habits of thinking that are strictly structured by binaries that oppose avant-garde writing and minority writing, what is "political" and what is not, and what is poetry and what is not. The paradox is that while Weinberger decries the idea of evaluating minority poets based on their "police-blotter profiles," he does exactly that. Not only does he racially profile the poets but he racially profiles the poetry: minority poetry is only that poetry that openly manifests its "minority" features, whether by phenotypic (thematic) markers or by customary political stances ("of blackness," "Asianness," etc.).

Thus, like the boy in "Carp and Goldfish" who takes it upon himself to decide what the Other (fish) is or likes, Weinberger grants himself the authority to designate who is a minority (or not) and what minority poetry is (or not), who is "race-baiting," and who belongs in an "innovative" poetry anthology—with much the same unquestioned privilege and cultural arrogance Pound and Eliot manifested when they took it upon themselves to decide what was "Chinese poetry," actual Chinese poets be damned.

White critics of the avant-garde, such as Weinberger, Perloff, and Al Filreis (who, in commenting on the controversy, writes "Yau doesn't have a political bone in his body"[83])—get to speak for and categorize Others and their poetry. These otherwise quite nuanced critics of poetry are not so innovative or "outsiderish" when it comes to race and poetry—their assumptions are actually quite conventional: "innovative" ("avant-garde" and "experimental") poetry is not racially marked (with the rare exception of the occasional African American "exceptional exception"; it is certainly not Asian American), and ethnicity is evinced in content, not form. For Perloff and Weinberger, race or ethnicity inheres in visible markers or themes—for Perloff, Yau's name, Chinese features, or something "Chinese" in his post–New York School poetry; for Weinberger, ethnic or minority themes in Yau's poetry and/or some sort of overt political identification. "New York School" or "innovative" or "experimental" poetry—these categories necessarily exclude racialized writing. This idea of what "minority" or "ethnic" poetry is is as narrow as a "police-blotter profile": and based on a similar sort of racial profiling.

As I have tried to show in my readings of poems in Yau's early and midcareer, even those poems and passages "unmarked" by explicit (autobiographical) references to ethnicity and self manifest the effect of Yau's history and subject position as a Chinese American poet. Unlike Weinberger, who, from his unacknowledged position of privilege, can uncritically declare, "I believe that, in this society, all poets are Others,"[84] Yau understands firsthand, as a racialized American poet, that "language offers no refuge from time. . . . It does not enable one to transcend one's circumstances."[85]

SIX

Genghis Chan

Parodying Private Eye

At the end of his *Corpse and Mirror*, in another two-part prose poem, "Two Kinds of Language," John Yau depicts a scene of a father and son driving on the back roads of North Carolina:

> The radio was on, a yellow eye blinking inside the car's concave shell. An electric heart. Neither of them spoke, as song after song filled the car. . . . All the songs seemed to tell a similar story, and yet the words and music never quite seemed to fit together. (82)

In his short story "The Sons of Chan," Frank Chin captures the power of the radio—what Yau calls "an electric heart"—as the protagonist, the Chinese American actor who plays Charlie Chan's son, recalls radio shows and hit songs from his childhood:

> The electricity of a thousand old radio shows loud with the voices of dead stars shuddered in my antenna bone from pole to pole, like ancestors, put my blood and me on like clothing, kept me company. . . .
> *A fiery horse with the speed of light, a cloud of dust and a hearty HI YO SILVER. I know many things for I walk by night. I have seen the men and women who have dared step into the shadows. Listen!. . . [original ellipsis] while traveling in the Orient I learned the mysterious power to cloud men's minds.*[1] (original italics)

> My flesh throbs from the beat of every radio show I'd ever heard inside out pole to pole blasting again. (157)

Even now I seem a creature out of an old hit tune. (161)

Like Frank Chin, Yau, who is ten years younger, recognizes the power of American popular culture, in its promulgation of "Oriental" characters such as Charlie Chan, to create not only a Frankenstein-like Asian American subjectivity but also Asian American masculinity and sexuality (note the phallic imagery of "shuddered in my antenna bone from pole to pole," "flesh throb[bing]"). The radio parts and the Asian American male's "equipment" have become conflated, man and machine, human and inhuman, a cobbled-together creature made from American popular culture. The "yellow eye" of the radio fuses the "yellow" listener and the "electricity of a thousand old radio shows" that "put my blood and me on like clothing."

At the same time, this Asian American subjectivity created by radio and television is inseparably linked by contrast to—and as the implicit antithesis of—a "normal" (white, heterosexual) "all-American" subjectivity—whether mundane (as in pop songs) or heroic (the Lone Ranger[2]).

Yau's passionate interest in old Hollywood movies—the silent films of Anna May Wong, yellowface movies (including Charlie Chan), horror movies (in which the monsters are played by many of the same actors who did yellowface), film noir—intersects with questions about what it means to be spoken for (and spoken by) others and the nature of subjectivity, with its splits and gaps. To explore these questions, Yau, in his poetry, uses various formal, rather than primarily thematic, means—and, arguably, no form more effectively than parody.

For Yau, parodic language not only provides a linguistic means by which to face and critique the many selves that he, as a particular Asian American poet, has internalized as a result of the normative discourses that attempt to write him (such as the stereotypical images of "Orientals" generated by Hollywood) but also serves as a rhetorical strategy—indeed, a weapon (not unlike Chin's use of irony)—which gives him agency to actively undermine these dominant racial and literary discourses. Like metaphor and irony, parody in its very structure and ideological pointedness reenacts and resists the assimilationist pressures that exert great force upon an Asian American poet/subject.

A Chinese American poet born in Lynn, Massachusetts, in 1950—the first year of the Korean War, five years after atomic bombs were dropped on Japan, and less than a year after the "loss" of China to Communism—would need whatever rhetorical weapons he had at his disposal as he entered the New York City poetry and art worlds, cultural realms hardly known for their racial diversity, then or now.

In this chapter, I examine Yau's use of parody, with particular attention to his series of forty-four "Genghis Chan: Private Eye" poems, spanning five books of poetry: *Radiant Silhouette* (1989), *Edificio Sayonara* (1992), *Forbidden Entries* (1996), *Borrowed Love Poems* (2002), and *Further Adventures in Monochrome* (2012).[3] While parody as a style or genre[4]—Linda Hutcheon calls it "probably a genre, rather than technique" in her 1985 book *A Theory of Parody: The Teachings of Twentieth-Century Forms*[5]—functions prominently in Yau's poetic oeuvre (with the possible exception of his first book, *Crossing Canal Street*), its use is most intensely sustained in the Genghis Chan poems. By means of a dry parodic wit, Yau expresses through the figure of Genghis Chan—more explicitly than in other poems in his oeuvre—the rage of an Asian American racialized male subject and poet.

Parody is not simply a formal style or genre but has "a hermeneutic function with both cultural and even ideological implications," writes Hutcheon in *A Theory of Parody* (2). In the most recent (2012) edition of *The Princeton Encyclopedia of Poetry and Poetics*, Hutcheon and Malcolm Woodland, who co-wrote the entry "Parody," call it "a form of . . . intertextuality" and also "a doubled structure" (1002). Parody infuses Yau's poetry and fiction in multiple ways and on multiple levels. Its deployment is one of the rhetorical strategies he uses as a means both to aggressively rewrite dominant representations of Asian Americans and to negotiate his own vexed attraction-repulsion to an "Asian American identity" and identification. Like irony, parody formally enables the simultaneous expression of various voices and subjectivities (angry, playful, witty, bitter, self-loathing, politically incisive, and so on). It reflects these multiple and contradictory internal voices and enacts what Bakhtin calls a "battle between two voices"[6]—that of the parodist and the parodied—and works as both a defensive strategy and an offensive weapon (not unlike Marilyn Chin's use of irony).

At the same time, parody, by definition, is "dependent" on the discourses it targets—thus, its structure captures effectively, and in effect, the sense of self-hatred and internalization of dominant racial/ sexual representations that Asian American and other minoritized subjects experience in American society, even as they may consciously try to resist them and subject them to détournement.

The hybrid conqueror/detective figure[7] of Genghis Chan was born out of popular Hollywood depictions of Asian men. Like Frank Chin and countless other Asian American boys,[8] Yau grew up in the shadow of the dual stereotypes of the shuffling asexual detective Charlie Chan and the marauding Asian invader on horse-back, Genghis Khan. Many critical discussions of parody assume a clearly identifiable "target" text or genre that is being parodied (for example, critics often refer to Cervantes's parody of romance tales in *Don Quixote*).[9] In the words of Margaret A. Rose: "[T]he work to be parodied is 'decoded' by the parodist and ordered again (or 'encoded') in a 'distorted' or changed form to another decoder, the reader of the parody."[10]

But what if parody's codes are multiple, intermixed, and difficult to "decode"? In Yau's work, these target discourses are not easily identifiable or locatable; they drift in the background, omnipresent, not as discrete texts but as something larger, more diffuse, and per-vasive—and, thus, like the criminals shadowed by Chan and other mystery novel detectives—more insidious. As Hutcheon points out in *A Theory of Parody*, "[P]arody always implicitly reinforces even as it ironically debunks"; "[p]arody is fundamentally double and divided" (xii, 26).

And what if, as with irony, readers do not "get" the parodic codes? Given the overwhelming power and ingrainedness of American racial representations and discourses, the degree to which any parodic text can effectually undermine or overthrow them remains an open question. Thus, parody is both a formal and a political issue. I will leave the question of parody's efficaciousness in intervening in and breaking the grip of target discourses open for now; nonetheless, Yau's poetry offers, I argue, examples of parodic writing and the deployment of parody that can contribute to and broaden critics' conceptions and discussions of parody.

Parody

In *Parody: Ancient, Modern, and Post-modern*, Margaret Rose defines parody "in general terms as *the comic refunctioning of preformed linguistic or artistic material*" (original italics; 52)[11]—with an emphasis on the comic aspect. In *A Theory of Parody*, Linda Hutcheon rightly critiques Rose for her "restrictive" emphasis on the "presence of comic effect" (20). Hutcheon defines parody more broadly as "repetition with difference" (32)—more specifically, "a form of repetition with ironic critical distance" (xii) or "imitation with critical ironic distance, whose irony can cut both ways" (37). Simon Dentith, too, goes for an even broader definition: "Parody includes any cultural practice which provides a relatively polemical allusive imitation of another cultural production or practice."[12]

The earliest found usage of the noun *parodia*, to which most lexicons relate our word for "parody," occurs in chapter 2 of the *Poetics* by Aristotle, who attributes its origins to the mock-epics of Hegemon (fifth century BC).[13] *Parodia* and the verb *parodeo* were applied by the "Aristophanic scholiasts and others to cover all sorts of comic quotation and textual re-arrangement."[14] "[I]t is clear," writes Dentith in *Parody*, "that ancient Greek culture was shot through with parodic forms" (40). The supreme parodist of antiquity may have been Aristophanes, who parodied dramatic tragedy for comic "meta-fictional" as well as satiric purposes in such "paratragedies" as his *Frogs* (405 BC).[15] Since antiquity, critics have debated whether the concept of parody embodies a comic function, a ridiculing function, or both.

One reason for the disagreement lies in the ambiguity of the prefix *para-*, which can be used to mean "like," "beside" and "opposite."[16] Rose argues that "[t]he majority of works to which words for parody are attached by the ancients, and which are still known to us in whole or in part, suggest that parody *was* understood as being humorous in the sense of producing effects characteristic of the comic, and that if aspects of ridicule or mockery were present these were additional to its other functions" (original emphasis; 25). Critics in the sixteenth century, says Rose, classified parody primarily as a form of ridicule; seventeenth-century theorists confused it with the burlesque. Likewise, modern and late-modern scholars, by ignoring the ancient roots and usages of the concept of parody (particularly the comic) have, she argues, misinterpreted parody, tending to dismiss it as a "lowly" form—that is, they have extended the "negative" (mis)understanding of parody as ridicule. Although postmodern theorists have revived interest in parody by praising its meta-fictional and intertextual aspects, Rose goes on to argue, they, too, misunderstand its background, functions, and structure and reduce it to "yet another meta-fictional or intertextual form" (113).[17] For Rose, parody is "*both* comic *and* 'double-coded'" (original emphasis; 242), not *either* comic *or* meta-fictional.

In a useful section of her book, "Distinguishing Parody from Related Forms," Rose shows how parody differs from burlesque, travesty, pastiche, satire, and irony, among others. For example: "In both its general and specific forms, parody, unlike forms of satire or burlesque which do not make their target a significant part of themselves, is ambivalently dependent upon the object of its criticism for its own reception. . . . Both by definition (through the meaning of its prefix 'para') and structurally (through the inclusion within its own structure of the work it parodies), most parody worthy of the name is ambivalent towards its target" (51). In *A Theory of Parody*, Hutcheon views irony as an "aspect" of parody and parody's "rhetorical miniature"; to her, both irony and parody are "form[s] of indirect as well as double-voiced discourse," and both are "intensely context- and discourse-dependent" (xi, xiv).

Rose makes the important point that "the popular definition of parody as the 'imitation of the forms of a work with a change to its content' is not very useful or meaningful" because "this [description] overlooks the fact that in some cases . . . the parody of a work may entail the changing, as well as the imitation, of both the 'form' and 'content,' or 'style' and 'subject-matter,' of the original" (43). It is difficult, she says, to "separate the imitation and changing of form from the imitation and changing of content" (43). And later: "[T]he ancient terms for parody were in general not defined, or used, on the basis of any hard and fast distinction between form and content" (64).

Rose also argues against narrow either-or definitions of parody: "Despite the fact that parodies may be *both* critical of *and* sympathetic to their 'targets,' many critics have continued to describe parody as being *only* critical, or *only* sympathetic, or playful, or agitatory, or engagé, or blasphemous, or ironic, or imitative, or counter-imitative, and so on. In addition to being a device which is able, because of its peculiar dual structure, to have an ambivalent, or ambiguous, relationship to its 'target,' parody is able to be used to demonstrate several of the above characteristics at once, if, or when, an author chooses" (original italics; 47). Despite this characterization, Rose's insistence throughout her book that the notion of the "comic" was inherent in the ancient concept of parody and is, thus, still fundamental to its present-day meaning has the effect of both limiting her discussion of parody and minimizing the extent to which parody, whether because of centuries of misunderstanding or not, has come to have more of a "bite" than she acknowledges. Throughout her book, Rose insists on a "positive" reading of parody and criticizes what she labels as "negative" views (that is, the view of parody as essentially "hostile" rather than comic).[18]

Such a Manichean distinction not only overshadows the potential ideological implications of parody—of course, parody itself can be used for a variety of different political ends, subversive and conservative—but also the question of how an audience receives an author's parodic efforts, especially when the writer and the reader come from different cultural contexts, as is often the case with minority writers, including Yau, and most of their readers. In other words, if parody is characterized as mainly comic, then Yau's parodies of pernicious racial stereotypes will tend to be read in the same light as "funny" ethnic jokes or other types of "ethnic" humor; after all, stereotypes are often kept in circulation by "comic" means—for example, Charlie

Chan's fortune cookie aphorisms[19]—and efforts to counter them are foreclosed with responses like "Can't you take a joke?" or "Stop being so sensitive—it's only a joke!"[20]

Unlike Rose, some other critics see parody's role primarily as subversive. The German critic Winfried Freund defines parody as "a literary instrument of ideological criticism. Parody destroys established ideologies, such as the heroic or fascistic, by searching them for symptomatic, verbally and structurally fixed constructs and tearing these structures down along with the ideologies manifested in them."[21] And film theorist Robert Stam writes, "By appropriating an existing discourse for its own ends, parody is especially well-suited to the needs of the powerless, precisely because it *assumes* the force of the dominant discourse only to deploy that force, through a kind of artistic jujitsu, *against* domination" (original emphasis).[22]

Mikhail Bakhtin on Parody

Although the most important theorist of parody, Mikhail Bakhtin, viewed parody as having played a crucial role in the history of the European novel—"One could even say that the most important novelistic models and novel-types arose precisely during this parodic destruction of preceding novelistic worlds."[23]—Donald Wesling is right to argue that "if we are careful to define our terms and our relation to what Bakhtin said, we can apply his most powerful ideas to poetic texts, to find them differently dialogic from the novel, but nonetheless dialogic."[24] I would go even further and argue that not only can Bakhtin's ideas on parody be fruitfully applied to poetry (with some caveats in mind) but, more specifically, John Yau's poetry can bring into more layered and nuanced relief the power of Bakhtin's ideas on parody. Hutcheon's call to "heed the teachings of art as well as criticism" is one I strongly second.[25]

That said, there are a few caveats to keep in mind when reading Yau's poetry in dialogue with Bakhtinian theory. First, there is no question that Bakhtin clearly privileges the novel over poetry as the site of heteroglossia and dialogism (indeed, he organizes his discussion of the history of parody as a narrative of progression that eventually finds full expression in the novel—not poetry). Second, the European novel's power to destroy preceding discourses differs quite markedly from Asian American literary texts' relative lack of power to dismantle, even when they are most bitingly parodying, American popular and literary discourses about Asian Americans.

Yau's poetry does, nonetheless, provide a compelling test case to disprove Bakhtin's assertions in "Discourse in the Novel" that "[t]he world of poetry, no matter how many contradictions and insoluble conflicts the poet develops within it, is always illumined by one unitary and indisputable discourse" and that "[t]he language of the poet is *his* language . . . that is, as a pure and direct expression of his own intention" (original emphasis; 286, 285). In "From the Prehistory of Novelistic Discourse," Bakhtin distinguishes between novelistic discourse, which he says is "always criticizing itself," and what he calls "all straightforward genres—the epic poem, the lyric and the drama (strictly conceived)" or "direct discourse" (49, 55):

> One who creates a direct word—whether epic, tragic or lyric—
> deals only with the subject whose praises he sings, or represents,
> or expresses, and he does so in his own language that is perceived
> as the sole and fully adequate tool for realizing the word's direct,
> objectivized meaning. This meaning and the objects and themes
> that compose it are inseparable from the straightforward language of
> the person who creates it: the objects and themes are born and grow
> to maturity in this language, and in the national myth and national
> tradition that permeate this language. (61)

It seems clear that this narrow description of poetry,[26] formulated at a particular moment in history in a specific European country, with a "national myth and a national tradition," cannot account for the poetic discourses of the late twentieth- and twenty-first-century United States, with its heterogeneous mix of cultures and languages, a reflection of an increasingly diasporic world. While the national myths of the United States hold a powerful lock on the majority of Americans—I acknowledge the coercive force of normativized national ideologies, say, of "freedom and "democracy"—this body politic is not homogeneous and unified, and different poets within the national body have radically different relationships to these myths. One could not generalize about the "straightforward language" of American poets in the twenty-first or twentieth century, especially not in the case of a minority American poet, whose parents spoke Chinese and English at home, who is imbricated in multiple discursive traditions, and for whom the English language (including American English) is not "his own." John Yau writes parodic poems that are anything but straightforward; they are multivoiced, dialogic, and heteroglossic—attributes that, for Bakhtin, privilege the novel.

In "Prehistory," Bakhtin, like Rose, begins his discussion of parody by examining its ancient uses, particularly the "fourth drama" or satyr play—"parodic-travestying counter-presentations of lofty national myths" (54), which the Greeks did not view as profanation or blasphemy but "an *indispensable* conclusion to the tragic trilogy" (original emphasis; 55): "any and every straightforward genre, any and every direct discourse—epic, tragic, lyric, philosophical—may and indeed must itself become the object of representation, the object of a parodic travestying 'mimicry'" (55). How did this mimicry function? Bakhtin explains:

> It is as if such mimicry rips the word away from its object, disunifies the two, shows that a given straightforward generic word—epic or tragic—is one-sided, bounded, incapable of exhausting the object; the process of parodying forces us to experience those sides of the object that are not otherwise included in a given genre or a given style. Parodic-travestying literature introduces . . . the corrective of reality that is always richer, more fundamental and most importantly *too contradictory and heteroglot* to be fit into a high and straightforward genre. (original emphasis; 55)

One can see why parody's subjunctive potential ("It is as if") to "[rip] the word away from its object" and its ability to reveal "those sides of the object that are not otherwise included in a given genre or a given style" would be compelling to an Asian American poet such as Yau, who feels that given discourses and literary traditions have not included his "reality that is always richer, more fundamental and most importantly *too contradictory and heteroglot* to be fit into a high and straightforward genre." For Bakhtin, "[i]t is precisely style that is the true hero of the [parodic-travestying] work" (51). In ancient Greece and ancient Rome, the different parodic forms were unified by both a common purpose—"to force men to experience beneath these categories a different and contradictory reality that is otherwise not captured in them"—and a shared subject: "language itself" (59). "On Hellenistic and Helleno-Roman soil," writes Bakhtin, "there became possible a maximal distance between the speaker (the creating artist) and his language, as well as a maximal distance between language itself and the world of themes and objects" (63).

Bakhtin's discussion of parody's importance during Roman times bears relevance, I argue, for a discussion of Asian American poets in the twentieth- and twenty-first-century United States:

> Roman literary consciousness was bilingual. . . . From start to finish, the creative literary consciousness of the Romans functioned against the background of the Greek language and Greek forms. From its very first steps, the Latin literary word viewed itself in the light of the Greek word, *through the eyes* of the Greek word; it was from the very beginning a word "with a sideways glance," a stylized word enclosing itself, as it were, in its own piously stylized quotation marks. (added emphasis; 61)

Obviously, one must be careful in drawing comparisons between the situations of current Asian American writers and those of ancient Roman writers. Most Asian American writers, while aurally exposed to another language, claim English as their first written language—certainly this is the case with Yau; he is not, by any means, bilingual. Asian Americans are also fully American, not foreign, despite continuing perceptions that they are not "truly" American.[27] Yet, like the Romans in their vexed (and productive) relationship to Greek language and culture, many Asian Americans, particularly writers, in the United States feel they are constantly being judged as inferior or derivative when compared to "native" (that is, white) speakers of English. Thus, the image of the "sideways glance" is incisively relevant.[28]

Bakhtin's observations about parody and the conditions in which it arose prove especially cogent for the work of Yau, who concerns himself with questioning language and what it means to be the one "looking," split off from the "I," an "'I' that is both object and subject, an 'I' seen in different profiles."[29] Bakhtin writes in "Prehistory,"

> Linguistic consciousness . . . constituted itself *outside* this direct word and outside all its graphic and expressive means of representation. A new mode developed for working creatively with language: the creating artist began to look at language from the outside, with another's eyes. . . . The creating consciousness stands, as it were, on the boundary line between languages and styles. (original emphasis; 60)

> The boundaries between semi-stylized and semiparodic discourse were very unstable: after all, one need only emphasize ever so slightly the conventionality in stylized discourse for it to take on a light overtone of parody or irony, a sense that words have "conditions attached to them": it is not, strictly speaking, *I* who speak; I, perhaps, would speak quite differently. (original emphasis; 65)

This last line ("it is not, strictly speaking, *I* who speak") might have been written by Yau, a Chinese American poet standing "on the boundary line between languages and styles" and acutely aware that words have "conditions attached to them."

During the Middle Ages, the struggle between the unifying discourse of Latin and national "folk" languages resulted in numerous parodies of Latin hymns, prayers, and grammar:

> The sacred Latin word was a foreign body that invaded the organism of the European languages. And throughout the Middle Ages, national languages, as organisms, repulsed this body. It was not, however, the repelling of a *thing*, but rather of a conceptualizing discourse that had made a home for itself in all the higher reaches of national ideological thought processes. (original emphasis; "Prehistory," 77)

This need to parody a dominant "conceptualizing discourse" has modern-day analogues in the efforts of marginalized writers to critique homogenizing national discourses and mainstream aesthetics—for example, avant-garde poets such as Language poets and Conceptual poets but also, or especially, minority writers, like Yau, who must resist not only these same national discourses and aesthetics but also the "conceptualizing discourse[s]" that ideologically bind and fix them along the axes of race (for example, by means of stereotypes). These hegemonic discourses originate at home (rather than abroad)—in "all the higher reaches of national ideological thought processes"—and are in the same language, and it is the "native-born" Asian American and other hyphenated Americans who are seen as the "foreign bod[ies]."

But, as with irony, how efficacious or subversive is parody if it is not recognized as parodic? In "Discourse in the Novel," Bakhtin reminds us that "[e]xcept in those cases where it is grossly apparent, the presence of parody is in general very difficult to identify . . . without knowing the background of alien discourse against which it is projected, that is, without knowing its second context. In world literature there are probably many works whose parodic nature have not even been suspected" (374). Parody's valences—its intent, targets, political thrust—in Yau's poetry prove especially difficult to characterize or pin down, because, as noted earlier, his poems lack the straightforwardness of the expected forms of minority political critique. Yau's work does not offer explicit polemical statements or easily decodable sarcasm or irony.

To turn the self into an object is to get some distance from and attempt to control one's subjectivity. Parody also works in this way—not only by ripping an object from the power of conceptualizing discourses but also by turning these languages into objects themselves, objects that can then be manipulated. Bakhtin writes in "Prehistory,"

> These parodic travestying forms . . . liberated the object from the power of language in which it had become entangled as if in a net; they destroyed the homogenizing power of myth over language; they freed consciousness from the power of the direct word, destroyed the thick walls that had imprisoned consciousness within its own discourse, within its own language. A distance arose between language and reality. (60)

To be a minority American—especially to be a minority American poet—is to almost always be made aware of the "distance" between language and reality. Asian American poets, who are constantly made acutely conscious that they are not (and will never be) native speakers or "real" minorities, often find themselves situated on the "boundary line" between discourses and languages, "look[ing] at language from the outside, with another's eyes" ("Prehistory," 60), a position that disempowers them but also possibly gives them a site from which to take shots at the "homogenizing power" of mainstream American myths and stereotypes, such as the powerful ones disseminated by Hollywood:

> As a living, socio-ideological concrete thing, as heteroglot opinion, language, for the individual consciousness, lies on the borderline between oneself and the other. The word in language is half someone else's. It becomes "one's own" only when the speaker populates it with his own intention, his own accent, when he appropriates the word, adapting it to his own semantic and expressive intention. Prior to this moment of appropriation, the word . . . exists in other people's mouths, in other people's contexts, serving other people's intentions: it is from there that one must take the word, and make it one's own. And not all words for just anyone submit equally easily to this appropriation, to this seizure and transformation into private property: many words stubbornly resist, others remain alien, sound foreign in the mouth of the one who appropriated them and who now speaks them; they cannot be assimilated into his context and fall out of it; it is as if they put themselves in quotation marks against the will of the speaker. . . . Expropriating it [language], forcing it to submit to one's own intentions and accents, is a difficult and complicated process. ("Discourse in the Novel," 293–94)

While Bakhtin acknowledges that "not all words for just anyone submit equally easily to this appropriation" and that this process is "difficult and complicated," his choice of words—"appropriation," "seizure," "private property," "assimilated," "expropriating"—indicates a model of discursive claiming that cannot adequately account for the personal or historical experience of Asian American subjects. Can the English language ever be made their "own" when it is they, not words, that are seen as constitutively "alien" and "foreign," and it is they, not words, that "cannot be assimilated" and that speak with ineradicable "accents"? It is Asian American poets themselves who are put "in quotation marks"—as English poets, as American poets, as avant-garde poets.

The power of Asian American writers' parodic efforts to "liberate" depictions of Asian Americans from homogenizing myths is more limited than what Bakhtin saw as the case for European novelistic discourse. One reason is that the novels Bakhtin describes had the power of the modern notion of *nation* behind them, while Asian Americans exist as relatively powerless minorities within a large nation-state that barely sees—indeed, devalues—them. In the case of modern European novels, the homogenizing myths they dismantled were seen as "alien" (for example, the Latin of the church or other transnational institutions), whereas Asian American writers have no recourse to depicting such American mainstream myths as alien because, as I have said, it is the Asian Americans themselves who are viewed as "alien" (and English assumed to be their foreign language), in need of assimilation, and because these very myths are what constitute "Americanness." Since the founding of the United States, what is "full-blooded American" has been defined against the alien (usually ethnic) Other: Native Americans, chattel slaves, and immigrants—notably, the "Asian threat" from without (as exemplified by the Chinese Exclusion Act, four wars with Asian countries) and within (Japanese American internment, antimiscegenation laws, zoning and employment laws, the murder of Vincent Chin, and countless more examples).

Genghis Chan, Private Eye/"I"

The figure of Genghis Chan embodies the conflation of two "Oriental" characters that figure in the American popular imaginary: Charlie Chan and Genghis Khan. As is so with other racial minorities, stereotypes of Asian Americans tend to be categorized along gender lines into two crude types: in the case of men, the "good," submissive Oriental (Charlie Chan, the houseboy) and the "evil" Oriental, represented by the barbaric invader (Genghis Khan) or the sinisterly devious despot (Fu Manchu) or a combination of the two (Ming the Merciless).[30] Whether "good" or "evil," all Orientals are viewed as equally "inscrutable."

Like his detective namesake, Yau's Genghis Chan works as a private eye. Through the Genghis Chan poems, Yau parodies numerous discourses that have written both himself and other Chinese (Asian) Americans: the mainstream media's racist/Orientalist rendering of "Orientals," the rhetoric of detective novels and film noir, ridiculing renditions of the "broken English" of early Chinese immigrants, clichéd homespun American maxims, and Orientalized poetic forms (most notably the haiku). Many of these discourses are themselves parasitic; for example, the character of Charlie Chan—created by the Ohioan novelist Earl Derr Biggers, based on an actual Chinese American detective in Honolulu and portrayed by three different white actors in forty-seven Hollywood films[31]—constitutes a grotesque caricature, intended or not, of "Oriental" behavior.

Biggers created the character of Charlie Chan after vacationing in Hawaii, where he read about a Chinese American detective in Honolulu named Chang Apana. Chan makes his first cinematic appearance in 1926, played by an Asian American actor, George Kuwa, in a small role in *House Without a Key*, but not until 1931, when Charlie Chan gets his own movie and is played by Warner Oland in yellowface (Sidney Toler takes over the role in 1938), does he really take off as a cinematic phenomenon, becoming permanently ingrained in the American psyche. The last Charlie Chan movie was released in 1949, not coincidentally the year that the United States "lost" China, and, in the American political imaginary, the little Asian "buddy" and World War II ally turned into a Red Communist threat.

Also noncoincidental was the casting of Eastern European actors who had been primarily known for their horror-film roles—Bela Lugosi, Boris Karloff, Lon Chaney, Peter Lorre—as "Orientals" in Charlie Chan and other early Hollywood films depicting Asians (such as *Shadows* [1922], *The Mask of Fu Manchu* [1932], *Shadow of Chinatown* [1936], and *Mr. Wong, Detective* [1938]).[32] Many of these actors relied on regular gigs playing these characters (Peter Lorre as Mr. Moto, for one) to make a living; at the same time, Asian American actors' careers and personal lives often ended tragically as a result of Hollywood's demeaning and exploitative use of them (for example, Anna May Wong).[33] Whether evil or "good," these Oriental characters always spoke broken English and were viewed as unredeemably alien. They were parodies themselves of some "Oriental" essence and culture: "I come from a China no Chinese from China comes from," says the Chinese American narrator who plays Charlie Chan's son in Frank Chin's story "Sons of Chan" (154). In Hollywood, Asian culture and customs were made ridiculous, sinister, and always inhuman. Needless to say, Asian Americans were never depicted as "regular Americans"—or as Americans at all, even if their roots in the United States went back to the mid-nineteenth century, as was not uncommon in California (Anna May Wong, born in 1905 in Los Angeles, was herself a third-generation American).[34]

Since Hollywood characterizations were the only widely disseminated depictions of Asians available to Asian Americans growing up in the United States, it is not an understatement to say that their sense of identity, ethnic and American and ethnic American, were formed to a great extent by these distorted mirrors-on-screen. As the narrator in Chin's "Sons of Chan" puts it, "God kicked Earl Derr Biggers in the head and commanded him to give us Chinamans [*sic*] a son, in almost His image. And Charlie Chan was born. And, in a sense, so was I. . . . I had a white man for a father" (132). ("Father" signifies a family patriarch but also God, the logos, the Word.) Yau told me during an interview that when he was around seven, his parents left him at the movies to watch double features instead of getting a babysitter; thus, in a real sense, he, too, was formed by the movies.

In contrast to the aphorism-spouting, effeminate, and subservient Charlie Chan—"led by a white man, speak[ing] with a broken tongue, and . . . docile and polite to a fault"[35]—another detective figure was emerging in American film: that of the (white) tough-guy private eye in film noir, inspired by the detective fiction of such writers as Raymond Chandler and Dashiell Hammett. This character was a taciturn, masculine loner, played in the movies by actors such as Humphrey Bogart and Robert Mitchum (one of Yau's favorites and whose laconic manner Yau's somewhat resembles). It is these two traditions—Orientalist/racist Hollywood depictions of the "Chinese," and the tough-guy American genres of detective fiction and film noir—that coalesce in the figure of Genghis Chan (whose first name evokes yellow-peril fantasies of invading, marauding "Asiatics"). The absurd conflation of Genghis Chan and Charlie Chan signals obvious parodic intent to the reader—or should.

The first seven poems in the "Genghis Chan: Private Eye" (hereafter, "GC") series appear in *Radiant Silhouette: New and Selected Work: 1974–1988*. What is being parodied in these poems is not so much discrete, specific, and localized "target texts" but amorphous and omnipresent popular discourses. In some cases, Yau parodies what are themselves already parodies (that is, parodies of "Asian" mannerisms and speech). The all-pervasiveness and diffuseness of these discourses make it difficult for the Asian American poet to fight them.

Parody provides one means of bringing close (or closer) these overweening ideologies, which manifest themselves in language, in an attempt to deconstruct and disarm them. In his genealogical account of the novel in "Prehistory," Bakhtin focuses on two factors—"one . . . *laughter*, the other *polyglossia*"—in the prehistory of novelistic discourse (original italics; 50). Laughter, as a root of parody, is important not just for its comic elements but also for its subversive ones, as Bakhtin delineates in his essay "Epic and Novel: Toward a Methodology for the Study of the Novel":

> It is precisely laughter that . . . in general destroys any hierarchical (distancing and valorized) distance. . . . Laughter has the remarkable power of making an object come up close, of drawing it into a zone of crude contact where one can finger it familiarly on all sides, turn it upside down, inside out, peer at it from above and below, break open its external shell, look into its center, doubt it, take it apart, dismember it, lay it bare and expose it, examine it freely and experiment with it. Laughter demolishes fear and piety before an object, before a world, . . . thus clearing the ground for an absolutely free investigation of it.[36]

Parody provides the "zone of crude contact" by literally *internalizing* the words of the dominant discourses in much the same way that minority Americans have internalized mainstream myths, stereotypes, and ideologies. Bakhtin explains that the first step toward liberating "one's own discourse and one's own voice . . . from the authority of the other's discourse" is first to assimilate that other discourse so that it is "tightly interwoven with 'one's own word,'" to "experience it physically as an object."[37]

Despite parody's potential power to bring a dominant discourse close so as to undermine it, Bakhtin's choice of the word "assimilate," as mentioned earlier, underscores the inadequacy of this model for Asian American writers. As subjects who are themselves assimilated by engulfing social, political, and cultural systems, Asian American poets such as Yau may attempt to "shadow" their enemy—the offending discourse—as a detective shadows the criminal, but ultimately, it is very difficult for them to clear the ground for "an absolutely free investigation of it" and to escape what David Lloyd calls the "dissymmetry of the specular relation." In speaking of the oppositional discourses generated by intellectuals who were formed under colonial state apparatuses, Lloyd writes that these intellectuals are "in the first place subjected to rather than the subjects of assimilation."[38] As for ethnic minorities,

> In the absence of any practicable recourse to territorial nationhood, being minority is defined specifically in becoming a citizen of the state and in strict, even logical, opposition to "being ethnic." . . . To adhere to what is called an ethnic culture is to refuse the cultural formation of the citizen; to be formed as a citizen is to undertake the impossible task of negating one's given ethnicity.[39]

Thus, no matter how parodic and subversive an ethnically Chinese detective can be, he must still choose between being "Chinese" or being a citizen. Indeed, two major problems with Bakhtin's discussion of the move from the internally persuasive word to "one's own discourse and one's own voice" in "Discourse in the Novel" is his assumption of the ease of this shift and his assumption that these "authoritative discourses" are ultimately quite benign and malleable: "A few changes in orientation and the internally persuasive word easily becomes an object of representation" (347). Bakhtin ignores both the power and the resistance of negative discourses, such as racial ste reotypes, to changes in orientation. As the character in Chin's "Sons of Chan" puts it, "I'd never spoken anything but the sacred words of somebody's spiritual ritual to you, never gotten out of the motion of somebody's magic plot" (160).

That Yau is aware of the fragmentation and contingent tenuousness of Chinese American subjectivity is signaled by his first description of Genghis Chan, who makes his inaugural appearance in this manner:

> I was floating through a cross section
> with my dusty wine glass, when she entered,
> a shivering bundle of shredded starlight. ("GC I")

This opening, with the jaded tough-guy rhetoric and appearance of a mysterious woman, clearly parodies classic detective mystery and film noir conventions. But there is something clearly incorporeal or disembodied about the main speaker ("floating through a cross section") and his perception of the woman ("bundle of shredded starlight"). Indeed, throughout this first group of Genghis Chan poems, words connoting fragmentation abound:

> . . . I'm nothing more
> than riffraff splendor drifting past the runway. ("GC I")

> She laughed,
> a slashed melody of small shrugs. ("GC I")

> I am just another particle cloud gliding across the screen ("GC VI")

Much of the language used to describe the male speaker's body—"floating," "nothing more / than riffraff splendor," "just another particle cloud"—would usually be used to depict women in noir films, not the tough-guy protagonists. One gets a material (phonic) instantiation of the gender reversals here in the line "I was floating through a cross section": one hears "cross sex" in "cross section."

The insubstantiality of the narrator's self and male body is underscored by the disconcertingly shredded "sh-," "shr-," "st-,"

"-ff," "spl-," and "scr-" sounds, which are intercut with the slicing (castrating?) "-ss," "sec-" and "sl-" syllables. The speaker's self
is blurred, shredded, and slashed into particles; the fragmented
quality is conveyed by these material phonemes and sounds. Yau
has spoken of his interest in the materiality of words and paint—
the "needlepoint basicness" of his word- and letter-switching
exercises. Here, language is manipulated in a manner not unlike
that in which paint is manipulated by visual artists ("I got that
thought from painters"): "And so I thought, why not just use
words as physical things in some way, literally cut them up and
play around with them?"[40] In his essay "The Phoenix of the Self,"
Yau writes about "paint's capacities to 'embody' . . . anxieties and
strictures."[41] Earlier in the essay, he commented on the project of
"speculative self-portrait":

> The struggle to locate a process of personal integration and rehabili-
> tation (of mind and body) in the context of an equally problematic
> rupture, that of the terrifying split/fragmentation of human experi-
> ence (the social body), is the implicit project of the speculative self-
> portrait. (147)

What better represents the "terrifying split/fragmentation of human
experience (the social body)" than the experience of watching movies that tell you one "truth" about yourself while knowing that
there is another truth or reality that has not been acknowledged by
mainstream culture—a reality that is "always richer . . . and . . . *too
contradictory and heteroglot* to be fit into a . . . straightforward
genre" (original emphasis)? "Our ideological development is," writes
Bakhtin, "an intense struggle within us for hegemony among various verbal and ideological points of view, approaches, directions and
values."[42]

Instead of a teleological development that results in a "winning"
assimilationist discourse, Genghis Chan's ideological formation
remains fragmented and frustrated. Instead of an affirming "hybridity," his hybridization is, to use David Lloyd's formulation, "an
unevenness of incorporation within a developmental structure rather
than an oscillation between or among identities."[43]

Genghis Chan perfectly embodies various types of "splits": between two types of "Oriental" stereotypes, the effeminate Charlie Chan and hyperaggressive Genghis Khan, one deferential, the other brutal; and between the more Americanized detective and the "Asiatic Hun" version. In Chin's "Sons of Chan," the narrator, a Chinese American actor who goes on his own mystery search, characterizes himself in this way:

> My other self comes alive secreted in back alleys and dark doorways. . . . A genius of violence and intrigue by night, and a meek Chinese-American actor playing Charlie Chan's comic lovably asshole son by day. (138)

In Yau's fictional piece "Hawaiian Cowboys," the narrator recounts reading a detective novel in which "[a]ll the detectives are thin, scarred loners moving silently through the maze of a terrified city" (*Hawaiian Cowboys*, 90). Yau has spoken of his "junk addiction" to detective novels with their loner figures.[44] He is most interested in the detective who is "marginalized whether by his moral stance or by his race" and is drawn to the "bleak visions" of film noir in which "you can't escape your past and there's no hope for the future" (personal conversation).

Both Chin's fictional son of Chan and Yau's Genghis Chan symbolize the split consciousness most hyphenated (slashed) Americans experience every day: the "I" as subject and object. The surrealism of this internal world becomes projected onto the surreal external world, the netherworld of a typical film noir detective—a world that for Genghis Chan, is culturally and racially marked. Words such as "slashed" and "yellow" do not operate neutrally.[45] Images of sexual impotence and the inability to speak—and their interconnectedness—pervade the first seven poems. These images cannot be read separately from stereotypes of Asian Americans in general and Asian American men in particular:

> A foul lump started making promises in my voice. ("GC I")

> I looked down,
> more slender

than I expected ("GC II")

I am the owner of one pockmarked tongue ("GC VI")

The speaker becomes a disgusting object (a "foul lump"), the possessor of a deformed and scarred ("pockmarked") tongue. Both his verbal and sexual appendages are impotent ("more slender / than I expected"). In these various poems, the "girl" is a white woman whom Genghis Chan wants to impress and seduce but cannot:[46]

Rusted pundit, throttled chin

I was turned by a tendril adrift,
pale freckled skin . . .
. . . .
Hours of sigh practice loomed ahead ("GC IV")

            She was
wearing white under white
gray blond curls dropped back ("GC II")

I wanted to tell you
about the bank teller and the giant,
the red moths hovering above their heads

I wanted to tell you
about the gizmo pit and kinds of sludge
I have catalogued during my investigation

I wanted to tell you
about how the sun
dissolved all of this long ago

leaving us in different rooms

registered under different names ("GC III")

Again, Genghis Chan's inability to seduce ("Hours of sigh practice loomed ahead") is linked to his inability to speak ("[r]usted pundit, throttled chin"). One could argue that his pursuit of the white woman ("pale freckled skin") parallels and is inextricably linked to the poet's pursuit of language—and the reader's search for the meaning of words in these poems. The sense that words are themselves as mysterious and desirable as the "shredded starlight" of the woman in the first poem is revealed in Yau's remark to Edward Foster:

> And poetry became this thing that I kept getting more deeply involved with—you know, you're alone in your room and you're writing, and you have this tiny *glimmer* that you might be able to shape words into a language, and therefore possibly communicate, at least to yourself, if not to anyone else, something that makes experience, your experience, understandable to you.[47] (added emphasis)

The anaphoric repetition of "I wanted to tell you" in "GC III" suggests frustration, incompletion, and, ultimately, impotence in Genghis Chan's attempts to approach the white woman, in his efforts to communicate with the "you" (who could be the woman and/or the reader), and in the poet's efforts to articulate meaning. Here, neither the detective nor the poet wins the girl. They are left "in different rooms / registered under different names" (a phrase that evokes the specter of earlier antimiscegenation laws). It is poetry itself, rather than the unattainable white woman, that proves to be the more loyal "mistress," as Yau implies in his statement to Foster that "poetry became this thing that I kept getting more deeply involved with."

In the seventh Genghis Chan poem (quoted in its entirety), this sense of impotence and ineffectualness is reiterated when the narrator must repeatedly tell himself—with the anaphoric repetition of "You will"—what to do:

> You will remember the tourist's jawbone
> and the end of the erotic age
>
> You will remember how to number
> the customized stones of Spartan psychoanalysis
>
> You will be nice to yourself and regret it
> You will undress in front of a window overlooking a prison
>
> You will speak to the driver of a blue horse
> You will grasp someone's tongue with your teeth and pull

You will prefer the one that bleeds on the carpet
to the one that drools on your sleeve

Several points about this passage can be noted: the use of the pronoun "you" to address the self (as we have seen, Yau also frequently
uses "he" instead of "I" to speak of the self) reemphasizes the self's
standing outside itself, the sense of the self as other. Here, the self
admonishes itself almost masochistically. The use of various pronouns blurs the boundaries between different speakers, thus emphasizing the interpenetration of multiple voices in parodic discourse.
Yau continues with depictions of the speaker's sexual impotence ("end
of the erotic age"). The masochistic "You will be nice to yourself and
regret it" and "You will undress in front of a window overlooking a
prison" feminize the speaker and slightly amp up a feeling of hysteria.
In the first Genghis Chan poem, the "I" says in lines 9–10, "I always
keep a supply of lamprey lipstick around, / just in case."[48] The desire
to master and possess the white woman's tongue finds extreme and
violent expression in "You will grasp someone's tongue with your
teeth and pull"—as if "Genghis Chan" could rip English from her
mouth and capture or swallow (internalize) it.

It is important to note that "GC VII," like the entire Genghis
Chan series, formally enacts the logic of parody, repetition with
difference, and punctures the myth of "originality," poetic or historical (for example, that "real Americans" are Pilgrims and their
descendants). Poets and citizens are all written by various preexist-
ing discourses:

> Indeed, any concrete discourse (utterance) finds the object at which
> it was directed already as it were overlain with qualifications, open
> to dispute, charged with value, already enveloped in an obscuring
> mist—or, on the contrary, by the "light" of alien words that have
> already been spoken about it. It is entangled, shot through with
> shared thoughts, points of view, alien value judgments and accents.
> The word, directed toward its object, enters a dialogically agitated
> and tension-filled environment of alien words, value judgments and
> accents, weaves in and out of complex interrelationships, merges
> with some, recoils from others, intersects with yet a third group:
> and all this may crucially shape discourse, may leave a trace in all

its semantic layers, may complicate its expression, and influence its entire stylistic profile.[49]

Again, what Bakhtin says here holds a particular historical and paradoxical resonance when thinking about Asian American writing. What is "homegrown" ("real American") and what is "alien" are clearly racially delineated in American discourses and ideologies. For Asian Americans, who are not seen as "real" or "original" Americans, their English is always constitutively seen as "shot through with . . . alien value judgments and accents." But in fact it is US history and American English that have always been "overlain with qualifications, open to dispute, charged with value, already enveloped in an obscuring mist" and always already "entangled, shot through with shared thoughts, points of view, alien value judgments and accents."

The myth of the "primacy" of white settlers (which necessitates the erasing of Indian genocide from history) has an analogue in the art world: the privileging of "originality" as one of the criteria often used to judge minority artists as derivative or imitative of great white artists—for example, Wifredo Lam in relation to Picasso, a framing Yau has strongly criticized in "Please Wait by the Coatroom: Wifredo Lam in the Museum of Modern Art,"[50] among other essays. The idea of originality remains powerful today, a legacy of a Romantic aesthetic that privileges "genius" and individuality.

The very form of parody embodies a deconstruction and critique of the idea of originality, especially the idea that artistic creations spring fully formed from the mind or imagination of the poet, straight from the Muses, as if there were no human or worldly context for this language. Parody involves acknowledging that

> [a]s a result of the work done by all these stratifying forces in language, there are no "neutral" words and forms—words and forms that can belong to "no one"; language has been completely taken over, shot through with intentions and accents. . . . All words have the "taste" of a profession, a genre, a tendency, a party, a particular work, a particular person, a generation, an age group, the day and hour. Each word tastes of the context and contexts in which it has

lived its socially charged life; all words and forms are populated by intentions. Contextual overtones (generic, tendentious, individualistic) are inevitable in the word.[51]

Yau has written approvingly that Jasper Johns "is not an inventive artist but a transformative one; he recontextualizes pre-existing images and articles" (*USJJ*, 72). Priscilla Wald characterizes Yau in this way: "'Revisionary' more accurately describes Yau's sensibility."[52] In his poetry, Yau is interested in the idea of series poems (an idea he borrowed from Jack Spicer), a form that is predicated on repetition with a difference, both continuity and change. Many of the images in Yau's poetry are themselves "versions" of a more "real" or bodily form: dream, corpse, mirror, shadow.

Parody works precisely as an altered version of an original text, as does caricature, which Yau describes as "deriv[ing] its power, of course, from the ways in which it emphasizes the norm by deviating from it." For Yau, the most powerful self-portraiture works by quotation: "For at the close of the 20th century, self-portraiture's goal, when imaginatively striven for, is not in clinging to the illusion of perfect self, but in exploring as both subject and subjected that which commodity culture is rapidly transforming into object."[53] That parody may signal an impulse to counter commodity culture is echoed by Hutcheon when she writes, "[I]t is likely that the Romantic rejection of parodic forms as parasitic reflected a growing capitalist ethic that made literature into a commodity to be owned by an individual."[54]

The next series of Genghis Chan poems, numbers VIII to XX, appears in *Edificio Sayonara* (1992). This group of poems differs in some respects from the earlier seven poems. As a whole they are more formally "experimental," often employing two-line stanzas that contain semantically confusing words or switched letters. There is a sense of things being "off" in most of the pieces. At the same time, some familiar themes recur: the inability to speak ("my mouth glued to my lips," "clumped tongues") or act ("Now I am clamped to the desk"; "I too am a yellow lamp / bolted to the elephant sky"). Markers of ethnicity become increasingly overt, as evidenced by the repetition of the word "yellow," phrases such as "slanted legs," and poems such as number XIII:

> It's hard to keep pretending
> you're a dusty chink
> in a hall of yellow linen
>
> You begin believing
> you're just another handkerchief
> wiping away the laundresses' tears

Of course, it is possible, as many critics prove, to read these poems without acknowledging the historical and ethnic resonances of terms such as "chink," "yellow," and "laundresses." One could talk about postmodern play and indecipherability or the lack of a self this poem seems to suggest ("you're just another handkerchief"). As Yau puts it in writing of the Whitney Biennial,

> It is easier and more comforting to discuss style than to address subject matter. . . . Either do what you are told or do it in a way we will accept because it conforms to our standards, and maybe, just maybe, we will acknowledge you. . . . Remember: The shock of style is one thing but the shock of subject matter is a very different thing.[55]

Perhaps that explains why many white experimental poets and poetry critics, while embracing Yau's style, tend to ignore discussing poems such as those in the Genghis Chan series.

Again, ideas about style are tied to the Romantic belief in the power of originality, a criterion that has often been wielded to denigrate minority artists as "derivative" or "secondary." In "Please Wait by the Coatroom," Yau makes this critique of the Museum of Modern Art's curators William S. Rubin's and Evan Maurer's decision to characterize Wifredo Lam's paintings as imitative of Surrealist art, such as Picasso's, and to place one of his paintings by the coatroom:

> Consequently, they believe that subject matter, which might be defined as the translation of the hybrid ingredients of consciousness into visual evidence, is of little importance, since the aesthetic tradition of Western art can only be renewed when an individual makes a

formal breakthrough. They [Rubin and Maurer] both define and use the sign of "originality" to determine their judgments. (59)

This description could be made of the attitude of avant-garde poetry critics toward minority poets such as Yau by simply substituting "linguistic" for "visual" and "poetry" for "art." For critics whose main focus is on formal "innovation" (invariably of a High Modernist sort), subject matter is dismissed and even the transmutation of "the hybrid ingredients of consciousness" into linguistic "evidence"—the subject matter of this book—is ignored, or simply not seen.

For example, a critic who can and does do perceptive formal readings of Yau's poetry but completely glosses over important cultural and ethnic markers is Charles Altieri. Here is the full text of "GC XIX," a poem in *Edificio Sayonara*, which Altieri explicates:

My stamped mother
used to fling to me

All stones lead to home
Go easy on the turtle pie

Gored down
at doom temperature

Cast a cold
and dirty style

On every yellow
leaf of lassitude

glistening beneath
the grappled fly

My stamped mother
used to fling me

and I
her lump of muck

would fling back
all the riveted bones

I could dandle
on my wasted plea

the chink of meat
we knew that linked us

to the junk
going by

In his essay "Images of Form and Images of Content in Contemporary Asian American Poetry," in which his reading of the Yau poem appears, Altieri's goal is to show how Yau's formally sophisticated poems can be contrasted with the "usual" clumsy ethnic autobiographical poem Altieri posits as their opposite. He describes "GC XIX" as "mak[ing] sharp contrasts with the family poems so common in the dominant testimonial mode" (83). Altieri reads the poem as centering on "how extreme are the emotions that the mother-son relationship can produce":

> Correspondingly, dealing with those emotions requires of poetry a deconstructive impulse that lets several layers of meaning cross, without imposing too much coherence, and above all without the illusion that somehow narrative memory could contain and order all the things it casts up. . . . For this poem, then, coming to terms with parents is a matter for modernist experiment, not for received forms that only confirm whatever "stamp" one has put on experience. (84)

Though Altieri does catch the "Chinese boat" connotation of "junk," he does so only to suggest that "poetry can be the Chinese junk boat capable of navigating all that detritus" (84). He concludes by saying that "the poem forms a single picture of the hostility between child and mother. . . . [A]ll this hostility may only be part of the junk that characterizes many parent-child relations" (85).

Here is an example of a fine poetry critic who, in effect, reduces Yau's poem to three "exemplars": (1) an experimental poet's deconstruction of narrative illusions; (2) an expression of an antisentimental and antinostalgic "good" Asian American poem that "makes sharp contrasts" with "bad" Asian American poems—that is, "family poems so common in the dominant testimonial mode";

and (3) a psychological commentary on the universal problematic-
ity of parent-child (mother-son) relationships. But none of these
accounts does justice to the layered meanings (and emotion) of the
poem's language, language that reflects the "hybrid ingredients of
consciousness"[56] that can never be delinked from the effects of history—the "terrifying split/fragmentation of human experience (the
social body)."[57]

For example, in the first line, the word "stamped" to describe the
speaker's mother connotes passport stamps, the stamping of "human
cargo" that has been inspected and crosses borders (a play on the
"chink of meat" that appears later and a reference to "inspection stations" at immigration ports of entry), and the frustrated or enraged
(stamping feet) or damaged/marked nature of the mother. "[U]sed
to fling me" is a distorted version of the common representation
of maternal love—"used to sing to me"—with the obvious violent
implications, which become amped up later in the poem (the mother
"fling[s] me").

"All stones lead to home" could be read as the poetic speaker's
puncturing of sentimental American beliefs about home—a parodying of the "folksy" (white) American homespun maxims and homi-
lies, such as "All roads lead home," "home sweet home," "there's no
place like home"; for nonwhite immigrants (and citizens), of course,
the sense of the United States as a cozy home is foreclosed to them.
The slightly clunky addition of the preposition "to" signals perhaps
that the speaker is not a "native speaker." The substitution of "stones"
for "roads" punctures the clichéd myths of the American Dream and
upward mobility—the cold hard reality of its illusory roads paved
with gold, its "paths of opportunity," and "roads to freedom."

Another reading of "All stones lead to home" is that the poetic
speaker is capturing his mother's misspeaking in English of the proverb "All roads lead home." Mishearing, misrecognition, and misstatement often characterize the nonnative speaker's relationship to
English. Or perhaps it is the speaker himself who has misheard and
mistranslated the mother's speaking of a Chinese saying. Or could
he also be mocking the traditional Chinese emphasis on "home,"
whether familial or the home country?

These multiple possibilities and voices—the speaker's parodic voice, the speaker's rendering of the mother's misstatement in English, the speaker's mistranslation of the mother's Chinese—are operating at once, in Bakhtinian fashion, in this line. What is clear is that the easy clichéd notion of home, whether American or Chinese, has been deconstructed and rendered into a disturbing, rather than comforting, "proverb."

Likewise, the lines following read as parodies of other types of American discourse: the folksy language of cookbooks ("Gored down / at doom temperature," "turtle pie") and sentimental song lyrics ("to the junk / going by" conjures up "as time goes by"). The invocation of the mother in the first line elicits the expectation of another ethnic "family" poem ("family poems so common in the dominant testimonial mode"), leading the reader to believe that what follows will be nostalgic remembrance—"my mother used to sing to me"—not the disturbing images of violence ("fling," "[g]ored," "riveted bones"), coldness (stones, "a cold . . . style"), disgust ("dirty," "muck"), and hopelessness "("doom," "wasted plea"). This home is no Joy Luck Club. Instead of all roads leading home, one gets only cold hard stones.

"Cast a cold / and dirty style / On every yellow / leaf of lassitude" is an imperative—the speaker's command to himself or to the reader? It could also be read as the poet's distancing look at himself—a rather self-hating judgment. The "I" is split into both subject and object (a "yellow / leaf" and, later, "the chink of meat"). Style here is not heroic as in Bakhtin's depiction of parodic style but "cold / and dirty." "[D]irty" and the "lump of muck" in stanza 8 capture the speaker's sense of self-disgust and mimic denigrating stereotypes of Chinese hygiene habits.

"[L]ump of muck" also echoes the "foul lump" in "GC I" and thus linguistically links the feeling of self-hatred to the speaker's linguistic and sexual impotence: his inability to speak (or speak "proper" English)—heard also in "wasted plea"—and his inability to win over the white woman object of his desire in "GC I" ("foul lump" also her judgment of him) or his mother ("I / her lump of muck"—Oedipal undertones).

The unpleasant monosyllabic sounds of "lump of muck" are often employed by Yau in the Genghis Chan poems—for example, in the lines "Duck walk / talk muck" in the later "GC XXV." These plopping sounds can be read as both the Chinese American speaker's uncomfortable relationship to the Chinese language he does not know (especially Cantonese)[58] and the poet's parodying of the racist renderings by Hollywood and American popular culture of "Chinese" and chop-suey English. One also hears midcentury Chinese American restaurant menu lingo ("sub gum wonton," "moo goo gai pan," "pu pu platter").

"[L]ump of muck" well captures the sense of the speaker's self-hatred of his mucky Chineseness and the shame of always being seen as speaking "ching chong" Chinese and subpar (broken) English. It is the "chink of meat"—hated Chineseness?—that "linked us," mother and son, to the "junk / going by." "[J]unk" here could signify, variously, the racist "crap" of American culture, the detritus of the immigrants' life in America, disappearing Chinese culture, the messy passing of time, and so on.

One could also read "chink of meat" as the Chinese American male speaker himself, who "dandle[s] / on my wasted plea" as an appositive. The "chink of meat" also connects to the "yellow / leaf of lassitude": both images of a small (and flaccid) "Asian" phallus "glistening beneath / the grappled fly." Genghis Chan himself, like the "grappled fly" (with its dual meaning of insect and male crotch), is often depicted in the poems as pinned to a wall (or a desk).

Thus, one can see that in "GC XIX," the social and the linguistic and the sexual are all linked—as they have always been, of course, in the American imaginary. History has "stamped" each of us. In Yau's case, the psychic and linguistic effects of migration, forms and processes of racialized interpellation, have left particular historicized marks on the poet's relationship to his mother, which in turn will, in various direct and indirect (and conscious and unconscious) ways, leave their "stamp" on the poetic speaker's relationship to his mother in "GC XIX"—marks that are not necessarily manifested in content. Any good reader of poetry (of all poetry, not just minority poetry) must take the "hybrid ingredients of consciousness," individual and social, into account.

What is patently clear is that the mother-son relationship in the poem is far from a "universal" or generic one. With his language, Yau highlights the conflicting and vexed feelings the speaker holds toward the mother (as was also evident in Yau's "Toy Trucks and Fried Rice" story); what he does not present is, as my readings have made clear, a "*single* picture of the hostility between child and mother" (added emphasis).

To read this poem in the light of the social context of the poet is not to *reduce* the poem to a flat, homogenous, or univocal "identity"-based reading or dreary social critique but to demonstrate how layered, multiple, and heterogeneous the voices and connotations are in this poem. Its parodying is not done in a gloomy manner. Margaret Rose points out in *Parody* that "[o]ne of the virtues of parody, besides its wit, is its mastery of cliché and convention" (243). One effect of Yau's parodying of quintessentially Middle American ways of speaking is that by tweaking a few words, he is able to show, in a darkly humorous manner, the banality and falsity at the heart of these seemingly commonsensical and normative homespun wisdoms. While American culture has often mocked the aphoristic style of Chinese philosophy by turning it into ridiculous "Confucius say . . ." and fortune cookie rhetoric, Yau here shows how easily he can turn "all-American" sayings into the same sort of gibberish.

One can see in Yau's parodying the idea that Bakhtin had articulated in "Prehistory" of "style . . . [a]s the true hero" of a parodying work or of parodic discourse (51). To détourn or parody a hegemonic (or any) discourse is to wrest agency from the tyrannizing criterion of style as "original"—an originality always already foreclosed to those who are constitutively seen as nonnative, secondary, alien.

"Another's sacred word, uttered in a foreign language, is degraded . . . and congeals to the point where it becomes a ridiculous image," writes Bakhtin in "Prehistory" (77). This type of parodying can be taken to its logical ends, as in Rabelais's work, where, says Bakhtin in "Discourse in the Novel," "a parodic attitude toward almost all forms of ideological discourse . . . was intensified to the point where it became a parody of the very act of conceptualizing anything in language . . . presuming that all language is conventional and false" (309). But this idea of parody's encompassing all language can erase the cultural and historical specificities motivating particular parodic acts (as we have seen with Altieri's almost completely ahistorical reading of "GC XIX") and, by doing so, foreclose more textured readings that would take social and historical context into account in the poem's *language*.

A major danger of parody is precisely that it is always dependent on the target texts it mocks. "Writing thus re-presents, as it mimics, cultural representation. . . . Yau expresses his concern with the dilemma of representation—how to keep mimicry from becoming recapitulation," writes Wald in discussing Yau's work.[59] This danger is highlighted by "GC XXIV" in the third series of Genghis Chan poems (*Forbidden Entries*, 1996):

Grab some
Grub sum

Sub gum
machine stun

Treat pork
pig feet

On floor
all fours

Train cow
chow lane

Dice played
trade spice

Makes fist
first steps

Here (and in many of the more recent Genghis Chan poems), Yau seems to be parodying the racist Hollywood rendering of "Chinese," the chop-suey broken English of countless movies, and perhaps of early Chinese settlers and Chinese American restaurant menus —for example, "sub gum wonton." One also hears ominous undertones of (American) war and violence—"Sub gum / machine stun" (submachine guns) and "On floor / all fours"—and the dictates of capitalism, not to mention the realities of the American Dream for immigrants: "Grab some / Grub sum."

This poem brings up several potentially problematic issues: First, to what extent will an audience unfamiliar with the parodic targets understand that this is a parody and not a faithful reproduction of "Chinese" English? One could think of Maxine Hong Kingston's idealistic attempts to reclaim the derogatory term "Chinamen" by separating the word into two (China Men), thus giving these men their humanity back—a subtlety that I doubt is picked up by most readers, even sophisticated ones in big cities. Second, is Yau himself not running the danger of seeming to indulge in racial mockery? There is a fine line between this parodying of "Chinese" sounds and the "ching-chong Chinaman" taunts of schoolchildren—thus, words like "Jap" and "Chinaman" can quickly be made to seem "all right" when put in the mouth of a "native informant" (as with Yunte Huang's spouting of Charlie Chan aphorisms). Not unrelatedly, Yau might be running the danger of recapitulating those prejudices voiced by his mother toward "lower-class" and working-class Cantonese and their loud and "crude" speech. As we see in "Toy Trucks and Fried Rice," the speaker's mother's Shanghainese snobbishness toward these Cantonese, who made up the majority of early (pre-1965) immigration to the United States, is both cultural and linguistic. Third, how many readers will catch the political resonances in lines such as "Sub gum / machine stun" and think of, say, the Vietnam War, the Korean War, and the various other wars in Asia and that other "Orient," the Middle East?

Finally, and perhaps most seriously, this type of poem allows certain critics to dismiss it as a clever word game, or worse, as Marjorie Perloff does, to conclude that Americans could not possibly hold such exaggerated stereotypes of Chinese people anymore:

Here ["GC XXIV"] the clever puns and specific images refer to the oldest of "Chinese" stereotypes: dim sum, chow mein, treated pork. . . . Yau is calling attention to the lingering orientalism [*sic*] of US culture, the labelling that continues to haunt Chinese-Americans. But his version of that labelling is itself guilty of reductionism. When, in the longer "Bar Orient," he gives us the old Hollywood movie version of the Chinese night spot as a drug den . . . the image of "China" seems as out of date as it is one-dimensional.[60]

While I would agree with Perloff that this poem is not one of Yau's strongest, I think she underestimates the shelf life of such exotic and sinister images of Chinese culture, whether as embodied by their strange food or bizarre cultural practices. In most parts of America, even in the larger metropolitan areas, such stereotypes are alive and well. The United States has yet to come to terms with its long and violent relationship to Asians and Asian Americans (the Philippine-American War, Hiroshima, Nagasaki, the 38th parallel, Dien Bien Phu, but also Rock Springs, Tule Lake, . . .).

In other poems in the Genghis Chan series, Yau parodies other types of discourses, not just the obvious racist Hollywood ones: for example, Orientalist renderings of Asian poetic forms—most explicitly in "GC XXIII (Haiku Logbook)," which consists of thirty "haiku"-like poems. Unlike the mellifluous "Zenlike" renderings of haiku by translators such as Robert Hass, Yau's "haikus" express his desire for a "certain ugliness to the very sounds I used."[61]

The experimental nature of many of the Genghis Chan poems, particularly in the second and third series, could also signal that Yau is parodying certain forms of avant-garde writing, particularly Language poetry, of which Yau has been openly critical. He has spoken out against what he sees as their implicit racism, evidenced by both their belief that the subject is dead—or, if it is still alive, that class is the major constitutive social force upon it, and race inconsequential—and their not including poets of color in their fold (personal conversation). Yau's Genghis Chan character, though not the unified "I" of the traditional lyric, *is* undoubtedly racially constituted and marked.

Yet he is not merely a passive victim. The fact that Yau joins the stereotypically weak Charlie Chan with the stronger masculine figure of Genghis Khan signals the production of a hybrid and potentially more powerful (and subversive) figure. Yau describes his Genghis Chan poems as an attempt to "turn the image of the obedient and polite Asian American male into something else, something less predictable, more sarcastic, aggressive, and more anarchic." He does this not only by his use of referents—"I use 'yellow' for example in different ways, but really that color comes loaded with social meaning, doesn't it?"[62]—but by formal means, as in his use of parody. "Yau makes 'slippage' apparent," writes Wald, "as his poetics *articulates* both the grammar of cultural subjectivity and grammar *as* part of the process of cultural subjecting" (original emphasis).[63] Or as Yau puts it in writing of artists' self-portraits in "Phoenix of the Self,"

> In contrast to the tradition of male self-portraiture as an act of assertion, that of the subject reinscribed within existing patterns, [Jasper] Johns posits the subject *in* and *as* those patterns, ultimately offering not an abstract but a concrete analogue for society's persistent projection of the male body as neutral, value-free turf. (original emphasis; 148)

The "persistent projection of the male body as neutral, value-free turf" in the visual arts sphere has its analogue, of course, in the poetry world and in American society. In American poetry from its beginnings to the present moment, the "neutral" and "value-free" speaker, the lyric "I," is undoubtedly presumed to be white and male—and universal. This "I" is de-tethered from history. He expresses his personal aperçus, no matter how trivial and pedestrian, presuming them to be weighty and universally resonant.

For all poets, racially marked or not, it is "*in* and *as* those patterns" of language" that these different intersecting (and contradictory) planes of subjectivity are embodied concretely and materially. Yet while all subjects are written in history and language, for those poets who are situated on the margins of the American body politic and the English poetic tradition, the questions of identity and language and the link between them are always fraught and anything but neutral and value-free. Identity is for Yau "an intricately political question."[64] "In the Genghis Chan poems," writes Yau, "I wanted something more unstable, more wobbly [than strict puns], as if language itself was beginning to collapse."[65]

As I have argued throughout this book, the politicized experience of being an Asian American poet and subject does not inhere only in the content or thematics of a writer's work but in formal structures and manifestations, such as rhetorical tropes, pronouns, syntax, verb tenses, moods, sounds, rhythms, and tone.

American history forms all American poets. It should not be simply Asian American poets and critics who, when reading the first two lines of "GC XXX"—"shoo war / torn talk"—hear the resonances of four American wars in Asia in the last century (and the avoidance of discussion about them, as they are "shoo[ed]" out of the American consciousness) and the "torn talk" that afflicts the language of not only racialized poets but also national discourses (on race, war, and so on). Why is that so many fine and otherwise perceptive readers of poetry completely miss these historical and social resonances and choose to read the work of Yau and other avant-garde Asian American poets as only "postmodern" or "deconstructive" or "nonsensical"? The chiasmic crossings of "war torn" and "shoo talk" are a shared American legacy, not just an Asian American one.

"Where I come from is a sentence which has not yet been written," writes Yau.[66] His sentence may never be completely written, but it is in the writing of sentences out of psychic and material experiences, by minority and racially "unmarked" poets alike, that poetry, like painting, becomes, in Yau's words, a "metaphorically charged site for inscription of the diminished imperfect self"[67]—and of our diminished imperfect American history.

SEVEN

Mei-mei Berssenbrugge's Poetics of Contingency and Relationality

Born in 1947, three years before John Yau, Mei-mei Berssenbrugge is the oldest of the poets examined in this study, yet her poetics are as challenging—difficult, abstract, opaque—as that of any of the younger contemporary avant-garde poets writing today. Berssenbrugge's career trajectory represents a unique case in Asian American literature and, indeed, in contemporary avant-garde poetry. Although critics now primarily associate her with white experimental women poets of the Language and New York Schools, such as Leslie Scalapino and Barbara Guest, Berssenbrugge, unlike Yau, publicly affiliated herself early in her career, in the 1970s and 1980s, with politically outspoken writers of color, many of whom, particularly the men, are viewed as cultural nationalists. Her third book, *Random Possession,* was published by Ishmael Reed in 1979,[1] and an early play, *One, Two Cups,* was directed by Frank Chin. Berssenbrugge became friends with Reed, Chin, and other politically vocal writers of color such as Leslie Marmon Silko; to this day, Berssenbrugge remains close friends with Silko in particular and speaks of the significant influence of these writers on her work: "I was part of the multi-cultural movement that was in the early 1970s. . . . It was important that the stories of people's immigrant experience got told."[2]

One could easily imagine a critic characterizing the arc of Berssenbrugge's four-decade career in developmental or evolutionary terms: "From naïve beginnings as a writer of ethnic identity poems,

Mei-mei Berssenbrugge has now arrived as a real poet who writes real poetry: rigorous avant-garde poems that lack the embarrassing residue of race and an autobiographical lyric 'I.'" Yet, as we see from the previous quote by Berssenbrugge and by many other statements she has made, Berssenbrugge herself would reject such a narrative. She sees no contradiction between her earlier and more recent poetic and political commitments.

In many respects, Mei-mei Berssenbrugge's life and poetic career, and poems, call into question various assumptions critics knowingly and unknowingly hold about minority writing, Asian American writing, avant-garde poetry, and the nature of the literary itself. Born in Beijing to a Dutch American father and a Chinese mother, her first language was Chinese, a fact that she considers crucial for her later development as a poet.[3] She moved to the United States at age one, was raised in Massachusetts, was educated at Reed College and Columbia University, and has spent decades living in New Mexico. She and her husband, the visual artist Richard Tuttle, now split their time between Abiquiu, New Mexico, and New York City (and in more recent years, Mount Desert Island, Maine). Berssenbrugge has written a dozen books of poetry, a few in collaboration with visual artists, including two with her husband and two with Kiki Smith. Her selected and new poems *I Love Artists* was published by the University of California Press in 2006. Her most recent volume of poetry, *Hello, the Roses*, was published by New Directions in 2013.[4]

Foreign born, a nonnative speaker of English, mixed race, a writer in the multicultural movement of the 1970s, fellow traveler of "avant-garde" poets, former assistant to Georgia O'Keeffe, winner of two Asian American Writers' Workshop annual awards for best book of poetry, wife of a famous minimalist artist, widely included in anthologies of avant-garde poets—Berssenbrugge, in her life and poetry, challenges the overly simplistic critical binary that pits "bad" identity poets of color against more evolved avant-garde poets (whether minority or white).[5] While sophisticated poetry critics have considered Berssenbrugge a poet worthy of critical attention,[6] this acceptance by avant-garde poets and critics does not come without certain unspoken but operative terms. Because the issue of race is seen as solely occupying the space of "content"—as opposed to form—and because minority poetry is viewed as constitutively "bad poetry" insofar as it deals only with racial identity—and thus, "content"—one might argue that it is precisely because Berssenbrugge's poems (seemingly) contain no markers of racial identity that she and Myung Mi Kim, among Asian American women poets, are singled out for notice by critics of avant-garde poetry.[7]

Indeed, when intelligent critics such as Charles Altieri and Linda Voris, who are otherwise subtle readers of poetry, discuss Berssenbrugge's work, they make absolutely no mention of her being Asian American and no mention of race (or that other verboten topic, "identity") in her work. A glance at recent reviews of Berssenbrugge's books yields the same result: race is completely erased.[8] Instead, critics focus on other concerns—mothering, feminism, affect, phenomenology, nature, ecology, science, among others—in her work.[9] These issues are not lacking in salience in Berssenbrugge's poetry, but to completely ignore the issue of her ethnicity amounts to a serious misreading of the larger context and issues at work in her poetry and a willful ignoring of her own avowed concerns and allegiances.

In 2002, Berssenbrugge stated straightforwardly, "I cherish the label 'Asian American poet' because I identify with other Americans who come from China, and with other Asian Americans."[10] What is one to do with such a quote? It seems shockingly unfashionable and out of step—not to mention rare—in this "post-race" era for a poet of color who has finally scaled the walls of the avant-garde inner sanctum to make such an identity claim. Why do avant-garde poetics seem so at odds with (self-)identification as a minority American poet? What are the underlying assumptions and categories that critics bring to the discourse and debates about poetry today?

Writing in an anthology on avant-garde poetics of the 1990s, the experimental poet Harryette Mullen speaks of what she dubs "aesthetic apartheid": "The assumption remains, however unexamined, that 'avant-garde' poetry is not 'black' and that 'black' poetry, however singular its 'voice,' is not 'formally innovative.'"[11] One could just as easily have replaced the word "black" with "Asian American." In that same essay, Mullen writes,

[B]ecause "women of color" seems to occupy a separate category apart from innovative or experimental poets . . . I become an example of "innovative women poets of minority background," along with Mei-mei Berssenbrugge and Myung Mi Kim, as well as Erica Hunt (in fact, at different times I have read on the same program with the latter two). (29)

In other words, Mullen, Berssenbrugge, Kim, and Hunt became—and to a certain extent, still are—*the* (token) innovative minority women poets. They were, and are, included in avant-garde poetry anthologies and events because they write "like us," not like those other Asians, Latina/os, and blacks who write those awful ethnic poems,[12] and because they happen to be Asian or black, one can feel virtuous about including them. Thus, even as avant-garde critics ignore any sign of race or identity in these women's writing, they can still pat themselves on the back for being open-minded enough to include people of color in their anthologies and readings.

Anyone who has spent any time in avant-garde poetry and/or critical circles in the States—whether in New York City, San Francisco, Los Angeles, Philadelphia, or Chicago—knows that these circles are overwhelmingly unpigmented. At the 2006 MLA convention, the first to coalesce around a theme—in this case, poetry, particularly avant-garde poetry—not a single minority poet was included in the keynote sessions, which comprised such writers as Charles Bernstein, Christian Bök, Caroline Bergvall, and Susan Stewart.[13] The only nonwhite writer included—and a fiction writer, not a poet—was Yoko Tawada from Japan, who writes in German. (Was it that hard to find even one "decent" Asian American poet who writes in English?) Among the critics, the only nonwhites were two China-born academics who work on experimental writing but by white, not minority, poets.[14] Where was Nathaniel Mackey? Fred Moten? Harryette Mullen? John Yau? Tan Lin? Mónica de la Torre? Will Alexander? C. S. Giscombe? Mei-mei Berssenbrugge? Myung Mi Kim? The list could go on.

Thus, while it might initially seem that critics of avant-garde poetry offer a more "liberating" approach to the experimental work of someone like Berssenbrugge—by choosing to focus on form and not solely autobiographical or ethnographic content, as some critics of more traditional lyric minority poetry are wont to do—these two groups of critics on opposite ends of the aesthetic spectrum, in fact, occupy two sides of the same problematic coin. By making no mention at all of race or identity simply because they are not thematized in the poems and by ignoring statements made by the poet herself, sophisticated critics of avant-garde writing can be as guilty of a willful misreading of Berssenbrugge as are those poets who read Li-Young Lee and Marilyn Chin primarily as "Chinese" (that is, not fully American) poets and focus solely on ethnic content. For this former group of critics, a lack of overt racial content in the poetry translates into the often unspoken conclusion that race is irrelevant.

Both sets of critics—on opposite poles of the aesthetic/poetic ideological spectrum but not the social/racial ideological one (they often share a certain familiar type of white liberalism)—fail to recognize how racial subjectivity can make itself felt *in* and *as* language and in what is not said or said obliquely. The imbrication of "form" and "content" is complex and subtle. Both groups of critics take at face value what appears on the page as thematic "content": for critics of more traditional ethnic poetry, everything is reducible to ethnic themes; for critics of avant-garde minority poetry, a lack of overt racial content in the poetry is proof of the irrelevance of race in the work. Both groups of critics in their treatment of minority poets also exhibit the liberal tendency to treat these writers as tokens of diversity.

But Mei-mei Berssenbrugge does not want to be thought of as *either* an identity poet *or* an avant-garde poet who has disavowed her Asian American "identity."

Because of these various misconceptions and knee-jerk assumptions that undergird much critical writing on minority poetry—no matter what the poet's aesthetic affiliations—one must proceed carefully when building a case about the relation between experiences, contexts, histories, and subjectivities, on the one hand, and poems, on the other. It is arguably most difficult to articulate this relation in the case of avant-garde or experimental minority poetry, such as Berssenbrugge's, whose language is not meant to be primarily mimetically representational—certainly not autobiographical or narrative or

unvexedly mimetic—and which exhibits no (or virtually no) markers
of ethnic identity.

Indeed, upon initial reading, Berssenbrugge's poems seem to shut
the world out: they come across as difficult, hermetic almost, and
their language does not offer many familiar handholds for the reader
to grab. The language seems overwhelmingly abstract, but upon
closer inspection, it is, one sees, actually quite concrete and precise
in its descriptions, especially of the natural world, with which she is
preoccupied. Except in her very early work, the lines are long. While
Berssenbrugge's poetry is "experimental," her syntax is not radically
disrupted; while clearly not conventionally lyric or autobiographical,
her poems do not shy away from using the pronouns "I" or "you" or
"we." There is almost no mention of ethnic or racial anything except
in three or four poems, and perhaps the only clearly autobiographical
poem is a very early one, "Chronicle."

Written when she was eighteen,[15] "Chronicle" is one of the few
early poems, albeit heavily revised, that Berssenbrugge chose to
include in her volume of selected poems, thus signaling its importance for her in her poetic oeuvre. Here is the poem in its entirety in
the version printed in *I Love Artists*, among Berssenbrugge's selected
poems:

My great-grandfather dozed after drinking
hot liquor in his dark room full of books
When she entered to wake him without knocking
as she did every night being the first grandchild
he was dead. One fur sleeve touched the floor
Once he carried her in his big sleeve through
cold halls to the kitchen where they were burning
straw. His daughter took her smelling of wormwood
behind the fireplace to feed. It wasn't the same robe
he died in, but the same color and cloth. My mother
really can't remember the smell of lynx, herbs
against moths, nor the slowness of his step
which must have been told.[16]

At first glance, the reader finds herself in familiar territory when
reading Asian American literature—an autobiographical first-person

lyric poem that recounts the memory of a great-grandfather in China[17]—but upon further inspection this "identity" poem is not as straightforward as it might first seem.

The poem's last few lines, the final sentence—"My mother / really can't remember the smell of lynx, herbs / against moths, nor the slowness of his step / which must have been told"—retrospectively frame the entire poem and deconstruct it by foregrounding the mediation of memory and language and the unreliability of both: "really can't remember" and "which must have been told." Furthermore, the speaker of the poem is not recounting her own memory but her mother's (the "she" in the poem), thereby introducing a third level of mediation. The speaker's Chinese mother, whom most readers would assume possesses a native informant's direct access to another culture and past,[18] "really can't remember." Those memories she does have are of things not typically Chinese or "Oriental"— such as "the smell of lynx" and "herbs / against moths." The latter detail suggests the mustiness of clothes that have been stored away for a long time, as if entombed, with time—and the larval moths' metamorphoses—suspended.

The olfactory and functional resonances of "herbs / against moths" are linked to the baby's "smelling of wormwood." Wormwood, according to the *OED*, was "used in medicine as a tonic and vermifuge, and for making vermouth and absinthe; formerly also to protect clothes and bedding from moths and fleas, and in brewing ale."[19] The herbs that kill off the moths and the antiparasitical wormwood evoke death and a temporal suspension. Indeed, the poem centers around the scene of discovery of death. This same baby, the speaker's mother, who was nursed behind her fireplace and carried in her grandfather's "big sleeve," is the one who discovers him dead in his "dark room full of books" ("It wasn't the same robe / he died in, but the same color and cloth"). The continuum between death and life and between past and present is marked by the absence of periods between the sentences in lines 2 and 5—the dead great-grandfather's fur sleeve is seamlessly joined to the "big sleeve" of the robe he wore when he was living; the granddaughter who sees the dead man's fur sleeve is the same baby he once held in the "big sleeve"—and by the shared temporality of the verb tenses: there is no past perfect, just one past tense. Even the one instance of the present tense, "My mother / really can't remember," gives no sense of what age the mother is when she can't remember. The "she" (the speaker's mother) occupies all stages of life in the poem: she is the baby carried in her grandfather's sleeve, the child (?) who finds her grandfather dead, the mother of the poem's speaker, the one who can't remember, and the one who will herself age and die, like her grandfather.

Thus, the baby "smelling of wormwood" can already be seen as part of the human continuum of life and death: after all, she is linked to the dead grandfather and to the "herbs / against moths." The baby can already be viewed as dead in the future perfect—worms suggesting the decomposition of a body in the grave—so that all three generations—the speaker's great-grandfather, grandmother, and mother—are narrated retrospectively by the poem's speaker. These ancestors are preserved on the page, in words, as the grandfather is in the "dark room full of books." Seen from another angle, this stasis on the page can be read not as eternal death but as eternal life: like the wormwood that kills the worms in the baby and the herbs that halt the development of the wormlike proto-moths, relegating them forever to a pre-state of being, the words of the poem stop time and hold the speaker's ancestors in permanent suspension.

The crucial last line, "which must have been told," and the poem's title, "Chronicle," provide an important clue that language is the governing structure here, not the unproblematized access to a "Chinese" memory. It *must* have been told: it is the telling that is key. Without the telling, there is no memory that is passed down—no Jungian "race memory" trickling down in Chinese blood. Instead, language is the primary means of contextualizing—and creating—this supposed cultural/ethnic memory. The choice of the word "must" also leaves open the possibility that "it" might not have been told. The "which" grammatically refers to the "slowness of his step," but the vagueness of the pronoun's antecedent also suggests that "which" could (or, instead) refer to the entire set of memories—that is, the body of the entire poem. In other words, perhaps these Chinese American "memories," which readers automatically assume are true and autobiographical even when represented in poetry or fiction, were indeed made up by the poet.

Berssenbrugge's recognition that all of this remembered family history took place in and through language—or was made up in language—saves the poem, in my opinion, from being another sentimental grandparent poem. In this and various other respects just detailed, "Chronicle" resists any tendency—either by the reader or by the poet herself—to fetishize or exotify this "ancient" Chinese tableau or memory. While the poem's seemingly straightforward autobiographical expository style, overt use of ethnic markers, and short lyric lines are unrepresentative of Berssenbrugge's larger body of work—later poems are almost evanescent in form, with long meditative lines that, with few exceptions, largely lack ethnic references, certainly autobiographical ones—its calling into question of the easy or unproblematic capturing of a person (or a thing or idea or memory or phenomenon) is not.

In proceeding through Berssenbrugge's poems, I want to temporarily set aside the question of her identity as Asian American poet or an Asian American experimental poet and, instead, begin by approaching her poetry from a broader perspective. I do so because I immediately recognize the difficulty in trying to talk about the link between the body of her work and her formation (and self-identification) as an Asian American poet. Trying to make an argument about the relationship between a poet's experiences, history, and formation, on the one hand, and her words on the page, on the other, is a difficult—some might say impossible—task for all critics. "No one can describe the relation between an experience / that needs to be communicated and the form of communication," says the speaker in section 5 of Berssenbrugge's poem "Irises" from her 1998 volume *Four Year Old Girl*.[20] The relation between "experiences" and poems is arguably most difficult to articulate in the case of avant-garde or experimental poetry, where mimetic representation is usually refused and language and meaning are stretched to their limits.

If I were to choose those few poems of Berssenbrugge's that do make overt mention of anything "Chinese"—poems such as "Chronicle," "Tan Tien," "Chinese Space," and "Nest," which span the course of her forty-year career—I might be accused of stacking the deck and focusing on only those poems that help make the point that her Asian American identity is crucial to her poetic production. Rather, I begin by making a few general observations about her poems and then look at specific examples from poems that are both "racially unmarked" and more overtly "racially marked." In other words, I will proceed speculatively, letting the poems themselves suggest specific arguments.

When one examines Berssenbrugge's oeuvre, certain patterns, recurrent images, themes, one might even say obsessions, gradually become apparent. Here are some words that say more precisely what I mean:

> light, edge, horizon, tide, wave, current, color, glass, mirror, shadow, silhouette, vapor, cloud, membrane, dawn, dusk, sunset, seasons, window, door, motion, silence, sound, distance, pulse, beat, rhythm, odor, fragrance, pattern, presence, absence, surface, reflection, infinity, feeling, sensation, haze, form, voice, mood, order, liveliness, serenity, smoke, dust, fog, ice, water, emotion, empathy, structure, energy, consciousness.

What do these words have in common? They can roughly be divided into those that describe phenomena or the natural world and those that describe states of consciousness and feeling—one might crudely say the binary between "objective" and "subjective" worlds.

Yet they share something in common: they all represent things, phenomena, states that are both embodied and disembodied, have form and are formless, are at once concrete and curiously abstracted. So we can see color, but it has no real materiality. We can see a horizon, but how do we grasp it? The same can be said of light, which occupies more than one state at once, as both a wave and a particle. Berssenbrugge writes of the atmospheric condition, fog, in her important long poem of the same name: "Though it is visible, it is / not a concrete substance" (43).[21] But fog, though amorphous, still has a form.

Material and immaterial can equally describe psychic and emotional states. In the list of words just enumerated, almost half have to do with mood, feeling, consciousness. "The mental impulse is a thought and a molecule tied together," Berssenbrugge writes in "The Four Year Old Girl," a poem from *Four Year Old Girl* (83). The consciousnesses of the speakers in Berssenbrugge's poems often find parallel in states of nature.

At other times, natural phenomena seem to merge with human states, as in these lines from "Fog":

> As lava burst from the ground to cover the planet, it also freed water, which escaped as massive billowing
> fog, a contradicting ambition of consciousness to acquire impressions and retain strong feeling (38)

It is not clear from the syntactical structure whether the phrase that ends the sentence ("a contradicting ambition of consciousness to acquire impressions and retain strong feeling") modifies "water" or "fog"—as its placement would grammatically lead one to believe—or whether the phrase functions paratactically so that a "contradicting ambition of consciousness" is made parallel to the process of bursting forth. In either case, nature, whether in the form of fog or lava, becomes endowed with human intentionality and energy. The lines tie human consciousness to natural phenomena in a manner that is neither metaphorical nor literal. Four stanzas later, the same language is used to describe a human, a "she": "Beautiful, unrepeatable, fleeting impressions can be framed only within the / contradicting ambitions of her consciousness to acquire impressions and to retain her feeling, a way of / repeating a dream" (39). By this repetition, Berssenbrugge signals her view that human consciousness and natural phenomena are not discontinuous. In a 2006 interview, she stated, "I try to expand a field by dissolving polarities or dissolving the borders between one thing and another."[22]

In another poem, "Forms of Politeness," also from *Empathy* (and included in *I Love Artists*), the speaker says:

> Because it's not possible to absorb more than one insight at a time, there seems to be a contradiction between the visual or space, and the context or meaning.

> She felt deep uneasiness with the image of this sunset of unnatural
>   energy, its sinister expression
> of an order of impossible beauty we thought we lost, accounting for
>   the intensity of yellow light on the hill,
> which is not a thing, *and* it is not a metaphor, the way your life is not
>   a metaphor to her. . . . (original emphasis; 55)

This idea of something's occupying a state of being that is "not a thing" and "not a metaphor"—in this case, "yellow light"[23]—is an important idea in Berssenbrugge's work.

She rejects the seeming contradiction: the false binary of abstract versus concrete, metaphor versus thing. It is not that Berssenbrugge rejects either metaphors[24] or things; she rejects the false binary. The multiple and shifting pronouns in this passage—"she," "we," "your"—could indicate different persons, but they could also be read as referring to the same person. The "she" is part of the "our"; the "your" could also be an address to the she's self, the she's "I."

Indeed, pronouns work at the level of both content and form. They refer to antecedents, yet, as Roman Jakobson says, they are "purely grammatical . . . units."[25] They shimmer, without forcing us to have to choose between content *or* form. In this respect, Berssenbrugge's use of pronouns reflects her belief that identity—including poetic identity—is not an either-or choice. Berssenbrugge does not want to have to choose between being either an Asian American poet, who is read by critics as operating only at the level of content, or a "formally innovative" poet, who supposedly operates only at the level of "form" or language.

For Berssenbrugge, it is possible to occupy different states of being ("yellow light") simultaneously without contradiction. She states explicitly in several interviews that "the continuum between material and immaterial" is one of her main subjects.[26] But we do not actually need to be told this—we can see it clearly from the poems themselves. The long twelve-part poem "Fog" is perhaps the best example of her continual exploration of ideas about the continuum between material and immaterial, between human consciousness and the natural world, between abstract and concrete.

The two middle sections of the poem, 5 and 6, deserve a closer look, as they raise issues central to Berssenbrugge's poetic practice. The phrase "as if" recurs in these two sections, as it does repeatedly throughout her poems over the decades (twenty-five of the thirty-nine poems in her *Selected Poems* contain the phrase):

It has no shape or color that is stable, as if I had fallen asleep. . . . (42)

. . . A part of
the person can become visible at a time, or parts of the people, and
  other parts rest in folds of the fog, as if
they were muffled sounds. (42)

At night, she could see as if the country were illuminated, as if it
  were day. . . . (43)

In the first example, the speaker perceives the unstable identity of shape and color (of the fog?) as if from the counterfactual perspective of one who is unconscious because asleep (yet perhaps dreaming so, therefore, also partly conscious?). The instability here inheres in both the object being perceived, the "It," and in the speaker herself—how can she perceive shape and color when she is asleep? Of course, in dreams, one can indeed have the experience of occupying various states and perspectival positions at once. Like the unconscious, dreams are the realm in which rational linear thinking is suspended.[27] So another reading of that first line is to see an analogy being made between the instability of the fog and the "instability" of the dream state itself or of states of being, temporality, and spatiality in dreams.

In the second example, the speaker understands that she can see only certain parts of other people's bodies, while other parts are hidden in fog—itself both visible and invisible—a state that is like ("as if") a hypothetical state of muffled sounds. So two sensory states, seeing and hearing, are brought into comparison without contradiction. As we have seen in earlier examples, human perception and the external world of natural phenomena are brought in contiguity (is the fog actual or metaphorical?). When speaking of "parts of the people," the poetic speaker is referring both to physical parts of their bodies and parts of their being or identity. The notion of visibility holds particular import, of course, for people of color, whose visible "parts"—skin color, the shape of a nose or an eye—are often read as metonyms *and* metaphors for some sort of racialized essence, while "other parts rest in folds," invisible to the eye. The line preceding this quote reads, "This is a realm or field in which other people exist in subtler forms than the body in daylight" (42).

In the third example, two states of the natural world—or rather, two phases of the same natural phenomenon—day and night, become merged by means of the speaker's perception; the diurnal and nocturnal become, in a manner of speaking, inseparable from the speaker's consciousness. Because she can see as if it were day, she has converted night into day by her perception of the landscape.

The natural phenomenon of fog exemplifies the simultaneous states of being material and immaterial, embodied and disembodied ("Though it is visible, it is not a concrete substance"). Water itself is one substance that can change quickly from one form to another or occupy two or even three states at once: "Fog is a kind of grounded cloud composed like any cloud of tiny drops of water or of ice crystals, forming / an ice fog" (38). At the same time, "fog" is a metaphor for human states of being or identity. The phrase "as if" opens the door to these other worlds, revealing to us the instability of knowing and of being—in other words, epistemological and ontological contingency, both of natural phenomena and of human states of being in the world.

The concept of contingency is crucial in Berssenbrugge's work. Contingency, the quality or condition of being contingent, has several senses: a close connection or affinity; uncertainty of occurrence (the condition of being liable to happen or not happen in the future); chance, fortuitousness; the condition of being free from predetermining necessity in regard to existence or action—hence, the being open to the play of chance or of free will; the quality or condition of being subject to chance and change, or being at the mercy of accidents; a possible or uncertain event on which other things depend or are conditional; a thing or condition of things dependent upon an uncertain event; a thing incident to something else.[28] Contingency thus suggests contiguity, affinity, connectivity but also dependency, uncertainty, chance. It contains within it the possibility of something fortuitous and/or something untoward, for the exercising of free will but also being at the mercy of chance.

Berssenbrugge is as interested in states of human contingency as in the contingency of natural phenomena. The idea that a person cannot be reduced to a fixed state of being (or "identity") is crucial in her body of work, as we saw in the previous examples. Neither human identity nor blood relations are fixed. Section 5 of "Fog" begins with these lines:

> It has no shape or color that is stable, as if I had fallen asleep and a
> long bridge appeared, where my
> relatives are like companions crossing a bridge.
>
> Her friends and family are like people you meet at the marketplace.
>
> When you look at your husband, you think of a floating flag of the
> roof.
>
> Even though he is your husband, he is not stable. . . . (42)

The indeterminate pronoun "It" that begins section 5 presumably refers to the fog, though the reader is not certain. As stated earlier, this "It" is analogized to the hypothetical subjunctive state of falling asleep. In the dream state, the speaker's relatives appear "like companions crossing a bridge." Thus, by means of a simile, the relatives are analogized to non-relatives ("companions"). In the next stanza, both non-blood but close relations ("friends") and blood relations ("family") are made identical in their analogizing, again by means of simile, to strangers one meets at the marketplace. Thus, what might seem essential human bonds—by blood or by affection—are shown to be not dissimilar from links with complete strangers. After all, is it not contingency that makes someone a relative? Or a friend? Or a spouse?

The various senses of "contingency" are captured here: the "chance" processes that join blood relatives, and the senses of affinity and closeness that bring friends together. Those who privilege "blood" relations over forms of nonbiological kinship invoke and impose a supposedly clear-cut distinction between the noncontingent nature of "blood" and the contingent and capricious nature of "non-blood" ties. But, as Berssenbrugge shows here, contingency cuts in different paradoxical ways. Blood is no more stable a concept as other natural entities and states of being.[29]

"Even though he is your husband, he is not stable," says the speaker (we are assuming here that she is not questioning his psychic health). When the speaker thinks of her husband, she thinks associationally, contingently, of a "floating flag of the roof." Because of the adjective "floating," "flag" here likely has its common meaning of a cloth desig-nation (a metonym or synecdoche or metaphor?) though it might also refer to a roof's flagstone that "wanders." What is stable in human bonds? Or within human identity itself? As with the earlier passage from "Forms of Politeness," the pronouns run from first to third to second person—and all three could be referring to the same "I."

As we have seen in several examples, Berssenbrugge's style is char-acterized by her frequent use of pronouns—not only personal pro-nouns but also deictic pronouns (literally, pronouns that point), such as "this" and "it" and "that," whose reference must be fixed through the context of the utterance. Roman Jakobson, after Otto Jespersen, called such words as deictic pronouns "shifters," words "whose mean-ing differs according to the situation."[30] Every shifter, in other words, has a general more existential or abstracted meaning (for example, "you" means the addressee) but also a specific meaning in the given situation (her husband, herself). "Shifters," says Jakobson, "are dis-tinguished from all other constituents of the linguistic code solely by their compulsory reference to the given message."[31]

It is not hard to determine, given what we can see of Berssenbrug-ge's approach to understanding the world, that such words, which represent two states of being at once, work in congruence with her epistemological and ontological inclinations. In the quote just cited, we can see that "this" can refer to the act of making, a process rather than a reified thing; "it" can refer to the fog; and "that" could refer to any number of things. The "you" could refer to someone else or to herself. The "she" is also likely a reference to herself—so the speaker occupies the position of both "I" and "she," observer and observed, subject and object. Identity is fluid, shifting, unstable. The pronouns here are truly contingent—affiliated and contiguous yet also dependent on others.[32]

This idea of relationality is both an aspect of pronouns—"[p]ronouns," in general, says Jakobson, "in contradistinction to all other autonomous words, are purely grammatical, relational units"[33]—and is also tied to Berssenbrugge's beliefs about the contingent nature of the world. One exists in relation to others and to the natural world, being both affiliated and dependent: everything connects and is in a continuum. Many of Berssenbrugge's poems invoke an unidentified "you" or "we" or obliquely refer to family or friends (such as "Four Year Old Girl"). At the same time, pronouns designating persons exist in close relation to pronouns designating objects and/or indefinite entities. Concrete and abstract are linked pronominally. Being relational does not mean being tied necessarily by blood or having some sentimental connection to family or others. "One of my themes is the possibility or impossibility of connections with others," Berssenbrugge has said.[34]

The idea of relationality exists not only at the level of social relations and of thought but is also inextricably tied to language. Poetry and language are, of course, ways of representing the world and of apprehending, knowing, it. Language mediates, but it also creates and intervenes. Like identity, poetry is performative, contingent— contingent in the sense of both relational and dependent upon something else. Neither language nor identity is given or fixed. In the poem "Health," from *Four Year Old Girl*, the speaker says, "Her self is constructed of units of meaning not given by nature, but successively constituted by how they're used" (81).[35] "[U]nits of meaning not given by nature" is an apt description of both language and human identity (subjectivity, psychic and bodily states).

"The problem is not to turn the subject, the effect of the genes, into an entity" (83), writes Berssenbrugge in the poem "Four Year Old Girl." Resisting the urge to turn "the effect of the [note the definite article here] genes into an entity" is not unlike resisting the idea that a self is constructed of "units of meaning . . . given by nature."

And here we circle back to the idea of race and racial identity because racialized thinking works precisely in this way: seeing racial identity as fixed. A being or self is reduced to an entity, a reified thing, which is read as an "effect of the genes." Racial interpellation, of course, allows neither contingency nor situational differences to alter one's view of the racialized other. Racial interpellation turns the other into a pronoun—"them"—but one that always stays at the level of the generic or abstract, never given a specific name or allowed to shift. It is a pronoun, unlike Jakobson's shifters, that absolutely does not allow for situational differences to inform or change its pointing.

I now turn to one final poem—one of Berssenbrugge's more overtly "Chinese" poems, "Tan Tien," also from the book *Empathy* (and also included in *I Love Artists*). The poem begins with the third-person pronoun but shifts to second person in the second stanza—another use of the second-person pronoun that actually seems to function as first person.

> As usual, the first gate was modest. It is dilapidated. She can't tell
> which bridge crossed the moat, which all cross sand now, disordered
>   with footsteps.
> It's a precise overlay of circles on squares, but she has trouble locating
> the main avenue and retraces her steps in intense heat for the correct
>   entrance,
> which was intentionally blurred, the way a round arch can give onto
>   a red wall,
> far enough in back of the arch for sun to light. (22)

In this first stanza, an unidentified "she" seems to be having some difficulty entering this Chinese site, which is likely a tourist site ("Tan Tien" sounds like a transposed version of the name of the famous Temple of Heaven, Tian Tan, in Beijing): She "can't tell / which bridge crossed the moat" (there are other bridges), and she has "trouble locating" the "main avenue" (there are other smaller avenues) and the "correct entrance" (there are "incorrect" ways to enter) that was "intentionally blurred" ("by whom?"). There is a modest "first gate" (so there must be other gates, too), and there is precision in the space—"a precise overlay of circles on squares"—which does not help her ("but she has trouble locating"). There are signs of a good deal of human presence—"disordered with footsteps"—but also of the inexorable passing of impersonal time: the moat is filled with "sand now"; the first gate is "dilapidated." (As in "Chronicle," the past and the present coexist in the space of the poem.)

If we were to assume, as many critics do with ethnic poems, that the Chinese American poet is the same autobiographical "she" trying to find her way into a Chinese temple, Berssenbrugge makes it clear that neither she nor the main actor in the poem has any given "Chinese" instinct or genetic knowledge about how to enter this "Chinese space."[36] The "tell" in "She can't tell" can mean either that the speaker cannot discern or discriminate the entrance to this Chinese space or that she cannot narrate it—or both.

The "can't" in "She can't tell" is echoed later by its positive double in "the way a round arch can give onto a red wall." In both instances, "can('t)" can indicate the capability, in the case of humans, or the capacity, in the case of inanimate objects, to do or be something—or the lack thereof, as in this case with "she." In the architectural description, the other possible meaning of "can"—may or could possibly—invokes states of contingency, possibility, and hypothetical states all at once. Through her use of the same modal auxiliary verb form in the same stanza, Berssenbrugge links in the reader's mind, whether consciously or not, the human and inanimate (though decidedly human-made) structure. The round arch is, in this respect, given almost humanlike capabilities.

One sees this linking or blurring of human and nonhuman in the title of the poem, "Tan Tien," which is actually a misnaming, as I said—a reversal of "Tian Tan," the famous Temple of Heaven in Beijing where the emperor made sacrifices to heaven ("tian" means "sky" or "heaven," and "tan" means "altar"). That Berssenbrugge has reversed the name is significant: by transposing "tan" and "tien," she also switches human and divine so that the human altar comes first: literally, "altar heaven." Besides invoking the contingency of human affairs upon nature or the divine (the emperor's offering sacrifices), the transposed title raises the possibility that abstract "places" such as heaven or nature, or inanimate objects, may all be endowed with quasi-human impulses, not unlike the lava in "Fog" that is not discontinuous with human consciousness, or the "round arch" that can "give onto" another inanimate but equally human-made structure. The two supposedly opposed states in "Tan Tien," heavenly and human-made, become continuous with each other—as with the merging of human consciousness and natural phenomena in "Fog"—their relationality and contingency further emphasized.

The poet's transposing or "erroneously" naming this sacred/human-made Chinese structure or space, not unlike the speaker's inability to find the "correct" entrance to this "Chinese space," again makes clear that the poet and the speaker have a contingent rather than a blood-given relationship to Chinese culture. The seemingly "mistaken" transcription of the Temple of Heaven in the title signals to us that Berssenbrugge is aware of this mediatedness. Likewise, the "correct entrance" to "Tan Tien" is "intentionally blurred." While the transposition inherent in "Tan Tien" may be the effect of not really knowing the Chinese language, or of memory's faulty transcription, there is no question that the representation of the entrance to this "Chinese space" is intentionally blurred, as in a photograph, and clearly shows the mediation of the artist's hand in the representation of "Chinese space," whether in words or as a visual image (here, rendered in words).

The second stanza begins with a conditional state ("If . . . ") in which a "you" who is alone "separates" from a state of symmetry:

> If being by yourself separates from your symmetry, which is
> the axis of your spine in the concrete sense, but becomes a
>   suspension
> in your spine like a layer of sand under the paving stones of a
>   courtyard
> or on a plain, you have to humbly seek out a person who can listen
>   to you,
> on a street crowded with bicycles at night, their bells ringing. (22)

One's symmetry is equated with the axis of the spine, a concrete bodily structure, but also likened by use of a simile to materials of nature ("a layer of sand") used in human-made constructions ("under the paving stones of a courtyard") or in the wild ("on a plain"). This sand is linked in the reader's mind to the sand that has filled the moat "now." The antidote to this conditional separation is the imperative to "humbly seek out a person who can listen to you, / on a street crowded with bicycles at night." Relationality, making connections in a human or social space, can "correct," the poem implies, this state of separation and asymmetry. The "can" of "a person who "can listen to you" indicates both capability and possibility.

The third stanza continues:

> And any stick or straight line you hold can be your spine,
> like a map she is following in French of Tan Tien. . . .

As in "Fog," even the body (not to mention the self) is not necessarily made up of "units of meaning . . . given by nature," for "any stick or straight line you hold *can* be your spine" (added emphasis); thus, the lines between human and human, living and nonliving—a spine and a stick—and the abstract ("straight line") are blurred. A nongenetically endowed (or "given") stick or line can function like a spine, like an axis. The stick and line are likened by means of a simile to a map of "Tan Tien" in French. So the thing that "orients" ("orient" = "east" in French[37]) this speaker in this "Chinese space" is not Chinese or even English but French.

Again, the poem shows us that the speaker has no genetically given (or "essential Chinese") access to this "Chinese space" (and Chinese past). Just as a stick or a straight line can function like the axis of a spine, so her orientation in this Chinese space is mediated by a European language not even her own. In fact, she is separated from "Tan Tien" by three languages: Chinese, French, and English. French, of course, conjures up the idea of Orientalism. The speaker comes to this Chinese place by the West's mapping of the "Orient," just as Yau, a Chinese American steeped in an English-language poetic tradition, came to "Chinese poetry" by means of Pound and Fenellosa, not by the Chinese language and certainly not by some Jungian "blood knowledge."

In the fourth stanza, we are told explicitly that the "she's" descriptions are recollected after the fact:

Later, she would remember herself as a carved figure and its shadow
   on a blank board,
but she is her balancing stick, and the ground to each side of her is
   its length,
disordered once by an armored car, and once by an urn of flowers at
   a crossing.
The stick isn't really the temple's bisection around her, like solstice
   or ancestor.
This Tang Dynasty peach tree would be parallel levitation in the
   spine
of the person recording it.

She not only "would remember" but "would remember herself,"
as if she has to consciously conjure herself as an object outside
herself—an object that is stylized and a representation: "a carved
figure." She would remember herself both as this carved figure
and its shadow. The figure is both concrete and material—a
carved thing—and abstract, a representation. A shadow is also
actual and real but also an abstracted silhouette, and it exists
solely contingently as a function of light and the thing it is the
negative of. The speaker would remember herself like or *as* a
carved figure and its shadow—similes—but she *is* her balancing
stick—a metaphor.

But what does it mean to say that she is her balancing stick? A
balancing stick can be both concrete and physical—like the carved
figure or a stick—or immaterial and abstracted—like the shadow or
"the axis of your spine" or "any straight line." In this passage, the
speaker occupies different "selves" and different states of being (simile
and metaphor, carved figure and shadow, representation and physical
object, concrete and abstract) at different temporal moments, both in
her memory (or is it her imagination?) and in "reality." It is not clear if
she has misremembered herself in the future, as the "but" would seem
to indicate. This sentence is set in the conditional tense—"she would
remember herself." She is a future self looking back in the past and
likely misremembering.

We are told that the stick "isn't the temple's bisection" (metaphor)
"like solstice or ancestor" (similes). What does the phrase "like sol-

stice or ancestor" modify? The temple's bisection or the stick? (The most important day of the year at the Temple of Heaven was the day when the emperor gave offerings during the winter solstice and divined what the coming year would bring.)

The conditional reappears in the last two lines of this stanza: "This Tang Dynasty peach tree would be parallel levitation in the spine / of the person recording it." The tree, one from an ancient Chinese dynasty, is invoked as a hypothetical state and abstract "parallel"—to what?—but also embedded bodily in her ("in the spine"). The natural but nonhuman living entity and the human being are joined once more.[38] The conditional "would" again calls into question the speaker's or poet's unmediated relation to "ancient China" because this Chinese tree would function in the spine of any "person recording it," anyone representing it. What does the "it" refer to? The tree (which is both inside and outside the body)? A poet is a person "recording." As in "Chronicle," "Tan Tien" foregrounds the mediation of language and memory: the retrospective act of recording or representing frames the entire experience of a "Chinese memory."

In stanza 6, the speaker imagines what a "he"—presumably the emperor in the past—felt when he gained "its confidence"—"its" presumably the Temple's (and not the same "it" as in stanza 4). The Temple is rendered humanlike. And then there is a reference to a prototypical Chinese image: "What she thought was her balance flattens into a stylized dragon / on the marble paving stones"—leading the reader perhaps mistakenly to assume that the speaker does have some essential "Chinese" connection to this historical space. But we have to remember that a dragon is a mythical creature, not an actual one, and that in Chinese culture, it has long been synonymous with the emperor, not a female commoner. It is important here, too, that the dragon is "stylized," the adjective reiterating the representational nature of this Chinese creature (like the "carved figure"). And if we look closely, we realize it is not "she" but her balance—abstract yet real—that is likened to a dragon. Her balance must be flattened from three dimensions to two, the plane of representation.

The poem concludes with this stanza:

Yet she's reluctant to leave the compound. Only the emperor
could walk its center line. Now, anyone can imagine how it felt
to bring heaven news. She is trying to remember this in Hong Kong
as the tram pulls suddenly above skyscrapers and the harbor
and she flattens against her seat, like a reversal occurring in the
     poles,
or what she meant by, no one can imagine how. (23)

Once, only the emperor was allowed to walk the center line, where
presumably the stylized dragon is carved, but now "anyone" can. Or
at least anyone can "imagine how it felt" to be the emperor, even the
speaker. The deictic "anyone" is important here as are "this" and "no
one" in the last line. The "she," like anyone else, can imagine what it
is like to be the Chinese emperor—she has no special essential link
to this Chineseness. Her link to these markers of "Chineseness" (the
Temple of Heaven, the emperor) is thoroughly mediated by faulty
memory, acts of will ("trying"), geographical displacement ("in Hong
Kong")—"She is trying to remember this in Hong Kong"—and language: "what she meant by, no one can imagine how." As she "flattens
against her seat" in a Hong Kong tram later, suspended above the
Anglo-Chinese city, she is linked in the reader's mind to the flattened
dragon—like that stylized dragon she, too, is "flattened" onto the
representational plane of a page of Berssenbrugge's book.

What does "this" she is trying to remember refer to? And what
does Berssenbrugge mean by the last line, "no one can imagine how"?
She is not saying that no one can imagine a concrete memory—a
"what"—but, rather, a "how"—or the process of remembering. And
not only is the speaker's relationship to "Tan Tien" contingent upon
memory and language but upon others, the reader ("no one").

Thus, we circle back: "Tan Tien"—like the early poem "Chronicle"—is one of the two of the very few more explicitly marked "Chinese" poems in Berssenbrugge's body of work, yet neither can be
reduced to "Chinese" content. They reveal the complexity of a "self"
and its contingent and mediated relationships to memory, an ancestral past, history, the natural world, the imagination, and language.
The concerns of "Tan Tien" and "Chronicle" are, as I have shown,
continuous with those in her seemingly "non–ethnically marked"

poems, such as "Fog." Though I structured my arguments and analyses in such a way as to bring ethnicity in through the back door, so to speak, there is no differentiation between "Fog" and "Chronicle" and "Tan Tien" in Berssenbrugge's oeuvre. They are all of a piece. "I would say the ethos and aesthetic of my poetry aspire to be holistic, continuous, or one thing," says Berssenbrugge.[39] The poems are equally concerned with similar issues—of processes, contingency, relationality, materiality and immateriality, abstraction and particularity, language and representation—and they are all equally Asian American poems, as they are "experimental" ones.

Reading any of these poems forces us to rethink our normative habits of reading and our falsely binary assumptions about ethnic writing and avant-garde writing. Berssenbrugge's poems, as "avant-garde" as they are, are poems that have everything to do with her formation as a racialized American, an Asian American. But racialized does not mean "fixed"—racial identity, like all identity, is contingent, not positivist. "[W]hen I think of myself in poetry, it is multifaceted. It's inside and outside. It is more like a force field than an entity. We are not one thing," says Berssenbrugge.[40]

It is language, not a fixed racial essence, that is so important: "I believe one experience that made me into a poet was switching from Chinese to English, because then you see everything is relational," said Berssenbrugge in 2005.[41] Language is relational and contingent. Three years earlier, Berssenbrugge was asked, "Do you think your sense of alienation has something to do with your being Eurasian?" and she answered "Absolutely." Then added:

> Images, identities, definitions try to simplify. You feel the pressure of being put in a package of what you are not. Any person in this country who is not white, that is a big part of your experience. And I think it crosses class. I was born in China, and I believe the trauma of going from one language to another has given me a sense of relativity of language that made me a poet.[42] The genetics is complex, as is the point of view.[43]

Even though, here at the very end of this chapter, I bring in Berssenbrugge's words to make my case, it is not really necessary to do so.

The poems tell us themselves, as we see when we do a close reading of them. Their language and their linguistic structures make their own arguments most forcefully.

Berssenbrugge's exploration of contingency and relationality calls into question the normalizing assumptions and categories that govern the way people read minority texts—and persons—in the United States and asks us to think about the relationship between race, writing, and the avant-garde. Her poems, while appearing abstract and largely devoid of racial markers, nonetheless strongly bear the impress of the racializing pressures and structures that shaped her subjectivity. To say this is not to make a reductive cause-and-effect argument. In other words, I am not claiming that the fact, for example, that Berssenbrugge grew up mixed race in Massachusetts is the main or sole "cause" of her frequent use of, say, qualifying participial phrases. One could note, as Marjorie Perloff does in her first book on Robert Lowell,[44] that a Massachusetts-born white poet might also frequently use qualifying participial phrases in his poems.[45] Thus, this formal feature in Berssenbrugge's work is not something uniquely or essentially "Chinese American." Berssenbrugge's phrasal structures are not the *direct* result of her having grown up as a racialized Chinese American nor, to put it in a slightly different way, is her being Chinese American the reductive sole cause of her use of clauses expressing contingency and relationality.[46]

But to make these negative claims does not necessarily entail then making the logical leap, as some critics do, to assert that Berssenbrugge's having grown up as a mixed-race American, whose first language was Chinese, has not had an influence *at all* on her subjectivity and her syntactical structures, that these facts of her life are irrelevant. This argumentative sleight-of-hand strikes me as logically fallacious: If A is not the sole and/direct cause of B, then A is not one of the determinants of B at all. Note that I say "one of" and also "determinant," not "cause."[47]

I am not claiming that a non–Asian American poet might not also use a similar syntax to express states of contingency,[48] but that there is no question that Berssenbrugge's being a mixed-race Asian American poet fundamentally underlies her sense of the contingency of identity and relations—not just of social identity but also of natural phenomena—and, thus, her use of a syntax of contingency in her poems (one way she expresses this sense of contingency is through participial phrases). Lowell's use of similar syntax emanates from and is informed by a different set of concerns.

What one says of Berssenbrugge can also be said of Lowell: his use of qualifying phrases is influenced by a particular constellation of personal, familial, social, and aesthetic experiences, histories, and interests. As Perloff argues in her careful analysis of Lowell's "Memories of West Street and Lepke"—his confessional poem from *Life Studies* about the shock of living in a mental institution among criminals and members of ethnic minorities and lower classes, a far cry from his Boston Brahmin upbringing—Lowell's use of qualifying participial phrases, his phrasal style, and not just the poem's thematic content, reflects the jarring nature of this experience:

> The syntactic structures of "memories of West Street" thus imply that only by viewing the self in terms of its surroundings, companions, and habitual actions can the poet come to grips with the world he inhabits: the piling up of participial phrases and adjective strings guarantees the authenticity of the poet's vision.[49]

Though I quibble with the phrase "authenticity of the poet's vision" (as, I suspect, Perloff herself might also now), her larger point about the link between the world the poet inhabits and the syntactic structures of the poem is well made and backed up by meticulous close readings.

All writing is situated. Like poetic subjectivities—and the histories and experiences that make up those subjectivities—poetry is contingent and relational. It not only represents but is a means of making sense of the world—it constructs and intervenes.

If natural and human states of being (what we label the "self") are not fixed, then the representation of those states, the rendering of them into words, must be approached with great care. Berssenbrugge is acutely aware of the poet's task:

You could try to make some fog into a piece of white cloth. This is
    impossible. Though it is visible, it is
not a concrete substance. She tried to make a delicate cloud into a
    cloth. . . . ("Fog," section 6, 43)

Anything with limits can be imagined, correctly or incorrectly, as an
    object. ("Empathy," 50)

Making something as amorphous as "fog" into a piece of cloth, an
object, is not unlike the act of making a poem from the ephem-
erality of human and natural life. The end products are concrete
things, a piece of cloth, words, which cannot possibly capture in full
that fog—or a life.[50] It is in the *trying* to make, the act of making,
that something from that cloud or the fog, even if only a color or
a memory or a texture, necessarily finds its way into the cloth—or
the poem. The critic's task is as delicate as the poet's and as weighty:
"How you look into . . . lit and unlit complexities . . . / is the complicated question of looking" ("Honeymoon," 63).

EIGHT

Subjunctive Subjects

Pamela Lu's Pamela: A Novel *and the Poetics and Politics of Diaspora*

An avant-garde minority poet is, as I have argued, not infrequently viewed as an oxymoron. If such poets are included in avant-garde poetry gatherings, they often figure as token bodies who "write like us" (and not like those "bad" identity-based brown or yellow poets).[1] This supposed dichotomy between the terms "avant-garde" and "ethnic" collapses in the case of Mei-mei Berssenbrugge, who, though now viewed as writing abstract and "difficult" poems and traveling alongside the Language poets, began her writing career in the late 1960s and early 1970s in league with "cultural nationalist" writers, such as Frank Chin, Ishmael Reed, and Leslie Marmon Silko. Berssenbrugge sees no need to disavow her past—indeed, she embraces it—and refuses the narrative that would cast her work as having "evolved" beyond her activist roots.[2]

While Berssenbrugge's current work does not thematize race, she can, nonetheless, be considered one of the generation of minority writers that came of age in the civil rights era. But now that we have entered the twenty-first century, complete with a two-term black president in the White House, one might reasonably ask whether thinking about race is even relevant in this "post-race" era. Is there any longer a need for categories such as "minority writing" and "Asian American poetry"? As more and more contemporary avant-garde minority writers write books that do not thematize race explicitly,[3] why not give up the category of race and minority literature entirely?[4]

Even before Barack Obama was first elected president in 2008, there was much talk at the end of the last century of moving "beyond race," both among academics and in the popular media.[5] Within the academy, one has seen certain trends and movements shifting toward a "post-race"—certainly post-identity—mind-set.[6] To escape the glamourlessness of US minority politics, usually associated with ethnic studies programs and identity politics, not a few academics have rushed headlong to embrace the rubric of diaspora studies,[7] with its sheen of the global and cosmopolitan. As the editors of a 2006 issue of *French Cultural Studies* dedicated to the topic noted, "The term 'diaspora' has become increasingly, and astonishingly, fashionable."[8]

The concept of diaspora can indeed offer new and exciting ways of thinking—for example, Brent Edwards's idea of the diasporic as interventionary and focusing on difference rather than similarity[9]—but, as some critics have pointed out, it might also have more disquieting consequences.[10] The "diasporic," for example, could be used, consciously or not, as a means to circumvent confronting the continuing traumas and discomforts of American racial politics and racism. We would do well to ask what is lost, as well as gained, by what Jana Evans Braziel and Anita Mannur identify as the "uncritical, unreflexive application of the term 'diaspora.'"[11] What are the benefits and costs of moving away from the notion of Asian American literature as a minor US literature and toward the idea of Asian American as part of the Anglophone Asian literary diaspora? What are the politics of the turn to diaspora?

Like the other "secondary" minority literatures—Latino/a and Native American—Asian American literature has yet to gain full legitimacy in English departments across the country, yet the category "Asian American" may soon face obsolescence, trailing clouds of the 1970s and 1980s behind it. With the "rise of China," English departments at prestigious institutions (such as the University of Chicago and Columbia) have hired scholars who are fluent in Chinese and/or other Asian languages to teach Asian American literature in a more transnational and "cosmopolitan" context, melding Asian American literature with Asian-language literatures and subsuming it under various rubrics such as "Pacific Rim," "Asian diasporic," "trans-

Pacific," or "pan-Pacific" literatures. This conflation of Asians and Asian Americans has long been a fact in the popular media.[12]

I am certainly not advocating a US-centered and monolingual approach to the study of Asian American literature—I, too, see the value of looking at horizontal affiliations among writers in various Anglophone Asian diasporas and have written on the topic[13]—and I acknowledge that many individual scholars working on Asian American literature in a transnational context are not motivated by such disguised ideological motivations. However, I remain wary of this move to conflate (or reconflate) Asian American and Asian. First, the greater American populace has never fully accepted that Asian Americans are indeed Americans and not Asian nationals. Second, conflating Asian and Asian American raises both old theoretical issues—for example, Asian Americans viewed as perpetual foreigners, "fresh off the boat"—and new ones, such as the ways in which Asian American studies might be (mis)apprehended disciplinarily, institutionally, and conceptually or simply eliminated in decades to come.

The rush to embrace something called the "Asian diasporic" does not obviate the difficult questions that vexed and continue to vex the category "Asian American." The fundamental questions remain: "What constitutes the very category 'Asian American' or 'Asian diasporic'"? "What are the fundamental assumptions underlying these two categories?" "What links the texts (horizontally and vertically) in both these categories?" In other words, the racial binding element— the "Asian" of the "Asian diasporic," or the "Chinese" in the "Chinese diasporic"—must still be contended with, even if untethered from the national boundaries of US racial politics.

If the study of, say, Chinese American literature presumes a shared history of racial interpellations and other experiences in the United States, then what is one to do with texts written in English by those of Chinese descent, spread across different continents?[14] These diasporic texts may share the two main qualities of having been written by ethnically marked (here, Chinese) subjects and having been written in the English language, but what happens to shared histories in a common societal and political context when the bonds and bounds of a specific national—or local or geographical—frame are "removed"? And if Chinese ethnicity and the English language are what Anglophone Chinese diasporic writers share, then what is one to do with, say, an Anglophone Chinese diasporic text that exhibits no ethnic markers at all except the author's last name or first name (or, in some cases, a photo) identifying her as "Chinese"?[15] Such texts—limit cases, if you will—push us to question the assumptions and criteria underlying the categories "Asian American" and "Anglophone Asian diasporic" as well as the nature of the literary.

Enter *Pamela: A Novel*,[16] published two years before the turn of the millennium and written by Pamela Lu (b. 1972), a Chinese American poet from California. Published by a small Bay Area press founded by the Language poet Lyn Hejinian, one of Lu's teachers, and Travis Ortiz, *Pamela: A Novel* is a text completely of its time (the last years of the last century), before its time (as, by definition, avant-garde texts are), and after its time (postmodern, post–Language poetry, "post-racial"). *Pamela: A Novel* is both experimental and deeply old-fashioned—its title self-consciously and somewhat ironically makes winking reference to Samuel Richardson's foundational novel. If it is a novel, it is one that is nonnarrative, with no "story" or clear-cut sequence of events to unfold; filtered solely through the consciousness of a Chinese American recent college graduate (denoted by the letter "P") living in the Bay Area; devoid of any plot or dialogue; lacking fully fleshed-out characters and, needless to say, character development; and speculative in multiple senses. It can be said to be "about" the doings of P and her circle of friends in the same way that *Molloy* is "about" an old man who tries to return to his mother.[17] Its sentences are philosophical, extremely "well written," almost self-consciously so, with a lot of subordinate clauses.[18] It has been acclaimed as "the last masterpiece of the twentieth century"[19] and "one of the finest books to emerge from the ardent, experimental writing scene in the Bay Area"[20] by critics familiar with that scene and has, for the most part, been taken up by poets and critics writing, and writing about, contemporary experimental poetry, and almost not at all by critics of Asian American literature.[21]

Pamela: A Novel refuses all attempts to categorize it along generic, identity-based, or "diasporic" lines. Though written in the first person, there are no overt declarations of the narrator's ethnicity, sexuality, or gender. In fact, within the text, the narrator and main character, P, criticizes those works that capitalize on marginalized identities:

> For it was never simply being sexual or being a minority or being a sexual minority that mattered in itself, but the various combinations thereof that produced confusion and triggered those politicized art-forms that repeated clichés of "displacement" and "diaspora." (18)

The narrator calls out these works for their confused, self-serving, clichéd depictions of identity. Yet never does she (or Lu) dismiss the significance of one's being a racial or sexual minority and retreat to the idea of the universal subject or its American corollary, the "individual," delinked from social and historical contexts. There is no question that the text unfolds and is entirely filtered through the consciousness of a racially and sexually minoritized American who at no point forgets her social interpellation in the world. Indeed, this minoritized consciousness is crucial to and inseparable from the tale the book tells—that of P and her friends, many of whom are also minorities or minoritized (racially, sexually, and/or classwise)—if the book can be said to tell any tale at all.

Pamela: A Novel is not, as some might have it—for example, Walter Benn Michaels[22]—a book refreshingly free of issues of racial identity. Rather, it is so deeply informed by a racialized (and diasporic) subjectivity that it need not announce its concerns with mere thematic markers because its very language—most notably, its syntax and tone—is inseparable from this subjectivity and worldview. It can be said that Lu forces the reader to inhabit P's consciousness and point of view so fully that we begin to see and feel the world *as* a minoritized (and diasporic) subject. But never in a clichéd manner.

Many critics have read Richardson's 1740 novel *Pamela; or, Virtue Rewarded* as both a founding text in the genre and a seminal novel of modernity, one embodying the constitution of the modern (female) subject. In many respects, Lu's *Pamela: A Novel*, written more than 250 years later, inaugurates a new postmodern millennial subjectivity, one that, like Richardson's main character, breaks forth not only from a subordinated subject position but also from certain oversimplified twentieth-century notions of ethnic identity within and outside the academy and along all points of the political spectrum:

> Our challenge was to break ourselves free of the political habits we had inherited over the past twenty years: the answer for us, if there was one, would not involve spiritual revolutions against the patriarchy, nor would it require tedious round-table affirmations of "identity-related" experiences. (18–19)

But *Pamela: A Novel* also calls into question certain knee-jerk assumptions literary and cultural critics bring to discussions of the snazzier, more twenty-first-century category of "diasporic literature"[23]— "clichés of 'displacement' and 'diaspora'"—that ostensibly replaces more old-fashioned conceptions of nation-bound and identity-based literatures. In both its content and form, *Pamela: A Novel* forces us to question this rush to embrace the diasporic and to question our usual assumptions about what is "diasporic." Running counter to what most would consider a diasporic text—one with identifiable ethnic markers—it offers the reader a more flexible, imaginative, yet socially grounded, conception of what diasporic writing is or can be.

What do the terms "diaspora" and "diasporic" mean exactly?" With the burst of interest in the past decade or so, the definition of "diaspora" has broadened from its original meaning—"the dispersion of Jews from their homeland"[24]—to a more general sense of any group of people living outside their homeland. Arif Dirlik writes, "'[D]iaspora' has come to cover such a broad range of phenomena that it has become vague, and perhaps meaningless."[25] In 1996, two years before *Pamela: A Novel*'s publication, Khachig Tololyan, editor of the journal *Diaspora*, found "diaspora" a term "in danger of becoming a promiscuously capacious category."[26]

Like the terms "cosmopolitan" and "transnational," "diasporic" is imbued with a certain global verve that the terms "minority," "ethnic," and "migrant" lack. Certainly by the late 1990s, the time of *Pamela: A Novel*'s writing, the term "diaspora" had not only accrued currency in academic and certain intellectual circles but—like the equally valorized (and evacuated) terms "multiplicity," "hybridity," and "heterogeneity"—was almost too easily invoked as a form of automatic shorthand for anti-nationalisms of various sorts, border crossings, and, by implication, anti-essentializing acts weighted with political significance. Diaspora studies' currency is still strong, as evidenced by the inauguration in 2011 of the Diasporas Programme at Oxford University. What the editors of *French Cultural Studies* wrote in 2006 holds true today: "More broadly, academics in the humanities are at the moment somewhat enamoured of terms such as 'hybridity,' 'créolité' and 'diaspora,' and we sometimes seem to be prematurely celebratory of the successful construction of such alternative modes of identification."[27]

Multiple scholars, such as Khachig Tololyan, William Safran, and Paul Gilroy, have attempted to pinpoint the characteristics of and criteria for diaspora, while recognizing the risks of a list that is too loose or too restrictive.[28] While subjects in the Chinese diaspora generally "fit" these criteria—for example, have a relationship to an actual or imagined homeland, are aware of the group's identity, are marginalized within the host country, face great pressures to assimilate into the dominant Anglo culture, and so on—there are great geographical, historical, cultural, national, political, class-based, religious, linguistic, educational, familial, and individual differences across the spectrum of Chinese living in the diaspora.[29] There is also the question of degree of self-identification, especially among those who are further removed both temporally and geographically from China and who no longer speak Chinese.

Pinning down what constitutes the "diasporic" in diasporic literature cannot be found in refining ever more exhaustive lists of shared characteristics.[30] Positivistic approaches overlook the territory of feeling, the unconscious, and the ineffable and discount the power of what is unsaid or only implied, as well as what is conveyed powerfully by language and style—in other words, all that distinguishes literary texts from ethnographic, scientific, or social-scientific ones. Stuart Hall, in explaining what he calls the *"Présence Africaine"* in Caribbean culture, speaks of "secret syntactical structures."[31] While I would resist Hall's implication of something essential or biological being passed down in language, I would agree with him that culture, history, and a myriad of other pressures on the writing subject and her subjectivity make themselves felt not only at the level of her writing's thematics but also crucially at the level of form, which includes syntax.

Obviously, "Africanness" or, in this case, "Chineseness" cannot be reduced to phenotype, physiognomy, or name—there are histories of migrations, racial interpellations, traditions, contexts, and many other factors to consider (for example, mixed-race writers obviously complicate these classificatory schemes). The ways in which scholars usually think of the "horizontal" connection among diasporic writers potentially runs the danger of unconsciously reifying "Chineseness" as some sort of racial essence. Arif Dirlik warns:

> *Because* of the fact that the very phenomenon of diaspora has produced a multiplicity of Chinese cultures, the affirmation of "Chineseness" may be sustained only by recourse to a common origin, or descent, that persists in spite of widely different historical trajectories, which results in the elevation of ethnicity and race over all the other factors.[32] (original emphasis)

> A term such as *diaspora* . . . [was] intended to break down boundaries and to deconstruct homogenizing essentializations of categories such as race and nation. . . . Nevertheless, used uncritically without due attention to differences of place, *diaspora* lends itself to cultural and racial reification in endowing populations that are products of different historical trajectories with identity on the basis of descent from a common "nation."[33] (original italics)

While Dirlik may underestimate the pervasive and persistent racial interpellation minority subjects face despite the multiplicity of cultures and contexts, it is true that within Chinese diasporic communities and in scholarship on the Chinese diaspora, the emphasis can fall on the "Chineseness" shared by, say, Chinese Australian, Chinese American, and Chinese British subjects, authors, and texts.[34]

If "Chineseness" can, and often does, prove a slippery path, what precisely *does* link works such as *The Woman Warrior* by Chinese American writer Maxine Hong Kingston, *Shanghai Dancing* by Chinese Australian writer Brian Castro, and *Sour Sweet* by Chinese British writer Timothy Mo if not primarily the Chinese ethnicity of their authors?[35] Most critics of diasporic writing are concerned with the sociological relationship of diasporic writers to both the "home" and "local" cultures,[36] and they pay much less attention to that other major element shared by diasporic writers: language (in this case, the English language).

To help us think about the conjunction between language and diasporic subject position, let us return now to *Pamela: A Novel*, a text deeply engaged with the link between language and subject position and the subjectivity engendered by that position. By its singularity, linguistic mastery, philosophical deftness, and unwavering examination of the "self" and the social, the text illuminates some of the pitfalls and possibilities in the notion of "diasporic." *Pamela: A Novel* calls into question fixed notions of a self, home, family, "we," time, memory—all the usual underpinnings of "identity" and its social connectedness—yet neither the narrator nor author chooses to argue for a wholly abstract or imaginary understanding of persons, for a "post-race" reading of hyphenated subjects, or for a retreat to the idea of a universal subject.

Pamela: A Novel does not overtly thematize race or ethnic identity. Yet their presence in the text is unmistakable:

> Often we felt tempted to page each other over the airport intercom system or to pick up the nearest White Courtesy Phone in response to any number of the muffled, unintelligible announcements that traveled over the airwaves of the intercom system, though R later pointed out, as soon as we were all reunited, that what we needed then was not the *White* Courtesy Phone but rather the *Other* Courtesy Phone, a nonexistent piece of technology that would cater to the demands of our marginalized discourse and bring us together against the dominant paradigm of airport static and confusion.
>
> R's search for these other forms of courtesy and communication had fueled her lifelong quest to find people who understood the truth she spoke and who could themselves speak the truth she felt the world was lacking. (original emphasis; 24–25)

Despite the rather ironic reference to "our marginalized discourse"— the tone throughout the book constantly balances and oscillates between states of irony, earnestness, playfulness, melancholy, among others—it becomes clear, nonetheless, as we enter into the thoughts of the narrator and main character, P (all the characters are denoted by initials[37]) that she is someone with a minoritized (and minority) point of view and sensibility, as are several of her friends who, along with P, constitute the "we." Without proclaiming her identity or using overt ethnic markers, P reveals her subject position by more oblique means, which, though less declarative or narrative, are all the more forceful for being so much a part of who she is that they cannot be separated from the way she thinks and talks.

P's use of the pronouns "we" and "our" conveys, with a light touch, who she is by self-declared association:

> Our position as late-twentieth-century post-colonial subjects meant that we were never at any time *not* in the world. . . . The world continued to foster our presence in a way that depended on this presence never being seen, and on denying any involvement with us. Hence we were awarded presence precisely because we were so conspicuously absent. . . . Our silence and invisibility was [*sic*] of the utmost importance to the state of the nation because the very suggestion of us challenged and undermined the simplicity of narrative on which the national identity depended. (original emphasis; 28–29)

Again, even with the ironic "meta-" invocation of clichéd academic speak—"[o]ur position as late twentieth-century post-colonial subjects"—the speaker's tone is wryly reflective, if not sincere, with a tinge of despondency. P is very aware, and makes the reader aware, of the ways in which language plays a crucial role in meting out presence and absence by those in power and those who control discourses and representation. National identity depends on narrative, a narrative in which "post-colonial subjects" are written into it by rendering them absent, silent, and invisible—silence and invisibility being particularly resonant for Asian Americans, who are stereotyped as quiet and submissive "model minorities." But the narrator shrewdly understands the paradoxical fact that this silence and invisibility were also "of utmost importance to the state of the nation" because by their presence and by their being allowed to challenge the "simplicity" of the national narrative, minorities ultimately end up reaffirming that narrative.[38]

The form and meaning of the sentences in this passage—the use of double negatives ("we were never at any time *not* in the world") and the invoking of paradox ("Hence we were awarded presence precisely because we were so conspicuously absent")—work to highlight the necessary and productive paradoxes embodied by state power, even as they highlight the absurdities inherent in the logic of these "simple" master narratives.

Lu's use of the first-person plural pronouns is important here, as it is throughout the text. While P and her friends R, YJ, and C walk "through the dark sand singly together" (16), it is their coming together as a "we" that links their separate experiences of marginalization. The first-person plural here does not coalesce around blood kinship but, instead, the shared experience as "late-twentieth-century post-colonial subjects" of having been rendered unseen. It is the coalescence of a group—"the very suggestion of us"—that has any remote possibility of challenging and undermining dominant narratives. Though they would not see themselves as bearing any similarity to activists of an earlier identity-based era—"political habits we had inherited over the past twenty years" (18)—the "we" in its solidarity and solidity, like the "we" of that earlier era, stands in contrast to the ineffectualness of the first-person singular (or worse, the imposition of the third-person plural) but with a more jaundiced (or realistic?) sense of the ineffectualness of their efforts:

> [W]e often went to great lengths to speak of ourselves in the first person, only to discover that we had not been speaking at all, and that we were in fact the "them" that someone else was talking about. (34)

> The persistent Romantic image of a lone hero impacting the world with his passion hardly applied to us because no matter how passionately we hurled ourselves at it, the world was always prepared to dodge. (29)

The "Romantic image of a lone hero" is of course, a Western ideal of a "universal" protagonist—an individual who is, needless to say, white, male, and heterosexual. By contrast, *Pamela: A Novel*'s "truths, ne'er so well expressed, are," writes reviewer Robert Glück, "emitted by

We, a glorious pronoun in which Lu builds a social space and founds a society." And, I would add, this "glorious" we coalesces, crucially, around common experiences of minoritization—racial and sexual, primarily—and alienation, not just friendship and affection (though those are important, too).[39]

Being Other occasions questioning and philosophizing about the state of being excluded from and menaced by "dominant paradigms," one of the major concerns of the text. Thus, while *Pamela: A Novel* does not resort to the usual autobiographical or sociological modes of handling minority experience—referentiality does not function straightforwardly here—being a member of a racialized and/or sexualized minority is so much a part of who many of these characters are and of their sense of the world that the ontology of a minoritized subjectivity cannot be reduced to mere theme or project.

Thus, while there are fewer than half a dozen moments in *Pamela: A Novel* in which Asian ethnicity is mentioned explicitly, that is not to say that the state of "being Asian American" is a throwaway detail. In one of the few straightforwardly painful passages in the book, P describes her friend C, who

> wrote with all the awful clarity and slenderness of someone who
> had grown up Asian in Indiana, the memory of anger and that daily
> experience of coming home single to watch the double of his face
> peel away from itself in the mirror. (17)

By contrast, the only instance in which P alludes specifically to being Asian herself, she does so in an oblique tongue-in-cheek manner, loaded with antic humor:

> [A]ncestral memory was what inspired me to renounce immediate
> fast-food gratification and spontaneously cook stir-fry while listening
> to a recording of an all-girl Taiwanese punk band. (79)

Here "ancestral memory" is being used parodically: while P seems to be "renouncing" twentieth-century American "fast-food" impulses in favor of something "Oriental," she is in fact cleverly resisting an Orientalist interpellation and discourse that might be forced upon her. It is clear that P's relationship to her "Taiwaneseness" is treated with a sidelong wink here, as if being Taiwanese were something that might be approximated by means of performing certain actions whose ontological nature is simultaneously being called into question.⁴⁰ The tone of the sentence teases the reader, who does not quite know whether to take the statement seriously or not. This depiction of a young Asian American woman listening to an "all-girl Taiwanese punk band" represents refusal along several axes, racial and sexual: for example, of the white heterosexual male Orientalist fantasy of the geisha from a premodern time, whose sexual and culinary skills are innate and atavistic; of traditional Chinese Confucian heteronormative expectations of her as a daughter, wife, and mother.

Later on the same page, P expresses a more unambiguous and unhappy stance toward her ancestry:

> I experienced my ancestral memory as a curse that afflicted both
> of my lower extremities, manifesting in my right foot as a chronic
> orthopedic misalignment which grew gradually into a mysterious
> tumor, and in my left foot as an array of multiple bone fractures
> resulting from being squashed beneath the double tire of a Mack
> tanker truck. (79)

The narrator's use of quasi-comic hyperbole reifies her ethnicized and racialized "ancestral memory" as a physical malady—which literally solidifies into a tumor—and again takes a swipe at Orientalist (and chop-suey) invocations of "ancient Chinese" memories and secrets. The humor of this passage does not disguise the seriousness behind the seeming flippancy. After all, racial difference is often pathologized and treated as a "disease," and the subject who suffers from the effects of such pathologizing does often come to see her "ancestral memory" as an affliction, one that must be "cured" by, say, various assimilative strategies. The material and psychic weight of living as a racial minority whose "ancestral" culture is experienced as trauma—because interpellated as inferior, un-American, and so on by the dominant culture—with psychic and material consequences can feel like the equivalent of "multiple bone fractures," the result of being squashed under the psychic equivalent of multiple Mack tanker trucks (which epitomize, like John Deere tractors, heterosexual male all-Americanness).

And what is "ancestral memory"? P goes out of her way to puncture conventional assumptions about both ancestral and individual memory:

> So we found it natural, if not imperative, to be assaulted and overwhelmed by memories which were not our own but which we nevertheless carried *as though* they had actually happened to us. In this sense, the history of our lives was always the history of something else. (added emphasis; 33)

Here, Lu succinctly and skillfully engages the questions of self-identification and external interpellation. First at the denotative level, the narrator's use of the pronouns "we" and "our" suggests not primarily the communal experiences and histories by members of the "we" but more the shared experience of having memories that "were not our own." In this respect, she is positing a certain shared experience of alienation from one's own histories and memories—one that many minorities and diasporics share in dominant cultures that have violently imposed their own representation of what those ancestral and individual memories should look like.

Second, P makes clear the inseparability of "personal" and social memories—history and the inescapable force of racial interpellation even if one does not "feel" minoritized (for example, consciously traumatized by racism): "[T]he history of our lives was always the history of something else."

Third, and perhaps more important, Lu renders this shared psychic alienation at the level of form. Her use of the subjunctive "as though" and P's paradoxical or seemingly illogical declarations ("the history of our lives was always the history of something else"), along with the tone of the passage, undercuts any tendency to impute ancestral memory (or any sort of canned ethnic group identity) to either the narrator or her friends. By saying that "we found it natural . . . to be assaulted and overwhelmed by memories which were not our own," Lu pushes at the notion of what, for racial Others, is "natural"—the imputation of biological determinism and/or Jungian archetypal memory but also an internalization of the stereotypes and expectations imposed by both the dominant culture (here, American) and the ethnic culture (here, Chinese).

To be marked as "minority" ("Chinese") and automatically read as possessing certain stereotyped traits and behaviors inevitably results in some degree of internalization so that memories are carried around *as though* they had happened to one.[41] This phrase "as though" is crucial.[42] The unsettling and slightly humorous image of carrying around memories that are not one's own—are not memories, by definition, one of the few things deeply personal to each individual?[43]— forces us to confront the larger issues behind the question "What is diasporic?" but also "What constitutes the self?"

Yet while P resists her interpellation into the category of identity implied by "ancestral memory," she does not find solace in that very American refuge, the privileged idea of the "self" or the "individual" (or its corollary reserved for ethnic Americans: "identity"). Indeed, P and her friends find the notion of the self vexing, if not illusory:

> The self was a mystery so consumed by its own questioning that it had no room left for us, a condition which we nevertheless preferred since we were totally unprepared for the alternative. . . . We desperately depended upon the spectacle of the large "I," with all its artifice and white noise, to keep us alive and functional in the world. We sometimes wondered who this "I" really was. Raw speculations placed "I" at the dawn of Western civilization. . . . [T]here was no way to find "I" without by definition losing it, and therefore losing ourselves. (33–34)

The narrator makes clear that the cohesive Cartesian "I" is a fiction, a powerful one that had a historical moment of origin—half-jokingly adduced to a vague but nevertheless not imaginary or ahistorical point: "the dawn of Western civilization." It is a large spectacle, one that is not unraced (characterized by "white noise"). Again, each member of the "we" has the shared experience looking for the "I": in the process they risk "losing [them]selves" and their minds ("losing it").

In other words, the usual American recourse of looking inward to find one's "self"—and the ethnic American writer's imposed obligation to write autobiographically[44]—not only does not lead to answers but results in more disjunctions:

Years of self-exploration had revealed a complex collection of personality traits, tendencies, habits, and passions, but I could never quite associate these characteristics with myself, much less imagine what such an individual might possibly be like. (57)

Since society could no longer correctly identify us, we had to identify ourselves even if we could not identify with ourselves— even if our identifications were inadequate and the self itself was wrong. (75)

"I could never quite associate these characteristics with myself" echoes the earlier claim that "the history of our lives was always the history of something else" (33) and P's description of C's "coming home single to watch the double of his face peel away from itself" (17)—both bring to mind W. E. B. Du Bois's famous concept of double consciousness. Lu has spoken of how the pronoun "I" functions as both pronoun and initial, as if "I" were another separate character in the text.[45] In his review of *Pamela: A Novel*, Aaron Benjamin Kunin writes, "The pronoun 'I' is effectively reactivated as an unfamiliar figure with richness and depth."[46]

Indeed, "I" is one of three characters, three speculative entities, the narrator suddenly invokes, or rather splits into, a little more than halfway through the book:

If I was at risk of suddenly becoming P in the midst of a plausible situation, then P was similarly at risk of becoming not me but Pamela, a project that I had invented to include both P and me, and that was expanding, day by day, into a larger persona than either of us could handle. (58–59)

If P was the wallpaper to the house that was Pamela, then I was the resident who paced restlessly through the halls. (61)

Here, "I" might be read as the "real" character of the narrator (suspending, for the moment, the paradox of calling a narrator "real"), "P" as the fictitious externalized character of "I" within the text, and "Pamela" as the literary representation or "project" (*Pamela* is, after all, the title of the work). "Pamela" is given a menacing agency of her own: "Pamela was smothering us" (59).

A few pages, earlier, Lu metaphorizes this condition of self-splitting and self-observation into what she calls "the condition of subjunctivity," a condition that, in her words,

> was heightened by the fact that it was all *relative*: there was the subjunctive of the real character speculating about the imaginary situation, the fictitious character speculating about the real situation, and then of the fictitious character speculating about the even more fictitious situation, which could prove to be either totally unimaginable or, equivalently, as unimaginative as the plain facts. Of these three subjunctives I could never settle on what I was, save that I lived regularly in the shadow of myself and only just managed to avoid falling in. (added emphasis; 57–58)

Here, sorting out what is "real," "the plain facts," is especially difficult if what is "totally unimaginable" comes parabolically close to being as "unimaginative as the plain facts." In a world in which reality itself is surreal, where one's "real self" is fragmented and refracted back in unrecognizable forms on a daily basis, settling on "what I was" is understandably difficult. Where does one locate the self or the "I"? What is a self? What is real? What is fictional? What is relative?

The word "relative" has particular resonance when thinking of diasporic subjects because it captures both the notion of descent by blood *and* affiliation by other nonbiological or nonessentializing means: "[a] thing or group (such as a species, language, etc.) which is related to another by common origin or (more loosely) by similarity of structure, properties, or purpose."[47] In grammar, a relative pronoun or clause refers back to an antecedent; in the diasporic context, that antecedent may be, and usually is, a blood ancestor, though he may not be (for example, in the case of the non-blood-related fathers of "paper sons" in the Chinese diaspora). As an adjective, the term "relative" embodies the notion of nonabsolute identity: "[e]xisting or possessing a specified characteristic only in comparison to something else; not absolute or independent"; "[co]nsidered in relation or proportion to something else or each other; comparative" (*OED*).

Like the relation among the various characters who become a "we" in the text, what links "I," "P," and "Pamela" as relative(s) is not blood but their being yoked—brought into being—primarily through and in language:[48] in this case, through the subjunctive. The subjunctive, the *OED* reminds us, is a grammatical term designating something "subjoined or dependent." The definition elucidates that the subjunctive precisely designates or relates to "a verbal mood that refers to an action or state as conceived (*rather than as a fact*) and is therefore used chiefly to express a wish, command, exhortation, or a contingent, hypothetical, or prospective event" (added emphasis).[49] The subjunctive lies in the realm of the "what if" or "as if," alternative possibilities, potential. In other words, there is potential inherent in the subjunctive (another name for the subjunctive mood is the potential mood). As P says of one of her friends, A: "A illustrated the possibility of taking grand tours of civilized thought within the space of a subordinate clause" (63).

At the same time that the subjunctive embodies potential and travel, its contingent nature raises the possibility of the mood tipping in less optimistic directions. Another dictionary tells us, "In English . . . the subjunctive mood [is used] to indicate doubt or unlikelihood."[50] Dependence, doubt, unlikelihood . . . Thus, not unlike the notion of the "diasporic," the subjunctive mood is a space in which one can reimagine identities and affective relationships that are usually defined according to customary categories, but in this mood is also the possibility of the failure of the wishing into being—the attendant and contradictory risks of contingency.

The subjunctive is literally a mood, the province of affect, suffused by what P highlights elsewhere in the text: tone. One is always wishing or hoping or imagining or doubting or dreaming or fearing an elsewhere that is not here—or an elsewhere that is always here.

In this regard, too—the here that is not here, the there that is both there and here—the logic of the subjunctive reminds one of the classic diasporic concerns about location, which haunts, or afflicts, the characters in *Pamela: A Novel*:

> This problem of location seemed to hound us constantly, as we
> found ourselves perpetually displaced by the very maps that were
> meant to locate us. Or perhaps, as A observed, the maps were by

their very design paradoxical and deceptive. For what other reason
would cartographers design a building map with the highlighted
phrase "You Are Here," accompanied by a large arrow indicating
the place you were supposedly standing? How can you be "Here," a
microscopic point on a map, and standing on the ground full-sized
at the same time? . . . Are you in both places at once, and if you *are*
pointing at "Here," where, as the sign says, you are, aren't you really
over "there"? (original emphasis; 21–22)

"Maps" that try to pinpoint or fix the placement of the diasporic self
are "by their very design paradoxical and deceptive." The diasporic
condition itself is paradoxical or, perhaps, contradictory—certainly
not fixed or stable. P muses at one point:

While R aspired to invoke her own reality through indirect reference, I attempted to build my foundation on a proof by contradiction—that is, I assumed that I could do without myself, and set out
to prove my assumption wrong. What I feared most was perhaps not
the difficulty of the proof but the unprovability of the claim, and
perhaps not so much the unprovability of the claim as the provability
of its paradox. (66)

What does it mean to build a foundation on a "proof by contradiction"? What sort of "shelter" is thus created? Actual homes in *Pamela:
A Novel* provide no shelter or certainty. Indeed, it is their home(land)s
that drive the various characters into uncertainty and flux:

[R] would return from school or work to find herself away from
home or, more to the point, herself at the center of home but home
itself nowhere to be found. Hers was more than a simple search for a
home or even a home away from home, but rather a yearning for an
abode that would not suddenly leave her in the lurch and in which
she could be herself all in one place. . . . R experienced homesickness
in the midst of her home, while I experienced it in spite of my home,
so that in the end it was the sickness of the home which drove us out
of the house altogether, into the broad, uncertain lines of some other
form of shelter. (61–62)

Like "I," "P," and "Pamela," the narrator P and her friends wander
anchorless in the world and in the text—diasporics par excellence.

Their "home," even if physically present, is "nowhere to be found" and not a place where one "could be [one]self." One could be homesick for a home (the *heimlich*) in the midst of a physical home (nation-state or country) or in spite of it.

P and her friends seek to find a home and a new form of community in language, even as they realize that there is no homeland, even a utopian one, to turn to. There is something uncharacteristically earnest and sincere about their strenuous attempts to find a place for themselves in the world, with their nonstop hyper-self-conscious philosophizing on even the most minute details of their daily lives. At times, all that seems to anchor them to "reality" is this outpouring of language (internal and external), nonstop monologues and dialogues. Lu herself has stated that "[t]he language of the book reflects . . .the realism of how a group of individuals from very different backgrounds succeeds in forming a community (a 'we') by developing a common language of synthesis, pet terminology, jokey one-liners, and experiential leaps in logic."[51]

Like many minoritized and diasporic subjects, P and her friends are marked by a desire for identificatory bonds with a larger group, but in this case they identify not along the lines of blood (kinship) or ethnicity but along the lines of shared marginalization and, crucially, shared language—or more precisely, literature: "And in fact it was literature that had brought us together in the first place" (81).[52] Literature creates a space that enables these isolated wanderers to find respite and create an imagined community.

Sentences are literally seen as abodes or forms of habitation. P speaks of her friend A who

> paced back and forth between the walls of his sentence in search of the perfect armchair or reclining futon in which to realize his insights . . . until he was eventually drawn to his purpose and promptly sat down, in the middle of his statement. (63)

Like the text of the "house that was Pamela," language is an abode for both P and A—a house if not a home. And because this language is English, it is necessarily not-home (*unheimlich*) for those characters in *Pamela: A Novel* who are minority Americans, especially so for Asian

Americans and Asian diasporics, who are seen as inherently foreign (non-American or un-American) and, thus, constitutively nonnative speakers of English.

The community that P and her friends form is fragile, contingent, somewhat hypothetical and utopian, and wished into being through language. This being wished into existence in and through language is not unlike the grammatical operation of the subjunctive. In trying to forge new bonds of "kinship," P and her friends tap into the more optimistic potential of the subjunctive's "as though." The subjunctive, of course, encompasses both the desire and wish for identification and the simultaneous awareness that the state wished into being through language is hypothetical.[53]

One might argue that this making subjunctive can also be said to be the situation of all subjects, especially postmodern ones, endlessly self-ironizing and "meta-", split into subject and object at once. Or that the making subjunctive can be said to be the necessary condition of all writing. (Here, we are reminded once again of Richardson's letter-writing maid who comes into subjecthood through the penning of her epistles.)

Colin Davis makes a not dissimilar claim for the diaspora: "Diaspora, then, can be taken as a figure for modern, spectral subjectivity, homeless and self-haunted."[54] In "Diasporic Subjectivities," he writes, "Language is bound up with the diasporic condition," then cites the biographical case of Derrida as an example:

> Derrida was brought up as French-speaking, without a native knowledge either of the Jewish languages of the Diaspora or other languages current in Algeria, notably Arabic or Berber; so French is his only language, but it is also not *his*. It is the language of a colonial power which denied him citizenship, and which therefore excluded him from owning the only language he knew well. (original emphasis; 339)

Like Derrida, P and her friends C and YJ "were using a borrowed language to add more words to our names, and to develop a picture of ourselves, the shape of which we could only infer from our surroundings" (18).

While Davis's more general deconstructive observation may or may not obtain, he is wise to ground the overly broad and abstract claim in a specific historical example—in this case, the particular diasporic situation of Jacques Derrida. Braziel and Mannur remind us in "Nation, Migration, Globalization":

> Theorizations of diaspora need not, and should not, be divorced from historical and cultural specificity. Diasporic traversals question the rigidities of identity itself—religious, ethnic, gendered, national; yet this diasporic movement marks not a postmodern turn from history, but a nomadic turn in which the very parameters of specific historical moments are embodied and—as diaspora itself suggests— are scattered and regrouped into new points of becoming. (3)

> Diaspora does not, however, transcend differences of race, class, gender, and sexuality . . . nor can diaspora stand alone as an epistemological or historical category of analysis, separate and distinct from these interrelated categories. (5)

Lu herself never forgets the historical, material, and local ground of these subjects even as she wings off into somewhat abstract speculative realms. Lu's narrator and main character P is a raced, queered, gendered, and classed character (similarly, Richardson's Pamela is a raced, gendered, and classed character).

The desire of P and her friends to form a community and find a "home," however tenuous and fragile, in language reflects their own specific historical situations as minoritized (and diasporic) subjects. P tells of how she became close friends with R, who, we learn from other statements in the book, is also a sexual and ethnic minority:

> I suddenly realized how we spoke not just a foreign language but the same foreign language, and how we had, unknowingly and seemingly without effort, become a "we." (27)

The "we" is necessary to fight against the world's dominant paradigms, which seek to write P and her friends in these narratives:

> [A]nd life there paralleled the experience of a badly written sentence . . . a non sequitur.

So we were fortunate, for the most part, to get through life holding onto a complete sentence, and luckier still if we could salvage
an entire paragraph, rescued from the wreckage that was the great
historical-cultural narrative. And even if we did, even if we found
ourselves with a fragment of the big picture or of the whole story,
it was still not our story. It was not our story, nor had it ever at any
time before or after our birth been our story. (41–42)

Their lives and their subjectivities are structured by a language
that is greater and more powerful than they are—the "great
historical-cultural narrative." "To get through life holding onto a
complete sentence" or "luckier . . . salvage an entire paragraph,"
is to acknowledge these minoritized subjects' subordinate relationship to these larger narratives, but it is also to see language
as a possible life raft—no matter how broken off, fragmented, or
incomplete—even if what they are holding on to is seen as "badly
written" (a charge usually lurking behind negative judgments of
minority writing).

Unlike those theorists who would glibly and abstractly celebrate
the transgressive potential of diasporic border crossings or who think
that the *jouissance* of wordplay can overcome the very real and material structures in states and nations,[55] Lu understands that the struggle in and through language is a starker matter about surviving in the
face of such dominant paradigms:

Extreme Asian American gaps in language, cultural experience, and
historical time open up opportunities for vocabulary play, invented
self-definitions, and appropriations of mainstream or canonical
cultural goods with a wink. But at the same time, this is not just
play but an almost desperate life-preserving attempt to really, really
"own" a form, to have and inhabit a form (both aesthetic and physical) of one's own.[56]

The language here is of life and death: "[e]xtreme," "desperate," "life-
preserving." To "own" a form is to possess it, be coterminal with it (to
have it be one's "own"), and to inhabit it as a true home. It is to claim
a room of one's own but also to resist, to the extent one can, being
captured by other people's interpellative forms (usually narratives).

P and her friends would rather function subjunctively on their own terms rather than on someone else's:

> For R was anything if not difficult to pronounce in terms of the world's known vocabulary, especially in terms of an official vocabulary that defined her as less than her own complete sentence, as if R could even think of serving as subordinate clause to a subject other than herself. (90)

Language is crucial to the production of oppressive structures—laws, stereotypes, and so on—though not interchangeable with them. Society's conceptions of minorities and minoritized peoples are limited by their known vocabulary. It is not only the names of "aliens" that are difficult to pronounce to mainstream America but their very being. P and R could never be a complete sentence to the dominant powers-that-be, so "from the wreckage" they must grasp, "in an almost desperate life-preserving attempt," the national language and "mainstream or canonical cultural goods" and détourn them. Language thus becomes the means both to survive and, if possible, to fight back.

Mastering language—in this case, English—becomes a mode of defense and aggression with a particular urgency. P speaks of her friend YJ who "continually hammered at hostile environments with the sheer force of her words" (82) or C, who "wrote with all the awful clarity and slenderness of someone who had grown up Asian in Indiana . . . the memory of anger . . . now sublimated into a stunning command of the English language that manifested itself as poetry, or a series of eloquent, articulate jabs at reality" (17).

The English of *Pamela: A Novel* and of P, C, and YJ is so self-conscious, so accomplished that its almost-too-perfect nature becomes both an explicit rebuttal to the imputation of faulty English and an implicit commentary on the constructedness and impossibility of perfect "proper English." In standard written English, one assumes an identity, one takes on drag, one becomes subjunctive by passing "as though" one "naturally" were a Western subject. We are reminded of the model sentences of eighteenth-century novels. The main character in Richardson's *Pamela* "masters" herself through writing and to some extent chooses her own subjection by marrying her employer and former attacker. In her letters, she writes as if she were a free subject, but ultimately she is not. P in Lu's *Pamela: A Novel* also chooses to master the master's tools, English, and potentially subjects herself to another form of subjunctive subordination—the "as if" of assimilation (Homi Bhabha's "almost the same, but not quite" of colonial mimicry).

Let me illustrate with two examples that hold salient force in the American context: "If I were to write English well, I would be a real American" and "If I were a real American, I would write English well." In both cases, the predicate of being (the subjunctive "were") expresses the wishing into being of a desired state (writing English well, being a real American). One must remember that the first definition of subjunctive is "that [which] is subjoined or dependent." Thus, in the subjunctive mood, the verb in the dependent clause is made subjunctive/subordinate to the verb in the independent clause. *Being* (a real American) is dependent upon *writing* (English well). And writing (English well) upon being (a real American).

The regulatory idea of a "standard" or "native" language, has, of course, been a primary weapon of exclusion and discrimination wielded against foreign-born and native-born Americans of the wrong race ("It was appalling to think that we could emigrate to Florida or California and continue to exist, much less bring a language other than English to the workplace, although there was no guarantee that we would ever be understood even when we used the proper language" [29]). To decide who a "real" American is based on one's command of English unmasks the inseparability of linguistic "standards" from racialized logics of exclusion. In a real sense, the most "proper" English *is* translator's English, both an imaginary English and an English that incorporates the eye and ear of an outsider or one who knows another language. One might even argue that in this respect the diasporic subject may be uniquely poised to out-master all those who "master" "standard" English.

By writing *Pamela: A Novel* in this almost-too-perfect translator's English, a form of English as Second Language (ESL), Lu demon-

strates that *all* English speakers are governed by a subjunctive relationship to English.[57] There is something cheeky in Lu's illustrating
that the most correct or proper form of English is precisely that of the
nonnative speaker: in so doing, she flies in the face of the customary
opposition of ESL, a denigrated form of English, to a (white) literary
artist's "native" command of English. Thus, in the very forms and
structures of her writing, Lu joins two areas that are often seen as
mutually exclusive—minority identity and avant-garde writing—and
thereby forces us to question how and why the avant-garde has been
implicitly raced as white all along. Against those critics who argue
that *Pamela: A Novel* is primarily avant-garde, post-racial, and post-
identity, I counter that the text instantiates in its very being—in its
writing, its form and tone and point of view—a fusing of the experimental and the minority/diasporic.

Let me make clear that I am not arguing that Lu has created a
particular racialized ("Asian") diasporic way of writing (in other
words, not something analogous to Black English). What I am saying is that in *Pamela: A Novel*—and this is true of this work, not
every Anglophone Asian text—we cannot fully understand the text
without understanding both the importance of the marginalized,
racialized, gendered subjectivity at work here and the inseparability
of the language—the syntax, mood, verb tenses, and tone—from this
subjectivity. Subjunctivity is both thematized (as in the passage about
"I," "P," and "Pamela") and enacted in language. I would go further
and say that the grammatical structure mirrors the structure of the
wishing into being of community—a diasporic identification with a
larger group—but also the more coercive operations effected by the
state, for example, in the disciplinary structure of assimilation—the
subordination, or willing subjection, to a hypothetical norm of an
"ordinary American" or a "real American." The citizen subject. The
citizen subjunct.

Subjunctivity not only appears in actual phrases but suffuses the
mood of the "novel" as well. We must not forget, after all, that the
subjunctive is in grammar a mood, not a tense (the conditional tense
is often dependent on the subjunctive mood). Just as mood or tone or
feeling cannot be quantified, neither can the subjunctive (or the dia-

sporic). In another passage about memory, P remembers—or rather, imagines remembering—

> [what] would have occurred had I actually been in a garden in the residential section of Pasadena with my mother 22 years ago, which I had not. This was the way in which I had come to understand the concept that A called "tone." R and I read "tone" as the underlying yet coherent feeling that accompanied any experience and encapsulated some unplaceable essence of it. In this sense, tone was neither here nor there, but everywhere all at once and therefore, nowhere where we could find it, point at it and call it a "thing." . . . Everything boiled down to "a feeling," which could be demonstrated but never named because its very precision existed on another level altogether, irrelevant to the field of names. (31–32)

This passage begins with a conditional perfect ("would have occurred had I actually been') that is then negated ("which I had not")—one is reminded of P's desire, described later in the book, for a "proof by contradiction." The negated conditional is followed by a deictic "This," which has an unclear antecedent. "This" refers not to a thing but to a "way" through which P had "come to understand" the concept of tone, which she and R read as "the underlying yet coherent feeling that accompanied any experience and encapsulated some unplaceable essence of it." "Tone" and "feeling" are not things, yet they are precise in capturing this "unplaceable essence" of an experience—their precision exists on "another level altogether."

This "underlying yet coherent feeling . . . everywhere all at once" and "irrelevant to the field of names" would be an apt description of the diasporic condition. The fact that Lu puts the phrase "a feeling" in quotation marks calls into question the stability or definability of any "feeling" or any attempt to pin down as a named "thing" something that is "unplaceable" ("[t]o formally express ethereal existence," in Berssenbrugge's words[58]). P's suspicion toward being named ("the field of names") or of being judged by one's name and toward pinpointing a subject's geographical location suggests that the conditions of P and her friends cannot simply be categorized as (or reduced to) "Asian American" or "postcolonial" or "late-twentieth-century" or even "minority" or "diasporic."

Being subjunctive means there is no connection to either "Chineseness" and an ancestral past or to any "placeable" replacements. Being subjunctive—like the multidimensional condition of being diasporic (not the trendy buzzword version)—resides not in a "here" or "there" but in the hoped-for, the contingent, the hypothetical, the impossible, the utopian, in the "as if." It expresses both desire and doubt, potential and subordination.

But this is not to say that the material social world, which constantly negates one as a hyphenated Chinese subject, can be wished away by invoking in a knee-jerk academic way "border crossings" and notions of hybridity. As *Pamela: A Novel* powerfully shows, interpellation has a major hand in creating the Chinese diasporic subjectivity—and it is that interpellation that largely drives its subjects to find a counter-weapon in language. While those in diasporic literary studies are usually interested primarily in ethnic literature that makes its diasporic nature denotative, Lu's work brings to light the real yet hard-to-capture aspects of diasporic subjectivity—the "unplaceable essence of it" and the psychic residues of, say, the affective (after)life of racism and the partially hidden or encoded traces of another culture or language.

To include *Pamela: A Novel* in the category of the diasporic (or the Chinese American or Asian American) despite—or, more crucially, because of—its lack of the customary markers and themes of "Chineseness" is to move beyond customary conceptions of Anglophone Chinese diasporic writing (those obviously marked as "ethnic") and to greatly expand the possibilities of what constitutes the diasporic itself. I would argue that *Pamela: A Novel* is a deeply diasporic work because it fuses so completely the two "sides" of the Anglophone Chinese diasporic coin—"Chineseness" and the English language—so that the two are inseparable. The evidence of P's Chinese Americanness does not reside in superficial citations of ethnicity. Being Chinese American (like being sexually minoritized and being a writer), and the difference and marginality that come with that state of interpellation, infuses every pore of P's subjectivity—her consciousness, her points of view, her sensibility, her history—and is coextensive with her every thought and utterance. Just as the tone of a novel or poem cannot be quantified, diasporic subjectivity is hard to capture with positivist criteria.

In a "world that was no place like home" (62), where "home" itself is nowhere to be found, Anglophone Chinese diasporic subjects are linked not only by being "Chinese" and speaking English, in the usual mundane senses of these "facts," but also by the processes of subjectification that have subordinated them to larger processes of interpellation and identification—namely, being hostilely hailed as Chinese but also having to position or imagine themselves in relation to an "ancestral" memory or culture. In both cases, the "I" becomes subjunctified and proceeds "as though." This process of splitting and subjunctification also takes place in relation to English. Being excluded from being a "native speaker" and from having a claim to the written literary tradition, the Anglophone Chinese diasporic writer must imagine herself as, or force herself into being, a master of English—or else be mastered in turn.

It is also in and through language—if not in the "real world"—that alternate conditions and futures can be imagined and perhaps made possible,

> like the time I walked through Berkeley with L shortly after the
> rains had stopped and suddenly became aware of the potential
> for travel—how the street tilted east and west in a line which one
> could follow indefinitely, walking straight into one's life as if it were
> one long distance culminating in freedom, leading away from and
> then back toward one's starting point in an orbit that magnified
> (or perhaps restored) the world to spectacular proportions. During
> moments like these I faltered. I tricked myself out of desolation: I
> could not tell if I was moving or moved. And such feelings seemed to
> contradict me, the way love seemed to contradict itself and its lovers
> with a sweeping gesture that traveled as much as it trapped. (50–51)

We see here the "potential for travel," streets tilting "east and west in a line which one could follow indefinitely," but also that the culmination in freedom can be illusory ("as if"). Again there is contradiction (and paradox): "leading away from and then back toward one's starting point," "not tell[ing] if I was moving or moved," "travel[ing] as much as . . . trapped." Yet it is precisely in these moments of "falter[ing]" that one can "trick [one]self" into a feeling akin to love (or being in love). Language—the space of a sentence or a paragraph—is a street "one could follow indefinitely."

In the subjunctive spaces of *Pamela: A Novel*, we enter the subjectivity and linguistic universe of P, a twenty-first-century diasporic subject who has an "unplaceable essence" but who is also never not a racialized (and sexually minoritized) Asian American. Lu's writing unfolds for readers the complex and contradictory modes of diasporic subjectivity ("tilted east and west"), experience, and writing—particularly those aspects that are not reifiable and quantifiable yet operate crucially and throughout, such as feeling and tone. In so doing, *Pamela: A Novel* reminds those of us in the academy—especially those who too quickly or comfortably embrace the "utopian promise" of diaspora[59]—to pay attention to the feelings that contradict us.

Epilogue

*American Poetry and Poetry Criticism
in the Twenty-First Century*

I want to end *Thinking Its Presence: Form, Race and Subjectivity in Contemporary Asian American Poetry* on an optimistic note, for there is reason to be hopeful as one looks ahead toward new poetic and critical horizons in the digital age.

Many innovative forms of writing are being produced today by minority poets, such as Will Alexander, Sherwin Bitsui, Mónica de la Torre, Sesshu Foster, C.S. Giscombe, Renee Gladman, Bhanu Kapil, John Keene, Maxi Kim, Janice Lee, Michael Leong, Tao Lin, Ed Roberson, Prageeta Sharma, James Thomas Stevens, Roberto Tejada, Edwin Torres, and Jenny Zhang. Many of these writers live in urban spaces such as New York City, L.A., Chicago, and the Bay Area, but also in Arizona, Colorado, Montana, upstate New York, Texas, and all over the country. They range in age from their twenties to their sixties. Some, such as Brian Kim Stefans, are highly conversant with new technologies, but, "high-tech" or not, their works are pushing into new formal and conceptual spaces. In many cases, this new work dissolves genre distinctions (as in Geraldine Kim's blend of poetry and novel, *Povel*, and Tan Lin's multiplatform works) and/or manifests the influence of digital culture—either in the form of digital poems themselves or in the use and echo of technology, such as social media, on the page.

At the same time, these twenty-first-century minority poets grapple with questions of race, culture, politics, and history but in a manner particular to their post-postmodern, "post-identity-politics" moment. As hip or "out there" as some of these works appear and are, their formal and rhetorical properties are, like those of the other poems studied in this book, not separable from, though not reducible to, the social and historical conditions of the works' making and of the authors' subject formations.

On the literary critical front, despite what I believe are the discouraging general tendencies of critics to view minority poetry in reductive and caricaturish ways, I do see some glimmers of change—mainly among those poets and poetry scholars who have been formed in their education by the post-1980s "opening of the canon" and critical race studies and increasingly in cyberspace, where poets and readers of poetry are more free to express views on poets and poetries that are not governed as strictly by rigid categories, assumptions, boundaries, and institutions. Here is where possibilities lie—possibilities that are fluid and less confined to narrow, outmoded definitions of what counts as "well crafted" or "rigorous" or "literary" or "avant-garde." Thus, while *Poetry* magazine still remains rather blandly middle of the road, its online forum, the Harriet blog, is filled with animated, sometimes heated debates by poets and readers of all different ideologies, subject positions, races, and aesthetic and political allegiances.[1] Likewise, many online magazines[2] and poetry books published by small presses— quite a few started by poets themselves[3]—all over the world offer some of the most bracing poetic writing and criticism available today.

I truly believe that the most cutting-edge poetry today is being produced by minority poets of all ages across the country. I read these writers with a sense of discovery and a deep sense of exhilaration in their (re)vivifying of the English language. Their works inform—and should be read in conversation with—the poetry of Shakespeare, Blake, Dickinson, Rilke, Eliot, Plath, Celan, Creeley. Contemporary experimental minority writing proves there is no simple either-or choice between "bad" identity poetry and great "purely literary" poetry. For example, the poetry of Harryette Mullen is as indebted to Gertrude Stein as to Bessie Smith and as influenced by the overlooked African American writer Fran Ross as by Oulipo. Contemporary avant-garde minority writing is formally innovative *and* politically informed (though ideas about race and identity are not expressed in the expected content-driven and thematic ways).

Within the academy, the possibility for new types of poetry criticism largely lies with those who take seriously the new modes of knowledge opened up by years of civil rights and institutional struggle and who learn from precisely those interdisciplinary fields that literary critics nostalgic for a lost literary Eden decry—ethnic studies, for example—even as they rigorously train themselves in literary analysis, theory, criticism, and poetics. The academy cannot stop these and other changes in the twenty-first century. This book offers an opening into the study of Asian American and minority poetry—"a field of possibility from which to begin," in Berssenbrugge's words[4]— and a radical rethinking of American poetry and poetics. But there is much more work to be done.

In order to do justice to and fully contextualize and understand the place of Asian American poetry within American and English-language literature (and Anglophone Asian diasporic writing), future studies need to examine the links between Asian American poetry and various contexts and histories—including American literary history, Asian American literary (for example, earlier Asian American avant-garde writings) and social history; its relationship to institutions, academic disciplines, and departments (Asian American studies and ethnic studies and English departments)—and the links between specific Asian American poets and their poetic forebears and peers, in the long tradition of English-language poetry and poetics, canonical and avant-garde.

In the case of John Yau, for example, one would look at his parents' immigration histories; their knowledge of Chinese; Yau's own relationship to the Chinese language and English; his having grown up Chinese American in Brookline, Massachusetts; his racialized position as an art critic in a very white New York City art world. One would look as well at the full range of his literary and artistic influences and ties: his links with other avant-garde poetic contemporaries; his ties to earlier poetic forebears, including Ezra Pound, Rimbaud, and French Surrealists, and his teachers Robert Kelly and John Ashbery; his position among other post–New York School poets; and his ties to visual artists, such as Thomas Nozkowski, and fellow art critics. Berssenbrugge, like Yau, has strong links to American avant-garde poets (in her case, Barbara Guest[5] and the Language poets) and to visual artists (such as Richard Tuttle, Kiki Smith, and Georgia O'Keeffe).

That said, scholars of minority poetry should resist the urge to always "validate" minority poets by reading them in relation to—or making the argument that they are "just as good as"—white poets. One should also examine the connections between Asian American poets and poets and writers from other minority groups—for example, the intersection of Berssenbrugge's poetry with the work of Ishmael Reed and Leslie Marmon Silko. Or simply devote entire volumes to the serious study of minority poetry.

By paying close attention to the full dimensionality—formal and social—of the poetry of that segment of the American population considered most "nonnative" to the production of English-language poetry, *Thinking Its Presence: Form, Race, and Subjectivity in Contemporary Asian American Poetry* builds an argument for the relation—sometimes mysterious but always abiding—between all poetic utterances and the subjectivities and histories from which they spring. My aim is to shine a light on the formal and social intertwining and complexity of all poetic production and the effect of ideologies, such as racialized thinking and racism, on all members of a society, not just those visible minorities seemingly most directly affected.[6]

I look forward to a time when minority poets will no longer have to struggle under the burden of a compensatory relationship to the English language and the English literary tradition that is much more than the usual "anxiety of influence"—of, say, having to prove that their writing is "as good as" that of "racially unmarked" writers by erasing race in their writing or having to always be read through the scrim of their physiognomy and putative "essences." I look forward to a time when the work of minority poets will be read with respect and full attention to its formal properties and when the work of "racially unmarked" poets will be read with an eye to its social and ideological formations and contexts.

It must change.

Notes

PREFACE

1. African American literature was finally granted the institutional recognition of being a "real" minority literature about three decades ago, institutionally validated by Harvard University's decision to found the Department of African American Studies, under the aegis of Henry Louis Gates Jr. For a cogent discussion of the terms "minority" and "minor," see Abdul R. Jan Mohamed's and David Lloyd's introduction to their edited volume *The Nature and Context of Minority Discourse* (New York: Oxford University Press, 1990).

2. Asian Americans' perceived alienness excludes them from very idea of what is "American" and from the possibility of a "native" relationship to the English language.

3. There are only a handful of exceptions, mostly embattled, such as the Departments of Literature at the University of California, San Diego, and the University of California, Santa Cruz, which include English literature among other literatures in the same department.

4. For example, Yale University's "Modern Poetry" course (English 310) covers Eliot, Stevens, Pound, Crane, Auden, Yeats, Williams, and Frost, as well as Marianne Moore and Elizabeth Bishop, among others; of the eighteen writers discussed, only one is nonwhite (Langston Hughes). The lectures are available on Open Yale Courses, thus spreading (implicit) ideologies about the Modernist canon to a much larger audience than just Yale undergraduates: http://oyc.yale.edu/english/engl-310#syllabus.

5. What is seen as "universal" is thought of as "racially unmarked," of course, but implicitly presumed to be white—whiteness is not seen as a racial category. At the same time, it is presumed that these "unmarked" universal poets are free, as *individual and fully three-dimensional* subjects, to have a range of human (emotional, aesthetic, etc.) experiences and stances, whereas ethnic poets are seen as sharing one undifferentiated, unidimensional, and homogeneous state of being: "blackness" or "Asianness," for example. Needless to say, this reductive view of racial persons translates into a reductive view of minority poetry, which is often apprehended in such terms. While "unmarked" (white) poets occupy the position of being universal and individual at once, the writing of minority poets is interpreted as speaking for nonuniversal (and, thus, marginal and irrelevant) experiences but also occupying a single abstract signifying category. The irony, of course, is that being read as an abstract signifier does not mean that the minority subject or poet is seen as capable of engaging in abstract thought—indeed, she is interpreted by means of concrete markers of visible racial difference and her poetry judged in terms of its sociological content, also manifested by concrete signifiers (details, motifs) of racial difference.

6. The exceptions include scholarship now being done by younger Asian American scholars who have been trained in both English literary studies and Asian American studies, such as Timothy Yu (a Perloff student) and Joseph Jonghyun Jeon and Warren Liu, both of whom wrote their dissertations under Charles Altieri. See Yu, *Race and the Avant-Garde: Experimental and Asian American Poetry Since 1965* (Stanford, CA: Stanford University Press, 2009); Jeon, *Racial Things, Racial Forms: Objecthood in Avant-Garde Asian American Poetry* (Iowa City: University of Iowa Press, 2012); and Liu, "The Object of Experiment: Figurations of Subjectivity in Asian American Experimental Literature," PhD diss., University of California, Berkeley, 2004.

7. Edward W. Said, *The World, the Text, and the Critic* (Cambridge, MA: Harvard University Press, 1983), 5; hereafter cited as *WTC*.

8. Raymond Williams, *The Politics of Modernism* (London: Verso, 1989), 80.

9. The number of scholars focusing on Asian American poetry can be counted on one hand. As is evidenced by the increasing occurrence of the word "form" in recent Asian American scholarship, more and more scholars such as Yu, Jeon, Liu, and myself are examining questions of formal innova-

tion and the contextualization of Asian American poetry in relation to twen-
tieth- and twenty-first-century American poetry. See also Josephine Nock-hee
Park, *Apparitions of Asia: Modernist Form and Asian American Poetics* (New
York: Oxford University Press, 2008). Even as I helped to inaugurate this sort
of critical reading of Asian American literature (see my "Necessary Figures:
Metaphor, Irony and Parody in the Poetry of Li-Young Lee, Marilyn Chin,
and John Yau," PhD diss., University of California, Berkeley, 1998), I do want
to caution strongly that simply invoking "form" *without* an awareness of history and political context, both in the academy and in society, runs the danger of being as reductive—and as reactionary—as reading solely in terms of
ethnic "content." The political valences of the recent "formal turn" in literary
criticism are varied, and both white and minority critics alike can be found
guilty of divorcing the text from the world.

10. "After all, meaning occurs / only in a context of conscious & non-
conscious, / recuperable & unrecoverable, dynamics," writes the poet-critic
Charles Bernstein in "Artifice of Absorption," in *A Poetics* (Cambridge,
MA: Harvard University Press, 1992), 13.

11. Ibid., 5.

CHAPTER I

1. See http://www.mla.org/about, which gives facts about the MLA and
its membership.

2. "The New Lyric Studies," *PMLA* 123 (2008): 181–234. Note the definite article.

3. Marjorie Perloff, "It Must Change," *PMLA* 122.3 (2007): 655, 654.

4. See, for example, Virginia Jackson, "Who Reads Poetry?," *PMLA*
123.1 (2008): 181–87; and *Dickinson's Misery: A Theory of Lyric Reading*
(Princeton, NJ: Princeton University Press, 2005).

5. All of the critics were asked to participate because they have a reputation in literary studies, many in the study of poetry, and all teach at elite
institutions: University of California, Berkeley; University of Chicago;
University of California, Irvine; Tufts; University of Michigan; Columbia
University; and Cornell University.

6. Beyond the thirty thousand MLA members who automatically
receive a subscription with their membership, other literature and language professors in the country and worldwide read the journal. It
is the one literary journal that most broadly crosses various literary
specializations.

7. Jonathan Culler, "Why Lyric?," *PMLA* 123.1 (2008): 201–6, quotes on 205.

8. Rei Terada, "After the Critique of Lyric," *PMLA* 123.1 (2008): 195–200, quotes on 196, 199.

9. Robert Kaufman, "Lyric Commodity Critique, Benjamin Adorno Marx, Baudelaire Baudelaire Baudelaire," *PMLA* 123.1 (2008): 207–15, quote on 211.

10. Stathis Gourgouris, "*Poiein*—Political Infinitive," *PMLA* 123.1 (2008): 223–28; Brent Edwards, "The Specter of Interdisciplinarity," *PMLA* 123.1 (2008): 188–94.

11. Oren Izenberg, "Poems Out of Our Heads," *PMLA* 123.1 (2008): 216–22, quotes on 217.

12. Jackson, "Who Reads Poetry?," PMLA 123.1 (2008): 181–87, quote on 183. Yopie Prins, "Historical Poetics, Dysprosody, and *The Science of English Verse*," *PMLA* 123.1 (2008): 229–34, quote on 233.

13. See Izenberg, "Language Poetry and Collective Life," *Critical Inquiry* 30.1 (2003): 132–59; reprinted as chapter 4 of his *Being Numerous: Poetry and the Grounds of Social Life* (Princeton, NJ: Princeton University Press, 2010).

14. Marjorie Perloff, "'Creative Writing' Among the Disciplines," *MLA Newsletter* 38.1 (2006): 4, http://www.mla.org/pdf/nl_spring06pdf.pdf.

15. One need only look at the curricula and major requirements in various English departments across the country to know that this description does not accurately reflect the current state of affairs in literary studies.

16. The terms of Perloff's characterization underscore my earlier point: "African American, other minorities, and postcolonial" are lumped in one abstract homogeneous category—"one subculture . . . and another"—while the "great" writers are individually named and represent a range of genres, styles, genders, sensibilities, and nationalities.

17. Though the only minority group she specifies is African American.

18. The prefix "sub-," of course, holds various, often simultaneous, meanings, such as "a part of," "subordinate to," and/or "inferior to." The *OED* lists this as the first meaning: "In prepositional relation to the noun constituting or implied in the second element, with the sense 'situated, existing, or occurring under, below, or at the bottom of.'" *OED* online, 3rd ed., June 2012, http://www.oed.com.

19. This rhetoric of a zero-sum game or a scarcity model in literature departments and universities echoes the rhetoric used historically and cur-

rently in debates about "illegal aliens," most notably Chinese and Mexican. Thanks to David Eng for this point.

20. One is reminded of Said's description of culture as "a system of discriminations and evaluations—perhaps mainly aesthetic, as Lionel Trilling has said, but no less forceful and tyrannical for that—for a particular class in the State able to identify with it. . . . For if it is true that culture is, on the one hand, a positive doctrine of the best that is thought and known, it is also on the other a differentially negative doctrine of all that is not best" (*WTC*, 11–12). "All that is not best" is relegated to what Perloff calls "subculture[s]," with all the less-than-elevating resonances that the prefix "sub-" carries (including subpar).

21. In my case, it was her indirect influence—by way of her student Craig Dworkin—that led me to begin reading experimental (minority) writing.

22. I recognize that several of the other contributors—Terada, Kaufman, Jackson, and Prins—do not fall neatly on either side of this implied binary of "the literary versus the social," but it is also true that Edwards is the only one who explicitly speaks out against Perloff's binarization. One might have thought that Kaufman, a Frankfurt School devotee, would have, or Jackson and Prins, with their strong historical commitments.

23. The other eight writers discussed are canonical, most considered "major" names—Baudelaire, Beckett, Cavafy, Dickinson, Frost, Lanier, Melville, Tolstoy (as evidenced by their being recognizable simply by their last names)—although Sidney Lanier, cited by Prins for his nineteenth-century work on prosody, is considered a minor poet, and Melville, cited by Jackson, is more famous for his prose than poetry. Emily Dickinson is the sole female poet in the group. The only twentieth-century American poet discussed (by Culler) is Robert Frost. Thus, of the four American poets named more than in passing, two—Melville and Lanier—are certainly not more important as poets, one could argue, than Langston Hughes or Amiri Baraka or, if one goes international (as many in this group of critics do, and as Perloff has often exhorted American literary critics to do), Aimé Césaire.

24. The number of poetry critics focusing *primarily* or *solely* on minority poetry remains dismally small: the most notable are Aldon Nielsen, Fred Moten, Nathaniel Mackey, and Brent Edwards—all writing on African American and African diasporic poetry. Within the group of critics

analyzing minority poetry, the number of those focusing on formal concerns is even smaller. In the United States, we have not had a poetry critic of the stature and influence of Raymond Williams to elevate the study of culture and society. Williams, who, despite his shortcomings in acknowledging the full significance of gender and race in British culture and literature, set a standard for both his close attention to literary language, deep knowledge of history, and his keen awareness of sociopolitical forces and structures.

25. It baffles me why a not insignificant number of literary scholars evince little feeling for or interest in literature or literary language—and I do not exempt scholars in Asian American studies and ethnic studies from this criticism. Literary examples can sometimes feel like add-on accessories to theoretically driven arguments that do not need such examples to exist. Why study literature specifically then? Why not just go out and do, say, economics or law instead? My hunch is that mastering the English language and having purchase on its illustrious literary tradition are still seen as signs that one has achieved full assimilation as an American. For immigrants and even more so for the children of immigrants (like myself)—particularly for Asian Americans, who are viewed as perpetually "alien" and non- or un-American—the route of literary studies as a means to becoming "fully American" exerts a forceful pull (as it did for an earlier generation of Jewish literary scholars, such as Harold Bloom and Stephen Greenblatt—though for them, only through the study of what Bloom calls the "strong poets," like Shakespeare). It is interesting to note that not a few of the contemporary major poetry scholars who resist discussing ethnicity and identity in relation to poetry are themselves the children or grandchildren of ethnicized European immigrants (e.g., Perloff, Bloom, Altieri). See Marjorie Perloff, *The Vienna Paradox: A Memoir* (New York: New Directions, 2004); Antonio Weiss, "Harold Bloom: The Art of Criticism No. 1," *Paris Review* 33.118 (1991): 178–232. See also Stephen Greenblatt, "The Inevitable Pit: Isn't That a Jewish Name?," *London Review of Books* 22.18 (2000): 8–12.

26. Perloff, "It Must Change," 656.

27. "The Claims of Rhetoric: Towards a Historical Poetics (1820–1900)," *American Literary History* 15.1 (2003): 15. See also her *Poetry and Public Discourse in Nineteenth-Century America* (New York: Palgrave Macmillan, 2010). In an earlier article on Paul Celan, Wolosky writes, "But the resistance to history, whether as sociological context or political commitment, . . . is

itself, as [Hans Magnus] Enzensberger warns, a historical phenomenon that occurs in historical contexts." From "The Lyric, History, and the Avant-Garde: Theorizing Paul Celan," *Poetics Today* 22.3 (2001): 652.

28. These tendencies echo and continue New Criticism's strictures against appealing to anything besides the "poem itself," the well-wrought urn. For proponents and practitioners of New Criticism—which, not coincidentally, came into being during the first Red Scare of the 1920s and reached its heyday during the second Red Scare of the 1940s and 1950s—any attempt to bring the social into a reading of a poem was viewed, of course, as "propagandistic," akin to declaring oneself a "Red Communist." (Despite the political implications of Derrida's and Foucault's work, deconstruction and other forms of poststructuralist high theory have done little to change most poetry critics' assumptions about the separation of the poetic and the social.) Though some extratextual concerns (e.g., gender, class, the environment) are perfectly acceptable for critics to discuss, race remains the one social issue that elicits the most intensely heated reaction when raised. Again, this is as true among those who write on avant-garde poetry as those with allegiances to more traditional forms. In other words, the divide between the poetic and the social feels most unbridgeable when "social" means racial.

29. Raymond Williams, *Culture and Society: 1780–1950* (1958; repr., New York: Columbia University Press, 1983), 30–31. It is not a coincidence that many of the poetry critics who do address the linking of aesthetic and political concerns are, or started as, Romanticists (Jerome McGann, David Simpson, Donald Wesling, Susan Wolfson, for example).

30. Not to mention scores of poets writing in other languages and other literary traditions: Leopardi, Baudelaire, Pasternak, Mayakovsky, Neruda, Césaire, and so on.

31. Steve Evans, "Introduction to *Writing from the New Coast*," in *Telling It Slant: Avant-Garde Poetics of the 1990s*, ed. Mark Wallace and Steven Marks (Tuscaloosa: University of Alabama Press, 2002), 13, 15. Evans's piece originally appeared as the introduction to *Oblek No. 12: Writing from the New Coast* (Spring/Fall 1993) 4–11.

32. Charles Bernstein similarly punctures the hollow claims of "diversity": "Within the emerging official cultural space of diversity, figures of difference are often selected because they narrate in a way that can be readily assimilated—not to say absorbed—into the conventional forms of the dominant culture" ("State of the Art," in *A Poetics*, 6).

33. Kenneth Goldsmith, *Uncreative Writing* (New York: Columbia University Press, 2011).

34. Later in the chapter, Goldsmith uses the same somewhat condescending (and familiar liberal) tone to write, "Surely one of the most inspiring identity-based narratives in recent history is that of Barack Obama" (ibid., 86).

35. "State of the Art," 4. Bernstein's analysis is on target, but such an attitude can also run the risk of sounding dismissive of all or most minority cultural production for being "packaged tours of the local color of . . . race [and] . . . ethnicity." In other words, the line between Bernstein's and Perloff's and Gourgouris's views may be finer than might first appear.

36. Or, some would argue, a narrow slice of the contemporary avant-garde scene: mainly founders, fellow travelers, and followers of Language poetry and two particular brands of post-Language writing: Conceptual writing and Flarf. See Kenneth Goldsmith's characterization of these two types of writing, which "fus[e] the avant-garde impulses of the last century with the technologies of the present," in his introduction to the July–August 2009 issue of *Poetry* that he guest-edited on the topic.

37. Though "Latino/a" includes Mónica de la Torre, who emigrated from Mexico as an adult, and Rodrigo Toscano, who does not identify as a Latino poet.

38. The question of race and poetry dates back to the founding of the United States: Thomas Jefferson in his *Notes on the State of Virginia* (published in London in 1787, the same year that the US Constitution was adopted) writes, "Misery is often the parent of the most affecting touches of poetry.—Among the blacks is misery enough, God knows, but no poetry. Love is the peculiar œstrum of the poet. Their love is ardent, but it kindles the senses only, not the imagination. Religion indeed has produced a Phyllis Whately [*sic*]; but it could not produce a poet. The compositions published under her name are below the dignity of criticism. The heroes of the Dunciad are to her, as Hercules to the author of that poem. . . . The improvement of the blacks in body and mind, in the first instance of their mixture with the whites, has been observed by every one, and proves that their inferiority is not the effect merely of their condition of life" (from section 14, "The Laws"). Note the particular oppositions Jefferson sets up in this passage. *Thomas Jefferson: Writings: Autobiography / Notes on the State of Virginia / Public and Private Papers / Addresses / Letters*, ed. Merrill D. Peterson (New York: Library of America, 1984), 266–67.

39. Six of the nine *PMLA* critics work primarily on American poets: Edwards, Izenberg, Jackson, Kaufman, Perloff, and Prins. Terada and Culler write mainly on literary theory, though both cite American poets in their essays. Gourgouris works on theory as well as Greek literature.

40. See, for example, Pauline Maier, *American Scripture: The Making of the Declaration of Independence* (New York: Vintage Books, 1997).

41. Charles Bernstein insists that "poetry be understood as epistemological/inquiry" ("Artifice of Absorption," 17–18).

42. From his poem "The Finger," in *Selected Poems* (Berkeley: University of California Press, 1996), 131.

43. One longtime US congressman agrees: after serving thirty-one years in the House, Barney Frank (Democrat from Massachusetts) said in an interview with *New York* magazine, "I still think race has been the most important problem for us to deal with." Jason Zengerle, "In Conversation: Barney Frank," *New York*, 23 Apr. 2012, http://nymag.com/news/features/barney-frank-full-transcript-2012-4/.

44. Said's description of humanistic study in American universities thirty years ago has, sadly, yet to become dated: "[E]verything that is nonhumanistic, nonliterary and non-European is deposited outside the structure" (*WTC*, 22).

45. Literary forms themselves are also thought to be timeless and universal, existing outside history.

46. Jefferson, *Notes on the State of Virginia*, 267.

47. Elaine Showalter, *Teaching Literature* (Malden, MA: Blackwell, 2003), 23.

48. Even as late as 1993, when I was an MA student in the Writing Seminars at Johns Hopkins University, the only minority text taught in that curriculum was Ralph Ellison's *Invisible Man*.

49. Note that Showalter's evolutionary narrative of progression from bad mimetic methods of reading "identity" literature by minorities to more sophisticated and revolutionary modes of theory reads almost as a mirror image of Gourgouris's postlapsarian narrative of the fall from self-interrogating (presumably theory-laden) literary critical methodology into careless identity-political approaches.

50. See Juliana Chang, *Quiet Fire: A Historical Anthology of Asian American Poetry, 1892–1970* (New York: Asian American Writers' Workshop, 1996).

51. See "Inventing a Culture: Asian American Poetry in the 1970s," chap. 3 in Yu, *Race and the Avant-Garde*, 73–99.

52. One could productively ask why jazz poetics, for example, does not count as avant-garde among poetry critics. An analogy in the music world: Cecil Taylor and Sun Ra are seen as belonging almost wholly in the (black) jazz world, not as having contributed to the new "classical music" of the twentieth and twenty-first centuries—descendants of Arnold Schoenberg, Pierre Boulez, John Cage, and György Ligeti, say—while Philip Glass and John Adams, in many ways, less formally experimental than Taylor and Sun Ra, are seen as part of that lineage. This is so even though Taylor was classically trained at the New England Conservatory and was influenced by modernist and postmodern classical composers, such as Ligeti and Xenakis, as much as he was by black jazz artists.

53. See Donald Wesling, *Bakhtin and the Social Moorings of Poetry* (Lewisburg, PA: Bucknell University Press, 2003).

54. While black or brown or yellow skin may be read as a signifier, a formal sign, it is a sign that is always affixed to a predetermined content, an essence, which remains static.

55. See, for example, Natalia Cecire, "Sentimental Spaces: On Mei-mei Berssenbrugge's 'Nest,'" *Jacket2*, 23 May 2011, https://jacket2.org/article/sentimental-spaces; Jennifer Scappettone, "Versus Seamlessness: Architectonics of Pseudocomplicity in Tan Lin's Ambient Poetics," *boundary 2* 36.3 (2009): 63–76; Charles Altieri, "Intimacy and Experiment in Mei-mei Berssenbrugge's Poetry," in *We Who Love to Be Astonished: Experimental Women's Writing and Performance Poetics*, ed. *Laura Hinton and Cynthia Hogue* (Tuscaloosa: University of Alabama Press, 2002), 54–68; Linda Voris, "A 'Sensitive Empiricism': Berssenbrugge's Phenomenological Investigations," in *American Women Poets in the 21st Century: Where Lyric Meets Language*, ed. Claudia Rankine and Juliana Spahr (Middletown, CT: Wesleyan University Press, 2002), 68–93.

56. "Content never equals meaning," Charles Bernstein reminds us ("Artifice of Absorption," 10).

57. When I taught Asian American literature at a private midwestern university, where students had held a hunger strike to get Asian American subjects included in the curriculum, my English department colleagues seemed to regard my role in the department as providing another form of student services to Asian American students. In my six years there (2000–2006), not one senior colleague besides my "official" mentor ever inquired about my intellectual work. An anecdote might explain why: A senior Modernist there, who taught and wrote mainly on Virginia Woolf

(and in the past, Pound), once asked me, "Why do you put yourself in a box?" When I responded, "Which box?"—I was not sure what she meant since what I work on, minority experimental poetry, is on the margins of various fields and categories—she replied, "The Asian American box," then quickly added, "I can't help it; I just love literature."

The hinged juxtaposition of her two remarks reveals the not uncommon view of the opposition between the narrow, artificially constructed, and nonliterary Asian American "box" to the universal category—clearly not a box—of "literature" (to which Woolf obviously belonged). The irony, of course, is that this English professor did not see herself as occupying any "boxes": whether that of a single-author focus, the literature of a slender chronological period, or women's literature. Though she might not have publicly described African American literature as occupying a box (she had once said to me that African Americans had "suffered more" than Asian Americans, and, thus, their literature was more worthy of study), it was clear that it was the *racial* aspect of Asian American writing—more specifically, its being a secondary ethnic literature, like Native American or Latino/a writing—that made its status as a literary category seem narrow, artificial, and unimportant, indeed, not literature at all. Other categories that were equally "narrow" and artificial in terms of breadth of time period (Modernism) or object of study (a single Modernist author) or social grouping (women) were not indicted as being boxlike.

As with avant-garde critics who deplore thematic justifications for readings of poetry yet use a thematic rationale—here, a negative rationale: the absence of racial markers in the poetry's content—to explain why they do not discuss race in their readings of minority poets, this former colleague saw no contradiction in expressing contempt for extraliterary modes of evaluation and categorization ("extraliterary" here meaning racial—in this case, presumably Asian American "identity") while simultaneously using extraliterary criteria ("degrees of suffering" in so-called real life) to discriminate which minority texts are "real" and worthy of study. One can hardly imagine this same scholar arguing that one should study Woolf and not Pound because Woolf "suffered more," or privilege the study of women's literature over Southern literature because, historically, women have suffered more than Southerners.

58. Equally helpful for rethinking these categories, assumptions, and preconceptions is to examine the contours of the reception of Asian American writing.

59. "The case that upheld the Chinese Exclusion Act to this day remains good law," writes legal scholar Ian Haney Lopez in his *White by Law: The Legal Construction of Race*, rev. ed. (New York: New York University Press, 2006), 28. The issue of class was intermingled—the main target of exclusion was Chinese laborers; merchants and students were exempted.

60. Harlan goes on to write, "But, by the statute in question, a Chinaman can ride in the same passenger coach with white citizens of the United States, while citizens of the black race in Louisiana, many of whom, perhaps, risked their lives for the preservation of the Union, who are entitled, by law, to participate in the political control of the State and nation, who are not excluded, by law or by reason of their race, from public stations of any kind, and who have all the legal rights that belong to white citizens, are yet declared to be criminals, liable to imprisonment, if they ride in a public coach occupied by citizens of the white race." *Plessy v. Ferguson*, 163 U.S. 537 (1896).

61. Compared to "unmodel" minorities—black, Latino/a, Native American—who do not "work as hard."

62. For example, Asian men are praised for not being "angry" like black men, and Asian women for being demure, rather than "brash" and "domineering" like black women. A typical stereotype of Asian Americans is that they are apolitical. These stereotypes shore up and also generate political realities. Concrete facts document the nonvisibility of Asian Americans in various realms of power: for example, the racial demographics of the US Supreme Court; the numbers of Asian Americans who are CEOs or heads of colleges and universities.

63. Not "real" or "true" compared to African Americans, in particular—who, given their history of chattel slavery and the cultural products that emerged from that painful history, are perceived as being more "authentically" and "interestingly" minority because "they suffered more"—a view (as noted earlier) that I have heard expressed, or implied, by academic colleagues numerous times. Comparative minority hierarchies are often invoked not only for suffering but also for cultural products. Asian Americans are perceived as not having produced what the dominant culture views as black culture's tantalizing musical and linguistic forms, such as blues, jazz, and Black English—products of ethnic culture that can be touristically enjoyed, consumed, and, in some cases, tapped into to mediate feelings of cultural and historical guilt. Baraka in his book *Blues*

People refuses to let us forget the larger, inseparable—and inseparably brutal—contexts and histories of African Americans from which this music springs. LeRoi Jones (Amiri Baraka), *Blues People: Negro Music in White America* (1963; repr., New York: Perennial, 2002).

64. Or in the case of African Americans, "standard" English.

65. As we know, not all accents are created equal. A British or French accent is an added bonus, whereas a Mexican or Chinese one devalues the person bearing it and functions as a mark of shame.

66. Even so nonconformist a spirit as Henry David Thoreau—the epitome of American independent thinking and free-spiritedness—in his famous essay on civil disobedience, "Resistance to Civil Government" (1849), cites the example of Asians to mark a group utterly foreign from him (and by implication, other Americans). In critiquing the herd-following, passive, and cowardly behavior of his fellow townspeople in Concord, Thoreau writes, "I saw . . . that they were a distinct race from me by their prejudices and superstitions, as the Chinamen and Malays are." In *Walden* (1854), he writes of the contrast between "Jonathan" (the average American Joe of the nineteenth century) and the "effeminate natives of the Celestial Empire, which Jonathan should be ashamed to know the names of." Henry David Thoreau, *Walden and Civil Disobedience* (New York: Penguin 1986) 406, 79–80.

67. Nightmarish visions of "Asiatic hordes" and the Yellow Peril extend far back in American and European history and continue today in the second decade of the twenty-first century, as China "threatens" to "take over the world," like a modern-day Genghis Khan.

68. While African Americans, Latino/as, and Asian Americans all came to this country from other foreign countries—under vastly different circumstances, to be sure—and share a history of racism and of being viewed as an inferior Other, blacks and Latino/as are not viewed as irredeemably foreign in the same way Asian Americans are. African Americans were cut off centuries ago from their "home" country and their African languages; while they face the continual pressure to speak "like a white person," English is still presumed to be their native tongue. And while Latino/as are denigrated and racialized as Spanish-speaking "illegal aliens," Spanish is nonetheless a European language (and Mexico and Puerto Rico, say, are not viewed as real economic threats in the way that China and Japan are and have been). Although comparing degrees of racial exclusion and discrimination on a scale of suffering is problematic, detailing historically

and differentially the experiences and assumptions various racial groups have been subjected to—their comparative racializations—is both illuminating and necessary for understanding American history and American literary history. Only by these historical differentiations can one begin to understand the ideological logics and specific workings of white settler colonies such as the United States.

69. And not just by uneducated and "ignorant" people. I was once asked by an Ivy League professor of philosophy whether English was my native language, though he had heard my completely American accent and knew I was an English professor; before I could even respond, he answered his own (rhetorical) question: "I think not."

70. From a 1996 interview with Tod Marshall, reprinted as "Riding a Horse That's a Little Too Wild for You," in *Breaking the Alabaster Jar: Conversations with Li-Young Lee*, ed. Earl G. Ingersoll (Rochester, NY: BOA Editions, 2006), 139. In an earlier interview that same year (reprinted as "Art and the Deeper Silence," in ibid., 82), Lee declared, "[S]yntax is identity"—a fact many nonnative speakers of English experience empirically (and not without varying degrees of shame) on a day-to-day basis.

71. One could argue that poetry is the one genre barred to those with a nonnative relationship to English (or any other language). English literary history would seem to demonstrate this idea: while Joseph Conrad and Vladimir Nabokov are the premier examples of first-rate nonnative prose writers in English, one is hard-pressed to name a poet of equivalent caliber who came to English as a second language.

72. A term that originated in the US imperialistic war in the Philippines and was used to refer to different Asian "enemies" in the subsequent wars in Japan, Korea, and Vietnam. During the Vietnam War, the "mere-gook rule" (or MGR) was followed in the US military. According to investigative journalist Nick Turse, MGR was "[t]he notion that Vietnam's inhabitants were something less than human. . . . This held that all Vietnamese—northern and southern, adults and children, armed enemy and innocent civilian—were little more than animals, who could be killed or abused at will." Nick Turse, *Kill Anything That Moves: The Real American War in Vietnam* (New York: Metropolitan Books–Henry Holt, 2013), 50. General Westmoreland tells director Peter Davies in his 1974 film *Hearts and Minds*, "The Oriental doesn't put the same price on life as does the Westerner. Life is plentiful, life is cheap in the Orient." Quoted in ibid., 50.

73. "The realities of power and authority—as well as the resistances offered by men, women, and social movements to institutions, authorities, and orthodoxies—are the realities that make texts possible, that deliver them to their readers, that solicit the attention of critics," writes Said (*WTC*, 5).

74. In a 2010 radio interview, Noam Chomsky stated, "The U.S. in the Philippines probably killed a couple hundred thousand people. It was a vicious brutal war with all kinds of atrocities." He went on to speak at length about the Vietnam War: "[T]he [Iraq] invasion itself, awful as it was—practically destroyed Iraq—never even began to come close to what happened—what we did to Indochina. What we did to Indochina is pretty astonishing. And it's remarkable how it's suppressed to this day. Take Cambodia. That's the latter part of the war after, long after South Vietnam was practically wiped out. In 1970, . . . Nixon, then President, told . . . Henry Kissinger that he wanted large-scale bombing of Cambodia so Kissinger obediently sent the message to—I think it was General Haig at the time—to the military, with classic words. He said, 'Massive bombing campaign of Cambodia. Anything that flies against anything that moves.' I don't think there's a comparable call for genocide anywhere in the archival record—at least I haven't seen one. And it was implemented. But a lot of this remains in the sort of semi-understood consciousness of plenty of people." "Noam Chomsky: The American Socrates on an Upbeat," interview with Christopher Lydon, Radio Open Source, 28 Oct. 2010, http://www.radioopensource.org/noam-chomsky-the-bright-side-of-the-american-socrates/. Chomsky's views are corroborated by Nick Turse in *Kill Anything That Moves*. Turse writes, "This was the real war, the one that barely appears at all in the tens of thousands of volumes written about Vietnam. This was the war . . . in which My Lai was an operation, not an aberration. This was the war in which the American military and successive administrations in Washington produced not a few random massacres or even discrete strings of atrocities, but something on the order of thousands of days of relentless misery—a veritable system of suffering" (22–23).

75. See Mae Ngai, *Impossible Subjects: Illegal Aliens and the Making of Modern America* (Princeton, NJ: Princeton University Press, 2005); and Erika Lee, *At America's Gates: Chinese Immigration During the Exclusion Era, 1882–1943* (Chapel Hill: University of North Carolina Press, 2007).

76. Cathy Song, *Picture Bride* (New Haven, CT: Yale University Press, 1983), x. Stereotypes of "Oriental" spirituality, timeless patience, and the endless ability to suffer, while seemingly much more "positive" than Westmoreland's abhorrent views, nonetheless still function to render one- or two-dimensional, actual Asian (American) lives and beings. See, for example, Jane Iwamura, *Virtual Orientalism: Asian Religions and American Popular Culture* (Oxford: Oxford University Press, 2011).

77. Personal e-mail, 27 Feb. 2011.

78. Rigoberto González, "Shout Out to Ken Chen," http://www.poetryfoundation.org/harriet/2010/04/shout-out-to-ken-chen/; Ken Chen, *Juvenilia* (New Haven, CT: Yale University Press, 2010).

79. See, for example, Charles Altieri, "Images of Form Vs. Images of Content in Contemporary Asian American Poetry," *Qui Parle* 9.1 (1995): 71–91. He compares the work of Marilyn Chin, with her "images of content," unfavorably to that of John Yau, with his "images of form."

80. From the review of Chen, *Juvenilia*, *Publishers Weekly*, 19 Apr. 2010, http://www.publishersweekly.com/978-0-300-16008-6. The reviewer does at least note Chen's use of language, though one cannot help noticing that classical Chinese poets—long-dead "great" writers—are juxtaposed to the mundane accounts of "U.S. immigrant life." Race and the realities of contemporary American society are, it seems, just not as sexy as Wang Wei and Li Yu.

81. Harryette Mullen, "Poetry and Identity," in Wallace and Marks, *Telling It Slant*, 27–31, quote on 31. Also reprinted in Harryette Mullen, *The Cracks Between What We Are and What We Are Supposed to Be: Essays and Interviews* (Tuscaloosa: University of Alabama Press, 2012), 9–12. Citations are to the Wallace and Marks volume.

82. Thus, attempts by, for example, the poet Marilyn Chin to bring classical Chinese forms into Asian American poetry would not count as "experimental."

83. Williams, *The Politics of Modernism*, 79.

84. Mei-mei Berssenbrugge, *Empathy* (Barrytown, NY: Station Hill Press, 1989). Sections of the poem are also included in her *I Love Artists: New and Selected Poems* (Berkeley, CA: University of California Press, 2006).

85. I choose to use the broader term "Asian American" to designate my project even though all of the poets in my book are Chinese American.

The reasons for this particular grouping of poets are various: I have specific cultural and historical knowledge of Chinese and Chinese American history and some familiarity with the Chinese language—all factors that contribute toward situating my readings and making them more nuanced; Chinese American writers have produced the largest and oldest body of literary work among Asian American writers over time (primarily a function of the demographics of immigration: Chinese Americans have been in this country the longest as a group and are the largest Asian American subgroup); and finally, as with all critics, I simply have my own proclivities and tastes. In addition, one major criterion I set for choosing poets to include was that a poet have published three or more books of poetry (Pamela Lu constitutes the only exception—her *Pamela: A Novel* is sui generis; it functions as a hinge between twenty- and twenty-first-century Asian American writing).

I see no fundamental differences between the issues faced by Chinese American poets and those faced by other Asian American ones. Just as Asian Americans tend to be seen as "all looking alike" in the popular imaginary, Asian American writers are generally viewed as monolithically and homogeneously "Asian" in the academic and literary realms. Understanding the shared and similar history of racial interpellation and mistreatment in the United States and of efforts by those in the Asian American movement of the late 1960s and early 1970s to forge strategic alliances and political identities based on these shared histories, I am convinced that my choice of the more general term "Asian American" is apt—even necessary—for the logic and larger implications of my arguments.

86. I would go further and argue that language works toward constituting and creating the poet's subjectivity; language, in a sense, makes the poet. Or, as Marilyn Chin envisions it in her poem "Rhapsody in Plain Yellow," the poet becomes language: "Say: I am the sentence which shall at last elude her." *Rhapsody in Plain Yellow* (New York: W. W. Norton, 2002).

87. That said, I agree with the Russian formalist critic Boris M. Ejxenbaum that "[l]iterature, like any other specific order of things, is not generated from facts belonging to other orders and therefore *cannot be reduced* to such facts" (original emphasis). Nonetheless, this observation does not negate the reality that facts belonging to other orders do exert pressures. Boris M. Ejxenbaum, "Literary Environment," in *Readings in Russian Poetics: Formalist and Structuralist Views*, ed. Ladislav Matejka and Krystyna

Pomorska (1971; repr., Normal, IL: Dalkey Archive Press, 2002), 61. The essay was originally published in Leningrad in 1929.

88. Paul Celan, "Speech on the Occasion of Receiving the Literature Prize of the Free Hanseatic City of Bremen," trans. Rosemarie Waldrop, in *Paul Celan: Collected Prose* (Riverdale-on-Hudson, NY: Sheep Meadow Press, 1986), 34.

89. Susan Wolfson, *Formal Charges: The Shaping of Poetry in British Romanticism* (Stanford, CA: Stanford University Press, 1997), 1.

90. One might ponder the relationship between the "It" here and the "It" in Perloff's "It Must Change."

91. My basic methodology of close reading is one that is deeply informed by the extratextual (social, historical, political) contexts that influence the formation of a poem. Like the critic Jerome McGann, I am well aware of the history and assumptions of this methodology.

92. One certainly can debate the coherence and logic of literary frames based on temporal segmentation or national boundaries or gender or race, but one cannot fault "Asian American literature" for being a more incoherent or artificially constructed category than these others. I understand that there might be some paradox in my arguing for paying close attention to the formal and aesthetic properties of texts grouped together under the nonliterarily organized category "Asian American," but this is no more or less a paradox than that confronting literary scholars who study "Restoration drama" or "Southern literature." They, too, come up against the tension between aesthetic styles, with their formal particularities, and the larger category's rubric of organization—in this case, temporal period or region.

93. Likewise, to argue that a particular aspect of a poet's worldly experience (e.g., Yau's having grown up Chinese American in Brookline, Massachusetts, the son of Shanghainese immigrants) is an influence on the poetic text is not to "reduce" the poem to that one extratextual aspect or to claim that that one aspect is the sole cause of a particular formal feature.

94. Such as "Chineseness" or "exile" or the "universal" experience of existential "homelessness" or the yearning to connect with a parent.

95. This formulation, attributed to Quintilian, begins the entry for "irony" in the latest edition of *The Princeton Encyclopedia of Poetry and Poetics*, 4th ed., ed. Roland Greene and Stephen Cushman (Princeton, NJ: Princeton University Press, 2012), 731. Clare Colebrook wrote the entry, but she does not subscribe to this simplistic view. See a fuller discussion of Colebrook's views on irony in Chapter 4.

CHAPTER 2

1. With the exception of those who teach Asian American literature, of course.

2. Tan's *The Joy Luck Club* (New York: G. P. Putnam's Sons, 1989) was on the *New York Times* bestseller list for over half a year and has sold millions of copies. See http://www.us.penguingroup.com/static/rguides/us/joy_luck_club.html for the publisher's description of the book, an interview with Tan, and "Discussion Questions." After more than a hundred years of writing by those of Asian descent in the United States, Tan's was the first (and in some ways, only) Asian American book that has broken through to a general audience and entered popular consciousness. Maxine Hong Kingston's *The Woman Warrior: Memoirs of a Girlhood Among Ghosts* (New York: Knopf, 1976) was the first Asian American book to gain critical acceptance among American cultural elites, as exemplified by the *New York Times* book reviewers, and the first to be taught widely on college campuses. Jhumpa Lahiri's book of short stories, *The Interpreter of Maladies* (New York: Houghton Mifflin, 1999), won the 2000 Pulitzer Prize for Fiction. Both Lahiri and Lee came to fame in the pages of the *New Yorker*, the publication that epitomizes the American literary establishment. Lee, a graduate of Yale, teaches at Princeton University. Both *The Joy Luck Club* and Lahiri's novel *The Namesake* (New York: Houghton Mifflin, 2003) were made into Hollywood movies, directed by Wayne Wang and Mira Nair, respectively.

Though these Asian American texts are now largely accepted by the literary establishment, their getting into college and university curricula was the result of decades of struggle—by student and community activists in the Third World Strike and the Yellow Power movements in California in the 1960s and 1970s; by students, professors, and others in the 1980s "canon wars"; and by ongoing efforts to question and open up the Anglo-American canon that continue in some form or another to the present moment.

3. What the writer Frank Chin has acerbically called "missionary narratives." Whatever one's disagreement with the ad hominen nature of Chin's attacks against Kingston and other successful Asian American woman writers, he does raise the issue of why publishers seem to favor autobiographical narratives by women who often end up marrying white men and touting the virtues of American society. Various Asian American critics have written at length on the Chin-Kingston controversy,

overwhelmingly indicting what they see as the misogynistic and cultural nationalist bent of his attacks. One could ask, for example, why the talented fiction writer Karen Tei Yamashita, who has published five serious and important books since 1990, has never received the same degree of recognition as Amy Tan in the culture-at-large. One might guess the reason: Yamashita's work is transnational, multiracial, critical of US corporate and governmental activity at home and abroad, formally inventive, and political. Karen Tei Yamashita, *Through the Arc of the Rain Forest* (Minneapolis: Coffee House Press, 1990), *Brazil-Maru* (Minneapolis: Coffee House Press, 1993), *Tropic of Orange* (Minneapolis: Coffee House Press, 1997), *I Hotel* (Minneapolis: Coffee House Press, 2010).

4. Examples include Linh Dinh's short stories in *Blood and Soap* (New York: Seven Stories Press, 2004) and *Fake House* (New York: Seven Stories Press, 2000); Sesshu's Foster's novel *Atomic Aztex* (San Francisco: City Lights, 2005); Bhanu Kapil's *Schizophrene* (Callicoon, NY: Nightboat Books, 2011); Janice Lee's *Daughter* (Seattle: Jaded Ibis Press, 2012); Tan Lin's *Insomnia and the Aunt* (Chicago: Kenning Editions, 2011); Tao Lin's novels *Richard Yates* (New York: Melville House, 2010) and *Eeeee Eee Eeee* (New York: Melville House, 2007) and his collection of short stories, *Bed* (New York: Melville House, 2007).

5. Christopher Beach, *Poetic Culture: Contemporary American Poetry Between Community and Institution* (Evanston, IL: Northwestern University Press, 1999), 19–36.

6. As poetry, as minority poetry, and as a "minor" or "secondary" minority poetry (compared to African American poetry).

7. Margaret Ferguson, Mary Jo Salter, and Jon Stallworthy, eds., *The Norton Anthology of Poetry*, 5th ed. (New York: W. W. Norton, 2004).

8. Bill Moyers's series aired on PBS stations nationwide in 1995; his interviews with the various poets is published as *The Language of Life: A Festival of Poets*, ed. James Haba (New York: Doubleday, 1995); Karen Brailsford, "Musing on the Poet's Plight: Li-Young Lee Puts Verse Things First," *Elle*, Nov. 1991, 162.

9. Gerald Stern's description of Lee's father as "personal physician to Mao, medical advisor to Sukarno, political prisoner in an Indonesian swamp and, finally, Presbyterian minister in a tiny western Pennsylvania town" in his foreword to Lee's first book of poems has been echoed in many subsequent descriptions of and interviews with Lee. Li-Young

Lee, *Rose* (Brockport, NY: BOA Editions, 1986), 9. Of course, what is left unsaid in that "personal history" of "exile" is the US (CIA) involvement in the overthrow of Sukarno. See Peter Dale Scott, "The United States and the Overthrow of Sukarno, 1965–1967," *Pacific Affairs* 58.2 (1985): 239–64, http://www.namebase.org/scott.html.

10. Liam Rector, a reviewer of Lee's first book, *Rose*, wrote, "Lee manages to take very personal materials and rend them into individuated yet generalized, even mythic themes." Liam Rector, "The Documentary of What Is," *Hudson Review* 41 (1988): 399–400, quote on 400. Claiming that Lee's poetry speaks for the mythic Immigrant erases the specific marks attesting to the violence of each racialized group's assimilation into American culture.

11. Or delves too deeply into the colonial and militaristic causes (usually instigated by the United States) of immigration to this country.

12. From a 1996 interview with Tod Marshall, originally published as "To Witness the Invisible: A Talk with Li-Young Lee" in *Kenyon Review* 22.1 (2000): 129-47, and reprinted in Ingersoll, *Breaking the Alabaster Jar*, 133. Citations will be to Ingersoll.

13. From an interview at Indiana University, originally published as "A Conversation with Li-Young Lee" in *Indiana Review* 21.2 (1999): 101–8, and reprinted as "The Pregnant Silence That Opens," in Ingersoll, *Breaking the Alabaster Jar*, 127. Citations will be to Ingersoll.

14. In Lee's family tree, one finds members on both sides of revolution in Asia. Lee's father had connections to Mao and the leftist Sukarno (who was toppled with CIA backing), but Lee's great-grandfather on his mother's side, Yuan Shikai, is an infamous reactionary character in modern Chinese history. After the overthrow of the Qing dynasty, whose rulers Yuan served, and the Chinese Revolution of 1911, Yuan served as the Chinese Republic's first president from 1913 to 1916 (historian Jonathan Spence calls his rule a "dictatorship") but then tried to reestablish imperial rule in 1915 by declaring himself emperor. See Jonathan Spence, *The Search for Modern China*, 3rd ed. (New York: W. W. Norton, 2013), 270. Lee often cites with pride his being a direct descendant of Yuan.

15. Roger Mitchell, review of *Rose*, by Li-Young Lee, *Prairie Schooner* 63.3 (1989): 135–37.

16. And even when an Asian American poet writes, as Lee does here, about those who are "daily defeated" in the American republic, these details are simply glossed over and ignored.

17. On the website for *The Joy Luck Club*'s publisher, Penguin, the first of the "discussion questions" provided asks, "Although the women in *The Joy Luck Club* are Chinese or Chinese American, and their heritage plays an important part in their lives, they also have experiences that all of us face, regardless of culture, even today. They struggle with raising their children, contend with unhappy marriages, cope with difficult financial circumstances, and are disheartened by bad luck. Which of the eight main characters did you identify with the most? Why?" Note the choice of the term "heritage," not "race." See http://www.us.penguingroup.com/static/rguides/us/joy_luck_club.html.

18. One could also argue that the prevalence of metaphors enhances the pleasurable draw of his poems: because metaphors work, arguably, by a process of reification—rendering an abstract thought or feeling into a graspable image or thing—they become nuggets of the "poetic" that readers can consume.

19. Williams, *Culture and Society*, 31. Williams is speaking here of British Romantic writers, but this view is one he more widely held about the essential connections between culture and society.

20. Theodor Adorno, "Commitment," in *Aesthetics and Politics*, afterword by Fredric Jameson (1977; repr., London: Verso, 1980), 190.

21. At the same time, one must be careful not to conflate "minority" and "Asian American" or even "Chinese American"—these are not homogeneous categories. While minority poets share certain experiences, their work encompasses vastly different styles and politics.

22. Frank Chin, Jeffery Paul Chan, Lawson Fusao Inada, and Shawn Wong, eds., *Aiiieeeee! An Anthology of Asian American Writers* (1974; repr., New York: Mentor, 1991), xii.

23. Not to mention mechanically inhuman and—like vermin—overwhelmingly numerous ("hordes," Yellow Peril), linked to various diseases.

24. Paul de Man, "The Epistemology of Metaphor," in *On Metaphor*, ed. Sheldon Sacks (Chicago: University of Chicago Press, 1979), 21. This essay also appears in a posthumous collection of de Man's writing, *Aesthetic Ideology*, ed. Andrzej Warminski (Minneapolis: University of Minnesota Press, 1996), 34–50.

25. Donald Davidson, "What Metaphors Mean," in Sacks, *On Metaphor*, 29.

26. Tropes such as irony, as we shall see in the next chapter, can also function more actively and aggressively as rhetorical strategies that allow the poet to fight back and intervene in dominant racial discourses.

27. If Confucianism were an influence on Lee's work, the reason would be that knowledge had been transmitted, say, by his father—and not by some "race memory"—in this case, a Chinese father who was a Presbyterian minister. A Chinese American poet who was adopted from birth by white parents would not have an "inborn" knowledge of Confucian ethics.

28. In this regard, I disagree with Steven Yao's conservative and Orientalizing readings of Lee's poetry. Yao, who was trained in Modernist studies (his first book was on Pound) and Asian studies, not ethnic or Asian American studies, views Lee's poetry as not being "truly" Chinese or Chinese "enough" because Lee's knowledge of Chinese is not pure but "flawed." This sort of depoliticized and essentializing approach sets the study of Asian American poetry back to a time before the 1960s civil rights struggles but fits well with Orientalist desires, not to mention the wish of those in English departments to believe that we are "post-race" (or as Yao puts it, "postethnic"). The title of his book speaks volumes with its emphasis on both the "foreign" *and* the "postethnic." Steven G. Yao, *Foreign Accents: Chinese American Verse from Exclusion to Postethnicity* (New York: Oxford University Press, 2010).

29. I would add that examining form as a means to reflect and think through larger "extratextual" issues—of assimilation, demands for "authenticity," the construction of the minority subject—points toward new and broader ways of theorizing not only minority and diasporic literature but "canonical" literature as well.

30. Li-Young Lee, *The City in Which I Love You* (Brockport, NY: BOA Editions, 1990), *The Book of My Nights* (Brockport, NY: BOA Editions, 2001), *The Winged Seed: A Remembrance* (St. Paul, MN: Hungry Mind Press, 1999). His most recent book of poems is *Behind My Eyes* (New York: W. W. Norton, 2008).

31. David Simpson, "Metaphor," in *Irony and Authority in Romantic Poetry* (London: Macmillan, 1979), 153.

32. Paul de Man, "Tropes (Rilke)," in *Allegories of Reading: Figural Language in Rousseau, Nietzsche, Rilke, and Proust* (New Haven, CT: Yale University Press, 1979), 47.

33. MacKinnon is talking about the nature of belief, but his remarks on metaphor in theology are apt for nontheological metaphors as well. Donald M. MacKinnon, "Metaphor in Theology," in *Themes in Theology* (Edinburgh: T. and T. Clark, 1987), 75.

34. Charles Altieri once remarked to me in the late 1990s that Lee is "in love with his own rhetoricity"—a judgment that in retrospect strikes me as not inaccurate.

35. One can view Lee's relationship to the English literary canon not dissimilarly, with "English poetry" and the "English language" possessing the same sort of absolute cultural authority as "Chineseness" (or God).

36. Though, of course, never recognized as fully American, as Homi Bhabha understood in the colonial context: "[M]imicry represents an *ironic* compromise. . . . [C]olonial mimicry is the desire for a reformed, recognizable Other, as *a subject of a difference that is almost the same, but not quite*" (original italics). Homi K. Bhabha, "Of Mimicry and Man: The Ambivalence of Colonial Discourse," in *The Location of Culture* (London: Routledge, 1994). 86. The essay originally appeared in *October* 28 (Spring 1984): 125–33.

37. Both in the types of metaphors used (concrete terms rather than abstract ones, linking family members and body parts to stable rooted nature, and vice versa—reflecting an urge to counter the fragmentation of exilic life) and in the overall striving to reach the unreachable "tenor."

38. To what extent is the poet's father also a synecdochic or metonymic stand-in for "China"? Since presumably the logic of metaphor and the logic of metonymy are seen as mutually exclusive or located on radically different axes, this question may blur the boundaries separating the two tropes.

39. One could argue that the discrete identifiable metaphors of desire—the father, China, an idea of "home," and so on—are themselves metaphors for the Absolute and that what Lee *really* desires is an unmediated relationship to God (the ultimate father), who constitutes the Logos and the Word. While Lee's father supposedly knew three hundred Tang poems by heart, he was also fluent, says his son, in six languages besides Chinese—Hebrew, Greek, and various modern European and Asian languages. His knowledge of the Bible and of languages inaccessible to his son necessarily gave him the aura of an Absolute Father: "In the beginning was the Word, and the Word was with God, and the Word was God."

40. Simpson, *Irony and Authority*, 152.

41. A list of individual works on metaphor would be lengthy, ranging from classical writers (e.g., Aristotle, Horace, Cicero, Quintilian), to Romantic ones (e.g., Schelling, Shelley, Nietzsche), to those in this century (e.g., Saussure, Benveniste, Heidegger, Richards, Empson, Jakobson, Kenneth Burke, Bloom, Groupe Mu, Genette, Ricoeur, Riffaterre, Derrida, and de Man). For a broader, theoretical, and useful single-volume discussion of metaphor by practitioners of New Criticism, deconstruction, and analytic philosophy, among others, see Sacks, *On Metaphor*, which includes essays by Paul de Man, Donald Davidson, Wayne Booth, and Paul Ricoeur. Even with the emergence of newer theories that discuss metaphor's more "embodied" usage in the everyday world (e.g., the work of George Lakoff on the use of metaphors in political discourse) and metaphor's links to cognitive science, this volume has held up well for thinking about literary metaphor. For more readings and a broad overview of the scholarship, see also Meredith Martin's entry on metaphor, in Greene and Cushman, *Princeton Encyclopedia of Poetry and Poetics*.

42. Greene and Cushman, *Princeton Encyclopedia of Poetry and Poetics*, 867, 864.

43. Ibid., 864. Meredith Martin, in her entry "Metaphor," makes the apt point that the "A is B" form of metaphor is not the most common; rather, "'the A of B' ('th' expense of spirit') and 'the A B' ('the dying year')" are the more frequent grammatical forms (865).

44. Donald Davidson, "What Metaphors Mean," 37.

45. Northrop Frye, "The Realistic Oriole: A Study of Wallace Stevens," in *Wallace Stevens: A Collection of Critical Essays*, ed. Marie Boroff (Englewood Cliffs, NJ: Prentice-Hall, 1963), 170. Originally published in *Hudson Review* 10.3 (1957): 353–70.

46. Wallace Stevens, "Three Academic Pieces," in *The Necessary Angel: Essays on Reality and the Imagination* (New York: Vintage Books, 1951), 72, 77.

47. Of course, identity itself is predicated on difference. See Samuel Taylor Coleridge on the imagination in his *Biographia Literaria*, vol. 7 of *The Collected Works of Samuel Taylor Coleridge*, ed. James Engell and W. Jackson Bate (Princeton, NJ: Princeton University Press, 1984).

48. David Lloyd argues that "[m]etaphor is not merely the oscillation between sameness and difference, but the process of subordinating difference to identity." See this essay for a cogent analysis of how the aesthetic and public spheres are inextricably linked in the representation of race—

"not only is race a cultural construct but . . . racism is the structure of culture"—and how metaphor is crucial to the discourse on the universal Subject and, concomitantly, racism, and assimilation. David Lloyd, "Race Under Representation," *Oxford Literary Review* 13.1–2 (1991): 62–94, quotes on 71, 82.

49. Kenneth Burke, "Four Master Tropes," in *A Grammar of Motives* (1945; repr., Berkeley: University of California Press, 1969), 503.

50. I. A. Richards, *The Philosophy of Rhetoric* (London: Oxford University Press, 1936), 94.

51. "On Truth and Lies in a Nonmoral Sense," trans. Daniel Breazeale, in *The Rhetorical Tradition: Readings from Classical Times to the Present*, 2nd. ed., ed. Patricia Bizzell and Bruce Herzberg (Boston: Bedford/St. Martins, 2001), 1177.

52. From "A Defence of Poetry" (written in 1821); quoted in Richards, 90.

53. Thanks to David Lloyd for pointing this out to me.

54. "The Formation of a Diasporic Intellectual: An Interview with Stuart Hall," with Kuan-Hsing Chen, in *Stuart Hall: Critical Dialogues in Cultural Studies*, ed. David Morley and Kuan-Hsing Chen (London: Routledge, 1996), 490.

55. Matt Miller, "Darkness Visible: Li-Young Lee Lights Up His Family's Murky Past with Poetry," *Far Eastern Economic Review*, 30 May 1996, 35.

56. Allen Grossman, "Summa Lyrica: A Primer of the Commonplaces in Speculative Poetics," in *The Sighted Singer: Two Works on Poetry for Readers and Writers* (Baltimore: Johns Hopkins University Press, 1992), 249.

57. Simpson, *Irony and Authority*, 158.

58. De Man, "Tropes (Rilke)," 55.

59. All quotations from "Persimmons" are from *Rose*.

60. From a 1991 interview with Anthony Piccione and Stan Sanvel Rubin, reprinted as "Waiting for a Final Shapeliness to Occur," in Ingersoll, *Breaking the Alabaster Jar*, 54.

61. Paul Ricoeur, "The Metaphorical Process as Cognition, Imagination, and Feeling," in Sacks, *On Metaphor*, 146.

62. Bhabha, "Of Mimicry and Man," 86.

63. See Otto Jespersen, *Language: Its Nature, Development and Origin* (New York: Henry Holt, 1924), 123.

64. Thanks to Craig Dworkin for this observation.

65. A consonant that is protoypically and painfully associated with Asian mispronunciation ("flied lice"). "Fright" could indeed lead to "flight."

66. While the boy thinks metaphorically by bringing disparate categories of things and words together, he does not do so by flattening difference, as with the logic of assimilation. And Mrs. Walker, while appearing to respect difference by distinguishing between these various pairs of words, actually enforces a false binary and offers no freedom of choice— just as there is no real "choice" when assimilating as an American between one's "alien," nonwhite culture and a white Anglo-European mode of dress, demeanor, and so forth.

67. Aristotle, *Poetics* (New York: Modern Library, 1954), 251.

68. De Man, "The Epistemology of Metaphor," 15.

69. I realize that, to some degree, all figurative language runs the danger of "prettifying" or making "poetic" even the most brutal human acts, but my point here about the potential issue with figurative language in Lee's poetry (Romantic, ethnic, lushly rhetorical) might not easily come to mind in a culture (and an academy) that prides itself on valuing "diversity" and "multiculturalism" and whose members feel virtuous about the mere act of consuming the literature (and suffering) of "Others."

70. A wisdom that, while shown to be more "true" than Mrs. Walker's American ignorance, nonetheless remains confined to the "private" space of the family.

71. The relative paucity of explicit countable metaphors in *City* might surprise readers who, beguiled into the lyricality of Lee's poetry, imagine a more pervasive perfume of figurative language (the volume title, after all, is itself a rich spatial metaphor).

72. Or to use another example from *Rose*: In the poem "Braiding," one of the key metaphors at work is that of braiding as a way to speak about poetic making. But nowhere in the poem can one identify a metaphoric phrase that says so explicitly in "A is B" form.

73. Ricoeur, "The Metaphorical Process as Cognition, Imagination, and Feeling," 144. Ricoeur's use of "whole utterance" refers to the sentence, but I think can just as well be applied to a body of sentences.

74. By contrast to the poet's father, wife, and sisters, his mother is never represented metaphorically. This fact can imply at least two divergent causes: in the poet's mind, she is seen more literally—the preparer of food, a woman washing her hair—without recourse to figurative lan-

guage; alternatively, she is rendered invisible by the absence of vivid figurative language to highlight her presence. In this scenario, she becomes a medium, not an agent, of expression.

75. Simpson, *Irony and Authority*, 159.

76. Lewis Coble and Kathleen Cusick, "The Poetry in the Poet: An Interview with Li-Young Lee," *Expressions* [Greenville, NC] (Spring 1991): 21.

77. Piccione and Sanvel Rubin, "Waiting For a Final Shapeliness to Occur," 47.

78. I am not arguing here for a poetics of "wholeness." I agree with Shelley Wong's arguments against a normalizing "discourse of wholeness," which the dominant culture posits as "an originary state from which humanity—or the particular minority group in question—has been estranged, or as the endpoint or *telos* of an eluctable, if ofttimes unsteady progress." See Wong, "Unnaming the Same: Theresa Hak Kyung Cha's *Dictée*," in *Writing Self, Writing Nation*, ed. Elaine H. Kim and Norma Alarcon (Berkeley, CA: Third Woman Press, 1994), 108.

79. In a 1996 interview, Lee spoke of being excluded from both Asian American and white culture in the United States: "[W]hen we were growing up, Asian Americans we knew wanted nothing to do with us. On the one hand, we would meet them and the ones who were born here felt we were too Chinese because we were very traditional, but the ones who were not born here felt we were too Western. The Asian-American community wasn't a refuge for us. . . . We were really outside, I mean, outside white culture, outside Asian-American culture. Outside. You know, just outside." Patty Cooper and Alex Yu, "Art Is Who We Are," in Sacks, *Breaking the Alabaster Jar*, 60. The interview originally appeared as "A Family Affair: Li Lin and Li Young [*sic*] Lee" in *Riksha*, no. 3 (1997): 28–47.

80. Simpson, *Irony and Authority*, 160. Coleridge reiterated his suspicion about metaphor as tending to present itself as reality (143).

81. Even in the long and sensual title poem, "The City in Which I Love You" (itself invoking a spatial metaphor), there are only four metaphors, all referring to his beloved wife, Donna: she is a bruise; her hair, "a torso of light"; her labia, "soft-finned fruit"; the poet's penis, a sword.

82. Death is a phrase ("Furious Versions"), an irregular postage stamp ("For a New Citizen of These United States"), a giant and a guest ("You Must Sing"); God is "that old furnace" ("This Hour and What Is Dead").

83. In the five poems between "The Interrogation" and "This Room and Everything in It," only two metaphors are used and then in the form of questions about death: "Was death giant?" and "Was death a guest?" ("You Must Sing").

84. This formulation also contradicts Roman Jakobson's famous mutually exclusive designation of metaphor as substitution and metonymy as combination. See his "Two Aspects of Language and Two Types of Aphasic Disturbances" (1956), in *Language in Literature*, ed. Krystyna Pomorska and Stephen Rudy (Cambridge, MA: Harvard University Press, 1987), 95–114.

85. One might consider the difference between the use of metaphors in the Bible (e.g., lamb, shepherd, son, Father) and the use of metaphor by the poet-son of an Old Testamental Presbyterian minister-father. Obviously, the wine and wafer in rites of communion are not considered symbolic or metaphorical by some Christians.

86. Simpson, *Irony and Authority*, 153.

87. Ibid., 158.

88. Yu, *Race and the Avant-Garde*, 146.

89. One might recall Coleridge's remark about metaphor being "grounded on an apparent likeness of things essentially different." Simpson, "Metaphor," 141.

90. Shelley Wong has argued convincingly that a "poetics of cleaving" characterizes the work of another Asian American poet, Theresa Hak Kyung Cha. Wong, "Unnaming the Same," 112.

91. Coble and Cusick, "The Poetry in the Poet," 22.

92. Aristotle, *Poetics*, 251.

93. Lloyd, "Race Under Representation," 72–73.

94. While all immigrants face some degree of suspicion and the pressure to assimilate into American culture and the English language, Asian American poets, in particular, are viewed as writing in a language that does not "belong" to them—a skepticism that a second-generation German American poet, for example, would never face.

95. Laura Ann Dearing and Michael Graber, "Working to Hear the Hum," in Sacks, *Breaking the Alabaster Jar*, 94. The interview originally appeared as "An Interview with Li-Young Lee," *Crab Orchard Review* 4.1 (1998): 107–21.

96. Lee, "The Pregnant Silence That Opens," 127.

97. Coble and Cusick, "The Poetry in the Poet," 22.

98. The entry is dated 6 April 1824. Keep in mind that Thoreau will be reading and quoting from Confucius's *Analects* and other Asian sources (most notably in *Walden*) only a couple of decades later. One sees in Emerson's arguments yet another example of the American tendency to hierarchize and divide racial minorities; his comparison of Chinese and Africans prefigures the current attitude that Asian Americans are not "real" minorities, as are blacks, who "have hewn the wood & drawn the water." *The Journals and Miscellaneous Notebooks of Ralph Waldo Emerson, Vol. 2, 1822–1826*, ed. William H. Gilman, Alfred R. Ferguson, and Merrell R. Davis (Cambridge, MA: Harvard University Press, 1961), 378–79. Some of Emerson's sentiments echo those of Samuel Johnson, who also brings up "crockery" (Chinese porcelain was an item that Westerners coveted; it constituted a large part of the China trade that led to Britain's enormous trade deficits to China in the eighteenth and nineteenth centuries). Boswell recounts a conversation from 1778: "Johnson called the East-Indians barbarians. Boswell: 'You will except the Chinese, Sir?' Johnson: 'No, Sir.' Boswell: 'Have they not arts?' Johnson: 'They have pottery.' Boswell: 'What do you say to the written characters of their language?' Johnson: 'Sir, they have not an alphabet. They have not been able to form what all other nations have formed.'" James Boswell, *The Life of Samuel Johnson*, ed. Christopher Hibbert (Harmondsworth, UK: Penguin, 1979), 259.

99. Piccione and Sanvel Rubin, "Waiting for a Final Shapeliness to Occur," 50–51.

100. Ricoeur, "The Metaphorical Process," 142.

101. Grossman, "Summa Lyrica," 250.

102. Compare Edward Said's idea of filiation and affiliation ("blood and design") in *The World, the Text, and the Critic*, especially in his introduction ("Secular Criticism"), 1–30.

103. Yet unlike in confessional poetry, in "The Cleaving" the relation between self and other is personal without focusing wholly on the individual speaking "I" to the exclusion of others.

104. Ralph Waldo Emerson, "Self-Reliance," in *Essays: First and Second Series* (New York: Vintage Books / Library of America, 1990), 45.

105. Walt Whitman, "Song of Myself," from *Leaves of Grass*. Reprinted in Donald McQuade, Robert Atwan, Martha Banta, Justin Kaplan, David Minter, and Robert Steptoe, eds., *The Harper American Literature*, 2nd ed., vol. 1 (New York: HarperCollins, 1994), 2441–86. One could, of course, criticize Whitman, as critics have done, for his overlooking the

fact that "you, me, all" are not "precisely the same." But his poetic vision of the United States, even if not actualized in history, is nonetheless a compelling and largely sympathetic one.

CHAPTER 3

1. "Now, through her mysterious beneficence," writes poetry critic Steve Evans, "[Ruth] Lilly had lifted Poetry from this place of squalor and cultural obsolescence: from a grandparent warehoused in a seedy retirement home, it had been transformed into the newest and richest kid on the block, its financial capital now far exceeding the dwindling symbolic capital it had been husbanding since the days of first-wave modernism." See Steve Evans, "Free (Market) Verse," 14 June 2010, www.thirdfactory. net/freemarketverse-all.html. A version appeared in the *Baffler* 17 (2006): 57–64.

2. Chin has been the recipient of Stegner, NEA, Rockefeller Foundation, Fulbright, and Radcliffe Institute fellowships, among others. She holds an MFA from the University of Iowa and is an active member of Yaddo. She is the author of three books of poetry—*Dwarf Bamboo* (Greenfield Center, NY: Greenfield Review Press, 1987); *The Phoenix Gone, the Terrace Empty* (Minneapolis: Milkweed Editions, 1994), rev. ed. published by Milkweed in 2009; *Rhapsody in Plain Yellow* (2002)—and one collection of prose, *Revenge of the Mooncake Vixen* (2009). Her last two books were both published by the major New York publishing house W. W. Norton.

3. *Poetry* 192.1 (Apr. 2008): 42.

4. *Poetry* 192.3 (June 2008): 251.

5. For example, Bednarik leaves unspecified who the "someone else" is—Ho Xuan Huong or Balaban?

6. In an e-mail to me on 26 Feb. 2011, Chin notes that "Nom is not a Romanised language and that it used Classical Chinese characters as the base language and added extra Chinese radicals to the characters to render sonic equivalences to the Vietnamese language. . . . The Vietnamese scholar/poets had a long relationship with Chinese poetry and wrote beautiful poems in classical Chinese for many years, long after the Chinese have stopped using classical Chinese. Remember that Ho Chi Min chose to write poems in Classical Chinese and did not choose to use the Romanized modern script. . . . Ho Xuan knew the Chinese quatrain

very well—and is well versed in the Tang and Sung era poetry." Chin's claims seem backed up, even on the website for Balaban's own Vietnamese Nôm Preservation Foundation: "The Vietnamese Nôm Preservation Foundation was founded in 1999 as a public charity devoted to preserving 1000 years of writing in Chữ Nôm, the Chinese-like script that Vietnamese used to record their own language and its vast heritage of poetry, history, medicine, and religion."See http://www.nomfoundation.org/About-the-Foundation/About-the-VNPF.

7. *Poetry* 192.4 (July–Aug. 2008): 421.

8. Balaban's choice of the word "entitlement" to indict Chin inevitably evokes the familiar discourse of contemporary debates—for example, about affirmative action—in which the specter of "entitled" minorities is raised.

9. Gayatri Spivak's oft-cited "[w]hite men are saving brown women from brown men"—from her seminal essay "Can the Subaltern Speak?," in *Marxism and the Interpretation of Culture*, ed. Cary Nelson and Lawrence Grossberg (Urbana: University of Illinois Press, 1988), 296.

10. Jane Perlez, "Hanoi Journal: Deciphering the Code to Vietnam's Old Literary Treasures," *New York Times*, 15 June 2006, sec. A, 4.

11. Turse, *Kill Anything That Moves*, 11–13.

12. After all, it was Bednarik who first took the offense, comparing Chin's translation unfavorably to Balaban's, while disingenuously invoking Eliot Weinberger's case for a multiplicity and diversity of translations.

13. *Poetry* 192.5 (Sept. 2008): 501.

14. *Poetry* 192.4 (July–Aug. 2008): 423.

15. While simultaneously failing to note the dual Western colonial traces in the group's name(s). Wiegers certainly cannot be accused of having a sense of irony.

16. Perlez, "Hanoi Journal."

17. John Balaban, *Spring Essence: The Poetry of Ho Xuan Huong* (Port Townsend, WA: Copper Canyon Press, 2000).

18. Linh Dinh, "Hồ Xuân Hương," Harriet blog, National Poetry Foundation, 17 May 2008, http://www.poetryfoundation.org/harriet/2008/05/hồ-xuan-hương/. Dinh also criticizes Balaban for exotifying not only Ho Xuan Huong and Vietnamese women (a bare-breasted woman "hiding her face behind a gong or a wok" appears on the cover of the book) but Vietnamese people in general. Dinh also takes on the claim that appears in a recently reissued edition of Balaban's 1980 *Ca Dao Vietnam: Bilingual Anthology of Vietnamese*

Folk Poetry: "During the Vietnam war, John Balaban traveled the Vietnamese countryside alone, taping, transcribing, and translating oral folk poems known as 'ca dao.' No one had ever done this before, and it was Balaban's belief that his project would help end the war." Dinh comments in response: "Nearly all the folk poems in Balaban's book could be found in Nguyễn Văn Ngọc's *Tục Ngữ Phong Dao*, however, published in Saigon in 1925, and reissued many, many times. A standard reference book, it is known to all scholars and many students and casual readers."

Marjorie Perloff rightly says, in an interview with Uppinder Mehan for the Society for Critical Exchange on 30 Jan. 2009: "*Poetry* magazine is just as dull as ever, pretty much, little better—the little tiny magazine, you know, which is the epitome of traditional poetry, but they have a very good blog . . . and on the blog they have fabulous things . . . all kinds of funny things and good arguments and good debates and all kinds of things go, so that has broadened the base enormously. . . . You can do a lot more on a blog than you can do in the magazine that comes out, you know, every month. . . . So the magazine remains the staid part for the sort of staid audience, but the blog is very lively and changes every day, has all kinds of things on it, and you can hear all kinds of talks on it. It's just really good." See http://www.youtube.com/watch?v=dUFubgOErMw &feature=related.

19. "Boo hoo" is both onomatopoeic and slang.

20. *Poetry* 192.4 (July–Aug. 2008): 422.

21. *Poetry* 192.5 (Sept. 2008): 502.

22. The irony, of course, is that pasta originated in China.

23. Though her having read literally was what got her into trouble with Bednarik and Grant in the first place.

24. Of course, racist "readings" of people based on phenotypic traits— for example, skin color, nose bridges, hair texture—are readings of the face value or surface meaning of bodily signifiers. They are at one and the same time overdeterminedly denotative (slanted eyes = "Asiatic" alien) and connotative (e.g., slanted eyes = inscrutability and untrustworthy sneakiness).

25. *Poetry* 192.4 (July–Aug. 2008): 422. The sincerity of this sentiment is undercut, of course, by the condescending tone of "makes perfect sense" and of the sentence that follows: "I hear her point, and thank her for it." The rest of the letter makes perfectly clear that he's not "thanking" her for anything.

26. Ibid.

27. Chin is one of the only Asian American poets writing today whose work can be considered overtly political; by contrast, in the late 1960s and early 1970s, when Asian American political consciousness was coming into being, there were several women poets (e.g., Janice Mirikitani, Faye Chiang) who were writing explicitly political poems and who were crucial to the gathering Yellow Power movement.

28. "Poetry gave me a safe place to grieve and contemplate," Chin said in 2002. Thom Tammaro and Kristin Garaas-Johnson, "The Rigorous Muse: A Conversation with Poet Marilyn Chin," *Bloomsbury Review*, Mar.–Apr. 2004, 17.

29. See Claire Colebrook, *Irony in the Work of Philosophy* (Lincoln: University of Nebraska Press, 2002).

30. Claire Colebrook, *Irony* (London: Routledge, 2004), 12.

31. Ibid. A few pages later, Colebrook writes, "Recognising irony, therefore, foregrounds the social, conventional and political aspects of language: that language is not just a logical system but relies on assumed norms and values" (16).

32. Arguably, this gulf between writer and readership may be even wider for Asian American writers—even compared to other minority writers—since Asians are seen as so alien and inscrutable.

33. Some people may want pizza, others may want the spicy indigestion-causing curry, a few may even try the strange and off-putting entrails, and so forth.

34. A more political reading would argue it is precisely in creating a counter-hierarchy of those who are excluded from ironic meaning and those who are not that Chin reverses the usual power hierarchies of included and excluded within society. As Colebrook writes, "Irony has a hierarchical dimension, excluding some members of the audience from its 'other' or implied sense" (Greene and Cushman, *Princeton Encyclopedia of Poetry and Poetics*, 732).

35. She is discussing Linda Hutcheon's work on irony. Colebrook, *Irony*, 159.

36. "*Meridians* Interview with Marilyn Chin," *Meridians: Feminism, Race, Transnationalism* 2.2 (2002): 69.

37. Ibid., 68.

38. Colebrook, *Irony in the Work of Philosophy*, 16, 22.

CHAPTER 4

1. From a 1996 interview with Laura Ann Dearing and Michael Graber, "Working to Hear the Hum," 93.

2. Anonymous, "An Interview with Marilyn Chin," *Indiana Review* 26.1 (2004): 113.

3. Ibid., 118. Chin continues the line of female and feminist activist poetry writing, such as that by Janice Mirikitani and Faye Chiang, which was so central to the formation of an Asian American consciousness in the 1960s and 1970s.

4. The larger and more existential forms of irony—Socratic, Romantic, and Kierkegaardian—are a slightly more complex matter.

5. Colebrook, *Irony*, 44–45; Colebrook, *Irony in the Work of Philosophy*, 15.

6. Paul de Man, "The Concept of Irony," in Warminski, *Aesthetic Ideology*, 178–79. De Man is quoting from Fragment 668 in Schlegel's *Zur Philosophie* (1797).

7. In her entry "Irony" in Greene and Cushman, *Princeton Encyclopedia of Poetry and Poetics*, Colebrook discusses irony's use as a trope by also citing this more familiar sense: "If other figures, such as metaphor, substitute like for like, irony substitutes opposites" (732).

8. Stuart Hall, "New Ethnicities," in Morley and Chen, *Stuart Hall: Critical Dialogues in Cultural Studies*, 446.

9. The metaphor here is tricky. These figures of speech do not simply or only "mirror" or "echo" or "parallel" the structures of Chin's Chinese American female subjectivity but contribute, as language does, toward the formation of this subjectivity; at the same time, irony also sheds light, as it were, on certain formal structures of the social and the political.

10. Indeed, Chin's poetry is marked as much by melancholy as by a sassy irony. This sadness and melancholy have become more pronounced over time and are felt most keenly in her most recent book of poetry, *Rhapsody in Plain Yellow*, with its elegies to her mother, grandmother, and lover.

11. Luce Irigaray, *Speculum of the Other Woman* (Ithaca, NY: Cornell University Press, 1985), 76; quoted in Linda Hutcheon, *Irony's Edge: The Theory and Politics of Irony* (London: Routledge, 1995), 34.

12. De Man notes, in "The Concept of Irony," that one of the ways that irony—here, Schlegelian irony—has been "defused" has been to reduce it "to an aesthetic practice or artistic device, a *Kunsmittel*. Irony is an artistic

342 <emphasis>Notes</emphasis>

effect, something a text does for aesthetic reasons, to heighten or to diversify the aesthetic appeal of this text. This is traditionally how authoritative books about irony deal with the problem" (169).

13. The other exceptions include Arthur Sze and Jeffrey Yang.

14. She dedicates her first book to one of her mentors, Ai Qing, the revolutionary mainland Chinese poet (and the father of the well-known artist-provocateur Ai Weiwei).

15. Tarisa Matsumoto, "Foxtrot with Marilyn: An Interview," in *Page to Page: Retrospectives of Writers from the Seattle Review*, ed. Colleen J. McElroy (Seattle: University of Washington Press, 2006), 212.

16. Personal e-mail, 26 Feb. 2011.

17. *OED* online, 2nd ed. (1989), Dec. 2012, http://www.oed.com. Other meanings include "[a] rude, wild, uncivilized person" and "[a]pplied by the Chinese contemptuously to foreigners." As an adjective, "barbarian" can mean "[a]pplied by nations, generally depreciatively, to foreigners; thus at various times and with various speakers or writers: non-Hellenic, non-Roman (*most usual*), non-Christian"; "[u]ncivilized, rude, savage, barbarous" (original emphasis).

18. Ibid., Mar. 2013.

19. Ibid. Likewise, the verb "barbarize" focuses on misuses of language and grammar: "1. *intr.* To speak or write like a barbarian; to violate the laws of Latin or Greek grammar. 2. *trans.* a. To render barbarous. . . . b. To corrupt or alter (language) from any classical standard or type (or what is so considered)." Like "barbarism," "barbarity" focuses on questions of culture (or, rather, the absence thereof): "4. a. Barbarism of style in art. . . . b. with *pl.* An instance of want of artistic culture." And "barbaric": "[p]ertaining or proper to barbarians or their art; in the characteristic style of barbarians, as opposed to that of civilized countries or ages."

20. Alex Preminger and T. V. F. Brogan, eds., *The New Princeton Encyclopedia of Poetry and Poetics* (Princeton, NJ: Princeton University Press, 1993), 633.

21. Ibid.

22. Colebrook, *Irony*, 1.

23. Colebrook's entry "Irony," in Greene and Cushman, *Princeton Encyclopedia of Poetry and Poetics*, 731–32. Colebrook writes, "In the 21st c., both celebrations and denunciations of Socratic irony remain in force" (732).

24. Ibid., 731.

25. O'Connor and Behler entry "Irony," in Preminger and Brogan, *New Princeton Encyclopedia of Poetry and Poetics*, 634.

26. Colebrook on irony, in Greene and Cushman, *Princeton Encyclopedia of Poetry and Poetics*, 732.

27. Preminger and Brogan, *New Princeton Encyclopedia of Poetry and Poetics*, 635. An example of a brilliant deconstructive work on irony: Paul de Man, "The Rhetoric of Temporality," in *Blindness and Insight: Essays in the Rhetoric of Contemporary Criticism* (Minneapolis: University of Minnesota Press, 1983), 187–228. His later lecture, "The Concept of Irony," given in 1977 at Ohio State University and transcribed in *Aesthetic Ideology*, is in many ways an *autocritique* (de Man's term) of "The Rhetoric of Temporality" ("Concept of Irony," 170).

28. Colebrook on irony, in Greene and Cushman, *Princeton Encyclopedia of Poetry and Poetics*, 732.

29. William Packard, *The Poet's Dictionary* (1989; repr., New York: Harper Perennial, 1994), 100.

30. Richard A. Lanham, *Handlist of Rhetorical Terms*, 2nd ed. (Berkeley: University of California Press, 1991), 92.

31. Wayne C. Booth, *A Rhetoric of Irony* (Chicago: University of Chicago Press, 1974), 7.

32. De Man, "Concept of Irony," 167.

33. Georgia Albert, "Understanding Irony: Three *essais* on Friedrich Schlegel," *MLN* 108.5 (Dec. 1993): 826.

34. Ibid., 828–29.

35. Burke, "Four Master Tropes," 512–13.

36. F. Chin et al., *Aiiieeeee!*, xii.

37. Her reference is to Sigmund Freud, "Jokes and Their Relation to the Unconscious," in *The Standard Edition of the Complete Psychological Works of Sigmund Freud. Jokes and Their Relation to the Unconscious*, ed. by James Strachey (New York: W. W. Norton, 1990).

38. Jennifer Reksovna Karyshyn, review of *Irony's Edge: The Theory and Politics of Irony*, *MLN* 110 (1995): 974.

39. Hutcheon, *Irony's Edge*, 9. The figure of the *eiron* was one "who does not and cannot speak directly," write William Harmon and Hugh Holman in their widely used *A Handbook to Literature*, 10th ed. (New York: Pearson/Prentice Hall, 2006), 283.

40. Hutcheon, *Irony's Edge*, 52. Fischer is quoted by Hutcheon (26). The phrase originally appeared in Fischer's "Ethnicity and the Post-modern

Arts of Memory," in *Writing Culture: The Poetics and Politics of Ethnography*, ed. James Clifford and George E. Marcus (Berkeley: University of California Press, 1986), 224.

41. Bhabha, "Of Mimicry and Man," 86.

42. Hutcheon, *Irony's Edge*, 50.

43. This term is Richard Terdiman's, quoted by Hutcheon from his *Discourse/Counter-Discourse: The Theory and Practice of Symbolic Resistance in Nineteenth-Century France* (Ithaca, NY: Cornell University Press, 1985), 13.

44. Hutcheon, *Irony's Edge*, 30.

45. Burke cites three: relativism, the "Pharisaic temptation" to feel superior, and "tendency towards the simplification of literalness" ("Four Master Tropes," 516).

46. Moyers, *Language of Life*, 73.

47. I would resist Chin's characterization of "doubleness" because I think this term does tend to oversimplify the multiple conflicting, contradictory, but also inseparable, aspects of herself and her work; there are not just two clear and differentiated "parts": "Chinese" and "white"/"Western"/"American."

48. The title "Exile's Letter" reflects a long tradition of Chinese exilic writing but also explicitly echoes a poem with the same title (sans subtitle) written by Ezra Pound in classical Chinese style to his friend Henri Gaudier-Brzeska, who was fighting at the front in World War I.

49. If they knew their (Asian) American history better, they would be aware that Asian labor was imported into the South to replace declining African American labor after the Civil War. See Ronald Takaki, *Strangers from a Different Shore*, updated and rev. ed. (Boston: Little, Brown, 1998), 94–95.

50. One sees, of course, the prefiguring of the "model minority" stereotype of Asian Americans that also functions to further capitalist profit in the twentieth and twenty-first centuries. This more "positive" view seems to run counter to Emerson's verdict on the relative merits of Chinese and black global labor (as noted in Chapter 2) and to the opinions of some academics who argue that, because Asian Americans did not "suffer" as much as blacks in US history (that is, were not chattel slaves), their literature is not as worthy of study. In reality, all three of these historical views share a similar logic and goal: to pit minorities against one another and divide them, in the interest of profit and white hegemony.

51. Takaki, *Strangers from a Different Shore*, 94–95.

52. In a clever rhetorical move, Madame Prevert begins by asking not whether the Chinese family has eaten (or eats) dogs but which dogs exactly did they "mistakenly" eat: her question is rhetorical, a pre-indictment, grounded in the common stereotype of Chinese as dogeaters.

53. John King Fairbank, *The Great Chinese Revolution 1800–1985* (New York: Harper Perennial, 1987), 147.

54. Note the play between "dessicated" (*sic*) and "cultivated." "Cultivated" also brings to mind the oppositional colonial rhetoric of the "civilized" (versus the "barbaric").

55. The shifting pronouns—"we," "I," "you"—function importantly in this poem, as they do in many of Chin's other poems (and in the work of the other poets in this volume): they not only express different points of view but clue the reader in to ironic language. *Who* is doing the talking affects our reading of lines as sincere or ironic.

56. The image here reminds us of Madame Prevert's dogs waiting behind the fence to devour the cabbages.

57. The "profitability" of the Asian female body does not function abstractly, metaphorically, or symbolically, as is concretely and amply demonstrated by the multi-billion-dollar sex industries—which include not only pornography, massage parlors, mail-order brides, and sexual tourism but also the commercial sex zones cultivated around, and by, the pervasive presence of US military bases in Asia.

58. The comparative literature critic Wai-lim Yip quotes the line in "Syntax and Horizon of Representation in Classical Chinese and Modern American Poetry" [hereafter, "Syntax and Horizon"] in his *Diffusion of Distances: Dialogues Between Chinese and Western Poetics* (Berkeley: University of California Press, 1993), 47.

59. See Arthur Waldron, *The Great Wall of China: From History to Myth* (New York: Cambridge University Press, 1990).

60. Kenneth Rexroth's and Ling Chung's *Women Poets of China* is the source for the Ts'ai Yen material (New York: New Directions, 1972), 134.

61. Ibid., 4–7.

62. In the eighth century, a new song lyric, the *ci*, appeared; it was composed for women singers and often represented, says Stephen Owen, a "stylized 'feminine' voice—although a feminine voice constructed by male writers." Thus, writes Owen, "we have the peculiar situation of men writing words, often explicitly, in the voices of women, to be sung back to

them [the men]." Many scholars believe that the rise of the new song lyric "came alongside new melodies and performance traditions, some from Central Asia." Stephen Owen, *An Anthology of Chinese Literature: Beginnings to 1911* (New York: W. W. Norton, 1996), 582. Hence, we can see that what many now consider "pure" (Han) Chinese classical poetry was influenced by "barbarian" cultures. Critics who have written cogently on traditional Chinese poetry and its intersection with Western poetics include Owen, James J. Y. Liu, and Wai-lim Yip.

63. Chin called *The Woman Warrior* "a very important book in my life. . . . I think it gave us permission to go on." Marilyn Chin, "Writing the Other: A Conversation with Maxine Hong Kingston," *Poetry Flash*, no. 198 (Sept. 1989): 5.

64. After the last line, a note in italics reads "after Cavafy"—a reference to the gay Greek poet Constantine Cavafy (1863–1933), who lived in Alexandria, also a diasporic subject.

65. De Man, "The Concept of Irony," 178.

66. See Michael Godley, "The End of the Queue: Hair as Symbol in Chinese History," *East Asian History*, no. 8 (1994): 53–72.

67. Slightly less plausible because the current American stereotype of Asian men is that they are sexless automatons, not virile horsemen—though, of course, the yellow-peril rhetoric of "hordes" of invading Asians still reverberates, as does the figure of Genghis Khan.

68. Takaki, *Strangers from a Different Shore*, 327–30.

69. In a later poem, "Horse Horse Hyphen Hyphen," which appears in *Rhapsody in Plain Yellow*, the speaker explicitly conflates herself with a horse: "He will press his tongue / Into my neighing throat" (69).

70. China, too, has always been a space of racial and cultural mixing, even within its "Han" borders: Mongol, Manchu, and other minority influences have profoundly affected the culture; Buddhism and Islam have done the same.

71. Moyers, *Language of Life*, 69.

72. Hall, "New Ethnicities," 445.

73. Ibid.," 444.

74. Moyers, *Language of Life*, 69.

75. In an e-mail to me on 26 Feb. 2011, Chin wrote, "My work is highly sexualized."

76. Marilyn Chin, "Happiness: A Manifesto," *Zyzzyva* 11.1 (1995): 55–59. A revised version appears in *Revenge of the Mooncake Vixen*, 195–201. I quote from her original version.

77. Here, she would find agreement from quite a few of the *PMLA*'s "New Lyric Studies" group.

78. In the modern world, which is to say for the last five hundred years at least, the model of masculinity and male beauty that has been deemed the proper object of female desire has been white, not Asian. This is a male beauty we *all* know.

79. Moyers, *Language of Life*, 67.

80. Diana Toy was an anorexic mental patient whom Chin tutored in 1983 at Crestwood Psychiatric Hospital. The irony of her situation is that in the land of plenty, where her family arrived to escape famine in China, she has chosen to starve herself. Her refusal to eat becomes an act of defiance against both her Chinese family, who would be appalled at the wastefulness, and the American myth that promises happiness amid overflowing supermarket aisles. But her slow starvation also symbolizes a spiritual hunger in this country of "asphalt loneliness."

81. One might ask whose voices are speaking in the italicized phrases "took precautions" and "[p]oor thang."

82. Chin, "Writing the Other," 6.

83. Moyers, *Language of Life*, 73.

84. I am not suggesting that all or even most white poets focus solely on the private "I"—there are plenty of counterexamples. However, the experience of growing up minority in the United States does seem to make it more difficult for a poet of color to be blind (except by an act of will or delusion) to the effects of larger political and social currents, though, of course, such acts of will and delusion occur every day.

85. James J. Y. Liu, "Some Grammatical Aspects of the Language of Poetry," in *The Art of Chinese Poetry* (Chicago: University of Chicago Press, 1962), 41.

86. The "universal" lyric "I" is implicitly thought to be "racially unmarked" (that is, white). For example, students tend to read a poem by Frank O'Hara, a gay poet, as spoken by a generic universal subject, not anchored by historical specificity, though O'Hara is also a member of a minority. Yet this imputing of universality simply does not happen with poems by ethnic writers, whose work is invariably read as autobiographical. Thus, it is race, not other forms of minoritization, that necessarily

preclude a lyric "I" in a poem from being read as "universal." Thanks to Henry Abelove for bringing this point to my attention.

87. Thus, while Pound fixates on the Chinese ideogram as both image and word, the truly far-reaching implications for English-language poetry lie in classical Chinese poetry's syntax and the elliptical nature of the I/eye and the multiple perspectives it can occupy at once.

88. Yip, "Syntax and Horizon," 31–32.

89. Celan, "Speech on the Occasion of Receiving the Literature Prize," 34.

90. James Baldwin, "The Negro Child—His Self-Image," *Saturday Review*, 21 Dec. 1963; reprinted in *The Price of the Ticket, Collected Nonfiction 1948–1985* (New York: St. Martin's Press), 1985.

CHAPTER 5

A shorter variant version of this chapter appeared as "Undercover Asian: John Yau and the Politics of Ethnic Self-Identification," in *Asian American Literature in the International Context: Readings on Fiction, Poetry, and Performance*, ed. Rocio G. Davis and Sämi Ludwig (Hamburg: LIT Verlag, 2002), 135–55.

1. Yau's Wikipedia entry describes him as having "published over 50 books of poetry, artists' books, fiction, and art criticism." See http://en.wikipedia.org/wiki/John_Yau. He is undeniably the poet with the largest corpus in the history of Asian American literature.

2. A speaker who is often automatically conflated with the author as if all poetry by Asian Americans were autobiographical, mimetic, and transparent.

3. From his poem "The Woman Across the Hall," in *Hawaiian Cowboys* (Santa Rosa, CA: Black Sparrow Press, 1995), 11.

4. John Yau, *The United States of Jasper Johns* (Cambridge, MA: Zoland Books, 1997), 53 (hereafter, *USJJ*). Yau is writing on Johns's work here, but his concurrence with this statement can be verified in numerous other statements and in his poetry.

5. Gerald L. Bruns, Introduction in Matejka and Pomorska, *Readings in Russian Poetics*, xi.

6. John Yau, "Between the Forest and Its Trees," *Amerasia Journal* 20.3 (1994): 40.

7. Liu, "The Object of Experiment," 5–6. While appearing in the unpublic pages of an unpublished doctoral dissertation, this line of argument is not dissimilar from those of senior poetry scholars, mostly white, some of whom have made similar points to me in conversation though not in print (primarily because they do not write on Asian American poetry). Critical work on Asian American avant-garde poetry is so meager and of such recent vintage that Liu's dissertation constitutes the only book-length project, besides Joseph Jeon's, devoted solely to Asian American avant-garde poetry. As in my earlier discussion of Perloff's statements on minority writing, my aim here is not to critique particular individual scholars—Perloff qua Perloff or Liu qua Liu—but, rather, the more widely held positions to which these scholars give voice.

8. Charles Bernstein, "Professing Stein / Stein Professing," in *A Poetics*, 142.

9. Liu's choice of the word "reflectively" indicates a questionable ascription or presumption on his part that what various Asian American poetry critics are assuming in seeing any link between racial subjectivity and the poetic text is what he calls "a reflective mimesis of a legibly conflicted subjectivity" ("The Object of Experiment,"124). This characterization—that any attempt to connect racial subjectivity and the formal properties of an avant-garde experimental poem assumes a simple (and simplistic) mimetic relationship—is itself problematic.

10. These scholars include, among others, Timothy Yu, Joseph Jeon, and myself. See Joseph Jonghyun Jeon's 2012 *Racial Things, Racial Forms*; Yu's 2009 *Race and the Avant-Garde*; and my 2002 essay "Undercover Asian."

11. Consider, for example, other more recent racial controversies in the poetry world: the Helen Vendler–Rita Dove dustup in the *New York Review of Books* over Vendler's review of Dove's *Penguin Anthology of Twentieth-Century American Poetry*. Marjorie Perloff, whose aesthetic preferences are vastly different from Vendler's, also weighed in against Dove's anthology. See Marjorie Perloff, "Poetry on the Brink: Reinventing the Lyric," *Boston Review*, 18 May 2012; Helen Vendler, "Are These the Poems to Remember?," *New York Review of Books*, 24 Nov. 2011; Rita Dove, "Defending an Anthology," *New York Review of Books*, 22 Dec. 2011. A nastier knockdown brawl occurred in February 2011 between Claudia Rankine and Tony Hoagland at the Association of Writers and Writing Programs (AWP) conference in Washington, D.C. See www.claudiaran-

kine.com for responses from poets and critics to Rankin's call for open letters on the topic "Race and the Creative Imagination." These are not the last of these sorts of poetry battles (even if the racial politics are almost always not made explicit).

12. John Yau, *Crossing Canal Street* (Binghamton, NY: Bellevue Press, 1976), and *Radiant Silhouette: New and Selected Work 1974–1988* (Santa Rosa, CA: Black Sparrow Press, 1989).

13. John Yau, *Borrowed Love Poems* (New York: Penguin Books, 2002), and *Paradiso Diaspora* (New York: Penguin Books, 2006). Yau is currently on the faculty of the Mason Gross School of the Arts at Rutgers University, where he teaches art criticism.

14. For example, Yau was included in the first Asian American anthology published by a major New York publisher, Garrett Hongo's *The Open Boat: Poems from Asian America* (New York: Anchor Books, 1993). He had not appeared in Joseph Bruchac's groundbreaking 1983 anthology *Breaking Silence: An Anthology of Contemporary Asian American Poets* (Greenfield Center, NY: Greenfield Review Press, 1983). His poem "Two Voices for Li Shang-Yin" did, however, appear in the poetry section of the literary issue of *Bridge*, an Asian American community magazine published in New York City: *Bridge* 8.4 (1983): 18.

15. Dorothy Wang, "Noir of the Self: A Talk with John Yau," *A. Magazine*, Nov. 1993, 61; personal interview, New York City, 13 May 1993.

16. *Sometimes* (New York: Sheep Meadow Press, 1979), *The Sleepless Night of Eugene Delacroix* (Brooklyn: Release Press, 1980), and *Broken Off by the Music* (Providence, RI: Burning Deck Press, 1981).

17. This invisibility in the white poetry world is not unlike, of course, the invisibility of Asian Americans in the media and in the American body politic.

18. The interview is reprinted in Brian Henry and Andrew Zawacki, eds., *The Verse Book of Interviews: 27 Poets on Language, Craft & Culture* (Amherst, MA: Verse Press, 2005), 177–98, quote on 185–86. Citations are to the Henry and Zawacki book.

19. John Yau, *Corpse and Mirror* (New York: Holt, Rinehart and Winston, 1983).

20. Rohrer, "John Yau," in Henry and Zawacki, *Verse Book of Interviews*, 186.

21. Richard Elman, "Three American Poets," review of *Corpse and Mirror*, *New York Times Book Review*, 18 Sept. 1983, 36.

22. Marjorie Perloff, review of *Forbidden Entries*, *Boston Review* (Summer 1997): 39; John Yau, *Forbidden Entries* (Santa Rosa, CA: Black Sparrow Press, 1996).

23. Yau, "Forest," 40.

24. Eliot Weinberger, "Letter," a reply to John Yau's "Neither Us nor Them," *American Poetry Review* (July–Aug. 1994): 43.

25. John Yau, "Neither Us nor Them," review of *American Poetry Since 1950: Innovators & Outsiders*, ed. Eliot Weinberger, *American Poetry Review* (Mar.–Apr. 1994): 45–54.

26. Weinberger delineates two familiar oppositional camps of poetry: establishment poets versus those "outsiders and innovators" in the Poundian tradition. Eliot Weinberger, ed., *American Poetry Since 1950: Innovators and Outsiders* (New York: Marsilio, 1993).

27. Weinberger, "Letter," 43–44; Tejada, "Letter," 46. The first six accusations are made by Weinberger; the last, by Tejada. *American Poetry Review* (July–Aug. 1994): Allen, 44–45; Hinton, 45; Gander, 45–46; Tejada, 46–47; Vicuña, 47. There are no letters by Yau's supporters, only letters by Yau himself that rebut letters by Weinberger and his five supporters.

28. Critic Al Filreis, writing on his blog in 2007 about the Yau-Weinberger showdown, felt that even "1994 [was] on the late side for straight-out Political Correctness fights of this sort—the mode was well worn and easily comprehended by this point; the rhetorical patterns would have been very, very familiar to readers." Filreis is much more optimistic about the evolution in critical sophistication of debates involving race and poetry than factual reality would give him reason to be. See http://afilreis. blogspot.com/2007/09/neither-us-nor-them-part-2.html.

29. John Yau, "Letter," a reply to Eliot Weinberger's letter, *American Poetry Review* (July–Aug. 1994): 44.

30. Aldon Nielsen, *Black Chant: Languages of African-American Postmodernism* (Cambridge: Cambridge University Press, 1997), 24.

31. Wang, "Noir of the Self," 61.

32. Speaking with Edward Foster, Yau admitted to feelings of "anger and self-hatred" as a young man and having "had trouble accepting who I was or what I was. You know, being Chinese-American and living in, but not belonging to, this homogeneous community." These feelings are certainly understandable in a society that privileges whiteness. When is an American artist rewarded for being a nonwhite person, especially one who refuses to be patronized and/or Orientalized? Edward Foster, "An

Interview with John Yau," *Talisman: A Journal of Contemporary Poetry and Poetics* 5 (Fall 1990): 40, 50.

33. George Uba, "Versions of Identity in Post-activist Asian American Poetry," in *Reading the Literatures of Asian America*, ed. Shirley Geok-lin Lim and Amy Ling (Philadelphia: Temple University Press, 1992), 46.

34. Foster, "Interview with John Yau," 48–49.

35. In an interview with Eileen Tabios, Yau also mentions having been interested, as a child, in the paintings of the Chinese abstract painter Zao Wou ki, who lived in Paris. "Approximating Midnight: Her Conversation with John Yau And," in *Black Lightning: Poetry-in-Progress*, by Eileen Tabios (New York: Asian American Writers' Workshop, 1998), 382.

36. What Marjorie Perloff calls, in reviewing *Forbidden Entries* (1996), "more overt representations of racial oppression" (39); these are Yau's poems that Perloff finds "least successful."

37. John Yau, *The Reading of an Ever-Changing Tale* (Clinton, NY: Nobodaddy Press, 1977), and *Notarikon* (New York: Jordan Davies, 1981).

38. Yau, "Forest," 40.

39. Ibid., 41.

40. Even as "unconventional" and stylized as Yau's early work is, reviewers (mis)read the poems as descending directly from Chinese poetry. For example, David Chaloner, writing in the countercultural poetry journal *Talisman*, said, "I suspect that the mysterious and potent resistance to complete exposure lies in an inheritance from the more ancient culture of China"; he later adds, "What now appears as an intricate and symbolic manifestation of the writer's past, alluded to in early, more autobiographical work, is the curiously timeless presence of an ancient sensibility." In that same issue, Kris Hemensley writes, "His writing is as funny as Wang Wei's, Tu Fu's, Li Po's." David Chaloner "On John Yau," *Talisman: A Journal of Contemporary Poetry and Poetics* 5 (Fall 1990): 113; Kris Hemensley, "A Further Note on John Yau," *Talisman: A Journal of Contemporary Poetry and Poetics* 5 (Fall 1990): 118.

41. In his review of Weinberger's *American Poetry Since 1950*, Yau is much harsher about Pound's Orientalizing and colonial tendencies, even as he acknowledges Pound's "considerable poetic genius": "Pound's aesthetics are based on the idea that anything and anyone can be appropriated, and, in this regard, he is very much a man of his times. For at the beginning of the twentieth century, imperialism and colonialism were still

going strong. Pound's belief that one can speak in the voice of the *Other* seems very much the aesthetic counterpart of colonialism; both can be understood as self-serving, paternalistic enterprises, which appropriate the raw materials, goods, and culture of the *Other* for themselves" (original italics). Yau sees Weinberger as having unquestioningly and unproblematically followed in Pound's footsteps, both in his aesthetics and in his view of racial Others. "Neither Us nor Them," 45.

42. I do not want to imply that Asian Americans can have a purely unmediated relationship to Asian culture—as the poetry of Li-Young Lee shows, this fantasy is an impossibility—but simply to emphasize the force with which dominant discourses write the Asian American subject and that what seems a "direct" relation to some essential "Chineseness" is in reality filtered through multiple scrims.

43. T. S. Eliot, Introduction in *Ezra Pound: Selected Poems* (London: Faber and Faber, 1928).

44. In the poem "An Old Chinese Gentleman Drops In to See His Cronies in a Coffeeshop (Mott Street)," Yau consciously cites "Li Po," "Chang Chien," "Tso Fu"—classical Chinese poets.

45. The novels are set in Tang-dynasty China. The magistrate, Judge Dee, serves as a detective (shades of Charlie Chan); his character is based on a historical figure, Di Renjie (ca. 630–ca. 700). See http://en.wikipedia.org/wiki/Judge_Dee.

46. One is reminded of the description by the Chinese American male narrator in Frank Chin's story "Sons of Chan" of the first time he had sex with a Chinese woman: "She smelled like Egyptian mummies. . . . She was old living things. . . . I was fucking a living fossil. . . . I am Charlie Chan's Son. I shall not want" (146–47). The first poem Yau includes in his 228-page *Radiant Silhouette* is "Cameo of a Chinese Woman on Mulberry Street," which, he notes, was first published as a postcard (in 1974 by Bellevue Press) and which appears in a slightly different version as "Suggested by a Chinese Woman Eating Alone on Mott Street" in *Crossing Canal Street*. In "Cameo," the "Chinese woman" is associatively linked to images of the moon and "pale fur and dark wings / the silver beak and silver talons" (15). In the earlier version, the moon and talons are present, but other details are slightly different: "long beak of a crane," "hummingbird dipping."

47. Classical Chinese poetry also lacks a subject, an "I," but unlike the poetry of Marilyn Chin (a Chinese American poet who has learned clas-

sical Chinese and consciously fuses Chinese poetic forms with English-language poetry to produce hybrid forms), Yau's poems in *Crossing Canal Street* feel more like imitations of Poundian imitations of what he imagined classical Chinese poetry to be. Since Pound did not read Chinese, his knowledge of classical Chinese poetry was itself filtered thirdhand through the work of the Orientalist Ernest Fenellosa, who himself read Japanese translations of Chinese poetry (indeed, the title page of Pound's *Cathay* reads: "Translations by Ezra Pound" followed by "For the most part from the Chinese of Rihaku [Japanese name for the famous Tang poet Li Bai], from the notes of the late Ernest Fenellosa, and the decipherings of the Professors Mori and Ariga"). Ezra Pound, *Cathay* (London: Elkin Mathews, 1915).

48. M. M. Bakhtin, "From the Prehistory of Novelistic Discourse," in *The Dialogic Imagination*, ed. Michael Holquist, trans. Caryl Emerson and Michael Holquist (Austin: University of Texas Press, 1981), 75.

49. Yau, "Forest," 38.

50. Oulipo, founded by François Le Lionnais and Raymond Queneau, is an acronym for *OUvroir de LIttérature POtentielle*, a "Paris-based group of writers and mathematicians who explore and extend the field of lit. through the practice of 'writing under constraint.'" See entry for "Oulipo" in Greene and Cushman, *Princeton Encyclopedia of Poetry and Poetics*, 987–88.

51. Yau, "Forest," 40.

52. Tabios, "Approximating Midnight," 387.

53. Yau's citing of Lowell, Plath, and O'Hara is not accidental: all are Massachusetts poets, like Yau, but unlike Yau, they are endowed with white privilege—in Lowell's case, class privilege, too—so that whatever their private psychic struggles, they did not also have to contend with the added stigma of race, though Plath did, of course, have to deal with the burden of gender.

54. In his 2002 interview with Rohrer, Yau said, "What I liked about painting was that it was not reducible. You couldn't say what the scheme was behind a Jackson Pollock, you couldn't say what the scheme was behind a Franz Kline. It didn't seem reducible to a narrative. It just hit you in the face. I thought 'gee, I wonder if poetry can do that?'" (Rohrer, "John Yau," 181).

55. One is also reminded of Williams Burroughs's cutups.

56. Tabios, "Approximating Midnight," 384–85.

57. Yau, "Letter," *American Poetry Review* (July–Aug. 1994): 44.

58. Indeed, the appeal of European surrealism for Yau and other minority poets is that it breaks down these hierarchies that distinguish between the "rational" and the "irrational," the "proper" use of a European language and the "substandard" languages of the colonized. Aimé Césaire's "Cahier d'un retour au pays natal" is the most stunning Surrealism-influenced example of the colonized poet writing back. Yau himself has spoken of Surrealism's being "politically and socially radical. Among modernist movements, surrealism is the only one who [*sic*] openly accepted people of color" (Tabios, "Approximating Midnight," 390).

59. Yu, *Race and the Avant-Garde*, 150.

60. Both pieces are reprinted in *Radiant Silhouette*. Citations are to *The Sleepless Night of Eugene Delacroix*.

61. Tabios, "Approximating Midnight," 386.

62. The issue of pronouns figures urgently in the work of all the Asian American poets in this study.

63. Yau related to me how his father would say, "'We're all foreigners. Don't believe those people—they don't know anything'"—statements that "definitely did not help when I took American history classes" (personal interview).

64. James Baldwin, "The American Dream and the American Negro," *New York Times*, 7 Mar. 1965, SM32.

65. M. M. Bakhtin, "Discourse in the Novel," in Holquist, *The Dialogic Imagination*, 341.

66. Yu, *Race and the Avant-Garde*, 149, 152.

67. Tabios, "Approximating Midnight," 384.

68. That said, as I have argued earlier, it is the race, not the sexuality, of a poet that bars his poems' speakers from occupying the position of a universal poetic "I." Compare, say, the ways in which readers approach the work of John Ashbery and Amiri Baraka.

69. It was precisely this exploration of the "I" as both subject and object, says Yau, that led him to create characters such as Genghis Chan (Tabios, "Approximating Midnight," 385).

70. Foster, "An Interview with John Yau," 42.

71. And, not uncommonly, the product of elite schools: the two most important New York School poets, Ashbery and O'Hara, and two of the most important Language poets, Charles Bernstein and Lyn Hejinian, graduated from Harvard.

72. John Yau, *In the Realm of Appearances: The Art of Andy Warhol* (Hopewell, NJ: Ecco Press, 1993), 4.

73. On the left is an abstract painting made up of sets of three or four or five crosshatched black lines repeated at various angles to one another, against a white background; the painting on the right appears to be a revised or draft version of the painting on the left: there is a big X on the top one-quarter of the painting and erased or smudged sections. The imprint of what seems to be the shadow or burn mark of a household iron appears on one of the blurry sections on the right-hand side of the painting.

74. Think of Surrealism's embrace of "primitive" African art forms.

75. Foster, "An Interview with John Yau," 45.

76. Tabios, "Approximating Midnight," 384.

77. In this respect, Yau and Li-Young Lee share a similar wariness of nostalgia—"I don't feel nostalgic because I don't know what to feel nostalgic *for*," says Lee (original emphasis; Moyers, *Language of Life*, 258)— though Lee, unlike Yau, does not mistrust sentiment.

78. Yau, *In the Realm of Appearances*, 40.

79. See the Wikipedia entries for "goldfish" and "carp." Carp are prized both as food and as ornamental (and symbolic) fish in China. By contrast, in the United States, they are viewed as invasive "pest species." More recently, there has been widespread media coverage of the frightening specter of the "Asian carp invasion"—one need only Google "Asian carp" to see the rhetoric—Asian fish presumably "taking over" American waterways and devouring "native" fish. To point out the obvious: the language echoes yellow-peril rhetoric around Asian immigration and the related rhetoric and hysteria around so-called Asian communicable diseases.

80. In both "Toy Trucks and Fried Rice" and in the second half of "Carp and Goldfish," the object and idea of a toy truck seem to stand for a certain "Americanness."

81. Foster, "An Interview with John Yau," 39.

82. Yau, "Forest," 40.

83. Filreis blog. He views the debate between Weinberger and Yau as really being about Poundian poetics and its legacies rather than race. Though not unsympathetic to Yau, Filreis's comments show yet again how impossible it is for poetry critics to address the issue of race even when it is put right in their face—as Yau does unequivocally.

84. Weinberger, "Letter," 43.

85. John Yau, *The Passionate Spectator: Essays on Art and Poetry* (Ann Arbor: University of Michigan Press, 2006), 70.

CHAPTER 6

1. Frank Chin, "The Sons of Chan," in *The Chinaman Pacific & Frisco R.R. Co.* (Minneapolis: Coffee House Press, 1988), 154–55.

2. Like the boy in "Toy Trucks and Fried Rice," who is taught one version of American history in school (the Indians were our enemies) and another by his father (the Indians were heroic, the only "true" Americans), an Asian American boy growing up in the 1950s had to figure out, consciously or not, where to situate himself in relation to the Lone Ranger and Tonto—or have it figured out for him, as James Baldwin points out ("although you are rooting for Gary Cooper, . . . the Indians are you").

3. *Further Adventures in Monochrome*, published in 2012 by Copper Canyon, reprints all thirty of the Genghis Chan poems from the other four books, with slight variations, and adds fourteen new "GC" poems (the book appeared too late to be included in this study). John Yau, *Edificio Sayonara* (Santa Rosa, CA: Black Sparrow Press, 1992), and *Further Adventures in Monochrome* (Port Townsend, WA: Copper Canyon Press, 2012).

4. The *OED* says parody can be either a style or a genre. *OED* online, 3rd ed., June 2012, http://www.oed.com.

5. Linda Hutcheon, *A Theory of Parody: The Teachings of Twentieth-Century Art Forms* (1985; repr., Urbana: University of Illinois Press, 2000), 19.

6. Mikhail Bakhtin, *Problems of Dostoevsky's Poetics* (Minneapolis: University of Minnesota Press, 1984), 193. I would say not always just two voices but often multiple ones.

7. Brian Kim Stefans, "Private Eye," review of *Edificio Sayonara*, by John Yau, *A. Magazine* 2.3 (1993): 60–61.

8. And unlike Yunte Huang—the author *of Charlie Chan: The Untold Story of the Honorable Detective and His Rendezvous with American History* (New York: W. W. Norton, 2010)—who was born and raised in China and immigrated to the United States in his twenties: this disparity in histories (and histories of racialization) makes all the difference in their respective attitudes toward the figure of Chan. Thus, while Huang finds Charlie Chan "beguiling," Chin understands, with more subtlety and insight, popular culture's forceful, if usually hidden (though nonetheless pernicious), ideological role in the formation of racial, national, and sexual identity: "And Charlie Chan was born. And, in a sense, so was I" (F. Chin, "Sons of Chan," 132).

9. Hutcheon's *Theory of Parody* is an exception.

10. Margaret A. Rose, *Parody: Ancient, Modern, and Post-modern* (Cambridge: Cambridge University Press, 1993), 39.

11. And until the most recent 4th edition (2012) came out, *The Princeton Encyclopedia of Poetry and Poetics* gave a not dissimilar definition: "Parody imitates the distinctive style and thought of a literary text, author, or tradition for comic effect." Preminger and Brogan, *New Princeton Encyclopedia of Poetry and Poetics*, 881; Greene and Cushman, *Princeton Encyclopedia of Poetry and Poetics*.

12. Simon Dentith, *Parody* (London: Routledge, 2000), 9.

13. Rose points out that the ambiguity of the word "mock," which can mean both "spoof" and "counterfeit," is often overlooked (*Parody*, 29).

14. Ibid., 19.

15. Ibid., 18, 280.

16. Ibid., 8, 46; Hutcheon, *A Theory of Parody*, 32.

17. Rose defines as "post-modern" only those theories and theorists who clearly "go beyond both the late-modern description of it [parody] as non-intentional and the modern depiction of it as *either* meta-fictional *or* comic" (original italics; *Parody*, 210).

18. For example, while Rose praises Mikhail Bakhtin for stressing the comic elements of parody, she also criticizes him for "further reduc[ing] parody to the burlesque" and for basing his analyses "on a largely negative modern view of parody as destructive or hostile to its target text" (ibid., 169).

19. Huang's *Charlie Chan* argues for the wittiness and cleverness of Charlie Chan's aphorisms. By assuaging white racial guilt, Huang—as a native informant, a "real" Chinese from China—in effect gives white audiences permission to continue enjoying Oriental minstrelsy and yellowface guilt-free, reassuring them that they are not "racist" for doing so. Not surprisingly, Huang's book became an American bestseller in 2010.

20. Or, as Marilyn Chin found out, it's only noodling.

21. Quoted in Preminger and Brogan, *New Princeton Encyclopedia of Poetry and Poetics*, 882. From Winfried Freund, *Die literarische Parodie* (Stuttgart: Metzler, 1981), 13.

22. Robert Stam, "Mikhail Bakhtin and Left Cultural Critique," in *Postmodernism and Its Discontents*, ed. E. Ann Kaplan (London: Verso, 1988), 139.

23. Bakhtin, "Discourse in the Novel," 309.

24. Wesling, *Bakhtin and the Social Moorings of Poetry*, 10. Shira Wolosky agrees: "Bakhtin's theories of dialogical language of course were developed mainly with the novel in mind. Yet they have important applications for poetry, despite Bakhtin's own hesitation to make this application" ("The Lyric, History, and the Avant-Garde," 660).

25. Hutcheon, *A Theory of Parody*, 3.

26. I would add that Bakhtin also exhibits a tone-deafness to and misunderstanding of poetic language.

27. Of course, white American writers once also felt as derivative in relation to English writers; English writers, before that, felt their writing could not be as glorious as that of "classical" Greece and Rome. And so on and so forth.

28. This image holds added resonance when one thinks of American stereotypes of the shifty-eyed, devious "Oriental."

29. Tabios, "Approximating Midnight," 385.

30. The Asian female counterparts are the geisha and the dragon lady.

31. For a background history of the figure of Charlie Chan, see Huang, *Charlie Chan*; and Ken Hanke, *Charlie Chan at the Movies: History, Filmography, and Criticism* (Jefferson, NC: McFarland, 1981). While Huang's history of Charlie Chan is highly readable, I strongly disagree with his attempts to redeem Charlie Chan as a clever Oriental version of Hercule Poirot. Huang views Chan as epitomizing "the creative genius of American culture" (283) and argues for the "strength of his character: his beguiling Oriental charm, his Confucian analects turned into singsong Chinatown blues" (xvii).

32. See, for example, "The Movies, Race and Ethnicity: Asians/Asian Americans" and "The Representation of Asians in Film and Television: A Bibliography of Materials in the UC Berkeley Libraries" at the UC Berkeley Media Resources Center website: http://www.lib.berkeley.edu/MRC/ imagesasians.html and http://www.lib.berkeley.edu/MRC/imagesasians-bib.html.

33. Yau has written poems on Wong ("No One Ever Tried to Kiss Anna May Wong," *Radiant Silhouette*), Peter Lorre (in the "Hollywood Asians" section of *Forbidden Entries* and in *Borrowed Love Poems*), and Boris Karloff (*Borrowed Love Poems*). For years, Yau has been gathering material for a book on Wong.

34. See Graham Russell Gao Hodges, *Anna May Wong: From Laundryman's Daughter to Hollywood Legend* (Hong Kong: Hong Kong University Press, 2012).

35. Gary Okihiro, *Margins and Mainstreams: Asians in American History and Culture* (Seattle: University of Washington Press, 1994), 143.

36. M. M. Bakhtin, "Epic and Novel: Toward a Methodology for the Study of the Novel," in Holquist, *Dialogic Imagination*, 23.

37. "Discourse in the Novel," 348, 345, 348. One major problem with Bakhtin's discussion of the "internally persuasive" word is that he characterizes it as mainly a "positive" type of discourse and fails to take into account that such internalized words can be pernicious (e.g., racial stereotypes).

38. David Lloyd, "Adulteration and the Nation: Monologic Nationalism and the Colonial Hybrid," in *An Other Tongue: Nation and Ethnicity in the Linguistic Borderlands*, ed. Alfred Arteaga (Durham, NC: Duke University Press, 1994), 78.

39. Ibid., 81.

40. Foster, "An Interview with John Yau," 44.

41. John Yau, "The Phoenix of the Self," *Artforum* 27.8 (Apr. 1989): 150.

42. "Discourse in the Novel," 346. Note Bakhtin's emphasis on both verbal and ideological points of view.

43. Lloyd, "Adulteration and the Nation," 91.

44. Foster, "An Interview with John Yau," 44.

45. While "slashed" here is used in the description of the female figure, the adjective's applicability to the fragmented Genghis Chan and the visual linkage of "slashed" to "slanted" further emphasizes his impotent, shattered, racialized, and feminized "self."

46. One might ponder the contrast between Genghis Chan, who is marked by failure to conquer sexually, and the Chinese American female speakers in Marilyn Chin's poems, who have no problem seducing white men. The difference lies in the history and the ideological constructions of stereotypes in which sex and race are always intertwined.

47. Foster, "An Interview with John Yau," 50.

48. In quite a few of Yau's poems and short stories (particularly in *My Symptoms*), the narrators are women. Assuming the subjectivity of another character is another means of distancing oneself from the personal and the autobiographical.

49. Bakhtin, "Discourse in the Novel," 276.

50. John Yau, "Please Wait by the Coatroom: Wifredo Lam in the Museum of Modern Art," *Arts Magazine* (Dec. 1988): 56–59. Reprinted as "Please Wait by the Coatroom," in *Out There: Marginalization and Contemporary Cultures*, ed.

Russell Ferguson, Martha Gever, Trinh T. Minh-ha, and Cornel West (Cambridge, MA: MIT Press, 1990), 133–39. Citations are to the original article.

51. Bakhtin, "Discourse in the Novel," 293.

52. Priscilla Wald, "'Chaos Goes Uncourted': John Yau's Dis(-)Orienting Poetics," in *Cohesion and Dissent in America*, ed. Carol Colatrella and Joseph Alkana (Albany: State University of New York Press, 1994), 152.

53. Yau, "Phoenix of the Self," 150, 151.

54. Hutcheon, *A Theory of Parody*, 4.

55. John Yau, "Official Policy: Towards the 1990s with the Whitney Biennial," *Arts Magazine*, Sept. 1989), 53.

56. Yau, "Please Wait by the Coatroom," 59.

57. Yau, "Phoenix of the Self," 147.

58. Cantonese was the dialect, until recently, of most Chinese immigrants, mostly working class; its sounds are more pronounced and can seem less mellifluous than Mandarin and Shanghainese.

59. Wald, "'Chaos Goes Uncourted,'" 151.

60. Perloff, review of *Forbidden Entries*, 40.

61. Personal e-mail, 20 July 1998.

62. Ibid.

63. Wald, "'Chaos Goes Uncourted,'" 158.

64. Priscilla Wald, "Guilt by Dissociation: John Yau's Poetics of Possibility," *Talisman: A Journal of Contemporary Poetry and Poetics* 5 (Fall 1990): 121.

65. Personal e-mail, 20 July 1998.

66. Yau, "Forest," 37.

67. Yau, "Phoenix of the Self," 150.

CHAPTER 7

1. Mei-mei Berssenbrugge, *Random Possession* (New York: I. Reed Books, 1979).

2. Zhou Xiaojing, "Blurring the Borders Between Formal and Social Aesthetics: An Interview with Mei-mei Berssenbrugge," *MELUS* 27.1 (2002): 199. See also Laura Hinton, "Three Conversations with Mei-mei Berssenbrugge," *Jacket* 27 (Apr. 2005), http://jacketmagazine.com/27/hint-bers.html. Reprinted in Elizabeth Frost and Cynthia Hogue, eds., *Innovative Women Poets: An Anthology of Contemporary Poets and Interviews* (Iowa City: University of Iowa Press, 2007).

3. She tells Hinton, "I feel very strongly that my first language was Chinese—my mother tongue" ("Three Conversations").

4. Mei-mei Berssenbrugge, *Hello, the Roses* (New York: New Directions, 2013).

5. See, for example, Altieri, "Images of Form Vs. Images of Content," 71–91.

6. See Charles Altieri, "Intimacy and Experiment in Mei-mei Berssenbrugge's Poetry," in Hinton and Hogue, *We Who Love to Be Astonished*, 54–68; and Voris, "A 'Sensitive Empiricism': Berssenbrugge's Phenomenological Investigations," in Rankine and Spahr, *American Women Poets in the 21st Century*, 68–93.

7. Berssenbrugge, along with Myung Mi Kim, is the most anthologized Asian American woman writer in experimental poetry volumes. See, for example, Frost and Hogue, *Innovative Women Poets*; Hinton and Hogue, *We Who Love to Be Astonished*; Claudia Rankine and Lisa Sewell, eds., *American Poets in the 21st Century: The New Poetics* (Middletown, CT: Wesleyan University Press, 2007); Rankine and Spahr, *American Women Poets in the 21st Century*; Mary Margaret Sloan, ed., *Moving Borders: Three Decades of Innovative Writing by Women* (Jersey City, NJ: Talisman House, 1998); Leslie Scalapino, ed., *O Two / An Anthology* (Oakland, CA: O Books, 1991).

8. A typical example is Ben Lerner's review of Berssenbrugge's *I Love Artists: New and Selected Poems* in *Rain Taxi*, online ed. (Summer 2006), http://www.raintaxi.com/online/2006summer/berssenbrugge.shtml#.

9. In addition to Altieri's "Intimacy and Experiment in Mei-mei Berssenbrugge's Poetry" and Voris's "A 'Sensitive Empiricism': Berssenbrugge's Phenomenological Investigations," cited previously, such essays include Jonathan Skinner's "Boundary Work in Mei-mei Berssenbrugge's 'Pollen,'" *How2* 3.2 (2008), included in a special "Ecopoetics" section of the issue, http://www.asu.edu/pipercwcenter/how2journal/vol_3_no_2/ecopoetics/essays/skinner.html; Megan Simpson, "Mei-mei Berssenbrugge's *Four Year Old Girl* and the Phenomenology of Mothering," *Women's Studies: An Interdisciplinary Journal* 32.4 (2003); Megan Adams, "Mei-mei Berssenbrugge and the Uses of Scientific Language," *HOW(ever)* 1.3 (Feb. 1984), http://www.asu.edu/pipercwcenter/how2journal/archive/print_archive/0284.htm.

10. Zhou, "Blurring the Borders," 199. Unlike critics of avant-garde poetry, critics of Asian American poetry have not ignored Berssenbrugge's ethnic identity in discussions of her work. See Jeannie Chiu, "Identities in Process: The Experimental Poetry of Mei-mei Berssenbrugge and Myung

Mi Kim," in *Asian North American Identities: Beyond the Hyphen*, ed. Elea-
nor Rose Ty and Donald C. Goellnicht (Bloomington: Indiana University
Press, 2004), 84–101; Liu, "The Object of Experiment." The Asian American Writers' Workshop has twice given Berssenbrugge its annual award
for the best book of poetry (in 2004 for *Nest* and in 1998 for *Endocrinology*). Mei-mei Berssenbrugge, *Nest* (Berkeley, CA: Kelsey Street, 2003),
and *Endocrinology* (a collaboration with artist Kiki Smith [Berkeley, CA:
Kelsey Street, 1997]).

11. Mullen, "Poetry and Identity," 30.

12. "Good" avant-garde poet versus "bad" identity poet. The house
Negro versus the field Negro. Mullen writes in "Poetry and Identity"
of her inclusion in an essay by Rachel Blau DuPlessis on contemporary
women's poetry: "I am not grouped with black women poets (of whom
Ntozake Shange is singled out as an exemplar of 'experimental' writing).
Instead, I am placed in a subcategory of formally innovative poets who
are also women of color" (29). Note the appearance of that familiar prefix
"sub-" yet again.

13. Age and seniority were not determining factors—the Canadian
poet Christian Bök was barely forty, and there was no shortage of senior
minority poets and scholars, such as Nathaniel Mackey. The theme of the
convention and almost all the main speakers were chosen by the president
of the MLA, who was Marjorie Perloff that year.

14. Yunte Huang and Ming-Qian Ma.

15. It appears in Berssenbrugge's second book, *Summits Move with
the Tides* (1974; repr., Greenfield Center, NY: Greenfield Review Press,
1982), and in *Random Possession* (1979). "Chronicle" was also included in
an anthology published by the UCLA Asian American Studies Center:
Emma Gee, ed., *Counterpoint: Perspectives on Asian America* (Los Angeles:
UCLA Asian American Studies Center, 1976), and in the 1983 anthology of
Asian American writing *Breaking Silence*, edited by Joseph Bruchac. It is
included in revised form among Berssenbrugge's selected poems in *I Love
Artists*.

16. Berssenbrugge, *I Love Artists*, 6. All subsequent references to Berssenbrugge's poems will be to this volume, unless otherwise noted, and will
be cited parenthetically by page number in the text.

17. While earlier versions of the poem seemed to manifest typical, almost
clichéd, signifiers of "Chineseness"—"year of the loon," "First Son," mother,
Chinese grandmother, ancestors, amahs, silk, slippers, robes, plum trees,

cherries, persimmons, crickets—language that Berssenbrugge edits out
of the final version in her *I Love Artists*, even those signifiers are not what
they appear. There is actually no "year of the loon" in the Chinese zodiac,
and the "First Son" is actually a first daughter. Thus, even in these earlier
versions, various disjunctions undercut the discursive tone of the poem and
call into question a Chinese (American) "memory."

18. Most readers seem to assume that Asian American writers,
even those born here and who lack fluency or even rudimentary
knowledge of an Asian language, can summon up this "home"
culture in a flash and present it, like Peking duck, on a platter.
The Asian American writer is posited as both the representer and
representative of that "home" culture: at once Chinatown tour guide
and native informant.

19. *OED* online, 2nd ed. (1989), Sept. 2012, http://www.oed.com.

20. Mei-mei Berssenbrugge, *Four Year Old Girl* (Berkeley, CA: Kelsey
Street Press, 1998). The poem is also included in *I Love Artists*.

21. From her breakthrough, and still best, book of poetry, *Empathy*.
Also reprinted in *I Love Artists*. "I made a leap to my mature work with
the book *Empathy*, in my late thirties," said Berssenbrugge in an interview with Michèle Gerber Klein. "Mei-Mei [*sic*] Berssenbrugge," *Bomb* 96
(Summer 2006), http://bombsite.com/issues/96/articles/2835.

22. Klein, "Mei-Mei Berssenbrugge."

23. The color of the light may also have other implications.

24. Though there are many more individual instances of similes than
there are of metaphors in her poems, metaphors do appear, but at the
larger level of the poem rather than at the level of the word or line (e.g., in
poems such as "Fog" or "Fragrance" or "Nest").

25. Roman Jakobson, "Poetry of Grammar and Grammar of Poetry," in
Verbal Art, Verbal Sign, Verbal Time, ed. Krystyna Pomorska and Stephen
Rudy (Minneapolis: University of Minnesota Press, 1985), 44.

26. See, for example, her interviews with Hinton, "Three Conversations," and Zhou, "Blurring the Borders."

27. "I'm making a unity in which the compositional rules are in the
unconscious. . . . When you go below the level of consciousness, it doesn't
matter if the concrete and the abstract are mixed" (Zhou, "Blurring the
Borders," 204).

28. See the definition in *OED* online, 2nd ed. (1989), June 2013, http://
www.oed.com.

29. Of course, the chimeric reality of "blood," especially as used in myths of race, has not prevented the concept from having very real and devastating material consequences over centuries—for example, from laws governing matrilineal inheritance of legal status under slavery and the "one-drop" rule to eugenics.

30. Otto Jespersen, *Language: Its Nature, Development and Origin* (New York: Henry Holt, 1924), 123.

31. Roman Jakobson, "Shifters, Verbal Categories, and the Russian Verb," in *Selected Writings*, vol. 2 (The Hague: Mouton, 1971), 132.

32. One might interject here, "But John Ashbery, too, uses pronouns widely. Why is Berssenbrugge special in this regard?" To which I would answer that Ashbery's abundant use of pronouns reflects his particular poetic and nonpoetic concerns, such as the question of who the self is. They are a different set of concerns from Berssenbrugge's, whose experiences and subject formation are, obviously, different from Ashbery's.

33. Jakobson, "Poetry of Grammar and Grammar of Poetry," 44.

34. Hinton, "Three Conversations." One is reminded of John Yau's remarks to Eileen Tabios that "my family spent hours talking about the importance of family" ("Approximating Midnight," 386), yet, as he once told me, the notion that members of the same family share the same or even a similar experience is "mythology, an idealism that doesn't speak the truth of family situations."

35. Berssenbrugge's interest in nature extends to an absorbing interest in the body, bodily systems, genetics, health—one of her books is titled *Endocrinology*.

36. The title of another important poem in *Empathy*.

37. Hence, "Oriental" as "east of" Europe.

38. In stanza 5, human and natural are joined by means of color: "blue tiers rise above the highest step, / the same color as the sky." Color, of course, is another natural phenomenon that occupies the state of being simultaneously concrete and abstract, material and immaterial.

39. Hinton, "Three Conversations."

40. Zhou, "Blurring the Borders," 211.

41. Hinton, "Three Conversations."

42. Note that Berssenbrugge shares with Li-Young Lee, Marilyn Chin, and John Yau the characterizing of emigration/immigration as traumatic, despite their very different poetic styles and aesthetics.

43. Zhou, "Blurring the Borders," 208.

44. Marjorie G. Perloff, *The Poetic Art of Robert Lowell* (Ithaca, NY: Cornell University Press, 1973). See her chapter "The 'Life-Blood of a Poem': The Uses of Syntax."

45. And one would be foolish to argue that because both Berssenbrugge and Lowell grew up in Boston, they use such phrases! Berssenbrugge's and Lowell's participial phrases serve different functions in their poetry and express different philosophical outlooks and renderings of the world.

46. Equally important influences, one could argue, are her relationships to the visual arts and visual artists, such as her husband, Richard Tuttle, and her immersion in the landscape of New Mexico. Berssenbrugge told the poet Leonard Schwartz on the radio show he hosts that "the length of the line corresponds to the wide horizon of the landscape where I live" (*Cross Cultural Poetics*, episode #109, 11 June 2006), http://writing.upenn.edu/pennsound/x/XCP.php.

47. Thanks to Henry Abelove for clarifying this point for me.

48. Nor do I overlook the fact that a non–Asian American poet may also use a similar syntax to write about fog or clouds or the other things Berssenbrugge writes about. Each poetic practice is different and springs from unique conditions.

49. Perloff, "The 'Life-Blood of a Poem,'" 109.

50. In the poem "Kali," Berssenbrugge writes, "We're made to believe she is the thing *per se*, she is the picture" (95). Included in *I Love Artists* and originally published in *Four Year Old Girl*.

CHAPTER 8

A different version of Chapter 8 was published as "Does Anglophone Chinese Diasporic Avant-garde Writing Exist?," in "Transnational Imaginaries: Reading Asian Australian Writing," special issue, *Journal of the Association for the Study of Australian Literature* 12.2 (2012), http://www.nla.gov.au/openpublish/index.php/jasal/issue/view/215/showToc.

1. See Mullen, "Poetry and Identity," 27–31.

2. See, for example, Berssenbrugge's remarks in her interview with Hinton, "Three Conversations."

3. For example, writers such as Renee Gladman, Tao Lin, Brian Kim Stefans, and Rodrigo Toscano.

4. As Kenneth W. Warren argues for the obsolescence of the category "African American literature" in *What Was African American Literature?* (Cambridge, MA: Harvard University Press, 2012).

5. Perhaps most notably Walter Benn Michaels, *The Trouble with Diversity: How We Learned to Love Identity and Ignore Inequality* (NY: Holt, 2007); and Paul Gilroy, *Against Race: Imagining Political Culture Beyond the Color Line* (Cambridge, MA: Harvard University Press, 2002). The examples in the popular press are too numerous to mention, but a typical instance would be *U.S. News & World Report*'s 25 Feb.–3 Mar. 2008 issue, whose cover featured a full-page photo of candidate Obama with the prominent headline "Does Race Still Matter?"

6. As I argued in my Introduction, the notion of "identity" as problematic is almost always conflated with the straw man of an essentializing/essentialized form of "identity politics" that exists mainly in the critics' imagination.

7. And/or its more conservative cousin, "world literature."

8. Katherine Astbury, Ingrid de Smet, and Jane Huddleston, "Introduction," *French Cultural Studies* 17.3 (2006): 251.

9. See Brent Edwards, "The Uses of Diaspora," *Social Text* 19.1 (2001): 45–73, and *The Practice of Diaspora: Literature, Translation, and the Rise of Black Internationalism* (Cambridge, MA: Harvard University Press, 2003).

10. The editors of *Theorizing Diaspora: A Reader* (Malden, MA: Blackwell, 2003), Jana Evans Braziel and Anita Mannur, rightly take a sober and cautious stance toward the term, arguing, as has Bruce Robbins, against the occasionally "ahistorical and uncritical manner" in which the term "diaspora" has been used. See their introductory essay to the volume, "Nation, Migration, Globalization: Points of Contention in Diaspora Studies," 1–22.

11. Braziel and Mannur, "Nation, Migration, Globalization," 3.

12. Examples include the infamous MSBNC website headline "American Beats Kwan," when figure skater Tara Lipinski defeated Asian American Michelle Kwan for the gold medal in the 1998 Winter Olympics. More recently, Oprah Winfrey, on her 25 Oct. 2010 show, described Seung-Hui Cho, the Korean American Virginia Tech shooter, as a "South Korean undergraduate student" (she also used the Asian form of his name, "Cho Seung-Hui," an odd designation for a US permanent resident who had come to this country at age eight). See "Colin God-

dard's Life After Virginia Tech," http://www.oprah.com/oprahshow/Virginia-Tech-Massacre-Survivor-Colin-Goddard.

13. See, for example, my essay "The Making of an 'Australian' Self in Simone Lazaroo's *The World Waiting to Be Made*," in "Diaspora: Negotiating Asian-Australia," ed. Helen Gilbert, Tseen Khoo, and Jacqueline Lo, special issue, *Journal of Australian Studies* 65 (2000): 44–49.

14. Anglophone Chinese literature tells only part of the story: we must not forget that there is also a sizable group of Chinese diasporic writings written in Chinese, by such writers as Eileen Chang (1920–95), who was a longtime resident of L.A.

15. Mixed-race authors, such as Berssenbrugge and the Chinese Australian writer Brian Castro, present obvious challenges to the physiognomy and name game.

16. Pamela Lu, *Pamela: A Novel* (Berkeley, CA: Atelos, 1998).

17. Indeed, since *Molloy* is driven by this rudimentary plotline, it can be said to have more of a plot than *Pamela: A Novel*. Lu herself calls *Pamela: A Novel* a "novel of characters and ideas, told in the monologue form by an obsessive-compulsive narrator à la Dostoyevsky or Thomas Bernhard" but also admits, "I'm none too strict about generic distinctions myself. Some of my favorite novels can be thought of as poetry encased in character and narrative. By the same token, *Pamela* might also be seen as an essay, spoken by fictional characters who exist in real life." From Rob Wilson, "Email Dialogue/Interview with Pamela Lu and Catalina Cariaga, *boundary 2* 28.2 (2001): 17–18.

18. In his review in a Seattle newspaper, Robert Glück describes the writing as "a pastiche of 18th-century style whose artifice is never broken and whose solemn periods are as measured as a Handel march." Review of *Pamela: A Novel*, *The Stranger*, 4–10 Nov. 1999, "Book Review Revue" section, http://www.thestranger.com/seattle/book-review-revue/Content?oid=2470.

19. Wilson, "Email Dialogue/Interview," 9.

20. Glück, Review of *Pamela: A Novel*.

21. The most prominent—and, as far as I can tell, the only—academic essay on the book is Sharon P. Holland's "When Characters Lack Character: A Biomythography," *PMLA* 123.5 (2008): 1494–1502.

22. Remarks made to the author on the occasion of a panel, "Postmodernism, Identity, Theory: A Conversation with Pamela Lu," at the University of Illinois, Chicago, 18 Apr. 2003.

23. As they do to the less glamorous categories of "Asian American literature" and "Chinese American literature."

24. The online edition of the OED based on the 3rd ed. (2014) still sticks to this definition: "1. The body of Jews living outside the land of Israel; the countries and places inhabited by these, regarded collectively; the dispersion of the Jewish people beyond the land of Israel. Also with reference to the early Christians: Christians of Jewish origin living outside the land of Israel, as recipients of the Gospels (see James 1:1, 1 Peter 1:1) (hist.)." (Sept. 2014, http://www.oed.com).

25. Arif Dirlik, "Intimate Others: [Private] Nations and Diasporas in an Age of Globalization," *Inter-Asia Cultural Studies* 5 (2004): 499.

26. Khachig Tololyan, "Rethinking *Diaspora*(s): Stateless Power in the Transnational Moment," *Diaspora* 5.1 (1996): 8.

27. Astbury, de Smet, and Huddleston, "Introduction," 253–54.

28. See, for example, William Safran, "Diasporas in Modern Societies: Myths of Homeland and Return," *Diaspora* 1.1 (1991): 83–89; Khachig Tololyan, "The Nation-State and Its Others: In Lieu of a Preface," *Diaspora* 1.1 (1991): 3–7, and "Rethinking *Diaspora*(s)," 3–35; Paul Gilroy, "Diaspora," *Paragraph* 17.1 (Mar. 1994): 207–12. See also Braziel and Mannur, "Nation, Migration, Globalization."

29. See Elaine Yee Lin Ho and Julia Kuehn, eds., *China Abroad: Travels, Subjects, Spaces* (Hong Kong: Hong Kong University Press, 2009).

30. The situation is made even more complicated when one necessarily needs to distinguish between or among literatures written by diasporics of the same racial/ethnic group but written in different languages—for example, Anglophone Chinese diasporic literature as differentiated from Chinese-language diasporic literature. See Wang Gungwu, "Within and Without: Chinese Writers Overseas," *Journal of Chinese Overseas* 1.1 (2005): 1–15.

31. Stuart Hall, "Cultural Identity and Diaspora," in Braziel and Mannur, *Theorizing Diaspora*, 240. The essay originally appeared in Jonathan Rutherford, ed., *Identity, Community, Culture, Difference* (London: Lawrence and Wishart, 1990), 222–37.

32. Arif Dirlik, "Bringing History Back In: Of Diasporas, Hybridities, Places, and Histories," *Review of Education, Pedagogy and Cultural Studies* 21.2 (1999): 99–100.

33. Arif Dirlik, "Race Talk, Race, and Contemporary Racism," *PMLA* 123.5 (2008): 1373.

34. In the case of writers in the Chinese-language literary diaspora, one would look more to writers in Taiwan, Hong Kong, and Southeast

Asia than those in the United States. See, for example, Wang, "Within and Without." In reality, these geographical boundaries cannot be drawn so neatly: Pai Hsien-yung (b. 1937) and Yan Geling (b. 1958) are just two examples of Chinese-language writers who live and write in the United States.

35. This question is further complicated by the fact that both Mo and Castro are of mixed race. Kingston, *The Woman Warrior*; Brian Castro, *Shanghai Dancing* (Artarmon, Australia: Giramondo, 2003); Timothy Mo, *Sour Sweet* (London: Deutsch, 1982).

36. See Elaine Ho's introduction in Ho and Kuehn, *China Abroad*, for a discussion of this danger in some scholarship on the Chinese diaspora.

37. The use of initials prevents the reader from ascribing to the characters a particular race, gender, or any other traits and qualities that names usually convey. Sharon Holland notes that "Lu's characters are literally *characters*: named for letters of the alphabet" (original emphasis; "When Characters Lack Character," 1497).

38. Noam Chomsky writes, "To escape the impact of a well-functioning system of propaganda that bars dissent and unwanted fact while fostering lively debate within the permitted bounds is remarkably difficult." *Necessary Illusions: Thought Control and Democratic Societies* (Boston: South End Press, 1989), 67.

39. As Lu is well aware, the first-person plural pronoun can also designate the majority and mainstream: "'transsexuals and gays are just like the rest of us' . . . which naturally led to the question of how the 'us' had gotten split in the first place. Who were we anyway, and what were we doing without the rest of us?" (*Pamela: A Novel*, 35).

40. Taiwanese identity is itself a complex topic, Taiwan having—depending on one's political point of view—a synecdochic or independent (if not oppositional) relationship to China.

41. An alternative, and perhaps more diaspora-affirming, reading of "memories which were not our own" might be that those in the Chinese diaspora do share a larger history of cultural practices, migration, and discrimination, which, while not personally experienced by a particular Chinese American individual in the twenty-first century, is carried around by her in her unconscious memory. Similarly, one might speak of memories and references "which were not our own" produced by the dominant culture and inherited and shared by those, including minoritized subjects, growing up and living in

that national culture—for example, the myths of foundational origins of the United States or of Western culture (in classical Greece).

42. One might consider its possible links to Berssenbrugge's "as ifs."

43. Lu may also be poking fun at the now-clichéd invocation of memory as a thematic and analytical focus of discussion by critics reading Asian American (and Asian diasporic) texts. In another passage in *Pamela: A Novel*, she suggests that even individual memory cannot be relied upon to be one's own: "For a while I had been struck by the passage of time as a spatial passage, which drowned me at random intervals in old familiar places I had never been" (31).

44. At one point in the text, the narrator muses, "I was expected to introduce myself into the story, and to identify with myself as a sympathetic subject, although I had deep-rooted difficulties with the notion of subjectivity to begin with" (58).

45. Remarks made at the panel "Postmodernism, Identity, Theory."

46. Aaron Benjamin Kunin, review of *Pamela: A Novel*, in *Rain Taxi*, online ed. (Fall 2000), www.raintaxi.com/online/2000fall/pamelalu.shtml.

47. The definition is based on *OED* online, 3rd ed., Dec. 2009 (updated online version June 2013), http://www.oed.com.

48. Note the reference to language in the *OED* definition of "relative": a "thing or group (such as a species, language, etc.)."

49. The definition is based on *OED* online, 3rd ed., June 2012 (updated online version June 2013), http://www.oed.com.

50. Entry for "mood" in the *American Heritage Dictionary of the English Language*, 5th ed. (Boston: Houghton Mifflin Harcourt, 2011).

51. Wilson, "Email Dialogue/Interview," 14.

52. That both Lu and her friends (and, in the novel, P and her friends) try to form their own community based along lines of shared interests, sensibilities, age, education, and most of all, a "common language"— rather than along more traditional lines of shared ethnicity, familial and kinship ties, and so on—highlights the difficulty of speaking about diasporic links among various peoples of Chinese descent across the world. Especially for young, well-educated, English-speaking, hyphenated Chinese, links based on ethnicity tend to be much weaker than other affiliations they share locally.

53. In this respect, the subjunctive reflects the nature of Kantian aesthetic freedom—the assent to subjective judgment that brings the universal subject into being. Thanks to David Lloyd for this insight.

54. Colin Davis, "Diasporic Subjectivities," *French Cultural Studies* 17.3 (2006): 341.

55. Braziel and Mannur write, "Theorizations of diaspora . . . must emerge from this base of scholarship, historically grounded in different diasporic locations, rather than purely postmodern theoretical abstractions of displacement and movement." "Nation, Migration, Globalization," 12.

56. Wilson, "Email Dialogue/Interview," 16.

57. Of course, this state of subjunctivity holds a particular (and particularly painful) resonance for Asian Americans, who, of all racial groups, have been burdened by being apprehended as constitutively nonnative speakers.

58. From Berssenbrugge's poem "Daughter," *I Love Artists*, 78. Originally published in *Four Year Old Girl*.

59. Dirlik, "Race Talk," 1373.

EPILOGUE

1. Though it must be noted that it is subject to the same problems to which any open forum of the Internet may give rise.

2. Such as Triple Canopy, The Volta, Hyperallergic, HTMLGIANT, among many others.

3. Such as Atelos; Counterpath; Dorothy, a publishing project; Fence Books; Letter Machine Editions; Ugly Duckling Presse, to name a few.

4. From Berssenbrugge's poem "Kisses from the Moon," *I Love Artists*, 110. Originally published in *Nest*.

5. For example, one interesting question would be to ask how Guest's influence manifests itself in Berssenbrugge's poems, especially when we consider that Guest, like many of the New York School poets, shows noticeable Orientalist tendencies in her work.

6. The history of the West since 1492 is one that is deeply and inescapably racialized. The foundations of the United States—and of US literature and literary criticism—were built to a not insignificant extent on the ideology of Anglo-European (white) supremacy. This fact remains, and remains separate from the "good intentions" held by well-meaning individuals.

Index

(2001), 56; "Braiding," in *Rose*, 72, 333n72;
The City in Which I Love You (1990), 56,
57, 58, 71, 74–75, 79, 333n71; "The City in
Which I Love You," in *City*, 79, 334n81;
"The Cleaving," in *City*, 40, 58–59, 71,
79–82, 84–91, 336n103; "Dreaming of
Hair," in *Rose*, 72; "For a New Citizen
of These United States," in *City*, 334n82;
"Furious Versions," in *City*, 334n82; "The
Gift," in *Rose*, 61, 71; "The Interrogation,"
in *City*, 335n83; "Mnemomic," in *Rose*, 72;
"My Sleeping Loved Ones," in *Rose*, 72,
73; "Persimmons," in *Rose*, 62–70, 74, 75,
82–84, 115; "Rain Diary," in *Rose*, 72; *Rose*
(1986), 51–52, 56, 57, 61, 71–74, 79, 80, 89;
"This Hour and What is Dead," in *City*,
334n82; "This Room and Everything in It,"
in *City*, 71, 75–79, 84, 335n83; "Water," in
Rose, 61, 72; *The Winged Seed* (1999), 56, 82;
"You Must Sing," in *City*, 334n82, 335n83
Lee, Wen Ho, 55
Leong, Michael, 302
Leopardi, Giacomo, 313n30
lesbian sexuality in Lu's *Pamela*, 276, 283, 293
Leverton, Denise, 171
Li Bai (Li Bo, Li Po, Rihaku), 138, 177, 352n40,
353n44, 354n47
Li Yu, 31, 322n80
liberalism/neoliberalism, 17, 26, 94, 105, 107, 114,
159, 169, 173–74, 248, 314n34
Ligeti, György, 316n52
Lilly, Ruth, 337n1
Lin, Tan, 23, 37, 247, 302, 326n4
Lin, Tao, 302, 326n4, 366n3
literary criticism. *See* critics and criticism
"Literary Environment," in *Readings in Russian
Poetics: Formalist and Structuralist Views*
(Ejxenbaum, 2002), 35, 323n87
literary magazines: *American Poetry Review*
(1994) controversy between Eliot
Weinberger and John Yau, 43, 166, 169,
170–76, 182, 203–4; *Bridge*, 350n14; Harriet
blog (Poetry Foundation), 29–30, 102, 303,
338–39n18; *Poetry* Magazine, 29–30, 41, 93,
102, 303, 314n36, 338–39n18. *See also* Copper
Canyon Press-Marilyn Chin controversy
Liu, James J. Y., 156, 163–66, 346n62
Liu, Timothy, 94
Liu, Warren, 163–66, 308n6, 308n9, 349n7,
349n9
Lloyd, David, 9, 64, 82, 83, 223, 225, 307n1,
331–32n48, 332n53, 371n53
Locke, John, 67, 83
Lone Ranger, 205, 357n2
loneliness, 73, 86, 160, 347n80

Lopez, Ian Haney, 318n59
Lorca, Federico García, 51
Lorre, Peter, 162, 220, 359n33
Los Angeles, 221, 247
Lowell, Robert, 36, 175, 181, 189, 196, 197,
269–70, 354n53, 366n45
Lu, Pamela, and *Pamela: A Novel* (1998), 44,
46–47; characteristics of *Pamela*, 275–76,
368n17; diaspora and, 275–77, 280, 285,
288–94, 296–300; initials used for characters
in, 281, 287, 370n37; lack of racial/ethnic
markers combined with awareness of
racialized subjectivity, 32, 46, 276, 280–87,
293, 299–301; language and diasporic subject
position in, 280, 291–99, 300–301; location,
home, and community, diasporic concern
about, 289–93, 300, 371n52; memory in,
283–86, 298, 300, 370–71n41; pronouns,
use of, 281, 282–83, 285, 286, 287, 295,
370n39; relationality in, 288–89, 291–93;
Richardson's *Pamela, or, Virtue Rewarded*
(1740), 275, 276, 292, 293, 295–96; the self
or "I" in, 286–88, 292, 300; significance of,
275–77; subjunctive mood in, 33, 46–47, 185,
214, 258, 288–89, 292, 295–99, 301, 371n53,
372n57; on "tone" and "feeling" in language,
297–98
Lugosi, Bela, 220
lyric poetry: arguments for specialness of, 2;
Chin's style of, 40, 161; conflation with
generic category of poetry, 1; Lee's style of,
49–50, 333n71; minority lyric poetry, critical
reading of, xx, xxii, 248; personal concerns,
as genre for addressing, 22; poetic speaker
or "I," 119, 154–57, 160–62, 178–82, 241–42,
245, 347–48n86, 347n84, 355n68. *See also*
"New Lyric Studies" forum, *PMLA* (January
2008)

Ma, Ming-Qian, 247, 363n14
Macbeth (Shakespeare), 153
Mackey, Nathaniel, 247, 311n24, 363n13
MacKinnon, Donald, 57, 330n33
Malcolm X, 165
male sexuality. *See* gender and sexuality
Mannur, Anita, 273, 293, 367n10, 372n55
Mao Zedong (Chairman), 326n9, 327n14
Martin, Meredith, 331n43
Marxism, 2, 8, 22
materiality: Berssenbrugge's poetry, materiality
and immateriality in, 253–57; of painting,
201, 202, 225; of words, 65–66, 182, 183, 225
Mathews, Harry, 175, 180
Maurer, Evan, 232–33
Mayakovsky, Vladimir, 313n30

to discuss, 8, 19–23, 36; Chin's remarks regarding, in Copper Canyon Press controversy (*See* Copper Canyon Press-Marilyn Chin controversy); comparison, hierarchization, and pitting against minorities, 25, 104–05, 132, 172–73, 188, 218, 316–17n57, 318–19n63, 318n61, 319–20n68, 336n98, 340n34, 344n60; poetry critics' inability to discuss, xxii, xxiv, 23, 29–31, 111–12, 174, 190, 204, 245–48, 317n57, 356n83; primacy of, in history and national identity of US, 19, 30, 36, 54; Rankine-Hoagland dispute at AWP conference (2011), 349–50n11; Vendler-Dove dispute (2012), 349n11; of white poets and critics, xxi, 292, 312n25; Yau's remarks regarding, in Weinberger-Yau face-off (1994), 170–76

"Race Under Representation" (Lloyd, *Oxford Literary Review*, 1991), 64, 82

racial interpellation: aesthetics versus identity and, 24–25, 30, 40; Asian Americans' shared history of, 323n85; in Berssenbrugge's poetry, 261; diasporic writing and, 274, 276, 279, 299, 300; in Lee's poetry, 57, 82, 91; in Lu's *Pamela*, 283, 285, 286, 299, 300; reasons for highlighting, xxiii, 24–25, 46; Yau's poetry and, 163, 166, 237

racial privilege, 15, 204, 354n53, 372n6

racial reification or racial essentialization, 16, 36–38, 59, 69, 70, 74, 88, 163, 165, 259, 261, 279, 284, 328n18, 367n5

racial self-hatred, 42, 43, 44, 110, 116, 169, 175, 191, 208, 236, 237, 351n32

"racially unmarked" (white) poets and poetry, xx, xxiii, 37, 197–98, 308n5

Racing Thoughts (Johns paintings, 1983 and 1984), 196–97

racism: affective afterlife of, 299; Asians and Asian Americans as targets of, 27–28, 51, 155, 163; Chin's calling out of, 41–42, 95, 99–100, 104–14, 115–16, 171; diaspora studies as means to circumvent discussion of, 28, 273; effect on all Americans of, 305; Hollywood depictions of Asians and Asian Americans and, 220, 222, 239, 241; inseparability from American history, 54, 127, 372n6; of Language poets, 241; psychic aspects of, 54, 299; recognized only if explicit, 100, 106, 113; shared by Asian Americans and racial minorities, 27–28, 42, 163, 319n68; structure and logic of, 82, 331–32n48, 339n24; as taboo topic, 108, 111–12, 171; traumas of, 155, 284, 285, 299; in United States, 127, 273, 305, 319n68; of white liberals, 16, 26, 105, 114, 159, 169,

173–74, 248, 314n34, 316–17n57; 339n25, 358n19; Yau and charges of, 169, 171, 174, 241

radicalism and minority writing, conflation of, 20–22

Rand, Archie, 42

Rankine, Claudia, 349–50n11

reception controversies: between Copper Canyon Press and Marilyn Chin (*Poetry* magazine, 2008) (*See* Copper Canyon Press-Marilyn Chin controversy); *PMLA* "New Lyric Studies" forum (January 2008) (*See* "New Lyric Studies" forum, *PMLA*); Rankine-Hoagland dispute at AWP conference (2011), 349–50n11; "Rethinking Poetics" conference (June 2010), 17–19; Vendler-Dove dispute (2012), 349n11; Weinberger–Yau face-off in *American Poetry Review* (1994), 43, 166, 169, 170–76, 182, 203–4

Rector, Liam, 327n10

Red Scares, 313n28

Reed, Ishmael, 244, 272, 305

relative, concept of, and relationality: in Berssenbrugge's poetry, 260–61; in Lu's *Pamela*, 288–89, 291–93

repetition, 118, 131, 140, 170, 228, 231–32, 254

repetition with difference, parody as, 209, 229, 231

"Resistance to Civil Government" (Thoreau, 1849), 313n66

Retallack, Joan, 18

"Rethinking Poetics" conference (June 2010), 17–19, 23

A Rhetoric of Irony (Booth, 1974), 123

rhetorical aspects of minority poetry, xxiii, 113

rhetorical questions, 7, 68, 320n69, 345n52

rhetorical strategies: irony as, 107, 118, 329n26; parody as, 206–07; tropes as, 329n26

rhyme, 15, 65

Rich, Adrienne, 12

Richards, I. A., 59, 60, 331n41

Richardson, Samuel, 275, 276, 292, 293, 295–96

Ricoeur, Paul, 64, 65, 71, 88–89, 331n41, 333n73

Riding, Laura, 175

Riffaterre, Michael, 331n41

Rilke, Rainer Maria, 303

Rimbaud, Arthur, 169–70, 304

"The River Merchant's Wife: A Letter" (Li Bo, translated by Ezra Pound), 138

Robbins, Bruce, 367n10

Roberson, Ed, 302

Robertson, Lisa, 18

Rock Springs massacre, 241

Rohrer, Matthew, 167, 168, 185, 354n54

Lightning Source UK Ltd.
Milton Keynes UK
UKHW010608090622
404134UK00005B/653